# Understanding
# Power

# Understanding Power

## The Indispensable Chomsky

*Explanatory footnotes available at*
*www.understandingpower.com*

Edited by Peter R. Mitchell
and John Schoeffel

THE NEW PRESS    NEW YORK

Requests for permission to reproduce selections from this book should be mailed to: Permissions Department, The New Press, 120 Wall Street, 31st Floor, New York, NY 10005.

Published in the United States by The New Press, New York, 2002
Distributed by Perseus Distribution

Explanatory footnotes available at www.understandingpower.com

ISBN 978-1-56584-703-3

CIP data available.

The New Press publishes books that promote and enrich public discussion and understanding of the issues vital to our democracy and to a more equitable world. These books are made possible by the enthusiasm of our readers; the support of a committed group of donors, large and small; the collaboration of our many partners in the independent media and the not-for-profit sector; booksellers, who often hand-sell New Press books; librarians; and above all by our authors.

www.thenewpress.com

Printed in the United States of America

19

# Contents

# Editors' Preface

This book brings together the work of one of the most remarkable political activists and thinkers of our time. The discussions span a wide array of topics—from the workings of the modern media, to globalization, the education system, environmental crises, the military-industrial complex, activist strategies, and beyond—and present a revolutionary perspective for evaluating the world, and for understanding power.

What distinguishes Noam Chomsky's political thinking is not any one novel insight or single overarching idea. In fact, Chomsky's political stance is rooted in concepts that have been understood for centuries. Rather, Chomsky's great contribution is his mastery of a huge wealth of factual information, and his uncanny skill at unmasking, in case after case, the workings and deceptions of powerful institutions in today's world. His method involves teaching through examples—not in the abstract—as a means of helping people to learn how to think critically for themselves.

The opening chapter introduces two themes that underlie nearly every aspect of the book: the progress of activism in changing the world, and the role of the media in staving off that activism and in shaping the way we think. The book follows a roughly chronological order, and begins with four discussions that took place in 1989 and 1990—the dawn of the post-Cold War era. These first chapters lay a foundation for Chomsky's subsequent analysis. The remaining chapters explore more recent developments in U.S. foreign policy, international economics, the domestic social and political environment, as well as activist strategies and problems. The book and its accompanying footnotes bring Chomsky's analysis right up to the present day.

The internet has enabled us to place extensive documentation in our footnotes, which appear at the book's website. These vast online notes go well beyond mere citation to sources: they include commentary on the text, excerpts from government documents, significant quotations from newspaper articles and scholarship, and other important information. Our goal was to make accessible much of the evidence supporting each of Chomsky's factual assertions. The notes also add additional depth for those interested in a given topic.

The complete footnotes—which are longer than the text itself—can be easily downloaded from the book's website, **www.understandingpower.com**

(they can also be accessed through www.thenewpress.com). Information about obtaining a bound printout of the notes is available on the website, or by writing us in care of the publisher.

The book was put together as follows. We transcribed tapes of dozens of question-and-answer sessions, edited them for readability, then reorganized and combined them to eliminate repetition and present the analysis in a coherent progression of topics and ideas. Our aim was to compile an overview of Chomsky's political thought that combines the rigor and documentation of his scholarly books with the accessibility of the interview format. Always we remained faithful to Chomsky's own language and answers—and he reviewed the text—but it was necessary to make superficial alterations for structural and stylistic reasons.

Most of the material is from seminar-style discussions with groups of activists, or from question periods after public talks, held between 1989 and 1999. Some of the answers in chapters 6, 7, 8 and 9 are taken from conversations between Chomsky and Michael Albert. Questioners are identified as "Man" or "Woman" because frequently this device reveals when the same person is pursuing a line of questioning, or whether somebody else has taken over.

We have personally checked and verified the sources cited in the footnotes, except for certain foreign language materials. Most of the sources are those Chomsky relied upon when making his comments in the text, but some are not. Emily Mitchell's assistance in retrieving reams of this material in the final months of our work on this project was invaluable. We direct readers to footnote 67 of chapter 1 for discussion of one common misunderstanding regarding the footnotes: that the frequent citation to articles from the mainstream media is at odds with the "Propaganda Model" of the media, which Chomsky outlines in chapter 1.

We want to thank our parents—Emily and George Mitchell and Ron and Jone Schoeffel—whose support made the book possible.

—The Editors

# A Note on the Events of September 11, 2001

As this book was going to print, hijacked airplanes hit the World Trade Center and Pentagon, killing thousands and potentially triggering major repercussions in U.S. society and in the world. The U.S. media devoted huge coverage to the attacks and their aftermath. But, overwhelmingly, the media omitted a critical, accurate discussion of the context in which they occurred.

When President Bush and U.S. officials announced that "America was targeted for attack because we're the brightest beacon for freedom and opportunity in the world," the mainstream media in the U.S. mostly echoed the refrains. A lead analysis in the *New York Times* stated that the perpetrators had acted out of "hatred for the values cherished in the West as freedom, tolerance, prosperity, religious pluralism and universal suffrage." [1] Glaringly missing from the U.S. media's coverage was a full and realistic account of U.S. foreign policy and its effects around the world. It was hard to find anything but a passing mention of the immense slaughter of Iraqi civilians during the Gulf War, the devastation of Iraq's population by U.S.-instigated sanctions throughout the past decade, the U.S.'s crucial role in supporting Israel's 35-year occupation of Palestinian territories, its support for brutal dictatorships throughout the Middle East that repress the local populations, and on and on. Similarly absent was any suggestion that U.S. foreign policy should in fundamental ways be changed.

This book was compiled before the events of September 11, 2001. But answers to many of the most important questions presented by those attacks will be found here. Why does the media provide such a limited and uncritical perspective, and such inaccurate analysis? What is the basis of U.S. foreign policy and why does it engender such widespread hatred of the U.S.? What can ordinary citizens do to change these situations?

As Chomsky noted right after the attacks, "The people in the advanced countries now face a choice: we can express justified horror, or we can seek to understand what may have led to the crimes. If we refuse to do the latter, we will be contributing to the likelihood that much worse lies ahead." From our frightening, current vantage point, the discussions collected in this book seem more urgent than ever. We hope that the book will provide a starting point for understanding, and will contribute to the critical debates—and changes—that must now occur.

# Understanding
# Power

# 1

# Weekend Teach-In: Opening Session

*Based primarily on discussions at Rowe, Massachusetts, April 15–16, 1989.*

## The Achievements of Domestic Dissidence

WOMAN: *Noam, I think the reason we've all come out here to spend the weekend talking with you is to get some of your perspectives on the state of the world, and what we can do to change it. I'm wondering, do you think activism has brought about many changes in the U.S.A. in the past few decades?*

Oh sure, big changes actually. I don't think the structure of the *institutions* has been changed—but you can see real changes in the culture, and in a lot of other ways too.

For instance, compare two Presidential administrations in the 1960s and 1980s, the Kennedy administration and the Reagan administration. Now, in a sense they had a lot in common, contrary to what everyone says. Both came into office on fraudulent denunciations of their predecessors as being wimpish and weak and letting the Russians get ahead of us—there was a fraudulent "missile gap" in the Kennedy case, a fraudulent "window of vulnerability" in the Reagan case. Both were characterized by a major escalation of the arms race, which means more international violence and increased taxpayer subsidies to advanced industry at home through military spending. Both were jingoist, both tried to whip up fear in the general population through a lot of militarist hysteria and jingoism. Both launched highly aggressive foreign policies around the world—Kennedy substantially increased the level of violence in Latin America; the plague of repression that culminated in the 1980s under Reagan was in fact largely a result of his initiatives.[1]

Of course, the Kennedy administration *was* different in that, at least rhetorically, and to some extent in practice, it was concerned for social reform programs at home, whereas the Reagan administration was committed to the opposite, to eliminating what there was of a social welfare system here. But that probably reflects the difference in international affairs in the two periods more than anything else. In the early 1960s, the United States was the world-dominant power, and had plenty of opportunity for combining international violence and commitment to military spending with social reform at home. By the 1980s, that same opportunity wasn't around anymore: the United States was just not that powerful and not that rich relative to its industrial rivals—in absolute terms it was, but not relatively. And there was a general consensus among elites, it wasn't just Reagan, that you had to break down the welfare state in order to maintain the profitability and competitiveness of American capital. But that difference apart, the two administrations were very similar.

On the other hand, they couldn't *do* the same things. So for example, Kennedy could invade Cuba and launch the world's to-date major international terrorist operation against them—which went on for years, probably still is going on.[2] He was able to invade South Vietnam, which he did after all: Kennedy sent the American Air Force to bomb and napalm South Vietnam and defoliate the country, and he sent troops to crush the peasant independence movement there.[3] And Vietnam's an area of minor American concern, it's way on the other end of the world. The Reagan administration tried to do similar things much closer to home in Central America, and couldn't. As soon as they started moving towards direct intervention in Central America in the first few months of the administration in 1981, they had to back off and move to clandestine operations—secret arms sales, covert funding through client states, training of terrorist forces like the contras in Nicaragua, and so on.[4]

That's a very striking difference, a dramatic difference. And I think that difference is one of the achievements of the activism and dissidence of the last twenty-five years. In fact, the Reagan administration was forced to create a major propaganda office, the Office of Public Diplomacy: it's not the first one in American history, it's the second, the first was during the Wilson administration in 1917. But this one was much larger, much more extensive, it was a major effort at indoctrinating the public.[5] The Kennedy administration never had to do that, because they could trust that the population would be supportive of any form of violence and aggression they decided to carry out. That's a big change, and it's had its effects. There were no B-52s in Central America in the 1980s. It was bad enough, hundreds of thousands of people were slaughtered—but if we'd sent B-52s and the 82nd Airborne, it would have been a lot worse. And that's a reflection of a serious rise in domestic dissidence and activism in the United States over the past twenty-five years. The Reagan administration was forced into clandestine tactics rather than direct aggression of the sort that Kennedy was able to use in Vietnam, largely in order to pacify the domestic population. As soon as Reagan indicated that he might try to turn to direct military intervention in Central America, there was a convulsion in the country, ranging from a massive flow of letters, to demonstrations, to church groups getting involved; people started coming out of the woodwork all over the place. And the administration immediately backed off.

Also, the Reagan military budget had to level off by 1985. It did spurt, pretty much along the lines of Carter administration projections, but then it leveled off at about what it would have been if Carter had stayed in.[6] Well, why did that happen? Partly it happened because of fiscal problems arising after four years of catastrophic Reaganite deficit spending, but partly it was just because there was a lot of domestic dissidence.

And by now that dissidence is kind of irrepressible, actually. The fact that it doesn't have a center, and doesn't have a source, and doesn't have an organizational structure, that has both strengths and weaknesses. The weaknesses are that people get the sense that they're alone—because you don't see things happening down the street. And it's possible to maintain the illusion that there's no activism going on, because there's nothing dramatically visible, like huge demonstrations or something; occasionally there are, but not most of the time. And there's very little in the way of inter-communication, so all sorts of organizing can be happening in parallel, but it doesn't feed into itself and move on from there. Those are all weaknesses. On the other hand, the strength is, it's very hard to crush—because there's nothing to cut off: if one thing gets eliminated, something else just comes up to take its place.

So looking over a long stretch, I don't think it's true that things have gotten more passive, more quiescent, more indoctrinated and so on. In fact, if anything, it's the opposite. But it's sort of neither more nor less, really, it's just different.

And you can see it in all kinds of ways. I mean, public opposition to the policies of the Reagan administration kept rising—it was always very high, and it rose through the Eighties.[7] Or take the media: there have been slight changes, there's more openness. It's easier for dissidents to get access to the media today than it was twenty years ago. It's not *easy*, like it's 0.2 percent instead of 0.1 percent, but it is different. And in fact, by now there are even people *inside* the institutions who came out of the culture and experiences of the Sixties, and have worked their way into the media, universities, publishing firms, the political system to some extent. That's had an effect as well.

Or take something like the human rights policies of the Carter administration. Now, they weren't *from* the Carter administration really, they were from Congress—they were Congressional human rights programs which the Carter administration was forced to adapt to, to a limited extent. And they've been maintained through the 1980s as well: the Reagan administration had to adapt to them somewhat too. And they've had an effect. They're used very cynically and hypocritically, we know all that stuff—but nevertheless, there are plenty of people whose lives have been saved by them. Well, where did those programs come from? Where they came from, if you trace it back, is kids from the 1960s who became Congressional assistants and pressed for drafting of legislation—using popular pressures from here, there and the other place to help them through. Their proposals worked their way through a couple of Congressional offices, and finally found their way into Congressional legislation.[8] New human rights organizations developed at the same time, like Human Rights Watch. And out of it all came at least a rhetorical commitment to putting human rights issues in the forefront of foreign policy concerns. And that's not without an effect. It's cynical, doubtless—you can show it. But still it's had an effect.

## The U.S. Network of Terrorist Mercenary States

WOMAN: *It's curious that you're saying that, because I certainly didn't have that impression. The only human rights issue the Reagan administration seemed to be concerned with was that of the Soviet Jews—I mean, they resumed funding the terror in Guatemala.*

But note how they did it: they had to sneak it in around the back. In fact, there was more funding of Guatemala under Carter than there was under Reagan, though it's not very well known. See, the Carter administration was compelled to stop sending military aid to Guatemala by Congressional legislation in 1977, and officially they did—but if you look at the Pentagon records, funding continued until around 1980 or '81 at just about the normal level, by various forms of trickery: you know, "things were in the pipeline," that kind of business. This was never talked about in the press, but if you look at the records, you'll see the funding was still going through until that time.[9] The Reagan administration had to stop sending it altogether—and in fact, what they did was turn to mercenary states.

See, one of the interesting features of the 1980s is that to a large extent the United States had to carry out its foreign interventions through the medium of mercenary states. There's a whole network of U.S. mercenary states. Israel is the major one, but it also includes Taiwan, South Africa, South Korea, the states that are involved in the World Anti-Communist League and the various military groups that unite the Western Hemisphere, Saudi Arabia to fund it, Panama—Noriega was right in the center of the thing. We caught a glimpse of it in things like the Oliver North trial and the Iran-contra hearings [Oliver North was tried in 1989 for his role in "Iran-contra," the U.S. government's illegal scheme to fund the Nicaraguan "contra" militias in their war against Nicaragua's left-wing government by covertly selling weapons to Iran]—they're international terrorist networks of mercenary states. It's a new phenomenon in world history, way beyond what anybody has ever dreamt of. Other countries hire terrorists, we hire terrorist states, we're a big, powerful country.

Actually, one significant thing came up in the North trial, to my surprise—I didn't think anything was going to come up. One interesting thing was put on the record, this famous 42-page document that they referred to; I don't know if any of you saw that.[10] See, the government would not allow secret documents to appear, but they did permit a summary to appear, which the judge presented to the jury saying, "You can take this to be fact, we don't question it anymore because it's authorized by the government." That doesn't mean it's not disinformation, incidentally; it means that this is what the government was willing to say is the truth, whether it's true or not is another question. But this 42-page document is kind of interesting. It outlines a *massive* international terrorist network run by the United States. It lists the countries that were involved, the ways we got them involved. All of it is focused on one thing in this case, the war in Nicaragua. But there were plenty of other operations going on, and if you expanded it to look at, say, Angola, and Afghanistan, and others, you'd bring in more pieces. One of the main players is Israel: they've helped the United States penetrate black Africa, they've helped support the genocide in Guatemala; when the United States couldn't directly involve itself with the military dictatorships of the southern cone in South America, Israel did it for us.[11] It's very valuable to have a mercenary state like that around which is militarily advanced and technologically competent.

But the point is, what was the need to develop this huge international terrorist network involving mercenary states? It's that the U.S. government couldn't intervene directly whenever it wanted to anymore, so it had to do it in what amounted to quite inefficient ways. It's a lot more efficient to do what Kennedy did, and what Johnson did—just send in the Marines. That's efficient, it's an efficient killing-machine, it's not going to be exposed and put a crimp in the works, you don't have to do it around the corners. So you're right: the Reagan administration *did* support Guatemala—but indirectly. They had to get Israeli advisers in there, and Taiwanese counterinsurgency agents and so on.

Just to take one example of this, the Chief of Intelligence for the F.D.N., the main contra force in Nicaragua, defected about six months ago, a guy named Horacio Arce; he's the most important defector yet. This was of course never reported in the United States, but he was very widely interviewed in Mexico.[12] And he had a lot of things to say, including details of his own training. He had been brought illegally to Eglin Air Force base in Florida, and he described in detail what the training was like there and then in San Salvador where he was sent for paratroop practice. The trainers were from all over the place: they had Spanish trainers, plenty of Israeli trainers, Puerto Ricans, Cubans, Taiwanese, Dominicans, separate Japanese trainers for the Misquito Indian recruits—they've got a huge operation running. And it's all clandestine, and all obviously illegal.

And it's lethal alright. I mean, in Guatemala alone maybe a hundred thousand people were killed during the 1980s, and the popular movements were decimated.[13] But lethal as it is, it would have been a lot worse without the restrictions that have been imposed by U.S. domestic dissidence in the last twenty-five years. I think that's the important point. If you want to measure the achievement of the popular movements here, you have to ask, what would things have been like if they hadn't been around? And things would have been like South Vietnam in the Sixties—when the country was wiped out, and may never recover. And remember, Central America's a much more significant concern for the United States than Vietnam: there's a historical commitment to controlling it, it's our own backyard, and American business wants it as the equivalent of what East Asia is to Japan, a cheap labor area for exploitation. Yet the Reagan administration was unable to intervene there at the level that Kennedy did in an area of marginal American concern, Vietnam. That's a big change, and I think it's primarily attributable to the domestic dissidence.

After all, what are the Iran-contra hearings about? What they're about is the fact that the government was driven underground. Well, why was the government driven underground, why didn't they just come out and do everything up front? They couldn't. They couldn't because they were afraid of their own population. And that's significant, you know. It's very rare that a government has had to go this deep underground in order to carry out its terrorist activities. It's an unusual situation; I don't even think there's a historical precedent.


## Overthrowing Third World Governments

WOMAN: *The Allende coup in Chile—that wasn't above ground. [Chilean President Salvador Allende was overthrown in a coup engineered by the C.I.A. in 1973.]*

The Allende thing was underground, that's true—but that was a one-shot affair. And even there, notice that it was done in a different style: it was done in the classic style, it was like the Iran side of the Iran-contra affair. See, there's a classic technique when you want to overthrow a government: you arm its military. That's the standard thing, for obvious reasons. You want to overthrow a government, who's going to overthrow it for you? Well, the military, they're the guys who overthrow governments. In fact, that's the main reason for giving military aid and training all around the world in the first place, to keep contacts with our guys in the place that counts, the army.

If you read American secret documents, this is all stated very openly, actually. For example, there's a now-declassified Robert McNamara [Secretary of Defense]-to-McGeorge Bundy [Special Assistant to the President for

National Security Affairs] intercommunication from 1965 with a detailed discussion of Latin America, in which they talk about how the role of the military in Latin American societies is to overthrow civilian governments if, in the judgment of the military, the governments are not pursuing the "welfare of the nation," which turns out to be the welfare of American multinational corporations.[14]

So if you want to overthrow a government, you arm its military, and of course you make it hard for the civilian government to function. And that's what was done in the Chile case: we armed the military, we tried to cause economic chaos, and the military took over.[15] Okay, that's sort of classic. In fact, that's almost certainly what the Iran part of the Iran-contra affair was about. The arms shipments to the Iranian military didn't have anything to do with a secret deal to release American hostages [held by pro-Iranian groups in Lebanon beginning in 1985], and they didn't have anything to do with "October Surprises" either, in my view [theory that the Reagan electoral campaign secretly promised arms to Iran if Iran delayed the release of earlier U.S. hostages until after the 1980 Presidential election]. What they had to do with was the classic device of arming the military so they would carry out a coup and restore the old arrangement that existed under the Shah. There's very good evidence for this; I can talk about it if you like.[16]

But Chile was a straight, classic operation—clandestine in a sense, but not all that clandestine. For instance, arming the Chilean military was completely public: it was in public records, it was never secret.[17] It's just that nobody in the United States ever looks, because the media and the intellectual class are too disciplined, and ordinary people out there don't have the time to go and read Pentagon records and figure out what happened. So it was clandestine in the sense that nobody knew about it, but the information was all available in public records, there was nothing hidden about it. In fact, Chile was kind of a normal C.I.A. operation, it was like overthrowing Sukarno in Indonesia [in a 1965 U.S.-backed coup].[18] There were some clandestine parts to it—and there are parts that still haven't come out yet—but it was not really deep covert action. And it was nothing like the Central American activities of the 1980s, they're just radically different in scale.

I mean, there *have* been clandestine operations—I don't want to suggest that it's novel. Like, overthrowing the government of Iran in 1953 was clandestine.[19] Overthrowing the government of Guatemala in 1954 was clandestine—and it was kept secret for twenty years.[20] Operation MONGOOSE, which so far wins the prize as the world's leading single international terrorist operation, started by the Kennedy administration right after the Bay of Pigs, that was secret.

MAN: *Which one was that?*

Operation MONGOOSE. Right after the Bay of Pigs invasion attempt failed, Kennedy launched a major terrorist operation against Cuba [beginning November 30, 1961]. It was huge—I think it had a $50 million-a-year budget (that's known); it had about twenty-five hundred employees, about five hundred of them American, about two thousand what they call "assets," you know, Cuban exiles or one thing or another. It was launched from Florida—and it was totally illegal. I mean, international law we can't even talk about, but even by domestic law it was illegal, because it was a C.I.A. operation taking place on American territory, which is illegal.[21] And it was serious: it involved blowing up hotels, sinking fishing boats, blowing up industrial installations, bombing airplanes. This was a very serious terrorist operation. The part of it that became well known was the assassination attempts—there were eight known assassination attempts on Castro.[22] A lot of this stuff came out in the Senate Church Committee hearings in 1975, and other parts were uncovered through some good investigative reporting. It may still be going on today (we usually find out about these things a few years later), but it certainly went on through the 1970s.[23]

Actually, let me just tell you one piece of it that was revealed about a year ago. It turns out that Operation MONGOOSE practically blew up the world. I don't know how many of you have been following the new material that's been released on the Cuban Missile Crisis [1962 U.S.-Soviet showdown over Soviet missiles in Cuba], but it's very interesting. There have been meetings with the Russians, now there are some with the Cubans, and a lot of material has come out under the Freedom of Information Act here. And there's a very different picture of the Cuban Missile Crisis emerging.

One thing that's been discovered is that the Russians and the Cubans had separate agendas during the course of the Crisis. See, the standard view is that the Cubans were just Russian puppets. Well, that's not true, nothing like that is ever true—it may be convenient to believe, but it's never true. And in fact, the Cubans had their own concerns: they were worried about an American invasion. And now it turns out that those concerns were very valid—the United States had invasion plans for October 1962; the Missile Crisis was in October 1962. In fact, American naval and military units were already being deployed for an invasion before the beginning of the Missile Crisis; that's just been revealed in Freedom of Information Act materials.[24] Of course, it's always been denied here, like if you read McGeorge Bundy's book on the military system, he denies it, but it's true, and now the documents are around to prove it.[25] And the Cubans doubtless knew it, so that was probably what was motivating them. The Russians, on the other hand, were worried about the enormous missile gap—which was in fact in the U.S.'s favor, not in their favor as Kennedy claimed.[26]

So what happened is, there was that famous interchange between Kennedy and Khrushchev, in which an agreement to end the crisis was reached. Then shortly after that, the Russians tried to take control of their missiles in Cuba, in order to carry through the deal they had made with the United

States. See, at that point the Russians didn't actually control the missiles, the missiles were in the hands of Cubans—and the Cubans didn't want to give them up, because they were still worried, plausibly, that there would be an American invasion. So there was a stand-off between them early in November—which even included an actual confrontation between Russian and Cuban forces about who was going to have physical control of the missiles. It was a very tense moment, and you didn't know what was going to happen. Then right in the middle of it, one of the Operation MONGOOSE activities took place. Right at one of the tensest moments of the Missile Crisis, the C.I.A. blew up a factory in Cuba, with about four hundred people killed according to the Cubans. Well, fortunately the Cubans didn't react— but if something like that had happened to *us* at the time, Kennedy certainly would have reacted, and we would have had a nuclear war. It came very close.

Alright, there's a terrorist operation which might have set off a nuclear war. That wasn't even reported in the United States when the information was released about a year ago, it was considered so insignificant. The only two places where you can find it reported are in a footnote, on another topic actually, in one of these national security journals, *International Security,* and also in a pretty interesting book by one of the top State Department intelligence specialists, Raymond Garthoff, who's a sensible guy. He has a book called *Reflections on the Cuban Missile Crisis,* and he brings in some of this material.[27]

Actually, other things have been revealed about the Crisis which are absolutely startling. For instance, it turns out that the head of the U.S. Air Force at the time, General Thomas Power, without consultation with the government—in fact, without even *informing* the government—raised the level of American national security alert to the second highest level [on October 24, 1962]. See, there's a series of levels of alert for U.S. military forces: it's called "Defense Condition" 1, 2, 3, 4, 5. Usually you're at "5"; nothing's going on. Then the President can say, "You can move up to '3,'" which means, get the Strategic Air Command bombers in the air, or "Go up to '2,'" which means you're ready to shoot, then you're at "1," and you send them off. Well, this guy just raised the level of alert unilaterally.

Now, when you raise the level of alert, the point is to inform the Russians and to inform the other major powers what you're doing, because they know something's happening—they can see what you're doing, they can see the S.A.C. bombers going up and the ships getting deployed: this stuff is all *meant* to be seen. So one of the top U.S. generals openly raised the level of security alert to just before nuclear war right in the middle of the Missile Crisis, and didn't inform Washington—the Secretary of Defense didn't even know about it. The *Russian* Secretary of Defense knew it, because his intelligence was picking it up, but Washington didn't know. And this general did it just out of, you know, snubbing his nose at the Russians. The fact that this happened was just released about a year ago.[28]

MAN: *At that point, did the Russians go up to the next level too?*

No, they didn't react. See, we would have seen if they'd reacted, and Kennedy probably would have shot off the missiles. But Khrushchev didn't react. In fact, throughout this whole period the Russians were very passive, they never reacted much—because they were scared. The fact is, the United States had an enormous preponderance of military force. I mean, the U.S. military thought there was no real problem: they *wanted* a war, because they figured we'd just wipe the Russians out.[29]

WOMAN: *But are you saying that the U.S. intentionally created the Cuban Missile Crisis?*

Well, I'm not quite saying that. These are things that happened in the course of the Crisis—how we got to it is a little different. It came about when the Russians put missiles on Cuba and the United States observed that missiles were going in and didn't want to allow them there. But of course, there's a background, as there always is to everything, and part of the background is that the United States was planning to invade Cuba at the time, and the Russians knew it, and the Cubans knew it. The Americans didn't know it—I mean, the American *people* didn't know it. In fact, even a lot of the American government didn't know it; it was only at a very top level that it was known.

## Government Secrecy

There's a point here to be made about government secrecy, actually: government secrecy is not for security reasons, overwhelmingly—it's just to prevent the population here from knowing what's going on. I mean, a lot of secret internal documents get declassified after thirty years or so, and if you look over the entire long record of them, there's virtually nothing in there that ever had any security-related concern. I don't know if Stephen Zunes [a professor in the audience], who's just done a dissertation on a lot of this stuff, would agree, but my impression from reading the secret record over a wide range of areas is that you virtually never find anything in there that had any connection to security whatsoever. The main purpose of secrecy is just to make sure that the general population here doesn't know what's going on.

STEPHEN ZUNES: *I concur completely.*

Yeah, that's your impression too? And you know, I'm at M.I.T., so I'm always talking to the scientists who work on missiles for the Pentagon and so on, and these guys also don't see any reason for it. Like, Stark Draper, who runs the big missile lab at M.I.T. and who invented inertial guidance and so on, says publicly, and he's told me privately, that he doesn't see any purpose in security classifications—because he says the only effect is to prevent American scientists from communicating adequately. As far as he's concerned, you can take the instruction book for building the most advanced missiles and just give it to China or Russia, he doesn't care. First of all, he says they can't do anything with it, because they don't have the technological and industrial level that would enable them to do anything. And if they *did* have that level, they'd have invented it too, so you're not telling them anything. All you're doing is making it harder for American scientists to communicate.

As for the secret diplomatic record, it's difficult to think of anything that has been released that was ever a secret which actually involved security—they involve marginalizing the population, that's what government secrets are for.

WOMAN: *You could apply that insight to the Rosenberg trial in the 1950s—they were supposed to have endangered the world by selling the Russians nuclear secrets. [Julius and Ethel Rosenberg were executed for treason by the U.S. government in 1953.]*

Yeah—the Rosenberg execution had nothing to do with national security; it was part of trying to destroy the political movements of the Thirties. If you want to traumatize people, treason trials are an extreme way—if there are spies running around in our midst, then we're really in trouble, we'd better just listen to the government and stop thinking.

Look, every government has a need to frighten its population, and one way of doing that is to shroud its workings in mystery. The idea that a government has to be shrouded in mystery is something that goes back to Herodotus [ancient Greek historian]. You read Herodotus, and he describes how the Medes and others won their freedom by struggle, and then they lost their freedom when the institution of royalty was invented to create a cloak of mystery around power.[30] See, the idea behind royalty was that there's this other species of individuals who are beyond the norm and who the people are not supposed to understand. That's the standard way you cloak and protect power: you make it look mysterious and secret, above the ordinary person—otherwise why should anybody accept it? Well, they're willing to accept it out of fear that some great enemies are about to destroy them, and because of that they'll cede their authority to the Lord, or the King, or the President or something, just to protect themselves. That's the way governments work—that's the way *any* system of power works—and the secrecy system is part of it.

Clandestine terror is a different part of it—if the public will not support direct intervention and violence, then you have to keep it secret from them somehow. So in a way, I think the scale of clandestine government activities is a pretty good measure of the popular dissidence and activism in a country—and clandestine activities shot way up during the Reagan period. That tells you something right there about popular "empowerment": it's a reflection of people's power that the government was forced underground. That's a victory, you know.

WOMAN: *Doesn't seem like much of a victory.*

Well, it depends what you look at. If you look at 200,000 corpses in Central America, it doesn't seem like much of a victory. But if you look at ten million people who are still alive, it does seem like a victory. It depends where you're looking. You don't win what you'd like to win, but you could have lost a lot more.

For example, take El Salvador in the 1980s. The purpose of U.S. policies there was to wipe out the popular organizations and support a traditional Latin American-style regime that would ensure the kind of business climate we expect in the region. So the independent press was destroyed, the political opposition was murdered, priests and labor organizers were murdered, and so on and so forth—and U.S. planners figured they had the problem licked. Well, today it's right back, it's right back where it was. New people came up, the organizations are forming again. It's at a lower level, of course, because there's been so much destruction, but they're right back. That wouldn't have happened if we'd sent in B-52s and the 82nd Airborne. So there is kind of a margin for survival in the Third World that relates to the degree of American dissidence.

Or take the hurricane in Nicaragua [in October 1988]. Well, it was devastating, the country may not survive in fact. But the possibility of survival will come from American dissidents. I mean, there's been a tremendous amount of hurricane relief raised—Quest for Peace, which is a dozen people at a Jesuit Center in Hyattsville, Maryland, has raised several million dollars in hurricane relief all by themselves, without any funds or any outreach, no media, nothing. Raising several million dollars with no resources is not easy—try it sometime. But that can be done because there's a large part of the American population which is just out of the system: they don't believe what the government tells them, they don't accept anything; they may not have any organization or any media or anything like that, but they're there, and they can be reached, by letter if nothing else. And that can provide a kind of margin for survival in the Third World.

## The Media: An Institutional Analysis

MAN: *You mentioned the media being only slightly open to dissidents. I'm wondering how long it has been the case that the American government and other powerful interests in the country could count on the participa-*

*tion of the major media when it comes to framing topics and reporting issues more or less the way they want them reported?*

Well, you know, I haven't looked at the entire history, but I would guess since about 1775.

MAN: *That long?*

If you look back at the Revolutionary War period, you'll find that Revolutionary War leaders, people like Thomas Jefferson (who's regarded as a great libertarian, and with some reason), were saying that people should be punished if they are, in his words, "traitors in thought but not in deed"— meaning they should be punished if they *say* things that are treacherous, or even if they *think* things that are treacherous. And during the Revolutionary War, there was vicious repression of dissident opinion.[31]

Well, it just goes on from there. Today the methods are different—now it's not the threat of force that ensures the media will present things within a framework that serves the interests of the dominant institutions, the mechanisms today are much more subtle. But nevertheless, there is a complex system of filters in the media and educational institutions which ends up ensuring that dissident perspectives are weeded out, or marginalized in one way or another. And the end result is in fact quite similar: what are called opinions "on the left" and "on the right" in the media represent only a limited spectrum of debate, which reflects the range of needs of private power—but there's essentially nothing beyond those "acceptable" positions.

So what the media do, in effect, is to take the set of assumptions which express the basic ideas of the propaganda system, whether about the Cold War or the economic system or the "national interest" and so on, and then present a range of debate *within* that framework—so the debate only enhances the strength of the assumptions, ingraining them in people's minds as the entire possible spectrum of opinion that there is. So you see, in our system what you might call "state propaganda" isn't expressed as such, as it would be in a totalitarian society—rather it's implicit, it's presupposed, it provides the framework for debate among the people who are admitted into mainstream discussion.

In fact, the nature of Western systems of indoctrination is typically not understood by dictators, they don't understand the utility for propaganda purposes of having "critical debate" that incorporates the basic assumptions of the official doctrines, and thereby marginalizes and eliminates authentic and rational critical discussion. Under what's sometimes been called "brainwashing under freedom," the critics, or at least, the "responsible critics" make a major contribution to the cause by bounding the debate within certain acceptable limits—that's why they're tolerated, and in fact even honored.

MAN: *But what exactly are these "filters" that create this situation—how does it actually* work *that really challenging positions are weeded out of the media?*

Well, to begin with, there are various layers and components to the American media—the *National Enquirer* that you pick up in the supermarket is not the same as the *Washington Post*, for example. But if you want to talk about presentation of news and information, the basic structure is that there are what are sometimes called "agenda-setting" media: there are a number of major media outlets that end up setting a basic framework that other smaller media units more or less have to adapt to. The larger media have the essential resources, and other smaller media scattered around the country pretty much have to take the framework which the major outlets present and adapt to it—because if the newspapers in Pittsburgh or Salt Lake City want to know about Angola, say, very few of them are going to be able to send their own correspondents and have their own analysts and so on.[32]

Well, if you look at these larger media outlets, they have some crucial features in common. First of all, the agenda-setting institutions are big corporations; in fact, they're mega-corporations, which are highly profitable—and for the most part they're also linked into even bigger conglomerates.[33] And they, like other corporations, have a product to sell and a market they want to sell it to: the product is audiences, and the market is advertisers. So the economic structure of a newspaper is that it sells readers to other businesses. See, they're not really trying to sell newspapers to people—in fact, very often a journal that's in financial trouble will try to cut *down* its circulation, and what they'll try to do is up-scale their readership, because that increases advertising rates.[34] So what they're doing is selling audiences to other businesses, and for the agenda-setting media like the *New York Times* and the *Washington Post* and the *Wall Street Journal*, they're in fact selling very privileged, elite audiences to other businesses—overwhelmingly their readers are members of the so-called "political class," which is the class that makes decisions in our society.

Okay, imagine that you're an intelligent Martian looking down at this system. What you see is big corporations selling relatively privileged audiences in the decision-making classes to other businesses. Now you ask, what picture of the world do you expect to come out of this arrangement? Well, a plausible answer is, one that puts forward points of view and political perspectives which satisfy the needs and the interests and the perspectives of the buyers, the sellers, and the market. I mean, it would be pretty surprising if that *weren't* the case. So I don't call this a "theory" or anything like that—it's virtually just an observation. What Ed Herman and I called the "Propaganda Model" in our book on the media [*Manufacturing Consent*] is really just a kind of truism—it just says that you'd expect institutions to work in their own interests, because if they didn't they wouldn't be able to function for very long. So I think that the "Propaganda Model" is primarily useful just as a tool to help us think about the media—it's really not much deeper than that.[35]

## Testing the "Propaganda Model"

WOMAN: *Could you give us kind of a thumbnail sketch of how you've used that tool?*

Well, essentially in *Manufacturing Consent* what we were doing was contrasting two models: how the media *ought* to function, and how they *do* function. The former model is the more or less conventional one: it's what the *New York Times* recently referred to in a book review as the "traditional Jeffersonian role of the media as a counter-weight to government"— in other words, a cantankerous, obstinate, ubiquitous press, which must be suffered by those in authority in order to preserve the right of the people to know, and to help the population assert meaningful control over the political process.[36] That's the standard conception of the media in the United States, and it's what most of the people in the media themselves take for granted. The alternative conception is that the media will present a picture of the world which defends and inculcates the economic, social, and political agendas of the privileged groups that dominate the domestic economy, and who therefore also largely control the government. According to this "Propaganda Model," the media serve their societal purpose by things like the way they select topics, distribute their concerns, frame issues, filter information, focus their analyses, through emphasis, tone, and a whole range of other techniques like that.

Now, I should point out that none of this should suggest that the media always will agree with state policy at any given moment. Because control over the government shifts back and forth between various elite groupings in our society, whichever segment of the business community happens to control the government at a particular time reflects only *part* of an elite political spectrum, within which there are sometimes tactical disagreements. What the "Propaganda Model" in fact predicts is that this entire *range* of elite perspectives will be reflected in the media—it's just there will be essentially nothing that goes beyond it.

Alright, how do you prove this? It's a big, complex topic, but let me just point out four basic observations to start with, then we can go into more detail if you like. The first point is that the "Propaganda Model" actually has a fair amount of elite advocacy. In fact, there's a very significant tradition among elite democratic thinkers in the West which claims that the media and the intellectual class in general *ought* to carry out a propaganda function—they're supposed to marginalize the general population by controlling what's called "the public mind."[37] This view has probably been the dominant theme in Anglo-American democratic thought for over three hundred years, and it remains so right until the present. You can trace the thinking on this back to the first major popular-democratic revolution in the West, the English Civil War in the 1640s [an armed conflict between supporters of the King and the Parliament for sovereignty over England from 1642 to 1648].

See, elites on both sides of the Civil War in England—on the one hand the landed gentry and rising merchant class, who were aligned with Parliament, and on the other the Royalists, who represented more traditional elite groupings—were very worried about all the popular ferment that was starting to develop in the context of the elite struggle. I mean, there were popular movements springing up which were challenging everything—the relationship between master and servant, the right of authority altogether; there was a lot of radical publishing taking place because the printing press had just been invented, and so on and so forth. And elites on both sides of the Civil War were very worried that the general population suddenly was beginning to get out of control. As they put it, the people are becoming "so curious and so arrogant that they will never find humility enough to submit to a civil rule." [38] So both the King and the Parliament were losing the capacity to coerce, and they had to react to that.

Well, the first thing they tried to do was to reintroduce the capacity to coerce: there was an absolutist state for a time, and then the King was restored [Charles II regained the throne in 1660 after several years of rule by Oliver Cromwell's military administration]. But they couldn't change everything back, they couldn't regain total control, and a lot of what the popular movements had been fighting for slowly began to work its way into the development of British political democracy [e.g. constitutional monarchy was established in 1689 and a Bill of Rights adopted]. And ever since then, every time popular movements have succeeded in dissolving power to a certain extent, there has been a deepening recognition among elites in the West that as you begin to lose the power to control people by force, you have to start to control what they think. And in the United States, that recognition has reached its apogee.

So in the twentieth century, there's a major current of American thought—in fact, it's probably the dominant current among people who think about these things (political scientists, journalists, public relations experts and so on)—which says that precisely because the state has lost the power to coerce, elites need to have more effective propaganda to control the public mind. That was Walter Lippmann's point of view, for example, to mention probably the dean of American journalists—he referred to the population as a "bewildered herd": we have to protect ourselves from "the rage and trampling of the bewildered herd." And the way you do it, Lippmann said, is by what he called the "manufacture of consent"—if you don't do it by force, you have to do it by the calculated "manufacture of consent." [39]

Back in the 1920s, the major manual of the public relations industry actually was titled *Propaganda* (in those days, people were a little bit more honest). It opens saying something like this: the conscious and intelligent manipulation of the organized habits and opinions of the masses is a central feature of a democratic system—the wording is virtually like that. Then it says: it is the job of the "intelligent minorities" to carry out this manipulation of the attitudes and opinions of the masses.[40] And really that's the leading doctrine of modern liberal-democratic intellectual thought: that if you lose the power to control people by force, you need better indoctrination.[41]

Alright, that's the first point about the "Propaganda Model"—it has traditionally been supported and advocated by a substantial part of the elite intellectual tradition. The second point I've already mentioned—it's that the "Propaganda Model" has a kind of prior plausibility: if you look at their institutional structure, you'd expect that the corporate media *would* serve a propaganda function in a business-dominated society like ours. A third point is that the general public actually tends to agree with the basic features of the "Propaganda Model." So contrary to what's usually said, if you look at poll results, most of the public thinks that the media are too conformist and too subservient to power—it's very different from the media's self-image, obviously, but that's the public's image of them.[42]

Well, from just these three initial observations—elite advocacy, prior plausibility, and the public's perspective—you would at least draw one conclusion: that the "Propaganda Model" ought to be a part of the ongoing *debate* about how the media function. You would think that would be enough grounds to make it a part of the discussion you often hear presented about the media's role, right? Well, it never is a part of that discussion: the "debate" is always over whether the media are too extreme in their undermining of authority and their criticism of power, or whether they are simply serving their "traditional Jeffersonian role" as a check on power. This other position—which says that there *is* no "traditional Jeffersonian role," and that the media, like the intellectual community in general, are basically subservient to power—is never part of the discussion at all. And there's a very good reason why that's the case, actually—because discussing the "Propaganda Model" would *itself* be dysfunctional to the institutions, so therefore it simply is excluded. The "Propaganda Model" in fact *predicts* that it won't be discussible in the media.

So, okay, those are the first three observations. The fourth has to do with the empirical validity of the "Propaganda Model"—and that's of course the meat of the matter. Is the "Propaganda Model" descriptively accurate? Is it true that the media serve the "traditional Jeffersonian role," or do they rather follow the "Propaganda Model"?

Well, to answer that question satisfactorily for yourself, you have to do a lot of investigation and examine an extensive amount of material on the question. But just to give you kind of an outline of how one can go about it, methodologically speaking—the first way we tested the model in *Manufacturing Consent* was to submit it to what is really its harshest possible test: we let the opponents select their own ground. See, if you don't do this, a critic can always attack you by saying, "Well, you're just picking examples that work." Fine, so you let the opponents select their own ground: you take the cases that people on the other side of the spectrum point to to show that the media go too far in their undermining of authority, you take the examples *they* select to prove *their* position—like the Vietnam War, or Watergate, or other cases like that—and you look at those examples to see whether they follow the "Propaganda Model." So that was the first thing we did: we let the opponents pick the ground, so there would be no question of taking the wrong sample or anything like that. And the result was, even when you let the opponents pick the ground, you still get very strong confirmation of the "Propaganda Model."

Another thing we've done is to document the range of permitted opinion in the media, just to discover what the bounds of expressible thought actually are in the mainstream. We've looked at crucial historical examples in detail. We've studied media treatment of closely paired examples—I mean, history doesn't construct controlled experiments for you, but there are lots of historical events that are more or less paired, and it's possible to compare how the media deal with them. So we've examined media coverage of atrocities committed by enemy states and compared it to coverage of atrocities which were roughly on the same scale, but for which the United States was responsible. We've compared coverage of elections in enemy states and in client states. We've looked at the treatment of problems of freedom of the press in official enemies and in client states. And there are a lot of other topics we've investigated as well.[43]

So we've studied a great number of cases, from every methodological point of view that we've been able to think of—and they all support the "Propaganda Model." And by now there are thousands of pages of similar material confirming the thesis in books and articles by other people too—in fact, I would hazard a guess that the "Propaganda Model" is one of the best-confirmed theses in the social sciences. There has been no serious counter-discussion of it at all, actually, that I'm aware of.[44] But that's all irrelevant within the mainstream culture—and the point is, it will all *stay* irrelevant, even if the level of proof were to reach way beyond what could ever be achieved in the social sciences. In fact, even if you could prove it at the level of physics, it would always remain irrelevant within the mainstream institutions. And the reason for that is that the "Propaganda Model" is in fact valid, and it predicts that it will be irrelevant—and in fact, not even be *understandable* within the elite culture—no matter how well it's proven. And that's because what it reveals undermines very effective and useful ideological institutions, so it's dysfunctional to them, and will be excluded.

## The Media and Elite Opinion

MAN: *But Mr. Chomsky, don't you think you might be making a bit of an intellectually lazy assumption as you draw up this analysis—namely, that there's this monolith "the media"? Isn't it a bit hypocritical to expect the media to be any different from the rest of the American population in the views it advocates?*

Well, the media *are* different from the general population—they're very much like American elites.

MAN: *I'm not necessarily sure that's true, I'm not sure how you could prove it one way or the other.*

I think you *can* prove it, actually: on major issues there is a very noticeable split between elite and popular opinion, and the media consistently reflect *elite* opinion. So for example, on things like, say, dismantling welfare state programs, or on a nuclear weapons freeze, or on U.S. policies in Central America in the 1980s, or on the nature of the Vietnam War, the views expressed in the media have always been very different from public opinion, and in line with elite opinion.[45]

MAN: *My point is that it's not necessarily a transformation of the media, but a transformation of society that you're looking towards. It can be a lazy diversion just to talk about the media as "them."*

Well, I think you *would* need a transformation of society to change the media—but I still think it's right to call the media "them."

MAN: *Take a look at the word "media," it is "us talking to us."*

OTHERS: *No, no.*

WOMAN: *You're wrong.*

There I really disagree. I mean, I think it's a good question to examine, but I don't agree. After all, what *are* the media? Who are they? Are they "us"? Take C.B.S., or the *New York Times*—who are they? They're among the major corporations in the country, they're not "us." They are no more "us" than General Motors is "us."

The question is: are the media like a sample of public opinion? Is it that the public has a certain range of beliefs and the media are just a sample of it? If that were the case, the media would be very democratic in fact.

MAN: *The only poll that I've seen about journalists is that they are basically narcissistic and left of center.*

Look, what people call "left of center" doesn't mean anything—it means they're conventional liberals, and conventional liberals are very state-oriented, and usually dedicated to private power.

MAN: *But if there is only a small percentage of the American population that is actively dissident, I think it's unfair to expect any greater percentage than that in the media.*

Again, you have to look closely: I think there's plenty of evidence that public opinion and media presentation have differed quite sharply. The general public regarded the media as much too easy on the Reagan administration, they thought there should have been *more* exposure. In fact, they thought that the media were too hard on Carter, but too easy on Reagan—it's exactly the opposite of what everybody says.

WOMAN: *Where do you get all this information?*

From polls. Actually, that point is made in a pretty interesting book by Mark Hertsgaard, called *On Bended Knee,* which is about media coverage of the Reagan administration.[46]

MAN: *You gave the example of the public being more in favor of welfare state programs than the media—but in Massachusetts right now, there's strong support in the general population for dismantling a lot of social services, and for no new taxes. Don't you agree the support's pretty strong for that these days?*

No. If you ask people, "Do you want new taxes?" they'll say no; but if you ask them, "Do you want better medical services?" they'll say yes.

MAN: *But there has been no strong popular response against a very austere state budget here which eliminates a lot of social services.*

But is there anybody pushing for developing *meaningful* social services? See, suppose there was somebody with a platform saying, "We want everybody in Massachusetts to have access to adequate medical care"—I'll bet you if somebody was pushing *that,* they'd get overwhelming support. But if you just come to people and say, "Do you want to have new taxes?" of course they'll say no. If you have something on the ballot saying, "Should we put a limit on property taxes?" the answer will be, "Sure, why should I pay more?" But you're not asking the right question. If you ask people, "Do you want your roads clean? Do you want good schools? Do you want medical services?" then they'll say yes. So part of the reason there isn't much response is that there's no one offering real alternatives.

Now, it's also true that there are a lot of people who just look at the world and say, "Don't confuse me with the facts, it's too painful," or "I don't want to know about reality, it's too ugly." But they're not even reading the news anymore—they only read the "Style" section, and the "Sports" and so on. However, if you take the people who still pay attention to the world, it's pretty striking: the population tends to regard the media as too conformist, too subservient to power. It's exactly the opposite of what everybody says.[47]

So just take a look at something like the nuclear freeze movement. The nuclear freeze had virtually no support in the media, no support among politicians, and certainly no support by business—but nevertheless, 75 percent of the American population supported it.[48] Well, *that's* certainly not reflected in editorial opinion or in opinion pieces in the media. Or take what's certainly the most discussed media issue of the 1980s, Nicaragua. I've done a lot of analysis of opinion pieces in the national media, like the *Washington Post* and the *New York Times,* and it's uniform—well over 99 percent of them are anti-Sandinista, and think the Sandinista Party government has to be eliminated; the only issue is how you do it: do you do it by attacking them with contra forces, or by some other means? Well, that does *not* reflect public opinion. I mean, most of the public thought we should just get out of Nicaragua and leave them alone—they didn't even know which side we were on, but thought we had no business there, so let's get away. That certainly wasn't reflected. Then among the minority of the population who in fact knew which side we were on, there was strong opposition to any method of overthrowing the government.[49] But that position is inexpressible in the media.

Let me just give you an illustration. Six months in early 1986 and six months in early 1987 happened to have been the periods of greatest debate over Nicaragua, right before the big contra aid bills came to Congress. The *New York Times* and the *Washington Post* in those two periods published only two columns that even raised the *possibility* that the Sandinistas should be permitted to survive. One was by the Nicaraguan Ambassador.[50] The other was by a guy named Kevin Cahill, a doctor at Lenox Hill Hospital in New York, who's a specialist in tropical diseases and who's worked extensively through the area. He had a column in which he said, there's only one country in Latin America where the government cares about the population, it's Nicaragua: here's what they're doing, we should let them do it.[51] That was the one exception of an opinion column even *considering* this position in practically a year of intensive coverage of the issue in the two most important newspapers in the country. Now, that certainly does not reflect popular opinion—in fact, it doesn't even reflect opinion in the academic profession in this case: the media do not accept contributions from Latin America scholars on this issue, just because they disagree.[52]

WOMAN: *There were people who lost their jobs in the media for reporting other points of view.*

Oh, that happens all the time. Ray Bonner is the famous case—he was a freelancer the *New York Times* picked up who made the mistake of actually reporting what was going on for about a year in El Salvador. He was bounced off to work in the "Metro" section or something, and then he just dropped out.[53] And there are lots of other reporters who have just ended up leaving: Sy Hersh, for example, left the *New York Times* because they wouldn't let him do the kinds of stories he wanted to do.

Look, I have a good friend who's one of the seven or eight main editors of a major American newspaper, and he happens to be very much opposed to U.S. policies towards Central America, and towards the arms race, as well as several other things. He tries to craft editorials which will just barely sneak through under the ideological barrier, but will sort of hint at some of the things he would like people to see—he has to make a very careful calculation as to what will make it in.

WOMAN: *But isn't that what this man over here is saying?*

No—that ideological barrier reflects *elite* opinion, it's not that the *public* is going to object. The public's not going to mind if the editor comes out with these things; in fact, this guy happens to be in a liberal city, the public will applaud—it's in Boston.

WOMAN: *So why is there that barrier?*

Well, I once asked another editor I know at the *Boston Globe* why their coverage of the Israeli/Palestinian conflict is so awful—and it is. He just laughed and said, "How many Arab advertisers do you think we have?" That was the end of that conversation.

MAN: *That's not true, unless he was joking.*

It *is* true, and he wasn't joking. That wasn't joking.

MAN: *The editor doesn't pay attention to the advertising—he doesn't care about the advertising.*

Are you kidding? If he doesn't care about the advertising, he will not be editor any longer.

MAN: *You're saying that the* Globe's *editorial decisions are based on trying to keep advertising revenue from—what?*

From dropping. It means retailers aren't going to advertise there and the *Globe's* going to go under.

MAN: *But the* Globe *has a monopoly market.*

They do not.

MAN: *What are they going to do, advertise in the* Herald *[second Boston newspaper]?*

Absolutely.

MAN: *I think that really is simplistic, I really do.*

This actually *happened,* it's happened a few times. Most of the time it never happens, because the newspapers never deviate. But in 1976 or '77, *New York Times* advertising and stock values began to drop very slightly. There were immediately articles about this in the *Wall Street Journal* and *Business Week,* pointing out what was going on—*Business Week* in fact said, if the *New York Times* doesn't realize that it's a business, it's not going to be in business any longer.[54]

Well, what was happening was that the *Times* had taken a mildly supportive editorial position on a New York tax bill that business was opposed to, and advertising started slipping off a little, stocks started dropping very slightly. And the *Times* then shifted its entire editorial staff: John Oakes went out, all the liberal editors went out, and a whole bunch of new people came in. All it took was a slight change on the stock market. Now, in that case it was a matter of such a slight deviation that you'd need a microscope to see it—suppose they took a major deviation, what would happen to their stock?

In countries that have a wider range of democratic politics than we do, where there really is a danger that some political party might impose different policies, this sort of thing happens all the time.

MAN: *I guess I don't know what it's like on a big paper. I have a great deal of autonomy as a reporter working for a small local paper.*

A small local paper's a different story. But suppose you start doing things that are harmful to local business interests—I think you'll find that it's not easy to keep doing it. You can probably do good reporting on international affairs if you want, just because they don't care so much in a small-town paper.

MAN: *I don't know—I don't take those interests into account at all. I'm the business writer for my county, and I can do what I want.*

You *think* you do what you want; see, Tom Wicker at the *New York Times* thinks he does what he wants, too—and he's right. But what he wants is what power wants.

MAN: *I've just followed my instincts, and I've never had any problems.*

Have you ever done things that caused an uproar in the business community?

MAN: *Possibly.*

But that's the question: I think if you had, you would have heard about it. I mean, if you expose corruption, that's fine . . .

## Filters on Reporting

WOMAN: *Is this a conscious effort on the part of the press, or would you say it just plays out economically because they want to sell newspapers and the public is buying it?*

It has nothing to do with the public.

WOMAN: *Advertisers?*

Well, yes, advertisers. See, the press does not make money on people buying newspapers, they lose money on people buying newspapers.[55] But the press *is* business interests—I mean, the major press is huge corporate interests, the small press is more local business interests, but either way it's kept alive by other businesses, through advertising.

MAN: *One of the biggest businesses around here is development, and I continually present both points of view, as far as environmental issues versus development issues.*

And business takes both points of view, business is on both sides—like, in this region, maintaining tourism is a huge thing for business, and that means maintaining the environment. And you know, the rich folk who move out here from New York also want to maintain the environment. So you've got very powerful, privileged interests on "the other side" of this issue. See, you happened to have picked an issue where the business community is split, and therefore the press will present "both sides." But try to start doing something that undermines *all* business interests as such—you will quickly find that you're not a journalist anymore. I mean, they may be willing to keep you on as a maverick just for the fun of it, but if you ever get to the point where you're influencing people's attitudes about public policy or power, you're not going to stay on. And that's exactly why people who say those things *don't* stay on.

MAN: *I posed this question to the president of the Chamber of Commerce: "Is economic growth really a desirable thing?" That's a radical question, and I got an answer to it.*

But it's *not* a radical question here, because preventing economic growth is helping business interests in this region. You happen to be in a special position on that issue. Suggest a redistribution of income, increase of business taxes for welfare purposes. Try that.

WOMAN: *But that's not reporting.*

Why not? He says, "opinions on both sides." That's an opinion on both sides.

Look, one of the things that Edward Herman and I did in *Manufacturing Consent* was to just look at the sources that reporters go to. In a part that I wrote, I happened to be discussing Central America, so I went through fifty articles by Stephen Kinzer of the *New York Times* beginning in October 1987, and just asked: whose opinions did he try to get? Well, it turns out that in fifty articles he did not talk to one person in Nicaragua who was pro-Sandinista. Now, there's got to be *somebody*—you know, Ortega's mother, *somebody's* got to be pro-Sandinista. Nope, in fact, everybody he quotes is anti-Sandinista. [Daniel Ortega was the Sandinista President.]

Well, there are polls, which the *Times* won't report, and they show that all of the opposition parties in Nicaragua combined had the support of only 9 percent of the population. But they have 100 percent of Stephen Kinzer—everyone he's found supports the opposition parties, 9 percent of the population. That's in fifty articles.[56]

MAN: *I think your indictment of subtlety is again simplistic. For instance, I read an article you wrote for* The Progressive *about reporters' dependence on government sources—that's really important, you have to get economic figures, you have to develop long-term sources, you can't get the information otherwise.[57] Why do you have such a low opinion of the readership to think that they're not going to pick up on the subtlety? It may be in the fifth or sixth paragraph, but you can see the reporter's own opinion there.*

I don't understand what you're saying. What I'm saying is that if you look at the sources reporters select, they are not sources that are expert, they are sources that represent vested interests: that's propaganda.

WOMAN: *But I don't think the journalists say that to themselves—they want to think they're doing an honest job.*

Sure they do, but you can see exactly how it works. Suppose that as a reporter you start going outside of vested interests. You will find, first of all, that the level of evidence that's required is far higher. You don't need verification when you go to vested interests, they're self-verifying. Like, if you report an atrocity carried out by guerrillas, all you need is one hearsay witness. You talk about torture carried out by an American military officer, you're going to need videotapes. And the same is true on every issue.

I mean, if a journalist quotes an unnamed "high U.S. government official," that suffices as evidence. What if they were to quote some dissident, or some official from a foreign government that's an enemy? Well, they'd have to start digging, and backing it up, and the reporter would have to have mountains of evidence, and expect to pick up a ton of flack, and maybe lose their job, and so on. With factors of that kind, it's very predictable which way they're going to go. And reporters generally pick the easy way; I mean, the laziness is phenomenal.

WOMAN: *Would you characterize this media analysis as a "conspiracy theory" at all?*

It's precisely the opposite of conspiracy theory, actually—in fact, in general this analysis tends to downplay the role of individuals: they're just replaceable pieces.

Look, part of the structure of corporate capitalism is that the players in the game try to increase profits and market shares—if they don't do that, they will no longer be players in the game. Any economist knows this: it's not a conspiracy theory to point that out, it's just taken for granted as an institutional fact. If someone were to say, "Oh no, that's a conspiracy theory," people would laugh. Well, what we've been discussing are simply the institutional factors that set the boundaries for reporting and interpretation in the ideological institutions. That's the opposite of conspiracy theory, it's just normal institutional analysis, the kind of analysis you do automatically when you're trying to understand how the world works. For people to call it "conspiracy theory" is part of the effort to prevent an understanding of how the world works, in my view—"conspiracy theory" has become the intellectual equivalent of a four-letter word: it's something people say when they don't want you to think about what's really going on.

MAN: *What role would you say the alternative media play in the "Propaganda Model"?*

Well, it varies. I think to some extent the alternative media play a role *within* the "Propaganda Model." So a lot of what's called the "alternative media" in the United States is really just a kind of commercialization of freakishness—like 95 percent of the *Village Voice*, for example, or maybe 99 percent. I regard that as just another technique of marginalization of the public: it's sort of another version of the *National Enquirer*, just for a different audience.

However, to a significant extent the alternative media play a very constructive role—often they present people with an alternative view of the world, and that does make a difference. For example, I travel around giving talks all over the country, and I've noticed that in places that have listener-supported radio, there's just a different feel in the community—there's a place that people can go to, and relate themselves to, and find out what's going on, and hear other people, and contribute, and construct a different conception of the world and how it works on a continuing basis. I mean, you feel it right away if something like that is going on, and you feel it if nothing's going on. The alternative political journals are the same.

But notice that anything that's alternative is going to be lacking in resources and lacking in outreach—it's like alternatives to automobile production: you can do it, but it's going to be extremely difficult. So I don't know the details, but I imagine that if you compare the resources behind, say, F.A.I.R. [Fairness and Accuracy In Reporting, a left-wing media-monitoring group] and A.I.M. [Accuracy In Media, a right-wing one], you'll come out with a very good estimate of what's involved.[58] And it's only natural that powerful interests wouldn't want to support genuinely alternative structures—why would an institution function in such a way as to undermine itself? Of course that's not going to happen.

WOMAN: *Recently on public television there was a series of programs about clandestine activities and the atomic bomb which brought out a lot of information that seemed to go against those powerful interests, though—it was very unusual, the kind of thing you almost never see. I'm wondering what you think its purpose might have been.*

*I was extremely surprised at the openness of what was being said: they mentioned Operation MONGOOSE, the assassination attempts on Castro, connections between the Kennedys and the Mafia; they talked about the U.S. recruiting some of the worst Nazis to work for us at the end of World War II.[59] I'm curious why those kinds of things are coming out now: why is it happening at this point, and in such a public forum? You were talking before about things sometimes slipping through the cracks—this is more than slipping through the cracks.*

Well, is it really? How many people saw it? See, and these are pretty activist people, people who are attuned to that sort of thing. And it's not the first time that this has happened—a lot of this material already appeared in the media, in 1975. So it would be interesting to know exactly why it is coming out now, but some things come to mind right off.

The first set of exposures was in 1975, which was right after Watergate; the second set of exposures is right now, which happens to be right after Iran-contra. And it's very typical that after government scandals like these, there's a period of relative openness in the media, which then closes up again. In fact, there are plenty of journalists who are very well aware of this fact, and who wait for government scandals to try to sneak through stories which they know they couldn't get published at other times. I can give you examples of that, if you'd like. And it's obvious why it's going to happen: there's a scandal, so the institutions want to legitimize themselves, and there's popular pressure, so journalists who want to write about things like this have a little bit of an opening to do it. That may be the reason.

Incidentally, there are going to be some more exposures in the media in a week or two on the show *Frontline*—which if P.B.S. runs it (they're now debating it), will be very interesting. It's an episode on the Middle East by Leslie and Andrew Cockburn, and from what I've heard, it's extremely well done. So it's not that these systems are *completely* closed to dissidents—even on commercial television, there are possibilities. For instance, when Leslie Cockburn was working at C.B.S., she was able to expose information of real importance about U.S. government involvement in drug-running through the contras. I don't know if some of you saw that, but this was on a national network program, *West 57th*—tens of millions of people were watching American pilots in jail testifying about how they would fly arms down to the contras and come back with their planes loaded with cocaine, land at Homestead Air Force base in Florida guided in by radar, then trucks would come up and unload the drugs and take them away, all right on the Air Force base. That was on C.B.S.[60]

So there *are* openings for investigative reporting, and there are people in the media who look for them and find them. In fact, some of the top investigative reporters in the country are very conscious of the way the system works and play it like a violin, just looking for moments when they can sneak stories through. Some of the best-known of them are even more cynical about the media than I am, actually—but they just find ways to work within the system, and often they get out material that's very important. So people will store up stories on topics they've researched, and wait for a time when it's going to be a little bit more lax and they can put them in. Or they'll look for the right editor, they write their points very carefully and frame them so they'll just get by.

Remember, there really are conflicting values in these systems, and those conflicts allow for possibilities. One value is service to power; another value is professional integrity—and journalists can't do their job of serving power effectively unless they know how to work with some integrity, but if they know how to work with some integrity, they're also going to want to exercise that value in other areas. It's extremely hard to control that conflict, and things certainly do get through sometimes.

Plus, you know, there also just is a need in the media to present a tolerably accurate picture of the world—and that also creates openings. So for example, take the *Wall Street Journal,* the prototypical business press: the editorial pages are just comical tantrums, but the news coverage is often quite interesting and well done, they have some of the best reporting in the country, in fact. And I think the reason for that is pretty clear. On the editorial page of the *Wall Street Journal,* the editors can scream and yell and foam at the mouth and nobody cares very much, but people in the business world have to have a realistic picture of what's happening in the world if they're going to make sane decisions about their money. Well, that also creates openings, and those openings can often be capitalized on.

So the main point is not total suppression of information by the media—that's rare, although it certainly exists. The main point is the shaping of history, the selection, the interpretation that takes place. I mean, just to give one illustration, I doubt that any story ever received the kind of fanatical level of coverage as the downing of Korean Air Lines Flight 007 by the Russians in 1983—that was presented as sure proof that the Russians were the worst barbarians since Attila the Hun, and that we therefore had to install missiles in Germany, and step up the war against Nicaragua, and so on. Well, for the month of September 1983 alone, the *New York Times* index—you know, the very densely printed index of articles that have appeared in the *Times*— has seven full pages devoted to this story. That's the *index,* for one month alone. The liberal *Boston Globe* on the first day of coverage had I think its first ten full pages devoted to that story and nothing else. I mean, I didn't check, but I doubt that even the outbreak of the Second World War had that much coverage.

Alright, there were other events that took place in the midst of all of the furor over the K.A.L. flight—for example, the *Times* devoted one hundred words and no comment to the following fact: U.N.I.T.A., who are the so-called "freedom fighters" supported by the United States and South Africa in Angola, *took credit* for downing an Angolan civilian jet plane with 126 people killed. Now, there were no ambiguities in this case: the plane wasn't off course, there was no R.C.-135 confusing the issue [K.A.L. Flight 007 had flown off course into Soviet airspace, and a U.S. Air Force R.C.-135 spy plane had been patrolling the same area earlier that day]. This was just premeditated mass murder—and that deserved a hundred words and no further comment.[61] A few years earlier, in October 1976, a Cuban airliner was bombed by C.I.A.-backed terrorists, killing 73 civilians. How much coverage was there of that?[62] In 1973, Israel downed a civilian plane lost in a sandstorm over the Suez Canal with 110 people killed. There was no protest, only editorial comments about—I'm quoting from the *Times*— how "no useful purpose is served by an acrimonious debate over the as- signment of blame."[63] Four days later, Golda Meir [the Israeli Prime Minister] arrived in the United States, and the press troubled her with few embarrassing questions—in fact, she returned home with new gifts of mili- tary aircraft.[64] Going back to 1955, an Air India plane carrying the Chinese delegation to the Bandung Conference was blown up in the air in what the Hong Kong police called "a carefully planned mass murder"; an American defector later claimed that he had planted the bomb in the service of the C.I.A.[65] In July 1988, the U.S. warship *Vincennes* shot down an Iranian civilian airliner in a commercial air corridor off the coast of Iran with 290 people killed—out of a need to prove the viability of its high-tech missile system, according to U.S. Navy Commander David Carlson, who was monitoring the event from a nearby ship and said that he "wondered aloud in disbelief."[66] None of these incidents was held to demonstrate "bar- barism," and in fact all have been quickly forgotten.

Well, one could offer thousands of such examples, and a lot of people, including me, have done so in print. These are the ways in which history is shaped in the interests of those in power—and that's the kind of thing I'm saying about the press. The information sometimes is *reported*, but the media isn't *presenting* it.[67]

## Honest Subordination

MAN: *I'm wondering how people inside the media tend to respond to this type of institutional critique.*

Well, to draw a broad brush-stroke through it, by and large the media love to be attacked from the right—they love it when they're attacked as being subversive, adversarial, going so far in their passion to undermine power that they're destroying democracy, and so on. They even love being told that they're *lying* in their commitment to undermine power—there are dramatic examples of this. And it's obvious why they like it so much: then they can come back and say, as Katharine Graham [owner of the *Washington Post*] did in a commencement address, well yes, it's true that in our anti-establishment zeal we sometimes go too far, but that's the price you have to pay in a free society. It makes great copy.

On the other hand, if they're criticized from the opposite side, saying: "Look, you may do your work with a good deal of integrity, but you're very subordinated to power—indeed servile, often—in the way that you select topics, and shape them, and adopt perspectives," *that* they hate. So they don't like to be told that they're doing their work honestly but subordinated to power—they much prefer to be told, "You're dishonest in your efforts to undermine power."

To give you a recent example, one of the major right-wing attacks on the media was a huge two-volume study published by an organization called "Freedom House" (nice Orwellian name) which criticized media coverage of the Tet Offensive in the Vietnam War, reaching the conclusion that the media basically lost the war for us by their lack of patriotism.[68] The thrust of the study was that the media had lied about the Tet Offensive and had presented a North Vietnamese/Viet Cong defeat as a great victory for the enemy, and had thereby undermined the American war effort. That was the fundamental claim, and to support it they alleged that the media had distorted what people had said, and had falsified the evidence, and so on and so forth. The media loved it, they just lapped it up—and ever since then, that's been the standard story.[69]

Well, the fact of the matter is that this Freedom House study was immediately exposed as a hoax, in a journalism review which was widely read. I wrote the article.[70] The study was almost a total fraud: when you corrected the hundreds of crucial errors and falsifications, what you were left with was the conclusion that American journalists had covered the Tet Offensive quite honestly, in a very narrow sense—that is, they had described accurately what was in front of their eyes—but they had done it within a framework of patriotic premises which distorted the whole picture quite considerably.

So for example, reporters would describe how the U.S. forces were wiping out towns in South Vietnam, and they'd say, "This is an unfortunate necessity, but we have to defend these towns from attackers." Well, there were no attackers except the Americans—there were no Russians, no Chinese, virtually no North Vietnamese, nobody but the American aggressors.[71] But of course, nobody in the press could say *that*. So, narrowly speaking, the media did an honest job, though always from a perspective very much shaped by U.S. government propaganda. And as to their depicting an enemy defeat as a victory, that's just totally false: the press was much more optimistic about the outcome of the Tet Offensive than official U.S. intelligence was—and we know that, because the intelligence reports appear in the *Pentagon Papers* [top-secret Defense Department planning record of U.S. involvement in Southeast Asia, leaked to the public in 1971].[72]

So in reality, what it comes down to is that Freedom House was accusing the media of not being sufficiently *upbeat and enthusiastic* in their adoption of the government propaganda framework. Well, that's pure totalitarianism. But the critique of their study disappeared, nobody pays the slightest attention to it. It's been reprinted a number of times and amplified, it's all thoroughly documented and supported, but nobody wants to hear it. The media do not want to hear that they did an honest job, but within the framework of state power; they'd much rather hear that they were so subversive they may have even undermined democracy.

## "Fight it Better": the Media and the Vietnam War

WOMAN: *I had the impression that during the anti-Vietnam War period there was more openness in the media to the progressive movements than there is now, for instance in the* New York Times *and the* Washington Post.

That's an illusion people have—actually, there was less openness. Look, I can tell you about that, because I was right in the middle of it, and also I've studied it in great detail . . .

WOMAN: *From reading today's newspapers, I think there's been a definite shift to the right.*

See, I don't agree with that. People do have that illusion, but I think it's because their perspective has shifted to the *left*—and that runs across most of the population, actually. So for example, the stance that most movement activists considered an anti-war position in 1969, they would today consider to be a *pro-war* position—accurately. I mean, in 1969 it was considered anti-war to say we're not fighting well enough: that was called "anti-war." So I don't know *you* of course, but if you're like the ordinary movement activist, I would guess that your perspective also has shifted in the last twenty years, and that's where this impression is coming from.

As for the *New York Times,* another of the things Ed Herman and I did in *Manufacturing Consent* was to spend about 150 pages reviewing mostly the *New York Times* on the Vietnam War from 1950 to the present—and the fact is, the *Times* was always to the hawkish side of the population, very far. They were never critical of it. There was never a critical columnist. They consciously suppressed U.S. government actions. When you look back at the reporters we thought of as critical, David Halberstam and others, Neil Sheehan, you'll discover that what they were criticizing was the *failure*—they were saying, "Of course it's a noble cause and we want to win, but you guys are screwing it up. Fight it better." It was that kind of criticism.[73]

This comes out very clearly in Sheehan's new book actually, this best-seller that just won the Pulitzer Prize, *A Bright Shining Lie.*[74] It's being highly touted everywhere as a big exposé of the Vietnam War, but if you look at it closely, what it's really exposing is the fact that the things American intelligence experts were saying in the field were not getting communicated back to Washington—that's the nature of Sheehan's criticism. And that's still considered the far-out anti-war position in the mainstream, even today: "You guys screwed it up, you should have fought it better." Sheehan's book is sort of a biography of John Paul Vann, who was an extreme hawk [he oversaw "civilian pacification" programs in Vietnam], but perceptive—he understood what was going on, and was on the scene in the field giving young reporters information that said things weren't going the way Washington said they were going (which was considered totally unpatriotic: how can you say it's not going the way Washington says?). And he's Sheehan's hero of the whole war.

Well, just take a look at Vann. He leaked some memoranda in 1965 which were used in the peace movement—like, I published them, and Ed Herman published them and so on, but the mainstream media would never publish them, and in fact Sheehan doesn't even mention them in his book. Basically they said something like this: in South Vietnam, the National Liberation Front—the so-called "Viet Cong"—has won the population over to their side, and they've won the population over to their side because they have good political programs. The peasants support them because they're the right people to support, we ought to be supporting their programs too. There's a social revolution in progress in South Vietnam, it's a badly needed social revolution, the N.L.F. is organizing it, and that's why they have peasant support; there's nothing we can do about that. Well, then comes the conclusion. The conclusion is, we've got to escalate the war, we have to wipe the N.L.F. out.[75] And the reason is essentially the same as what's argued by people like Walter Lippmann and the whole rest of this main tradition of "democratic" thinkers in the West—that democracy requires a class of elites to manage decision-making and "manufacture" the general population's consent for policies that are supposedly beyond their capacity to develop and decide on themselves.[76]

So for Vann, the thinking was, these stupid Vietnamese peasants are making a mistake—it's us smart guys who are the ones who can run the social revolution for them. They think the N.L.F. can run it, these people running around villages organizing them, but *we're* really the only ones who can run it. And out of our duty to the poor people of the world, we can't let them have their own way, because it'll just be a stupid error on their part. So what we have to do is wipe out the N.L.F., win the war, smash up Vietnam, and then we'll run the social revolution for them—like we've always done in history, you know. That's basically Vann's line, and that's also the message of Neil Sheehan's book. That's what made Vann a hero.

Or just take a look at the guy who was certainly the most critical columnist at the *Times*, Anthony Lewis. I mean, if you look at Anthony Lewis's *record* during the war, you'll really learn something about the peace movement, about ourselves—because we actually regarded Anthony Lewis as an *ally*. Let's remember what happened. The hard work in the peace movement was from 1964 through '67. By February 1968, corporate America had turned against the war—and the reason was, the Tet Offensive had taken place in late January. In late January 1968, there was this huge popular uprising in every city in South Vietnam; it was all South Vietnamese, remember, it wasn't the North Vietnamese who were doing it. And by early February 1968, it was obvious to anybody with their head screwed on that this was just a massive popular movement. I mean, the American forces in Saigon were never even *informed* that Viet Cong troops were infiltrating into the city—nobody told them. And it was simultaneous, and coordinated, it was just a huge popular uprising—there's nothing like it in history.

Well, you know, people who care about their money and their property and so on realized that this war was just money going down the drain—it was going to take a huge effort to crush this revolution. And by that point, the U.S. economy was actually beginning to suffer. That's the great achievement of the peace movement, in fact: it harmed the American economy. And that's not a joke. The peace movement made it impossible to declare a national mobilization around the war—there was just too much dissidence and disruption, they couldn't do what was done during the Second World War, for example, when the whole population was mobilized around the war. See, if they could have gotten the population mobilized like that, then the Vietnam War would have been very good for the economy, like the Second World War was during the Forties, a real shot in the arm. But they couldn't, they had to fight a deficit-spending war, what's called a "guns-and-butter" war. And the result was that we got the beginnings of stagflation [inflation without a concurrent expansion of the economy], and weakening of the U.S. dollar, and our main economic competitors, Europe and Japan, began raking off huge profits as offshore producers for the war—in short, the war changed the economic balance of power between the U.S. and its major industrial rivals. Well, American business could understand that, they saw what was happening, and when the Tet Offensive came along and it was clear that there was going to be a big problem putting down this revolution, corporate America turned against the war.

Also, they were worried about what was happening at home at the time—very worried. See, here we have exposed secret documents, which are extremely enlightening. If you look at the very tail end of the *Pentagon Papers*, for example, the part that deals with the weeks after the Tet Offensive, the top American military brass said that they were concerned about sending more troops to Vietnam, because they were afraid they wouldn't have enough troops left over for what they called "civil disorder control" at home—they were afraid of a revolution breaking out if they continued escalating the war. And they referred to the problems: youth, women, ethnic minorities, all these groups were starting to get involved in protest.[77]

And actually, there was also another factor here that I should mention: the American army was falling apart. Remember, this was a citizens' army, and it was the first time in history that a citizens' army was being used to fight a colonial war—and that doesn't work. I mean, you cannot take kids off the street and turn them into professional killers in a couple months—for that you need Nazis like the French Foreign Legion [an army of foreigners used to fight in France's colonies], or peasants that you mobilize and give guns to and turn into cold-blooded killers, like the contras, say. That's the way every imperial power in history has run its empire. But the United States tried to do it with a citizens' army, and by 1968 it was already collapsing: drugs, lack of discipline, shooting your officers. And all of that was also a reflection of the popular movement at home: this is a youth culture, after all, and the guys who were going into the army were not all that different from the ones at home who were getting involved in the various movements. So the American army was falling apart, and the top Pentagon brass didn't like it: they in fact wanted the army out.[78]

Alright, let's go back to the *New York Times*. All this time the *New York Times* had no criticism of the war: nothing. Anthony Lewis is a bellwether, because he was their most extreme critic. More than a year after the Tet Offensive, in mid-1969, Anthony Lewis was the *Times*'s Bureau Chief in London, and at that point he was unwilling even to *speak* to people in the American peace movement. I remember this personally. I was in Oxford in the spring of 1969 as John Locke Lecturer, and I was all over the British media talking about the war. Some of the British anti-war groups tried to get Anthony Lewis just to have a private discussion with me—he wouldn't do it, said he's not going to talk to anyone connected with this peace movement. And this wasn't even in the United States, it was in *England,* where the pressures and the political climate were different. Finally by late 1969, he did begin to write mildly critical stuff about the war. Then he went to

North Vietnam and discovered that bombs actually hurt: you walk through Haiphong, you see a lot of buildings knocked down, people torn apart; big surprise. At that point Anthony Lewis started to write critical material about the war—but bear in mind that that's about a year and a half after corporate America turned against the war.

Or take the My Lai massacre [the March 1968 shooting of 504 unarmed Vietnamese civilians by an American Army unit], which became a big issue in the United States. When? My Lai became a big issue in November 1969—that's a year and a half after the killings took place, and about a year and a half after corporate America had turned against the war. And of course, My Lai was a triviality—it was such a triviality that the peace movement knew about it right away and didn't even talk about it. Like, the Quakers in Quang Ngai Province where it took place [working with the American Friends Service Committee] didn't even bother reporting it—because the same sort of thing was happening all over the place.[79]

MAN: Life *magazine made My Lai famous.*[80]

My Lai, they did—but first of all, note the timing: it's a year and a half after it happened, a year and a half after corporate America turned against the war. And the reporting was falsified. See, My Lai was presented as if it was a bunch of crazy grunts who got out of control because they were being directed by this Lieutenant Calley, who was kind of a madman. *That* you can handle. But that's not what My Lai was about. My Lai was a footnote, My Lai was an uninteresting footnote to a military operation called Operation WHEELER WALLAWA—which was a huge mass-murder operation, in which B-52 raids were targeted right on villages. That wasn't Lieutenant Calley, that was a guy in Washington plotting out coordinates. You know what a B-52 raid is? That means wipe out everything—and it was targeted right on villages. In comparison to that, My Lai doesn't exist.

In fact, there was a military commission that reviewed My Lai, the Piers Commission, and their most dramatic finding was that there were massacres like My Lai all over the place. For instance, they found another massacre in My Khe, which is about four kilometers down the road—everywhere they looked they found another massacre.[81] Well, what does that tell you? What does that suggest to you, if everywhere you look you find a My Lai? Well, it suggests something, but what it suggests was never brought out in the media.

WOMAN: *You mentioned that we had a citizens' army in Vietnam. Do we still have a citizens' army?*

No, now it's a professional army.

WOMAN: *I know, that's what's scary.*

Exactly.

WOMAN: *Ironically, not having a draft . . .*

It's not ironic. I think the peace movement made a mistake there. I mean, personally I was never in favor of ending the draft, although I was all involved in resistance activities: when it turned to anti-draft activities, I pulled out of them.

WOMAN: *Me too.*

Look, there is no such thing as a "volunteer army": a "volunteer army" is a mercenary army of the poor. Take a look at the Marines—what you see is black faces, from the ghettos.

WOMAN: *And the officers are white.*

Yeah, and the officers are white, of course. That's like South Africa: the officers are white, the grunts who actually carry out most of the atrocities in places like Namibia are black.[82] That's the way empires have always been run. And sometime in the Seventies, the American army shifted to a traditional mercenary army of the poor, which they call a "volunteer army." People in power learn, you know. They're sophisticated, and they're organized, and they have continuity—and they realize that they made a mistake in Vietnam. They don't want to make that same mistake again.

And as for the *New York Times* being anti-war—well, we *thought* of it as anti-war at the time, but that was because our standard was so low. Nowadays we would consider that same sort of "criticism" to be pro-war. And that's just another reflection of the increase in political consciousness and sophistication in the general population over the last twenty years. If you look back at the *Times* in those days, that's what you'll find I think.

# 2

# Teach-In: Over Coffee

*Based primarily on discussions at Rowe,*
*Massachusetts, April 15–16, 1989.*

### "Containing" the Soviet Union in the Cold War

WOMAN: *Dr. Chomsky, it seems the terms of political discourse themselves are a tool for propagandizing the population. How is language used to prevent us from understanding and to disempower us?*

Well, the terminology we use is heavily ideologically laden, always. Pick your term: if it's a term that has any significance whatsoever—like, not "and" or "or"—it typically has two meanings, a dictionary meaning and a meaning that's used for ideological warfare. So, "terrorism" is only what other people do. What's called "Communism" is supposed to be "the far left": in my view, it's the far *right*, basically indistinguishable from fascism. These guys that everybody calls "conservative," any conservative would turn over in their grave at the sight of them—they're extreme statists, they're not "conservative" in any traditional meaning of the word. "Special interests" means labor, women, blacks, the poor, the elderly, the young—in other words, the general population. There's only one sector of the population that *doesn't* ever get mentioned as a "special interest," and that's corporations, and business in general—because they're the "*national* interest." Or take "defense": I have never heard of a state that admits it's carrying out an aggressive act, they're always engaged in "defense," no matter what they're doing—maybe "preemptive defense" or something.

Or look at the major theme of modern American history, "containment"—as in, "the United States is containing Soviet expansionism." Unless you accept that framework of discussion when talking about international affairs in the modern period, you are just not a part of accepted discourse here: everybody has to begin by assuming that for the last half-century the United States has been "containing" the Soviet Union.

Well, the rhetoric of "containment" begs all questions—once you've accepted the rhetoric of "containment," it really doesn't matter what you say, you've already given up everything. Because the fundamental question is, is it true? Has the United States been "containing" the Soviet Union? Well, you know, on the surface it looks a little odd. I mean, maybe you think the Soviet Union is the worst place in history, but they're conservative—whatever rotten things they've done, they've been inside the Soviet Union and right around its borders, in Eastern Europe and Afghanistan and so on. They never do anything anywhere else. They don't have troops stationed anywhere else. They don't have intervention forces positioned all over the world like we do.[1] So what does it mean to say we're "containing" them?

We've been talking about the media and dumping on them, so why not turn to scholarship? Diplomatic history's a big field, people win big prizes, get fancy professorships. Well, if you look at diplomatic history, it too is in the framework of "containment," even the so-called dissidents. I mean, *everybody* has to accept the premise of "containment," or you simply will not have an opportunity to proceed in these fields. And in the footnotes of the professional literature on containment, often there are some revealing things said.

For example, one of the major scholarly books on the Cold War is called *Strategies of Containment*, by John Lewis Gaddis—it's the foremost scholarly study by the top diplomatic historian, so it's worth taking a look at. Well, in discussing this great theme, "strategies of containment," Gaddis begins by talking about the terminology. He says at the beginning: it's true that the term "containment" begs some questions, yes it presupposes some things, but nevertheless, despite the question of whether it's factually accurate, it still is proper to adopt it as the framework for discussion. And the reason why it's proper is because it was the *perception* of American leaders that they were taking a defensive position against the Soviet Union—so, Gaddis concludes, since that was the perception of American leaders, and since we're studying American history, it's fair to continue in that framework.[2]

Well, just suppose some diplomatic historian tried that with the Nazis. Suppose somebody were to write a book about German history and say, "Well, look, Hitler and his advisors certainly *perceived* their position as defensive"—which is absolutely true: Germany was under "attack" by the Jews, remember. Go back and look at the Nazi literature, they had to defend themselves against this virus, this bacillus that was eating away at the core of modern civilization—and you've got to defend yourself, after all. And they were under "attack" by the Czechs, and by the Poles, and by European encirclement. That's not a joke. In fact, they had a better argument there than we do with the Soviet Union—they *were* encircled, and "contained," and they had this enormous Versailles debt stuck on them for no reason after World War I. Okay, so suppose somebody wrote a book saying: "Look, the Nazi leadership *perceived* themselves as taking a defensive stance against external and internal aggression; it's true it begs some questions, but we'll proceed that way—now we'll talk about how they defended themselves against the Jews by building Auschwitz, and how they defended themselves against the Czechs by invading Czechoslovakia, how they defended themselves against the Poles, and so on." If anybody tried to do that, you wouldn't even bother to laugh—but about the United States, that's the *only* thing you can say: it's not just that it's *acceptable*, it's that anything else is *unacceptable*.

And when you pursue the matter further, it becomes even more interesting. So for example, in this same book Gaddis points out—again, in sort of a footnote, an aside he doesn't elaborate on—that it's a striking fact that when you look over the American diplomatic record since World War II, all of our decisions about how to contain the Soviet Union, like the arms build-ups, the shifts to détente, all those things, reflected largely domestic economic considerations. Then he sort of drops the point.[3] Well, what does that mean? What does Gaddis mean by that? There he's beginning to enter into the realm of truth. See, the truth of the matter, and it's very well-supported by declassified documents and other evidence, is that military spending is our method of industrial management—it's our way of keeping the economy profitable for business. So just take a look at the major declassified documents on military spending, they're pretty frank about it. For example, N.S.C. 68 [National Security Council Memorandum 68] is the major Cold War document, as everybody agrees, and one of the things it says very clearly is that without military spending, there's going to be an economic decline both in the United States and world-wide—so consequently it calls for a vast increase in military spending in the U.S., in addition to breaking up the Soviet Union.[4]

You have to remember the context in which these decisions were being made, after all. This was right after the Marshall Plan had failed, right after the post-war aid programs had failed. There still had been no success as yet in reconstructing either the Japanese or Western European economies—and American business needed them; American manufacturers needed those export markets desperately. See, the Marshall Plan was designed largely as an export-promotion operation for American business, not as the noblest effort in history and so on. But it had failed: we hadn't rebuilt the industrial powers we needed as allies and reconstructed the markets we needed for exports. And at that point, military spending was considered the one thing that could really do it, it was seen as the engine that could drive economic growth after the wartime boom ended, and prevent the U.S. from slipping back into a depression.[5] And it worked: military spending was a big stimulus to the U.S. economy, and it led to the rebuilding of Japanese industry, and the rebuilding of European industry—and in fact, it has continued to be our mode of industrial management right up to the present. So in that little comment Gaddis was getting near the main story: he was saying, post-war American decisions on rearmament and détente have been keyed to domestic economic considerations—but then he drops it, and we go back to talking about "containment" again.

And if you look still closer at the scholarship on "containment," it's even more intriguing. For example, in another book Gaddis discusses the American military intervention in the Soviet Union right after the Bolshevik Revolution—when we tried to overthrow the new Bolshevik government by force—and he says *that* was defensive and *that* was containment: our invasion of the Russian land mass. And remember, I'm not talking about some right-wing historian; this is the major, most respected, liberal diplomatic historian, the dean of the field: he says the military intervention by 13 Western nations in the Soviet Union in 1918 was a "defensive" act. And why was it defensive? Well, there's a sense in which he's right. He says it was "defensive" because the Bolsheviks had declared a challenge to the existing order throughout the West, they had offered a challenge to Western capitalism—and naturally we had to defend ourselves. And the only way we could defend ourselves was by sending troops to Russia, so that's a "defensive" invasion, that's "defense." [6]

And if you look at that history in more detail, you'll find the point is even more revealing. So for example, right after the Bolshevik Revolution, American Secretary of State Robert Lansing warned President Wilson that the Bolsheviks are "issuing an appeal to the proletariat of all nations, to the illiterate and mentally deficient, who by their very numbers are supposed to take control of all governments." And since they're issuing an appeal to the mass of the population in other countries to take control of their own affairs, and since that mass of the population are the "mentally deficient" and the "illiterate"—you know, all these poor slobs out there who have to be kept in their place, for their own good—that's an attack on us, and therefore we have to defend ourselves.[7] And what Wilson actually *did* was to "defend ourselves" in the two obvious ways: first by invading Russia to try to prevent that challenge from being issued, and second by initiating the Red Scare at home [a 1919 campaign of U.S. government repression and propaganda against "Communists"] to crush the threat that anyone here might answer the appeal. Those were both a part of the same intervention, the same "defensive" intervention.

And it's the same right up until today. Why do we have to get rid of the Sandinistas in Nicaragua? In reality it's not because anybody really thinks that they're a Communist power about to conquer the Hemisphere—it's because they were carrying out social programs that were beginning to succeed, and which would have appealed to other people in Latin America who want the same things. In 1980 the World Bank estimated that it would take Nicaragua ten years just to get back to the economic level it had in 1977, because of the vast destruction inflicted at the end of the Somoza reign [the four-decade Nicaraguan family dictatorship ousted by the Sandinista revolution in July 1979]. But nevertheless, under the Sandinista government Nicaragua was in fact beginning economic development: it was establishing health programs, and social programs, and things were starting to improve for the general population there.[8] Well, that set off the alarm bells in New York and Washington, like it always does, and we had to stop it—because it was issuing an appeal to the "illiterate and mentally deficient" in other desperate countries, like Honduras and Guatemala, to do the same thing. That's what U.S. planners call the "domino theory," or the "threat of a good example," and pretty soon the whole U.S.-dominated system starts to fall apart.[9]

## Orwell's World and Ours

Well, all of that is within the rhetoric of "containing" Communism—and we could easily go on. But there's one word. You look at any other term of political discourse, and you're going to find the same thing: the terms of political discourse are designed so as to prevent thought. One of the main ones is this notion of "defense." So look at the diplomatic record of any country you want—Nazi Germany, the Soviet Union, Libya, pick your favorite horror-story—you'll find that everything they ever did was "defensive"; I'm sure if we had records from Genghis Khan we would find that what he was doing was "defensive" too. And here in the United States you cannot challenge that—no matter how absurd it gets.

Like, we can be "defending" South Vietnam. I have never seen in the media, *never* in thirty years that I have been looking carefully, one phrase even suggesting that we were not defending South Vietnam. Now, we weren't: we were *attacking* South Vietnam. We were attacking South Vietnam as clearly as any aggression in history. But try to find one phrase anywhere in any American newspaper, outside of real marginal publications, just stating that elementary fact. It's unstatable.[10]

It's unstatable in the scholarly literature. Gaddis again, when he talks about the battle of Dienbienphu, where the French made their last stand to keep colonial control over Indochina, he describes it as a defensive struggle.[11] McGeorge Bundy, in his book on the history of the military system, talks about how the United States toyed with the idea of using nuclear weapons in 1954 to help the French maintain their position at Dienbienphu, and he says: we were thinking about it to assist the French in their "defense" of Indochina.[12] He doesn't say defense against *whom*, you know, because that would be too idiotic—like, was it defense against the Russians or something? No. They were defending Indochina against the *Indochinese*.[13] But no matter how absurd it is, you cannot question that in the United States. I mean, these are extremes of ideological fanaticism—in other countries, you could at least *raise* these kinds of questions. Some of you are journalists: try talking about the American "attack" on South Vietnam. Your editors will think you came from Mars or something, there was no such event in history. Of course, there *was* in real history.

Or take the idea that the United States is supporting "democracy" all over the world. Well, there's a sense in which that's true. But what does it mean? When we support "democracy," what do we support? I mean, is "democracy" something where the population takes part in running the country? Well, obviously not. For instance, why are El Salvador and Guatemala "democratic," but Nicaragua [i.e. under the Sandinista Party] not "democratic"? Why? Is it because two of them had elections and the other one didn't? No. In fact, Nicaragua's election [in 1984] was a hundred times as good as any election in El Salvador.[14] Is it because there's a lack of popular political participation in Nicaragua? No. Is it because the political opposition can't survive there? No, the political opposition is barely harassed in Nicaragua; in El Salvador and Guatemala it's just murdered.[15] Is it that there can't be an independent press in Nicaragua? No, the Nicaraguan press is one of the freest presses in the world, much more so than the *American* press has ever been—the United States has never tolerated a newspaper even *remotely* like *La Prensa* in Nicaragua [opposition paper supported by the U.S. during the contra war], not even close: in any time of crisis here, the American government has shut down even tiny dissident newspapers, forget a major newspaper funded by the foreign power that's attacking the country and which is openly calling for the overthrow of the government.[16] That degree of freedom of the press is absolutely inconceivable here. In El Salvador, there *was* an independent press at one time—it was wiped out by the U.S.-backed security forces, who just murdered the editor of one newspaper and blew up the premises of the other.[17] Okay, that takes care of that independent press.

So you know, by what criteria are El Salvador and Guatemala "democratic" and Nicaragua not? Well, there *is* a criterion: in Nicaragua [under the Sandinistas], business elements are not represented in dominating the state much beyond their numbers, so it's not a "democracy." In El Salvador and Guatemala, the governments are run by the military for the benefit of the local oligarchies—the landowners, rich businessmen, and rising professionals—and those people are tied up with the United States, so therefore those countries *are* "democracies." It doesn't matter if they blow up the independent press, and kill off the political opposition, and slaughter tens of thousands of people, and never run anything remotely like a free election—all of that is totally irrelevant. They're "democracies," because the right people are running them; if the right people *aren't* running them, then they're not "democracies." And on this again there is uniformity: try to find anyone in the American press, *anyone*, who is willing to break ranks on the idea that there are four democracies in Central America and one totalitarian state [i.e. Sandinista Nicaragua] that never had a free election—just try to find one statement rebutting that. And if the killings in El Salvador and Guatemala *are* ever mentioned in the American press, they'll always call it "Death Squads Out of Control," or "Extremists Out of Control." Now, the fact of the matter is that the extremists are in Washington, and what they're controlling are the Salvadoran and Guatemalan militaries—but you'll never find *that* in an American newspaper.

Or just take this phrase "peace process," which we hear all the time. The phrase "peace process" has a dictionary meaning, it means "process leading to peace." But that's not the way it's used in the media. The term "peace process" is used in the media to refer to whatever the United States happens to be doing at the moment—and again, that is without exception. So it turns out that the United States is *always* supporting the peace process, by definition. Just try to find a phrase in the U.S. media somewhere, anywhere, saying that the United States is opposing the peace process: you can't do it.

Actually, a few months ago I said this at a talk in Seattle, and someone from the audience wrote me a letter about a week or so later saying he was interested, so he'd done a little research project on it. He took the *New York Times* computer database from 1980 (when it begins) up to the present, and pulled out every article that had the words "peace process" in it. There were like nine hundred articles or something, and he checked through each of them to see if there was any case in which the United States was opposing the peace process. And there wasn't, it was 100 percent. Well, you know, even the most august country in history, let's say by accident sometime, might not be supporting the peace process. But in the case of the United States, that just can't happen. And this is a particularly striking illustration, because during the 1980s the United States was the main factor in blocking two major international peace processes, one in Central America and one in the Middle East.[18] But just try to find that simple, obvious fact stated anywhere in the mainstream media. You can't. And you can't because it's a logical contradiction—you don't even have to do any grubby work with the data and the documents to prove it, it's just proven by the meaning of the words themselves. It's like finding a married bachelor or something—you don't have to do any research to show there aren't any. You can't have the United States opposing the peace process, because the peace process is what the United States is *doing*, by definition. And if anybody is opposing the United States, then *they're* opposing the peace process. That's the way it works, and it's very convenient, you get nice conclusions.

MAN: *Can I throw in another one? When you have a country which you can't even pretend is a democracy—there's no constitution, no parliament, there's an absolute monarch—you use the word "moderate."*

Yeah, "moderate" is a word that means "follows U.S. orders"—as opposed to what's called "radical," which means "doesn't follow U.S. orders." "Radical" has nothing to do with left or right; you can be an ultra-right-winger, but you're a "radical" if you don't follow U.S. orders.

MAN: *I have yet to see a single reference to Morocco's King Hassan as an "absolute monarch." He has the worst human rights record in the Arab world, torture widespread, he invaded Western Sahara, disobeyed the World Court, one of the nastiest characters anywhere—I have never seen an article that didn't refer to him as a "moderate."* [19]

That's right, because we have U.S. airbases in Morocco, and we get plenty of minerals from there, and so on. Or just take Saudi Arabia—Saudi Arabia is even described as "moderate" now. [20] In fact, even *Iraq* is sometimes described as "moving towards moderation": Iraq is probably the worst terror-state in the world—death camps, biological warfare, anything you like. [21]

MAN: *How about Suharto [Indonesian dictator]—he's called a "moderate" too.*

Suharto, yeah—that's the most extreme case I've ever seen, in fact, I'm glad you mention it. This is a really astonishing one, actually. For example, there was an article in the *Christian Science Monitor* a couple years ago about the great business opportunities in Indonesia, and it said: after the Indonesian government stopped a Communist revolt in 1965, the West was very eager to do business with Indonesia's "new moderate leader, Suharto." [22] Well, who's Indonesia's "new moderate leader, Suharto"? Suharto is the guy who, no doubt with the backing of the United States, carried out a military coup in 1965 after which the Indonesian army slaughtered about 500,000 people within four months. Nobody knows the exact numbers—I mean, *they* gave 500,000, pick your number; it was mostly landless peasants. [23]

Well, that was very much welcomed in the West, the American media just loved it. For instance, James Reston, the *New York Times*'s liberal columnist, had a column I remember called, "A Gleam of Light in Asia"— things are really looking up. *U.S. News and World Report* had a story called, "Hope Where There Once Was None." [24] These were the kinds of headlines that were running throughout the U.S. press—and the reason was, Suharto had wiped out the only mass-based political party in Indonesia, the Communist Party, which had about fourteen million members at the time. The *Times* had an editorial saying basically: it's all great stuff, but the United States is right not to become too openly involved, because it doesn't look too good to wipe out 500,000 people—but it's going the right way, let's make sure it keeps going the right way. This was right at the time of the massacre. [25] Well, that's Indonesia's "new moderate leader," Suharto. This is probably the most extreme case I've ever seen: this guy is one of the biggest mass murderers since Adolf Hitler.

## Contemporary Poverty

WOMAN: *Noam, I want to change gears for a moment if we could. You've said that you were politically aware as a young kid in the 1930s—I'm wondering, do you have any impressions of the differences between that time and today, in terms of general outlook and attitudes? How would you compare the two periods?*

Well, the Thirties were an exciting time—it was deep economic depression, everybody was out of a job, but the funny thing about it was, it was hopeful. It's very different today. When you go into the slums today, it's nothing like what it was: it's desolate, there is no hope. Anybody who's my age or more will remember, there was a sense of hopefulness back then: maybe there was no food, but there were possibilities, there were things that could be done. You take a walk through East Harlem today, there was nothing like that at the depths of the Depression—this sense that there's nothing you can do, it's hopeless, your grandmother has to stay up at night to keep you from being eaten by a rat. That kind of thing didn't exist at the depths of the Depression; I don't even think it existed out in rural areas. Kids didn't come into school without food; teachers didn't have to worry that when they walked out into the hall, they might get killed by some guy high on drugs—it wasn't *that* bad.

There's really something qualitatively different about contemporary poverty, I think. Some of you must share these experiences. I mean, I was a kid back then, so maybe my perspective was different. But I remember when I would go into the apartment of my cousins—you know, broken family, no job, twenty people living in a tiny apartment—somehow it was hopeful. It was intellectually alive, it was exciting, it was just very different from today somehow.

WOMAN: *Do you attribute that to the raised political consciousness of that era as compared to now?*

It's possible: there was a lot of union organizing back then, and the struggles were very brutal. I remember it well. Like, one of my earliest childhood memories is of taking a trolley car with my mother and seeing the police wade into a strike of women pickets outside a Philadelphia textile mill, and beating them up—that's a searing memory. And the poverty was extreme: I remember rag-pickers coming to the door begging for money, lots of things like that. So it was not pretty by any means. But it was also not hopeless. Somehow that's a tremendous difference: the slums are now hopeless, there's nothing to do except prey on one another.

In fact, a lot of life is hopeless today, even for middle-class kids. I mean, for the first time in I think human history, middle-class kids now assume they are not going to live as well as their parents—that's really something new, that's never happened before.[26] My kids, for example, assume that they are probably not going to live the way that we live. Think about it, that's never happened before in history. And they're probably right, except accidentally—like, some of them may, but on average they won't.

MAN: *Do you have an explanation of what's happened to the cities?*

I don't entirely understand it, to tell you the truth.[27] You could see it beginning in the late 1940s—New York City, for example, started to become a hostile place around then. I mean, as a kid when I would go to New York, I would think nothing of walking through Central Park alone at night, or walking along Riverside Drive by the river alone at night—the kinds of things you wouldn't do now without a platoon of Marines around you, you just took for granted back then; you didn't even give it a second thought. You never thought twice about taking a walk through Harlem, let's say— what the heck, you know? But that all began to change after the Second World War, and it changed throughout the whole United States: cities just became hostile.

I mean, New York always had the *reputation* of being hostile, like there were always jokes about the guy lying in the street and everybody walking over him. But you just didn't feel that you were taking your life into your hands and that people there were going to kill you, the sense you get when you walk through a lot of the city today. And also, you didn't have the same sense of super-wealth right next to grinding poverty—like today you see people sitting at a fancy restaurant drinking wine, and some homeless person lying on the street right in front of them. There wasn't quite that kind of thing either.

WOMAN: *Is the change maybe related to the internationalization of the economy, and the broadening of the super-rich class here?*

Maybe. I really don't know, to tell you the truth, and I don't want to pretend that I know. But my feeling is, it's beyond just economics. I mean, there were radical differences in wealth at that time, and people in the slums were extremely poor—it's just that they weren't desolate.

WOMAN: *It wasn't such a consumer culture at the time.*

Yeah, certainly not to the extent that it is now—like, everybody didn't have a television set where they were seeing some impossible life in front of their eyes all the time. Although you had something like it, don't forget: in those days the movies were what television is today; you'd go to the movies for a dime, and that's where you'd get your fantasy world. And the movies were all glitter, all upper-class fake glitter. But it just didn't have the same devastating effect, I don't know why. There's something really hopeless about contemporary life that's new, I think.

MAN: *The bomb had a lot to do with it.*

Maybe—but does that really account for what happens in the slums? Look, I mean, I never see much of it. In the late 1960s, I was with a mainly white group, RESIST [a national draft-resistance movement], but we had good contacts with the Black Panthers, and with them I did get into slum areas. In general, though, I don't tend to see the slums very much. But from the few times I've walked around poor areas of Harlem and other places like that since then, I just can't recall anything remotely like it in the 1930s, even in the poorest parts of Brownsville [a low-income section of Brooklyn]. Also, older friends of mine who've been teachers in New York since the 1920s tell me they think it's totally different today as well—kids were poor in the Thirties, but they weren't rat-bitten.

WOMAN: *For myself, as a radical who does a lot of political work in my community, the despair is unbelievable—what we have to fight against at the lowest rung is just incredible, I can really understand just giving up. Don't you have some explanation of how we've come to this point?*

Well, I think if you look over American history, you can point to at least a few factors behind it. This is an immigrant society, and before the Depression virtually every wave of immigrants who came here was more or less absorbed, at least the ones who wanted to stay—a lot of them didn't, remember; in fact, the rate of return was rather high during the peak periods of immigration.[28] But for the immigrants who did stay, the United States really *was* a land of opportunity. So, my father could come from Russia and work in a sweatshop, and manage finally to get to college, and then see his son become a professor—that stuff was real. And it was real because there was a lot of manual labor around which could absorb the waves of immigrants: people could work in sweatshops for sixteen hours a day and make enough to live on, then accumulate a little excess, and things would gradually start to get better. But in the 1930s, there was a big break in this system—the Depression ended those opportunities. And the United States has basically never gotten out of the Depression.

See, the post-World War II economic boom has been a different sort of economic growth from anything that ever happened before. For one thing, it's been basically state-funded and primarily centered in high technology-based industries, which are tied to the military system. And that kind of economic growth just does not allow for absorbing new waves of immigrants. It allowed for it briefly during the Second World War, when there was a labor shortage and people could come off the farms in the South and work in the war industries. But that ended. And since then, the jobs have mostly been in high-tech or in the service sector—which is rotten, you don't go anywhere. So there just aren't the same possibilities for people to move up: if you can get into high-tech industry, you probably were there already, and if you're working at sweeping the streets or something, that's where you're going to stay.

Now, maybe that situation would have been livable if there hadn't been a new wave of immigration, but there was. There was a huge wave of immigration. It happened to have been *internal* immigration this time, but from the point of view of the society it was like a foreign wave: it came from rapid mechanization of agriculture in the South, which drove the black population, the former slaves, off the land. Then on top of that, there's also been a major influx of Hispanic immigration. So you had these two big waves of immigration coming up to the Northern cities, and nothing for them to do: they couldn't do what my father did, because there wasn't the same kind of manual labor going on which could occupy millions more workers. So what in fact happened is these two huge waves of immigrants were just herded into concentration camps, which we happen to call "cities." And the vast majority of them are never going to get out—just because there's nothing for them to do. The economy simply is not growing; I mean, the Gross National Product goes up, but it goes up in a way which does not constitute economic growth for a poor urban population.

And with the decline of the traditional manufacturing industries in recent years, it's getting worse, not better. As capital becomes more fluid and it becomes easier for corporations to move production to the Third World, why should they pay higher wages in Detroit when they can pay lower wages in Northern Mexico or the Philippines? And the result is, there's even more pressure on the poorer part of the population here. And what's in effect happened is they've been closed off into inner-city slums—where then all sorts of other pressures begin to attack them: drugs, gentrification, police repression, cutbacks in limited welfare programs, and so on. And all of these things contribute to creating a very authentic sense of hopelessness, and also to real anti-social behavior: crime. And the crime is mostly poor people preying on one another, the statistics show that very clearly—because the rich are locked away behind their barricades.[29]

You can see it very clearly when you drive through New York now: the differences in wealth are like San Salvador. I mean, I was giving a talk there a little while ago, and as you walk around it's kind of dramatic: there are these castles, and there are guards at the gate, and a limousine drives up and the people go inside; inside I guess it's very elegant and beautiful. But it's like living in a feudal system, with a lot of wild barbarians outside—except if you're rich, you don't ever see them, you just move between your castle and your limousine. And if you're poor, you've got no castle to protect you.

MAN: *You mentioned drugs having an impact on the problem—I'm wondering whether you agree with the theory that drugs were maybe intro-*

*duced to the ghettos intentionally, to try to demoralize people there and keep them from coming together to organize to change things?*

It's a good question—activists who work in the ghettos and slums have been charging that for years. I mean, a lot of people have pointed out that just at the time when you started to get serious organizing in the urban ghettos in the 1960s, all of a sudden there was this huge flow of drugs which absolutely devastated the inner-city communities. And the communities just couldn't defend themselves against it: the parents couldn't do it, the churches couldn't do it, you've got guys hanging around on street corners giving ten-year-olds free drugs, and in a couple of months the neighborhood's gone. And the timing, in fact, *was* about when serious political organizing was beginning to take place. Beyond that, I don't know: maybe it was planned, maybe it just happened.[30] But I think you can make a good case that the way the criminal justice system has been set up ever since then *does* have a lot to do with social control.

So just take a look at the different prosecution rates and sentencing rules for ghetto drugs like crack and suburban drugs like cocaine, or for drunk drivers and drug users, or just between blacks and whites in general—the statistics are clear: this is a war on the poor and minorities.[31] Or ask yourself a simple question: how come marijuana is illegal but tobacco legal? It can't be because of the health impact, because that's exactly the other way around—there has never been a fatality from marijuana use among 60 million reported users in the United States, whereas tobacco kills hundreds of thousands of people every year.[32] My strong suspicion, though I don't know how to prove it, is that the reason is that marijuana's a weed, you can grow it in your backyard, so there's nobody who would make any money off it if it were legal. Tobacco requires extensive capital inputs and technology, and it can be monopolized, so there are people who can make a ton of money off it. I don't really see any other difference between the two of them, frankly—except that tobacco's far more lethal and far more addictive.

But it's certainly true that a lot of inner-city communities have just been devastated by drugs. And you can see why people would want them—they do give you a sense of temporary relief from an intolerable existence, whatever else they might do. Plus I'm just convinced that by now a lot of the drug stuff is around mainly because people can make money off it—so I don't really think there's much hope for dealing with the problem without some form of decriminalization to remove that incentive. It's not a pretty solution, but it's probably part of the solution, I suspect. And of course, decriminalization doesn't have to mean *no* regulation—like, in England over the years, they've tried to regulate alcohol through tax policies and so on, to encourage use of more benign products like beer rather than more dangerous ones, and something like that could be looked into here. But obviously something should be tried, I think.

## Religious Fanaticism

WOMAN: *Fundamentalist religion has really taken off in the last decade, maybe as an outlet for some of this despair. Do you have any thoughts about the significance of that development in the U.S.?*

It's pretty amazing what's happened, actually. There have been a lot of cross-cultural studies of what social scientists call "religious fanaticism"—not people who just believe in God or go to church, but they're really kind of fanatic about it, it's the kind of fanatic religious commitment that permeates your whole life. And what these studies demonstrate is that this is a typical characteristic of pre-industrial societies—in fact, it correlates very closely with industrialization: as industrialization goes up, this kind of religious fanaticism goes down. Well, there are two countries that are basically off the curve. One of them is Canada, which has more fundamentalist commitment than you would expect given its level of industrialization. The other is the United States—which is totally off the chart: we're like a shattered peasant society. I mean, the last study I saw of it was done in around 1980, and the United States was at the level of Bangladesh, it was very close to Iran.[33] Eighty percent of Americans literally believe in religious miracles. Half the population thinks the world was created a couple thousand years ago and that fossils were put here to mislead people or something—half the population. You just don't find things like that in other industrial societies.[34]

Well, a lot of political scientists and others have tried to figure out why this aberration exists. It's one of the many respects in which the United States is unusual, so you want to see if it's related to some of the others—and there *are* others. For instance, the United States has an unusually weak labor movement, it has an unusually narrow political system. Think: there is no other industrialized Western country that doesn't have a labor-based political party, and we haven't had one here since the Populist Party in the 1890s. So we have a very depoliticized population, and that could be one cause of this phenomenon: if social and political life don't offer you opportunities to form communities and associate yourself with things that are meaningful to you, people look for other ways to do it, and religion's an obvious one. It's strikingly the case in the black communities, actually, where the black churches have been the real organizing center which holds life together: I mean, there's terrible oppression, a lot of families are falling apart, but the church is there, it brings people together and they can get together and do things in that context. And the same is true in many white communities as well.

Now, I don't think you can draw too many sweeping conclusions from religion itself—it's kind of like technology, it depends what you use it for. Like, even among the fundamentalists, you've got Sojourners [a politically progressive religious group], and you have Jerry Falwell [a right-wing televangelist]. But it certainly does carry with it the potential of aligning with other forms of fanaticism—and that's a big danger in the United States, because it's a very significant movement here. In fact, by now just about every major political figure in the country has to associate himself with it in some way. In the 1980 election, for example, all of the three candidates [i.e. Carter, Reagan, and independent candidate John Anderson] advertised themselves as Born Again Christians. In the 1984 election, one of the candidates advertised himself as a Born Again Christian, and the other was a Methodist minister or something.[35] In the 1988 election, Dukakis was secular, which is unusual, but Bush said he was religious.

Actually, Bush, technically speaking, is not really President—because he refused to take the Oath of Office. I don't know how many of you noticed this, but the wording of the Oath of Office is written in the Constitution, so you can't fool around with it—and Bush refused to read it. The Oath of Office says something about, "I promise to do this, that, and the other thing," and Bush added the words, "so help me God." Well, that's illegal: he's not President, if anybody cares.[36]

ALL: *All right! Yeah!*

Happy? Yeah, let's impeach him.

I mean, it wasn't because Bush is religious—Bush knows where the nearest church is . . . because he has to show up there every once in a while. Or take Reagan: what does it mean to say he was a Born Again Christian? It means somebody told him he's a Born Again Christian. In Bush's case, though, I presume he's totally secular, he just knows that by now you've got to make a nod to this huge fundamentalist constituency—and since you're not going to offer them anything they really want, you offer them symbolic things, like saying "so help me God" or something like that.

But the point is, if things ever really come to a crunch in the United States, this massive part of the population—I think it's something like a third of the adult population by now—could be the basis for some kind of a fascist movement, readily. For example, if the country sinks deeply into a recession, a depoliticized population could very easily be mobilized into thinking it's somebody else's fault: "Why are our lives collapsing? There have to be bad guys out there doing something for things to be going so badly"—and the bad guys can be Jews, or homosexuals, or blacks, or Communists, whatever you pick. If you can whip people into irrational frenzies like that, they can be extremely dangerous: that's what 1930s Fascism came from, and something like that could very easily happen here.

## "The _Real_ Anti-Semitism"

MAN: *Do you know about the connections between the Republican Party and the neo-Nazis which were revealed a few months ago—and could you talk a bit about what might be the significance of that in this context?*

That was sort of an interesting phenomenon; it's hard to know exactly how seriously to take it, but it's certainly very real. I don't know how many of you followed what happened with the Nazis in the Bush campaign around last August—do you know about that stuff?

There's this part of the Bush campaign called the "Ethnic Outreach Committee," which tries to organize ethnic minorities; obviously that doesn't mean blacks or Hispanics, it means Ukrainians, Poles, that sort of business. And it turned out that it was being run by a bunch of East European Nazis, Ukrainian Nazis, hysterical anti-Semites, Romanians who came out of the Iron Guard, and so on. Well, finally this got exposed; some of the people were reshuffled, some were put into other positions in the Republican Party—but it all just passed over very quietly. The Democrats never even raised the issue during the election campaign.[37]

You might ask, why? How come the Democrats never even raised the issue? Well, I think there was a very good reason for that: I think the Jewish organizations like the Anti-Defamation League basically called them off. The point is, these organizations don't ultimately care about anti-Semitism, what they care about is opposition to the policies of Israel—in fact, opposition to their own hawkish *version* of the policies of Israel. They're Israeli government lobbies, essentially, and they understood that these Nazis in the Bush campaign were quite pro-Israel, so what do they care? The *New Republic,* which is sort of an organ for these groups, had a very interesting editorial on it. It was about anti-Semitism, and it referred to the fact that this committee was being run by anti-Semites, Holocaust deniers, Nazis and so on, and then it said: yes, that's all true, but this is just "antique and anemic" anti-Semitism. Nazism is just "antique and anemic" anti-Semitism, not terribly important, we shouldn't get too upset about it. And then it said: the *real* anti-Semitism that we ought to be worried about is in the Democratic Party, which is filled with "Jew-haters"—that was the phrase they used. And part of the proof is, the Democrats were actually willing to debate a resolution calling for Palestinian self-determination at their National Convention, so therefore they're "Jew-haters" and that's the "real" anti-Semitism in America. (That was in fact the title of a book by the Director of the A.D.L., Nathan Perlmutter.)[38] Well, the Democrats got the message that they weren't going to win any points with this, so they never raised a peep about it.

Incidentally, this is only one of the things that happened at that time—there's another story which got even less publicity, and is even more revealing. The Department of Education has a program of grants that it dispenses to fund projects initiated by local school systems, and for the last four or five years the school board in Brookline, Massachusetts, has been trying to get funding for a project on the Holocaust which always gets very favorably reviewed, but is always turned down. Again in 1988—also right before the election—the federal reviewing committee had to deal with their proposal. As usual it got very favorable reviews, but instead of just turning it down, this time the government simply eliminated the entire program category under which it was being submitted. Well, at that point some information began to surface as to *why* the project kept getting turned down—and it turned out that it was being refused every year because of letters the Department was getting from people like Phyllis Schlafly [a right-wing activist] attacking it for being unfair because it didn't give adequate space to Nazis and Ku Klux Klan members. Besides, they said, it's kind of brainwashing children, and turning them against things like the Holocaust, it's just more of this neo-liberal tampering with people's thoughts. Parts of these letters actually got published in the *Washington Post* and the *Boston Globe*.[39]

Well, you'd have thought there'd be an uproar. A program on the Holocaust gets turned down by the government, by the Reagan administration, because it doesn't give enough space to Nazis and Klan members? Not a peep, not a peep. And the point is, Phyllis Schlafly and that whole gang are adequately pro-Israel—and therefore it doesn't matter what they think. They can be in favor of the Klan, they can be in favor of the Nazis, they can say you shouldn't be allowed to teach the Holocaust, it doesn't matter, as long as they remain sufficiently supportive of hawkish Israeli policies. As long as they meet that qualification, it's fine, they can say whatever they want.

## Ronald Reagan and the Future of Democracy

WOMAN: *You mentioned Reagan—I've heard you say his administration was the first time the United States didn't really have a President. Would you enlarge on that, and tell us what your thoughts are on the future of that kind of government?*

I think it has a big future, myself—in fact, I think the Reagan administration was sort of a peek into the future. It's a very natural move. Imagine yourself working in some public relations office where your job is to help corporations make sure that the annoying public does not get in the way of policy-making. Here's a brilliant thought that nobody ever had before, so far as I know: let's make elections completely symbolic activities. The population can keep voting, we'll give them all the business, they'll have electoral campaigns, all the hoopla, two candidates, eight candidates—but the people they're voting for will then just be expected to read off a teleprompter and they won't be expected to know anything except what somebody tells them, and maybe not even that.

I mean, when you read off a teleprompter—I've done it actually—it's a very odd experience: it's like the words go into your eyes and out your mouth, and they don't pass through your mind in between. And when Reagan does it, they have it set up so there are two or three of them around, so his head can keep moving and it appears as though he's looking around at the audience, but really he's just switching from one teleprompter to another. Well, if you can get people to vote for something like that, you've basically done it—you've removed them from decision-making. It won't work unless you have an obedient media which will fall over themselves with what a wonderful, charismatic figure he is—you know, "the most popular President in history," "he's creating a revolution," "the most amazing thing since ice cream," and "how can we criticize him, everybody loves him?" And you have to pretend that nobody's laughing, and so on. But if you can do that, then you'd have gone a very long way towards marginalizing the public. And I think we probably got there in the 1980s—pretty close to there, anyway.

In all of the books that have come out by people in the Reagan administration, it's been extremely difficult to hide the fact that Reagan didn't have the foggiest idea what was going on.[40] Whenever he wasn't properly programmed, the things that would come out of his mouth were kind of like—they weren't *lies* really, they were kind of like the babbling of a child. If a child babbles, it's not lies, it's just sort of on some other plane. To be able to *lie*, you have to have a certain degree of competence, you have to know what truth is. And there didn't seem to be any indication that that was the case here. So in fact, all of the fuss in the Iran-contra hearings about "did Reagan know or didn't he know" [about the National Security Council's illegal dealings with Iran and the Nicaraguan contras], or "did he remember or didn't he remember?" I personally regarded as a cover-up. What's the difference? He didn't know if nobody told him, and he didn't remember if he forgot. And who cares? He wasn't supposed to know. Reagan's whole career was reading lines written for him by rich folk. First it was as a spokesman for General Electric, then it was for somebody else, and he just continued to the White House: he read the lines written for him by the rich folk, he did it for eight years, they paid him nicely, he apparently enjoyed it, he seems to have been quite cheerful there, had a good time. He could sleep late. And they liked it, the paymasters thought it was fine, they bought a nice home for him, put him out to pasture.

It's very striking how he disappeared. For eight years, the public relations industry and the media had been claiming that this guy revolutionized America—you know, the "Reagan Revolution," this fantastic charismatic figure that everybody loved, he just changed our lives. Okay, then he finished his job, they told him to go home—that's the end. No reporter would even *dream* of going out to see Reagan after that to ask him his opinion on anything—because everybody knows he *has* no opinion on anything. And they knew it all along. In the Oliver North trial, for example, stuff came out about Reagan telling—I don't like to use the word "lie," because, as I say, you have to have a competence to lie—but Reagan producing false statements to Congress, let's put it that way. The press didn't even care: okay, so Reagan lied to Congress, let's go on to the next thing. The point is, his job was done, so therefore he became irrelevant. Sure, they'll trot him out at the next Republican Convention so everybody can applaud, but that's it.

In a way it was like royalty. I mean, the imperial family in England plays a real role in depoliticizing the place, and Reagan reminded me a bit of that.[41] For instance, every session of Parliament in England opens with the Queen reading a message written by the ruling political party, and everybody pretends to take it seriously. But in another part of your brain, you don't ask, "Did the Queen believe what she was saying?" or, "Did she understand what she was saying?" or "Will she remember what she was saying?" or, "Did she lie to the Parliament?" Those are just not relevant questions—because the Queen's job is to be royalty, and to be revered, and to be admired, and to be the model woman that everybody's supposed to be like. It's kind of like playing a game in the political system, even though people there do in fact take it seriously in a sense—like they *care* if the Princess Diana is having a spat with Something-Or-Other, they think about it, and they talk about it, and so on. But of course, at some other level of their intelligence, they know that it has nothing to do with life.

Well, the British have it sort of institutionalized, and you don't vote for Queen. But suppose you could get to the point where elections in England were not for Prime Minister and Parliament, but instead people voted for Queen, and then things ran the way they do now, except the Prime Minister is just appointed by the banks and the corporations. And in the election campaign you'd ask, "Who's got the nicest hairdo?" you'd ask, "Who can say things nicer?" "Who's got the best smile?" Well, then you'd have gone a long way towards the desired goal of maintaining the formal functioning of the system, but eliminating the substance from it. And that's pretty much what we had with Reagan, I think.

Now, I don't know whether Reagan was contrived for that purpose or whether it just worked out that way, but once having seen it in operation, I expect that people will learn from it. And in fact, I think you could see signs of it in the 1988 election as well. I mean, everybody—the media and everyone else—agreed that there were no real issues in the campaign: the only issue was whether Dukakis was going to figure out a way of ducking all the slime that was being thrown at him. That's about the only thing anybody was voting about, did he duck or didn't he duck? That's like saying, "Don't bother voting."

MAN: *But doesn't it make* any *difference who wins? I mean, suppose they gave us Ollie North as President?*

Yeah, look, I don't want to say that it makes *no* difference. The figure who's there makes *some* difference—but the less difference it makes, the more you've marginalized the public.

WOMAN: *Do you vote?*

Do *I*? Well, differentially. I mean, I almost always vote for lower-level candidates, like school committee representatives and things like that—because there it makes a difference, in fact. But as you get more and more remote from popular control, it makes less and less of a difference. When you get to the House of Representatives—well, it's sort of academic in my case, because I live in one of these single-member districts where the same guy always wins, so it doesn't really matter whether you vote or not. When you get to Senator, it begins to become pretty symbolic anyway. At the level of President, half the time I don't even bother—I think those are usually very subtle judgments. I mean, it's a difficult judgment to try to figure out whether Nixon or Humphrey is going to end the Vietnam War sooner [in 1968], that's an extremely subtle judgment to make; I actually didn't vote on that one, because I figured Nixon probably would. I did vote against Reagan, because I thought the guys *around* Reagan were extremely danger-ous—Reagan himself was irrelevant, but the people in his administration were real killers and torturers, and they were just making people suffer too much, so I thought that might make a difference. But these are usually not very easy judgments to make, in my opinion.

WOMAN: *What do you think stopped the impeachment drive against Rea-gan after the Iran-contra scandal?*

It would just embarrass the hell out of everybody—I mean, nobody in power wants that much disruption for something like that. Look, why don't they bring every American President to trial for war crimes? There are things on which there is a complete consensus in the elite culture: the United States is *permitted* to carry out war crimes, it's *permitted* to attack other countries, it's *permitted* to ignore international law. On those things there's a complete consensus, so why should they impeach the President for doing everything he's supposed to do?

In fact, you can ask all kinds of questions like that. For instance, at the time of the Nuremberg trials [of Nazi war criminals after World War II], there was a lot of very pompous rhetoric on the part of the Western prose-cutors about how this was not just going to be "victor's justice": it's not just that we won the war and they lost, we're establishing principles which are going to apply to *us* too. Well, by the principles of the Nuremberg trials, every single American President since then would have been hanged. Has anyone ever been brought to trial? Has this point even been raised? It's not a difficult point to demonstrate.[42]

Actually, the Nuremberg trials are worth thinking about. The Nazis were something unique, granted. But if you take a look at the Nuremberg trials, they were very cynical. The operational criterion for what counted as a war crime at Nuremberg was *a criminal act that the West didn't do*: in other words, it was considered a legitimate defense if you could show that the Americans and the British did the same thing. That's actually true. So part of the defense of the German submarine commander Admiral Doenitz was to call an American submarine commander, Admiral Nimitz, to testify that the Americans did the same thing—that's a defense. Bombing of urban areas was not considered a war crime at Nuremberg; reason is, the West did more of it than the Germans. And this is all stated straight out—like if you read the book by Telford Taylor, the American prosecutor at the trials, this is the way he describes it; he's very positive about the whole thing.[43] If the West had done it, it wasn't a crime; it was only a crime if the Germans had done it and we hadn't. I mean, it's true there were plenty of such things, but still there's something pretty cynical about it.

In fact, even worse than the Nuremberg trials were the Tokyo trials [of Japanese war criminals]: by the standards of the Tokyo trials, not just every American President, but *everyone* would be hanged [at Tokyo, those who failed to take affirmative steps to prevent war crimes or to dissociate themselves from the government were executed]. General Yamashita was an extreme case: he was hanged because during the American conquest of the Philippines, troops that were technically under his command, although he had already lost all contact with them, carried out crimes—therefore *he* was hanged. Ask yourself who's going to survive that one. Here's a guy who was hanged because troops he had no contact with whatsoever, but which theoretically in some order of battle had to do with his units, committed atrocities. If those same principles apply to us, who's going to survive? And that was just one case, I think we killed about a thousand people in the Tokyo trials—they were really grotesque.[44]

WOMAN: *Just going back to elections for a second—would you say the '84 elections were the same as '88: no substance?*

Well, in the 1984 elections there was still an issue. In the 1984 elections, the Republicans were the party of Keynesian growth [the economist Keynes advocated government stimulation of the economy]—they said, "Let's just keep spending and spending and spending, bigger and bigger deficits, and somehow that will lead to growth"—whereas the Democrats were the party of fiscal conservatism: they had this sad-looking son of a minister [Mondale] saying, "No, no good; we can't keep spending, we're going to get in trouble, we've got to watch the money supply."

Okay, for anybody who gets amused at these things, the Republicans and the Democrats had shifted their traditional positions 180 degrees; historically, the *Democrats* have been the party of Keynesian growth, and the *Republicans* have been the party of fiscal conservatism. But they shifted totally—and what's interesting is, nobody even noticed this, I never even saw a single comment on it in the press. Well, that tells you something: what it tells you is, there are different sectors of the business community in the country, and they sometimes have slightly different tactical judgments about the way to deal with current problems. And when they differ on something, it'll come up in the election; when they don't differ on anything, there won't be any issues.

## Two New Factors in World Affairs

MAN: *To move to a more general level, Professor—I'm interested whether you think that there are any developments over the past few decades that are new on the international scene, which people should be aware of as we analyze things that are taking place in the world?*

Well, in my view, there are at least two really major things that are coming along that are new: one is a shift in the international economy.[45] And the other is the threat to the environment—which just can't be ignored much longer, because if facing it is delayed too much longer there isn't going to be a lot more to human history.

I'll start with the environment. The reality is that under capitalist conditions—meaning maximization of short-term gain—you're ultimately going to destroy the environment: the only question is when. Now, for a long time, it's been possible to pretend that the environment is an infinite source and an infinite sink. Neither is true obviously, and we're now sort of approaching the point where you can't keep playing the game too much longer. It may not be very far off. Well, dealing with that problem is going to require large-scale social changes of an almost unimaginable kind. For one thing, it's going to certainly require large-scale social planning, and that means participatory social planning if it's going to be at all meaningful. It's also going to require a general recognition among human beings that an economic system driven by greed is going to self-destruct—it's only a question of time before you make the planet unlivable, by destroying the ozone layer or some other way.[46] And that means huge socio-psychological changes have to take place if the human species is going to survive very much longer. So that's a big factor.

Quite apart from that, there have been major changes in the international economy. The world has basically been moving into three major economic blocks; the United States is no longer the sole economic power like it was after World War II. There's a Japan-based system, which involves Japan and the countries around its periphery, like Singapore and Taiwan, the old Japanese empire. There's Europe, which has been consolidating into the European Common Market—and that could be a powerful economic unit; if Europe gets its act together, it'll outweigh the United States: it's got a larger economy, a bigger population, a more educated population, and they've got their traditional colonial interests, which are in fact being reconstructed. Meanwhile the United States has been building up its own counter-block in North America through so-called "free trade" agreements, which are turning Canada into kind of an economic colony and basically absorbing Northern Mexico into the United States as a cheap-labor area. The three regions are roughly comparable by most measures, with the Asian region still far ahead in capital reserves.

No one understands quite how this situation will be affected by the financial liberalization that has been so harmful to the global economy since the mid-1970s. And there are also other intriguing issues. For example, the European powers, especially Germany, are attempting to reconstruct the traditional colonial relations between Central Europe and Eastern Europe that existed before the Cold War—Central Europe has the industry and technology and investment capital, and Eastern Europe and Russia provide them with cheap manpower and resources. Meanwhile Japan is doing precisely the same thing with Russia on the Asian side, trying to construct colonial relations with Siberia: Japan has plenty of extra capital, and Siberia has plenty of resources that the Russians can't exploit properly because they don't have the capital or the technology, so it's like a natural combination. And if these efforts work, then we're going to have the two major enemies of the United States, Japan and Europe, integrating with the Soviet Union, it becoming kind of a semi-colonial area related to them. And that realizes the worst nightmares of American planners.

See, there is an American geopolitical tradition which treats the United States as an island power off the mainland of Europe; it's a bigger version of British geopolitics, which treats England as an island power off the mainland of Europe. I mean, Britain throughout its whole modern history has tried to prevent Europe from becoming unified—that was the main theme of British history, prevent Europe from being unified, because we're just this island power off of Europe, and if they ever get unified we're in trouble. And the United States has the same attitude towards Eurasia: we've got to prevent them from becoming unified, because if they are, we become a real second-class power—we'll still have our little system around here, but it'll become kind of second-class.[47] By "the United States," I mean powerful interests in the United States, U.S.-based capital.

WOMAN: *Then do you think it's possible that the U.S. may not be considered a superpower someday?*

Well, you know, despite the *relative* decline in U.S.-based power, it's still powerful without historical precedent.

WOMAN: *I know it is militarily.*

No, even economically. Look, it's a real scandal of the American economic system that the general economic level here is so low. I mean, by world standards, in terms of, say, infant mortality or lifespan, or most other measures like that, people are not terribly well-off here—the United States is well down the list. I think we're twentieth of twenty industrial powers in infant mortality, for example. We're at about the level of Cuba, which is a poor Third World country, in terms of health standards.[48] Those are absolute scandals—the general population of the United States ought to be better off than that of any other country in the world by just a huge margin. No other industrial power has anything like our resources. We've got an educated population, like basic literacy is relatively high. We have a comparatively uniform population: people speak English all over the place—you can't find that in too many areas of the world. We've got enormous military power. We have no enemies anywhere nearby. Very few powers in history have ever had that situation. So these are just incomparable advantages, and our economic system has not turned them to the benefit of the population here, particularly—but they're there, and they're going to stay there.

Now take Japan: Japanese corporations and investors can collect a lot of capital, but they're never going to get their own resources—they don't have their own energy resources, they don't have their own raw materials, they don't have agricultural resources. And we do: that makes a big difference. In fact, American planners back in the late 1940s were very well aware of this difference when they sort of organized the post-war world—so while they helped Japan to reindustrialize, they also insisted on controlling its energy resources: the Japanese were not allowed to develop their own petrochemical industry, or to obtain their own independent access to petroleum resources. And the reason for that is explained in now-declassified U.S. internal documents: as George Kennan [State Department official and diplomat], who was one of the major planners of the post-war world, pointed out, if we control Japan's energy resources, we will have veto power over Japan—if they ever get out of line, we'll just choke off their energy supply.[49] Now, whether or not that plan would still work you don't know, because the world is changing in unpredictable ways. But for the moment, the United States is still overwhelmingly powerful in world affairs—that's why we can get away with so much.

## Democracy Under Capitalism

MAN: *You mentioned that we're going to need participatory social planning to save the environment. I'm wondering, doesn't decentralization of power also somehow conflict with trying to save the environment—I mean, that can't be done without some sort of central agreement, don't you think?*

Well, first of all, *agreements* don't require centralized authority, certain *kinds* of agreements do. One's assumption, at least, is that decentralization of power will lead to decisions that reflect the interests of the entire population. The idea is that policies flowing from any kind of decision-making apparatus are going to tend to reflect the interests of the people involved in making the decisions—which certainly seems plausible. So if a decision is made by some centralized authority, it is going to represent the interests of the particular group which is in power. But if power is actually rooted in large parts of the population—if people can actually participate in social planning—then they will presumably do so in terms of their own interests, and you can expect the decisions to reflect those interests. Well, the interest of the general population is to preserve human life; the interest of corporations is to make profits—those are fundamentally different interests.

MAN: *In an industrial society, though, one might argue that people need to have jobs.*

Sure, but having jobs doesn't require destroying the environment which makes life possible. I mean, if you have participatory social planning, and people are trying to work things out in terms of their own interests, they are going to want to balance opportunities to work with quality of work, with type of energy available, with conditions of personal interaction, with the need to make sure your children survive, and so on and so forth. But those are all considerations that simply don't *arise* for corporate executives, they just are not a part of the agenda. In fact, if the C.E.O. of General Electric started making decisions on *that* basis, he'd be thrown out of his job in three seconds, or maybe there'd be a corporate takeover or something—because those things are not a part of his job. His job is to raise profit and market share, not to make sure that the environment survives, or that his workers lead decent lives. And those goals are simply in conflict.

MAN: *Give us an example of what exactly you mean by social planning.*

Well, right now we have to make big decisions about how to produce energy, for one thing—because if we continue to produce energy by combustion, the human race isn't going to survive very much longer.[50] Alright, that decision requires social planning: it's not something that you can just decide on yourself. Like, you can decide to put a solar-energy something-or-other on your own house, but that doesn't really help. This is the kind of decision where it only works if it's done on a mass scale.

MAN: *I thought you might have been referring to population control.*

Yeah, population control is another issue where it doesn't matter if *you* do it, everybody has to do it. It's like traffic: I mean, you can't make driving a car survivable by driving well yourself; there has to be kind of a social contract involved, otherwise it won't work. Like, if there was no social contract involved in driving—everybody was just driving like a lethal weapon, going as fast as they can and forgetting all the traffic lights and everything else—you couldn't make that situation safe just by driving well yourself: it doesn't make much difference if you set out to drive safely if everybody else is driving lethal-weapon, right? The trouble is, that's the way that capitalism works. The nature of the system is that it's supposed to be driven by greed; no one's supposed to be concerned for anybody else, nobody's supposed to worry about the common good—those are not things that are supposed to motivate you, that's the principle of the system. The theory is that private vices lead to public benefits—that's what they teach you in economics departments. It's all total bullshit, of course, but that's what they teach you. And as long as the system works that way, yeah, it's going to self-destruct.

What's more, capitalists have long understood this. So most government regulatory systems have in fact been strongly lobbied for by the industries themselves: industries want to be regulated, because they know that if they're not, they're going to destroy themselves in the unbridled competition.[51]

MAN: *Then what kind of mechanism for social planning do you think would work? Obviously you're not too sanguine about our current form of government.*

Well, there's nothing wrong with the *form*—I mean, there are *some* things wrong with the form—but what's really wrong is that the *substance* is missing. Look, as long as you have private control over the economy, it doesn't make any difference what forms you have, because they can't do anything. You could have political parties where everybody gets together and participates, and *you* make the programs, make things as participatory as you like—and it would still have only the most marginal effect on policy. And the reason is, power lies elsewhere.

So suppose all of us here convinced everybody in the country to vote for us for President, we got 98 percent of the vote and both Houses of Congress, and then we started to institute very badly needed social reforms that most of the population wants. Simply ask yourself, what would happen? Well, if your imagination doesn't tell you, take a look at real cases. There are places in the world that have a broader range of political parties than we do, like Latin American countries, for example, which in this respect are much more democratic than we are. Well, when popular reform candidates in Latin America get elected and begin to introduce reforms, two things typically happen. One is, there's a military coup supported by the United States. But suppose that doesn't happen. What you get is capital strike—investment capital flows out of the country, there's a lowering of investment, and the economy grinds to a halt.

That's the problem that Nicaragua has faced in the 1980s—and which it cannot overcome, in my view, it's just a hopeless problem. See, the Sandinistas have tried to run a mixed economy: they've tried to carry out social programs to benefit the population, but they've also had to appeal to the business community to prevent capital flight from destroying the place. So most public funds, to the extent there are any, go as a bribe to the wealthy, to try to keep them investing in the country. The only problem is, the wealthy would prefer *not* to invest unless they have political power: they'd rather see the society destroyed. So the wealthy take the bribes, and they send them to Swiss banks and to Miami banks—because from their perspective, the Sandinista government just has the wrong priorities. I mean, these guys hate democracy just as much as Congress hates democracy: they want the political system to be in the hands of wealthy elites, and when it is again, then they'll call it "democracy" and they'll resume investing, and the economy will finally start to function again.

Well, the same thing would happen here if we ever had a popular reform candidate who actually achieved some formal level of power: there would be disinvestment, capital strike, a grinding down of the economy. And the reason is quite simple. In our society, real power does not happen to lie in the political system, it lies in the private economy: that's where the decisions are made about what's produced, how much is produced, what's consumed, where investment takes place, who has jobs, who controls the resources, and so on and so forth. And as long as that remains the case, changes inside the political system can make *some* difference—I don't want to say it's zero—but the differences are going to be very slight.

In fact, if you think through the logic of this, you'll see that so long as power remains privately concentrated, everybody, *everybody*, has to be committed to one overriding goal: and that's to make sure that the rich folk are happy—because unless they are, nobody else is going to get anything. So if you're a homeless person sleeping in the streets of Manhattan, let's say, your first concern must be that the guys in the mansions are happy—because if they're happy, then they'll invest, and the economy will work, and things will function, and then maybe something will trickle down to you somewhere along the line. But if they're *not* happy, everything's going to grind to a halt, and you're not even going to get anything trickling down. So if you're a homeless person in the streets, your first concern is the happiness of the wealthy guys in the mansions and the fancy restaurants. Basically that's a metaphor for the whole society.

Like, suppose Massachusetts were to increase business taxes. Most of the population is in favor of it, but you can predict what would happen. Business would run a public relations campaign—which is true, in fact, it's not lies—saying, "You raise taxes on business, you soak the rich, and you'll find that capital is going to flow elsewhere, and you're not going to have any jobs, you're not going to have anything." That's not the way they'd put it exactly, but that's what it would amount to: "Unless you make us happy you're not going to have anything, because we own the place; you live here, but we own the place." And in fact, that's basically the message that *is* presented, not in those words of course, whenever a reform measure does come along somewhere—they have a big propaganda campaign saying, it's going to hurt jobs, it's going to hurt investment, there's going to be a loss of business confidence, and so on. That's just a complicated way of saying, unless you keep business happy, the population isn't going to have anything.

MAN: *What do you think about nationalization of industry as a means of allowing for this kind of large-scale social planning?*

Well, it would depend on how it's done. If nationalization of industry puts production into the hands of a state bureaucracy or some sort of Leninist-style vanguard party, then you'd just have another system of exploitation, in my view. On the other hand, if nationalization of industry was based on actual popular control over industry—workers' control over factories, community control, with the groups maybe federated together and so on—then that would be a different story. That would be a *very* different story, in fact. That would be extending the democratic system to economic power, and unless that happens, political power is always going to remain a very limited phenomenon.

## The Empire

WOMAN: *Then is the basic goal of the United States when it intervenes in Third World countries to destroy left-wing governments in order to keep them from power?*

No, the primary concern is to prevent *independence*, regardless of the ideology. Remember, we're the global power, so we have to make sure that all the various parts of the world continue serving their assigned functions in our global system. And the assigned functions of Third World countries are to be markets for American business, sources of resources for American business, to provide cheap labor for American business, and so on. I mean, there's no big secret about that—the media won't tell you and scholarship won't tell you, but all you have to do is look at declassified government documents and this is all explained very frankly and explicitly.

The internal documentary record in the United States goes way back, and it says the same thing over and over again. Here's virtually a quote: the main commitment of the United States, internationally in the Third World, must be to prevent the rise of nationalist regimes which are responsive to pressures from the masses of the population for improvement in low living standards and diversification of production; the reason is, we have to maintain a climate that is conducive to investment, and to ensure conditions which allow for adequate repatriation of profits to the West. Language like that is repeated year after year in top-level U.S. planning documents, like National Security Council reports on Latin America and so on—and that's exactly what we do around the world.[52]

So the nationalism we oppose doesn't need to be *left-wing*—we're just as much opposed to *right-wing* nationalism. I mean, when there's a right-wing military coup which seeks to turn some Third World country on a course of independent development, the United States will also try to destroy that government—we opposed Perón in Argentina, for example.[53] So despite what you always hear, U.S. interventionism has nothing to do with resisting the spread of "Communism," it's *independence* we've always been opposed to everywhere—and for quite a good reason. If a country begins to pay attention to its own population, it's not going to be paying adequate attention to the overriding needs of U.S. investors. Well, those are unacceptable priorities, so that government's just going to have to go.

And the effects of this commitment throughout the Third World are dramatically clear: it takes only a moment's thought to realize that the areas that have been the most under U.S. control are some of the most horrible regions in the world. For instance, why is Central America such a horror-chamber? I mean, if a peasant in Guatemala woke up in Poland [i.e. under Soviet occupation], he'd think he was in heaven by comparison—and Guatemala's an area where we've had a hundred years of influence. Well, that tells you something. Or look at Brazil: potentially an extremely rich country with tremendous resources, except it had the curse of being part of the Western system of subordination. So in northeast Brazil, for example, which is a rather fertile area with plenty of rich land, just it's all owned by plantations, Brazilian medical researchers now identify the population as a new species with about 40 percent the brain size of human beings, a result of generations of profound malnutrition and neglect—and this may be unremediable except after generations, because of the lingering effects of malnutrition on one's offspring.[54] Alright, that's a good example of the legacy of our commitments, and the same kind of pattern runs throughout the former Western colonies.

In fact, if you look at the countries that have developed in the world, there's a little simple fact which should be obvious to anyone on five minutes' observation, but which you never find anyone saying in the United States: the countries that have developed economically are those which were not colonized by the West; every country that was colonized by the West is a total wreck. I mean, Japan was the one country that managed to resist European colonization, and it's the one part of the traditional Third World that developed. Okay, Europe conquered everything except Japan, and Japan developed. What does that tell you? Historians of Africa have actually pointed out that if you look at Japan when it began its industrialization process [in the 1870s], it was at about the same developmental level as the Asante kingdom in West Africa in terms of resources available, level of state formation, degree of technological development, and so on.[55] Well, just compare those two areas today. It's true there were a number of differences between them historically, but the crucial one is that Japan wasn't conquered by the West and the Asante kingdom was, by the British—so now West Africa is West Africa economically, and Japan is Japan.

Japan had its own colonial system too, incidentally—but its colonies developed, and they developed because Japan didn't treat them the way the Western powers treated their colonies. The Japanese were very brutal colonizers, they weren't nice guys, but they nonetheless developed their colonies economically; the West just robbed theirs. So if you look at the growth rate of Taiwan and Korea during the period of Japanese colonization, it was approximately the same as Japan's own growth rate through the early part of this century—they were getting industrialized, developing infrastructure, educational levels were going up, agricultural production was increasing. In fact, by the 1930s, Formosa (now Taiwan) was one of the commercial centers of Asia.[56] Well, just compare Taiwan with the Philippines, an American colony right next door: the Philippines is a total basket-case, a Latin American-style basket-case. Again, that tells you something.

With World War II, the Japanese colonial system got smashed up. But by the 1960s, Korea and Taiwan were again developing at their former growth rate—and that's because in the post-war period, they've been able to follow the Japanese model of development: they're pretty closed off to foreign exploitation, quite egalitarian by international standards, they devote pretty extensive resources to things like education and health care. Okay, that's a successful model for development. I mean, these Asian countries aren't pretty; I can't stand them myself—they're extremely authoritarian, the role of women you can't even talk about, and so on, so there are plenty of unpleasant things about them. But they have been able to pursue economic development measures that are successful: the state coordinates industrial policy, capital export is strictly constrained, import levels are kept low. Well, those are exactly the kinds of policies that are    *impossible* in Latin America, because the U.S. insists that those governments keep their economies *open* to international markets—so capital from Latin America is constantly flowing to the West. Alright, that's not a problem in South Korea: they have the death penalty for capital export. Solves that difficulty pretty fast.[57]

But the point is, the Japanese-style development model works—in fact, it's how every country in the world that's developed has done it: by imposing high levels of protectionism, and by extricating its economy from free-market discipline. And that's precisely what the Western powers have been preventing the rest of the Third World from doing, right up to this moment.

WOMAN: *Is there any hope for disbanding America's empire, do you think?*

Well, it seems to me the situation is kind of like what one concludes from looking at the very likely potential of ecological catastrophe: either control over these matters is left in the hands of existing power interests and the rest of the population just abdicates, goes to the beach and hopes that somehow their children will survive—or else people will become sufficiently organized to break down the entire system of exploitation, and finally start putting it under participatory control. One possibility will mean complete disaster; the other, you can imagine all kinds of things. For example, even profitability would no longer be all that important—what would be important is living in a decent way.

Look, the general population here does not gain very much from holding on to our imperial system—in fact, it may gain nothing from it. If you take a look at imperial systems over history, it's not at all clear that they are profitable enterprises in the final analysis. This has been studied in the case of the British Empire, and while you only get kind of qualitative answers, it looks as if the British Empire may have cost as much to maintain as the profits that came from it. And probably something like that is true for the U.S.-dominated system too. So take Central America: there are profits from our controlling Central America, but it's very doubtful that they come anywhere near the probably ten billion dollars a year in tax money that's required to maintain U.S. domination there.[58]

WOMAN: *Those costs are paid by the people, though, while the profits are made by the rich.*

That's it exactly—if you ask, "Why have an empire?" you've just given the answer. The empire is like every other part of social policy: it's a way for the poor to pay off the rich in their own society. So if the empire is just another form of social policy by which the poor are subsidizing the rich, that means that under democratic social planning, there would be very little incentive for it—let alone the obvious moral considerations that would become a factor at that point. In fact, all kinds of questions would just change, radically.

## Change and the Future

MAN: *Mr. Chomsky, you present a very powerful view of the problems of capitalism, which I totally accept. When you start talking about the dissidence of the American population and the possibilities for large-scale change, though, I've got to admit that I have a little bit of trouble. I don't see the same general disillusionment with the system that you describe. I think people maybe see things that are wrong in certain areas, maybe see that they're powerless, but on the whole still really seem to buy into it— they think Reagan was a hands-off guy, not a figurehead created by the public relations industry.*

Well, people aren't out in the streets revolting, that's true—you can just look outside the door and see that. But by any index I know, the fact of the matter is that the public has become dramatically more dissident and skeptical. So for example, about half the population thinks that the government is just run by "a few big interests looking out for themselves."[59] As to whether Reagan was a hands-off guy or a figurehead, frankly that doesn't matter very much. The reality is that people either know or can quickly be convinced that *they* are not involved in policy-making, that policy is being made by powerful interests which don't have much to do with them. Now, I think they sometimes misidentify the powerful interests—for instance, they include labor unions as among them; well, that's propaganda. But when they mention corporations, big media, banks, investment firms, law firms that cater to their interests, things like that, okay, then I think they're on target.

So, yeah, people aren't out revolting in the streets, that's for sure. But I think there's plenty of potential. I mean, the environmental movement is big, and remember, it's a movement of the Seventies, not the Sixties. The Third World solidarity movements are movements of the Eighties. The anti-nuclear movement is a movement of the Eighties. The feminist movement is Seventies and Eighties. And it's way beyond movements—there are all kinds of people who are just cynical: they don't have any faith in institutions, they don't trust anybody, they hate the government, they assume they're being manipulated and controlled and that something's going on which they don't know about. Now, that's not necessarily a move to the *left*: that could be the basis for fascism too—it's just a question of what people do with it. I mean, this kind of depoliticized, cynical population could easily be mobilized by Jimmy Swaggart [a televangelist], or it could be organized by environmentalists. Mostly it just depends on who's willing to do the work.

WOMAN: *But do you actually believe that these positive changes will come?*

I don't know, I really haven't the slightest idea. But nobody could ever have predicted any revolutionary struggle—they're just not predictable. I mean, you couldn't have predicted in 1775 that there was going to be an American Revolution, it would have been impossible to have predicted it. But there was. You couldn't have predicted in 1954 that there was going to be a Civil Rights Movement. You couldn't have predicted in 1987 that there was going to be an uprising on the West Bank. I don't think at any stage in history it has ever been possible to decide whether to be optimistic or pessimistic, you just don't know—nobody understands how change happens, so how can you guess?

Let me just take a concrete case. In 1968, M.I.T. [the Massachusetts Institute of Technology] was the deadest place in the world—there was no anti-war activity, nothing was going on. And this was *after* the Tet Offensive: Wall Street had turned against the war, M.I.T. still hadn't heard about it. Well, a small group of students who were in a little collective on campus decided they would set up a sanctuary for a soldier who deserted; that was the kind of thing activists were doing back then. There was this working-class Marine kid who wanted to desert as an anti-war gesture, so the idea was, people would stay with him until the cops came, then they'd try to make a public issue out of it. There was a discussion about this among ten or fifteen students and two or three faculty members—and I came out against it, because I was totally pessimistic; I thought it couldn't possibly work, I thought that it would be a complete fiasco. But they went ahead with it.

Well, it turned out to be an *incredible* success. I mean, within about two days, the whole of M.I.T. was totally shut down—there weren't any classes, nothing was going on, the whole student body was over in the Student Center. It turned into a 24-hour mixture of seminars, and you know, this horrible music that people listen to, all that kind of stuff—it was very exciting. And it just changed the whole character of the place; ever since then, M.I.T. has not been the same. I mean, it's not that it turned into Utopia or anything, but a lot of concern developed and a lot of activity started up, which still continues, on issues which people didn't even consider before. Well, could you have guessed? I mean, I guessed wrong, they guessed right. But as far as I can see, it was basically like flipping a coin.

# 3

# Teach-In: Evening

*Based primarily on discussions at Rowe,*
*Massachusetts, April 15–16, 1989.*

## The Military-Industrial Complex

WOMAN: *What's been the point of the arms race, Dr. Chomsky?*

Well, there are a lot of things, it's served a number of crucial functions. Remember, any state, *any* state, has a primary enemy: its own population. If politics begins to break out inside your own country and the population starts getting active, all kinds of horrible things can happen—so you have to keep the population quiescent and obedient and passive. And international conflict is one of the best ways of doing it: if there's a big enemy around, people will abandon their rights, because you've got to survive. So the arms race is functional in that respect—it creates global tension and a mood of fear.

It's also functional for controlling the empire: if we want to invade South Vietnam, let's say, we have to be able to make it look as if we're defending ourselves from the Russians. If we're not able to do that, it's going to be a lot harder to invade South Vietnam. The domestic population just won't accept it—it's costly, it's morally costly if nothing else, to do these things.

The arms race also plays a crucial role in keeping the economy going—and that's a big problem. Suppose that the arms race really did decline: how would you force the taxpayers to keep subsidizing high-technology industry like they've been doing for the past fifty years? Is some politician going to get up and say, "Alright, next year you're going to lower your standard of living, because you have to subsidize I.B.M. so that it can produce fifth-generation computers"? Nobody's going to be able to sell that line. If any politician ever started talking that way, people would say: "Okay, we want to start getting involved in social and economic policy-making too."

In fact, that danger has been very openly discussed in the business literature in the United States for forty or fifty years.[1] Business leaders know perfectly well what every economist knows: that spending for civilian purposes is maybe even *more* efficient, *more* profitable than spending for military purposes. And they also know that there are any number of ways to have the population subsidize high-technology industry besides through the Pentagon system—business knows that perfectly well, and it also knows the reasons against it. They remain what they always were.

If you take an economics course, they'll teach you, correctly, that if the government spends *n* dollars to stimulate the economy, it doesn't really matter what it's spent on: they can build jet planes, they can bury it in the sand and get people to dig for it, they can build roads and houses, they can do all sorts of things—in terms of stimulating the economy, the economic effects are not all that different.[2] In fact, it's perfectly likely that military spending is actually a *less* efficient stimulus than social spending, for all kinds of reasons. But the problem is, spending for civilian purposes has negative side effects. For one thing, it interferes with managerial prerogatives. The money that's funneled through the Pentagon system is just a straight gift to the corporate manager, it's like saying, "I'll buy anything you produce, and I'll pay for the research and development, and if you can make any profits, fine." From the point of view of the corporate manager, that's optimal. But if the government started producing anything that business might be able to sell directly to the commercial market, then it would be interfering with corporate profit-making. Production of waste—of expensive, useless machinery—is not an interference: nobody else is going to produce B-2 bombers, right? So that's one point.

The other point, which is probably even more serious from the perspective of private power, is that social spending increases the danger of democracy—it threatens to increase popular involvement in decision-making. For example, if the government gets involved, say around here, in building hospitals and schools and roads and things like that, people are going to get interested in it, and they'll want to have a say in it—because it affects them, and is related to their lives. On the other hand, if the government says, "We're going to build a Stealth Bomber," nobody has any opinions. People *care* about where there's going to be a school or a hospital, but they don't care about what kind of jet plane you build—because they don't have the foggiest idea about that. And since one of the main purposes of social policy is to keep the population passive, people with power are going to want to eliminate anything that tends to encourage the population to get involved in planning—because popular involvement threatens the monopoly of power by business, and it also stimulates popular organizations, and mobilizes people, and probably would lead to redistribution of profits, and so on.

MAN: *How about just reducing taxes, instead of sending all this money into the military-industrial complex?*

You can't reduce taxes much—because what else is going to keep the economy going? Remember, it's been known since the Great Depression that anything like free-market capitalism is a total disaster: it can't work. Therefore every country in the world that has a successful economy is somewhere close to fascism—that is, with massive government intervention in the economy to coordinate it and protect it from hostile forces such as too much competition. I mean, there just is no other way to do it really: if you pulled that rug out from under private enterprise, we'd go right back into the Depression again. That's why every industrial economy has a massive state sector—and the way our massive state sector works in the United States is mainly through the military system.

I mean, I.B.M. isn't going to pay the costs of research and development—why should they? They want the taxpayer to pay them, say by funding a N.A.S.A. program, or the next model of fighter jet. And if they can't sell everything they produce in the commercial market, they want the taxpayer to buy it, in the form of a missile launching system or something. If there are some profits to be made, fine, they'll be happy to make the profits—but they always want the public subsidies to keep flowing. And that's exactly how it's worked in general in the United States for the past fifty years.

So for example, in the 1950s computers were not marketable, they just weren't good enough to sell in the market—so taxpayers paid 100 percent of the costs of developing them, through the military system (along with 85 percent of research and development for electronics generally, in fact). By the 1960s, computers began to be marketable—and they were handed over to the private corporations so they could make the profits from them; still, about 50 percent of the costs of computer development were paid by the American taxpayer in the 1960s.[3] In the 1980s, there was a big new "fifth-generation" computer project—they were developing new fancy software, new types of computers, and so on—and the development of all of that was extremely expensive. So therefore it went straight back to the taxpayer to foot the bills again—that's what S.D.I. [the Strategic Defense Initiative] was about, "Star Wars." Star Wars is basically a technique for subsidizing high-technology industry. Nobody believes that it's a defense system—I mean, maybe *Reagan* believes it, but nobody whose head is screwed on believes that Star Wars is a military system. It's simply a way to subsidize the development of the next generation of high technology—fancy software, complicated computer systems, fifth-generation computers, lasers, and so on.[4] And if anything marketable comes out of all that, okay, then the taxpayer will be put aside as usual, and it'll go to the corporations to make the profits off it.

In fact, just take a look at the parts of the American economy that are competitive internationally: it's agriculture, which gets massive state subsidies; the cutting edge of high-tech industry, which is paid for by the Pentagon; and the pharmaceutical industry, which is heavily subsidized through public science funding—those are the parts of the economy that function competitively. And the same thing is true of every other country in the world: the successful economies are the ones that have a big government sector. I mean, capitalism is fine for the Third World—we love *them* to be inefficient. But we're not going to accept it. And what's more, this has been true since the beginnings of the industrial revolution: there is not a single economy in history that developed without extensive state intervention, like high protectionist tariffs and subsidies and so on. In fact, all the things we *prevent* the Third World from doing have been the *prerequisites* for development everywhere else—I think that's without exception. So to return to your question, there just is no way to cut taxes very much without the entire economy collapsing.

## The Permanent War Economy

MAN: *I'm a little surprised to hear you say that the Pentagon is so important to our economy.*

There's hardly an element of advanced-technology industry in the United States that's *not* tied into the Pentagon system—which includes N.A.S.A., the Department of Energy [which produces nuclear weapons], that whole apparatus. In fact, that's basically what the Pentagon's *for*, and that's also why its budget always stays pretty much the same. I mean, the Pentagon budget is higher in real terms than it was under Nixon—and to the extent that it's declined in recent years, it's in fact had the effect of what they call "harming the economy." For instance, the Pentagon budget started to decline in 1986, and in 1987 real wages started to fall off for skilled workers, in other words for the college-educated. Before that they'd been declining for unskilled workers, and they started to go down for the college-educated a year after the Pentagon budget began to drop off a bit. And the reason is, college-educated people are engineers, and skilled workers, and managers and so on, and they're very dependent on the whole Pentagon system for jobs—so even a slight decline in military spending immediately showed up in real wage levels for that sector of the population.[5]

Actually, if you look back at the debates which went on in the late 1940s when the Pentagon system was first being set up, they're very revealing. You have to examine the whole development against the background of what had just happened. There was this huge Depression in the 1930s, worldwide, and at that point everyone understood that capitalism was dead. I mean, whatever lingering beliefs people had had about it, and they weren't very much before, they were gone at that point—because the whole capitalist system had just gone into a tailspin: there was no way to save it the way it was going. Well, every one of the rich countries hit upon more or less the same method of getting out. They did it independently, but they more or less hit on the same method—namely, state spending, public spending of some kind, what's called "Keynesian stimulation." And that did finally get countries out of the Depression. In the Fascist countries, it worked very well—they got out pretty fast. And in fact, every country became sort of fascist; again, "fascism" doesn't mean gas chambers, it means a special form of economic arrangement with state coordination of unions and corporations and a big role for big business. And this point about everyone being fascist was made by mainstream Veblenite-type economists [i.e. after the American economist Veblen] right at the time, actually—they said, everybody's fascist, the only question is what form the fascism takes: it takes different forms depending on the country's cultural patterns.[6]

Well, in the United States, the form that fascism took at first was the New Deal [legislative programs enacted in the 1930s to combat the Depression]. But the New Deal was too small, it didn't really have much effect—in 1939, the Depression was still approximately what it had been in 1932. Then came the Second World War, and at that point we became *really* fascist: we had a totalitarian society basically, with a command economy, wage and price controls, allocations of materials, all done straight from Washington. And the people who were running it were mostly corporate executives, who were called to the capital to direct the economy during the war effort. And they got the point: this worked. So the U.S. economy prospered during the war, industrial production almost quadrupled, and we were finally out of the Depression.[7]

Alright, then the war ended: now what happens? Well, everybody expected that we were going to go right back into the Depression—because nothing fundamental had changed, the only thing that had changed was that we'd had this big period of government stimulation of the economy during the war. So the question was, what happens now? Well, there *was* pent-up consumer demand—a lot of people had made money and wanted to buy refrigerators and stuff. But by about 1947 and '48, that was beginning to tail off, and it looked like we were going to go back into another recession. And if you go back and read the economists, people like Paul Samuelson and others in the business press, at that point they were saying that advanced industry, high-technology industry, "cannot survive in a competitive, unsubsidized free-enterprise economy"—that's just hopeless.[8] They figured we were heading right back to the Depression, but now they knew the answer: government stimulation. And by then they even had a theory for it, Keynes; before that they'd just done it by instinct.

So at that point, there was general agreement among business and elite planners in the United States that there would have to be massive government funneling of public funds into the economy, the only question was how to do it. Then came kind of an interesting . . . it wasn't really a *debate*, because it was settled before it was started, but the issue was at least raised: should the government pursue military spending or social spending? Well, it was quickly made very clear in those discussions that the route that government spending was going to have to take was military. And that was not for reasons of economic efficiency, nothing of the sort—it was just for straight power reasons, like the ones I mentioned: military spending doesn't redistribute wealth, it's not democratizing, it doesn't create popular constituencies or encourage people to get involved in decision-making.[9] It's just a straight gift to the corporate manager, period. It's a cushion for managerial decisions that says, "No matter what you do, you've got a cushion down there"—and it doesn't have to be a big portion of total revenues, like maybe it's a few percent, but it's a very important cushion.[10]

And the public is not supposed to know about it. So as the first Secretary of the Air Force, Stuart Symington, put the matter very plainly back in 1948, he said: "The word to use is not 'subsidy,' the word to use is 'security.'"[11] In other words, if you want to make sure that the government can finance the electronics industry, and the aircraft industry, and computers, and metallurgy, machine tools, chemicals, and so on and so forth, and you don't want the general public trying to have a say in any of it, you have to maintain a pretense of constant security threats—and they can be Russia, they can be Libya, they can be Grenada, Cuba, whatever's around.

Well, that's what the Pentagon system is about: it's a system for ensuring a particular form of domination and control. And that system has worked for the purposes for which it was designed—not to give people better lives, but to "make the economy healthy," in the standard sense of the phrase: namely, ensuring corporate profits. And that it does, very effectively. So you see, the United States has a major stake in the arms race: it's needed for domestic control, for controlling the empire, for keeping the economy running. And it's going to be very hard to get around that; I actually think that's one of the toughest things for a popular movement to change, because changing the commitment to the Pentagon system will affect the whole economy and the way it's run. It's a lot harder than, say, getting out of Vietnam. That was a peripheral issue for the system of power. This is a central issue.

In fact, I've been arguing for years with friends of mine who are campaigning for "conversion" of the economy from military production to social spending that they're basically talking nonsense. I mean, it's not that business has to be *told* "for this many jet planes we could have this many schools, isn't it awful to build jet planes?" You don't have to convince the head of General Motors of that: he knew that forty years before anyone started talking about "conversion," that's why he wanted jet planes. There is no point in explaining to people in power that "conversion" would be better for the world. Sure it would. What do they care? They knew that long ago, that's why they went in the opposite direction. Look: this system was designed, with a lot of conscious and intelligent thought, for the particular purpose that it serves. So any kind of "conversion" will just have to be part of a total restructuring of the society, designed to undermine centralized control.

And I mean, you're going to need an *alternative*—it's not enough just to cut off the Pentagon budget, that's just going to make the economy collapse, because the economy is dependent on it. Something else has to happen unless you just want to go back to the Stone Age. So the first thing simply has to be creating both a culture and an institutional structure in which public funds can be used for social needs, for human needs. That's the mistake that a lot of the "conversion" people make, in my opinion: they're just identifying what's obvious, they're not focusing enough on creating the basis for an alternative.

WOMAN: *What is the hope, then, for dismantling the whole military system?*

There have to be large-scale institutional changes, we need a real democratization of the society. I mean, if we continue to have domination of the economic and political system by corporations, why should they behave any differently? It's not that the people *in* the corporations are bad people, it's that the institutional necessity of the system is to maintain corporate domination and profit-making. I mean, if the Chairman of General Motors suddenly decided to start producing the best quality cars at the cheapest prices, he wouldn't be Chairman any longer—there'd be a shift on the stock market and they'd throw him out in five minutes. And that generalizes to the system as a whole. There is absolutely no reason why the people who own the economy would want it to be set up in a way that undermines or weakens their control, any more than there's a reason why they would want there to be a political system in which the population genuinely participates—why would they? They'd be crazy. Just like they'd be crazy if they opened up the media to dissident opinion—what possible purpose would there be in that? Or if they let the universities teach honest history, let's say. It would be absurd.

Now, that doesn't mean that there's nothing we can do. Even within the current structure of power, there's plenty of latitude for pressure and changes and reforms. I mean, any institution is going to have to respond to public pressure—because their interest is to keep the population more or less passive and quiescent, and if the population is *not* passive and quiescent, then they have to respond to that. But really dealing with the problems at their core ultimately will require getting to the source of power and dissolving it—otherwise you may be able to fix things up around the edges, but you won't really change anything fundamentally. So the alternative just has to be putting control over these decisions into popular hands—there simply is no other way besides dissolving and diffusing power democratically, I think.

## Libyan and American Terrorism

WOMAN: *Switching to current events a bit, Mr. Chomsky—"terrorism" is a phenomenon that really took off in the media in the 1980s. Why do you think all of a sudden Libya became such a great threat to us?*

Well, because from the very first minute that the Reagan administration came into office, it immediately selected Libya as a punching bag.[12] And there were very good reasons for that: Libya's defenseless, Qaddafi is sort of hateful and kind of a thug—a very small-time thug, I might say, but nevertheless a thug—and he's also an Arab, and there's a lot of anti-Arab racism around.[13] And the Reagan administration needed to create fear: it had to mobilize the population to do things they didn't want to do, like support a massive increase in military spending.

I mean, Reagan could *talk* about the "Evil Empire," but he couldn't get into any confrontations with the Evil Empire—because that's dangerous; the Soviets can fight back, and they've got missiles and things like that. So the trick was to find somebody who's frightening enough to scare Americans into accepting a huge military build-up, but nevertheless weak enough so you could beat him up without anyone fighting back. And the answer was Qaddafi, and international terrorism generally.

International terrorism by Arabs is certainly real. I mean, overwhelmingly international terrorism comes out of Washington and Miami, but there is a relatively small amount of it that comes from the Arab world.[14] And people don't like it—they blow up planes, and it's scary, and it's Arabs, it's weird-looking guys who have dark faces and mustaches. How does it become a big enough threat that we have to build more missiles and so on? Well, it's *Kremlin-directed* international terrorism.[15] This stuff was crafted from the first moment—and furthermore, it was all utterly transparent right from the very beginning, like I was writing about it as early as 1981.[16] The media pretend they don't understand it, scholarship pretends it doesn't understand it, but it's been as predictable as a broken record: they put it on in 1981, and it's still playing.

The whole media campaign on terrorism started with a series of C.I.A. disinformation releases about Libya. In 1981 the C.I.A. leaked a story to the press about U.S. efforts to assassinate Qaddafi, in the hope that this would lead Qaddafi to some kind of erratic reaction which we could then use as an excuse to bomb him. Okay, that was exposed: the first reference to C.I.A. disinformation about Libya appeared in *Newsweek* in August 1981, when *Newsweek* stated that it had been subjected to a disinformation campaign by the government.[17] Since then, there have been about a half-dozen similar cases in which Washington floated some lunatic story about Libya and the media bought it, then discovered later that it was disinformation and pretended they were all surprised; I mean, at some point you'd think they would begin to ask what's going on, but apparently not. And some of these cases were completely crazy—there was a story about Libyan hitmen wandering around Washington, S.W.A.T. teams on alert patrolling the White House, that kind of thing. It was all total madness.[18]

Well, every one of these confrontations with Libya has been timed for some domestic purpose. The big one, the bombing of Libya in April 1986, was timed for the contra aid vote in Congress—the point was to build up a lot of hysteria beforehand, and it kind of worked: they rammed through a big aid package a month or two later.[19] It was all a complete set-up, totally prefabricated. First, a confrontation was arranged in which Libyan artillery guns fired at a U.S. fighter plane. You'll notice that somehow it's always the *U.S.* Navy or the *U.S.* Air Force that Libya is shooting at—they never shoot at *Italian* planes, or *French* planes, or *Spanish* planes, it's always American planes. Well, what's the reason? One possibility is the Libyans are insane: they go after the people who are going to wipe them out. The other possibility is that the Americans are *trying* to get shot at, which is of course the truth. The reason the Libyans only shoot at American planes is because American planes are sent over there to *get* shot at; nobody else sends planes into the Gulf of Sidra, because there's no point in doing it, so therefore they *don't* get shot at.

See, Libya says the Gulf of Sidra is a part of its territorial waters, and the United States refuses to accept that. Well, there's a way that countries can resolve such disputes: you take them to the World Court and get a ruling; a law-abiding state does it that way. Alright, that option was raised in the United States, but the State Department said, no, we can't do it, it's much too desperate a situation; getting a decision from the World Court will take two years. You know, we can't put off for two years whether the U.S. Navy can go into the Gulf of Sidra, the United States will collapse. All this stuff is so ludicrous you can barely repeat it.[20]

The beginning phase of the 1986 confrontation occurred when American planes penetrated Libyan territorial air space and finally got shot at—happily, because they know they're never actually going to be hit by the Libyan air defenses. They then flew back to the fleet, and the American Navy bombed a bunch of Libyan navy vessels and killed lots of Libyans. That was great, a real victory.

Following that, on April 5th, 1986, a discotheque in West Berlin was bombed; two people were killed. Rather crucially, one of them was a Turkish woman and the other was a black American G.I.—the reason was, this was a black Third World bar, not an insignificant fact. The White House immediately announced that they had evidence, intercepts and so on, that showed that this terrorist act was perpetrated by Libya, though they never presented any of this evidence.[21] Then nine days later, on April 14th, we bombed Libya.

It was completely obvious that we *were* going to bomb them. In fact, I have a way of monitoring the Associated Press wires on my personal computer, and there were dispatches coming out all day because it was evident we were going to bomb them. So I don't know if you've ever looked at a ticker-tape, but a story comes out about every minute, and all through the day there were tons of stories coming out about Libya; the last one before the bombing came through at 6:28 P.M. It was bylined West Berlin, and it said: West German and U.S. military intelligence say they have no information about any Libyan connection to the disco bombing, but they suspect a possible Libyan connection.[22]

Okay, half an hour later, at precisely 7 P.M.—rather crucial, it was at 7 P.M. *precisely*—the United States started bombing Libya. Why 7 P.M.? Because that's when the national news started on the three U.S. television networks: this was the first bombing in history ever timed for prime-time television, and I mean that literally. It was a tricky operation to arrange: you had to synchronize a six-hour flight from England so that a squadron of F-111 bombers would arrive in Libya precisely at 7 P.M., when the three national networks began their newscasts. They had to travel all the way across the Mediterranean, two planes had to turn around and so on, but still they hit it precisely at 7—that means there had to have been extremely careful planning: they didn't want the bombing to start at ten after seven, say, because that would have lost the effect.

Now, every journalist who isn't totally insane knew that this was a set-up: I mean, how likely is it that you would get a bombing at 7 P.M. Eastern Standard Time, precisely on the nose? And if you watched the news that evening, some of you will remember that the anchormen, Peter Jennings and those guys, started off by saying: "Alright, we're going to switch over to Tripoli"—then they switched over to Tripoli, and there was the whole A.B.C. news team. What the hell were they doing in Tripoli? They're never in Tripoli. Well, they were in Tripoli because they knew perfectly well there was going to be a bombing, that's why. I mean, they didn't know the exact minute, but everybody was in place in Tripoli because they knew the place was going to be bombed. Of course, they all pretended it was this big surprise.

So, 7 P.M., the United States bombs Tripoli and Benghazi, kills plenty of people: you go to the exciting events live, you hear the loud noises, the television news is preempted because this is so exciting. Then they flash back to Washington, and the Reagan administration spokesman, Larry Speakes, gets on T.V., and for the next twenty minutes they preempt the destruction to give you the State Department line. Meanwhile, the whole Washington press corps is just sitting there, these pussycats like Sam Donaldson and the rest of them, who would never ask an embarrassing question in a million years. Speakes gets up and says, "We knew for certain ten days ago that Libya was behind the disco bombing"—and nobody asked the obvious question: if you knew for certain ten days ago, how come you didn't know half an hour ago? Barring colossal incompetence in the newsrooms, every journalist there knew what I knew—they read the A.P. wires at C.B.S. as much as I do, I guess, so that means they knew that up until a half-hour be-

fore the bombing, American and West German intelligence had no information about a Libyan connection. But Larry Speakes gets up and says,
"We knew for certain ten days ago"—and none of them even batted an eyelash.[23] Nobody asked another obvious question: how come the bombing
was scheduled for 7 P.M. Eastern Standard Time? How did you set it up so
that a six-hour flight from London happened to arrive in Libya at precisely
the instant when the television news started in the U.S.? Nobody asked that
question. In fact, there's a whole series of questions which nobody asked—
everyone in the press just swallowed the absurdities. Then Reagan got on
and pontificated for a while. Next day's news, a hundred percent—everybody said, this is terrific, we finally showed these Libyans. Not a note of
discord.[24]

Now, let me go on with the personal side of this. Two weeks later, I happened to go to Germany—where, incidentally, I was giving a talk at a conference on terrorism. When I got off at the airport in Frankfurt, the first
thing I did was pick up the German newspapers, and I also picked up *Der
Spiegel,* which is kind of like the German *Newsweek*. The front cover of
*Der Spiegel* was a picture of Reagan looking like some kind of madman
with missiles going over his head, and at the bottom was the phrase: "Terror Against Terror."[25] Now, that happens to be an old Gestapo slogan:
when the Gestapo went after the anti-Nazi resistance, they called it "terror
against terror." And I assume that everybody in Germany knew that it was
a Gestapo slogan—I guess that was the point, and especially when you
looked at the picture, the associations were pretty obvious: they were saying, "This is like the Nazis." And the whole journal basically was devoted
to exploding the theory that Libya had anything to do with the disco bombing. They said, there's no evidence for this, it's a total fabrication, Washington has never provided any evidence. There were speculations as to who
might have done it, like it might have been drug-related, some people
thought it was Ku Klux Klan-related—the Klan is very strong there, coming
out of the American army—but there didn't seem to be any reason why
Libya would bomb a German Third World bar. And in fact, while I was in
Germany, I didn't meet a single person who thought that there was any
plausibility whatsoever to the Libyan connection.

Okay, I went to the conference on terrorism, and afterwards there was a
press conference. At the press conference, I was asked by German reporters
what I thought about all of this, and I told them the little bit I knew. After it
ended, a guy came up to me, a black American from Dorchester [in Boston],
and introduced himself. He was a G.I. who'd been living in Germany for
about twenty-five years—he'd served there, then decided he didn't want to
come back, so he stayed; a fair number of black Americans have done that,
actually. Now he was working as a reporter for *Stars and Stripes,* the American army newspaper. Well, he told me that what I had said about the
bombing was part of the story, but that I didn't know the half of it—it was
much worse than I had said. I asked him what he meant, and he said that as
a reporter for *Stars and Stripes,* he had regularly been interviewing the head

of the hundred-person West German investigating team which was studying the disco bombing [Manfred Ganschow], a man who also happened to
be the director of the West Berlin equivalent of the F.B.I. [the Berlin Staats-
schutz]. And he said that ever since the first day he began interviewing him,
this guy had been telling him: "There's no Libyan connection, there's no
evidence for it, we don't believe it." I asked him if he could get me something on paper about this that I could publish, and he said he would.

He flew to Berlin and conducted another interview with this guy, then
came back to Frankfurt where I was, and gave me the transcript of the interview. In it, he asked the guy: "Do you have any new information about a
Libyan connection?" And the guy said, "You've been asking me that ever
since the first day. I told you then we don't have any evidence, we still have
no evidence." The reporter kept pressing. He said, "Look, Helmut Kohl,
the Chancellor of Germany, now agrees that there's some plausibility to
Reagan's Libya story." And this guy said, "Well, politicians have to do
what they have to do, and they'll say their stuff, but I'm just telling you
what the facts are; the facts are, there's no evidence." [26] And it goes on from
there. There never was any evidence. A couple months later it even began to
be *conceded* that there was no evidence. So maybe Syrians did it, or maybe
it was some other thing, but the idea that there was any credible Libyan
connection just disappeared. [27]

Actually, on the first anniversary of the bombing, the B.B.C. [British
Broadcasting Corporation] did a retrospective on the story in which they
reviewed all the background and went to European intelligence agencies for
assistance: their conclusion was that all of the European intelligence agencies—including those from the most conservative governments—say they
see no plausibility to the idea that there was a Libyan connection to the
disco bombing. [28] The whole thing was a lie. Nevertheless, it continues to
be repeated in the U.S. press. [29]

In fact, the B.B.C. also presented some further interesting information. If
you were following all of this at the time, you'll remember that there was a
very dramatic story told in the U.S. media after the disco bombing about
how the United States had picked up secret intercepts that Libya was going
to bomb some target in West Berlin just before the bombing, so they had declared an alert and were running around to all the places U.S. soldiers go in
West Berlin, and they got to the discotheque just fifteen minutes too late—
you remember that story? [30] It turns out it was a total fabrication. The
B.B.C. investigated it: neither the German intelligence and police nor any
Western embassy had ever heard about it—it was all completely fabricated.

Well, the point is, all of this stuff was known to American reporters. The
*New York Times* had a top-flight correspondent in Germany, James
Markham, and he was interviewing the head of West German intelligence
too, except he was never reporting any of this. [31] In fact, none of it was
ever reported, the press played the whole thing as if they were completely
blind—they pretended all the way through that they didn't understand the
business about the timing; they didn't mention the fact that there was no ev-

idence of a Libyan connection to the disco bombing right up to the moment of the Tripoli attack; and they have yet to inform people that West Germany itself never saw any evidence of a connection, and has always regarded it as a total fabrication. All of that is just unstatable in the U.S. media—and in this context, it's not very surprising that the American population still believes the official line. Well, here's an example of real brainwashing—and it's just got to be conscious in this case, I can't believe that the press is that incompetent.

Actually, there's even one more part to the Tripoli bombing story, that I know of at least. Remember the Pentagon's version of why we had to bomb Libya the first time: it was that American planes had been flying over the Gulf of Sidra to establish our right to be there, they were in international waters forty miles off the Libyan coast, they detected Libyan planes pursuing them, they disabled the Libyan radar, then in international waters, the Libyans shot at our planes—therefore we had to shoot them down and sink their naval boats, and ultimately bomb Tripoli a few days later and kill lots of Libyan civilians. That was the Pentagon's story. Well, a couple days after that, a very good, highly respected British correspondent, a guy named David Blundy, went to Libya to investigate the story, and he discovered the following. It turns out that at the time of the first American attack, there were a bunch of British engineers in Libya who were there making repairs on the Libyan radar systems—it was Russian radar, but the Russians couldn't figure out how to fix it, so they had to call in British engineers to fix it. So these engineers were there working on the radar, and by the time of the incident with the American fighter planes, the radar was working perfectly well and they were in fact monitoring the whole episode right as it transpired. And what they claim is that the American planes were not in international waters, they had in fact flown directly over Libyan ground territory: they had followed Libyan commercial jets at first so they wouldn't be picked up on radar, then they revealed themselves when they were over Libyan ground territory, and at that point they picked up ground fire.[32] And the purpose just had to be to *elicit* Libyan ground fire. Then when they'd been shot at, they went back out to sea and bombed the boats and shot down the planes and so on.

Well, that has never been reported in the United States. And that was very cautious non-reporting—because the *New York Times* and others just had to have been aware of this story, they just never mentioned any of this information.

MAN: *I have a student who was on active duty in the Mediterranean at that time, and he says that the American Navy went within a very short physical distance of the Libyan shoreline—not only within twelve miles, but within three miles. He was right there on the deck and saw it.*

That's probably the same story; that's interesting.

WOMAN: *What was the point of it, though?*

The immediate point was pretty clear: right then the Reagan administration was trying to create fanaticism in time for the Congressional vote on aid to the Nicaraguan contras, which was coming up a few days later. In fact, if anyone didn't understand this, Reagan drew the connection explicitly in a speech he made. He said: you know these Libyans, they're even trying to set up an outpost in our Hemisphere—namely, in Nicaragua.[33] In case anybody didn't understand . . .

MAN: *I understand the operation was a real military fiasco as well.*

Yes, there's a very good study of that by Andrew Cockburn, who's quite a good military correspondent.[34] A couple of the planes broke down, the bombs were going all over the place. I mean, they used laser-guided bombs—"smart" bombs—and when laser-guided bombs miss, it means that something got screwed up in the control mechanism, so they can go ten miles away, they can go anywhere. I mean, no high-technology works for very long, certainly not under complicated conditions, so all of these gadgets were screwing up and the servicemen couldn't figure out where they were. The night radar didn't work, a plane was shot down—it goes on and on. And remember, this was with no enemy opposition.

It was the same with the Grenada invasion [in 1983], actually—that was also a military fiasco. I mean, seven thousand American elite troops succeeded, after three days, in overcoming the resistance of about three dozen Cubans and a few Grenadan military men; they got 8,000 Medals of Honor for it.[35] They mostly shot themselves, or shot each other. They bombed a mental hospital. The airplanes were on a different radio frequency than the ground troops. They didn't know there were two medical campuses. In fact, there was an official report about it later by some Pentagon guy [William Lind], who just described it as a total fiasco.[36]

MAN: *They had to use tourist maps.*

They had the wrong maps—and this is like bombing the Rowe Conference Center [i.e. where Chomsky and the group were meeting], about that hard.

MAN: *Are these military planners rational?*

There's a kind of rationality. But remember, they're not really expecting to fight a war against anybody who can fight back—like, they're not planning on fighting the Russians or anything like that. They're mostly doing counterinsurgency stuff against defenseless targets like Libya and Grenada, so it doesn't really matter whether the equipment works. The top brass in the Pentagon, they basically want a lot of high-powered, heavily automated gadgetry that's expensive, because that's what makes you a big bureaucracy and able to run a lot of things. I mean, there's an *economic* purpose to the Pentagon, like I was talking about before: it's a way to get the public to fund the development of high technology, and so on. But the generals also want all this stuff too—it's kind of a power play. So these generals would rather have high-tech fancy aircraft than simple aircraft which just do the job, because you're more powerful if you control more complicated stuff. The perception they encourage is that everything's getting fancier and fancier, and more and more complicated, so they need more and more money, and more and more assistance, and more and more control—and it doesn't really matter very much whether it works properly or not, that's kind of secondary.[37]

WOMAN: *Gore Vidal refers to us as "the proud victors of Grenada."*

Yeah, that's when Reagan got up and said, "We're standing tall again." [38] We're laughing—but remember, people didn't laugh at the time. The Grenada invasion was considered a big shot in the arm: we're standing tall, they're not going to push us around anymore, all hundred thousand of them. We overcame their nutmeg.

## The U.S. and the U.N.

MAN: *Noam, do you see any positive role that the U.N. can play, for instance sending U.N. peacekeeping forces to places instead of U.S. intervention forces?*

Well, the U.N. can only play a positive role if the great powers let it play a positive role. So where the great powers more or less agree on something and they just need a mechanism to effect it, the U.N. is useful. But if the great powers are opposed—like, say the United States is opposed to something—okay, then it just doesn't happen.

MAN: *What about if the U.N. didn't have a Security Council, or didn't give veto power to the five permanent Security Council members? [The U.N. Security Council has 15 seats, 5 of which are permanently assigned to the U.S., Britain, France, Russia, and China, and for "substantive" Security Council resolutions to go into effect none of the 5 permanent members can have voted against them; unlike the General Assembly, the Security Council has enforcement powers.]*

It couldn't happen—because the great powers will not allow any interference with their affairs. Take the United States, which has been by far the leader in vetoing U.N. Security Council resolutions since the 1970s: if we don't like what the U.N. is doing, the U.N. can go down the tubes—we just ignore them, and that ends the matter.[39] You don't kid around with an eight-hundred-pound gorilla, you know.

In fact, it's quite interesting to trace the changes in the U.S. attitude towards the U.N. over the years. In the late 1940s, the United States just ran it completely—international relations of power were such that the U.S. just gave the orders and everybody followed, because the rest of the world was smashed up and starving after the Second World War. And at the time, everybody here loved the U.N., because it always went along with us: every way we told countries to vote, they voted. Actually, when I was a graduate student around 1950, major social scientists, people like Margaret Mead, were trying to explain why the Russians were always saying "no" at the U.N.—because here was the United States putting through these resolutions and everybody was voting "yes," then the Russians would stand up and say "no." So of course they went to the experts, the social scientists, to figure it out. And what they came up with was something we used to call "diaperology"; the conclusion was, the reason the Russians always say "no" at the U.N. is because they raise their infants with swaddling clothes [bandages wrapped around newborn babies to restrain and quiet them]. Literally—they raise their infants with swaddling clothes in Russia, so Russians end up very negative, and by the time they make it to the U.N. all they want to do is say "no" all the time. That was literally proposed, people took it seriously, there were articles in the journals about it, and so on.[40]

Well, over the years, U.S. power over the U.N. began to drop—at least relatively speaking. A lot of Third World countries entered the U.N., especially in the 1960s as a result of decolonization, so there was a lot more independence—and the U.N. just got out of control, we couldn't order it around as much anymore. And as that happened, you could just trace the U.S. attitude towards the U.N. getting more and more negative. For instance, they started using this phrase which I'm sure you've heard, "the tyranny of the majority." What's the tyranny of the majority? It's what's known as "democracy" elsewhere, but when *we* happen to be in the minority, it becomes "the tyranny of the majority." And starting around 1970, the United States began vetoing everything that came up: resolutions on South Africa, on Israel, on disarmament—you pick it, the United States was vetoing it. And the Soviet Union was voting right along with the mainstream.[41] Okay, all of a sudden it turns out that the U.N. is a total disaster.

I'll never forget one article about this in the *New York Times Magazine*, by their U.N. correspondent, Richard Bernstein. He went through this whole business about how the entire world votes against the United States all the time. He wasn't asking, "How do they raise American children?" What he asked was, "Why is the world out of step?" Literally: "What's the matter with the world, it's all out of step, it doesn't understand—what is it with the world?" Then he began looking for defects in the world. I'm not exaggerating, that's exactly what it was like—and all of this stuff is done without any self-consciousness, it's just said straight.[42]

It's the same with the World Court [the popular name for the International Court of Justice, the judicial organ of the U.N.]. When the World Court issued an explicit decision against the United States in June 1986 ordering—*ordering*—the United States to terminate what it called "unlawful use of force" and illegal economic warfare against Nicaragua, we just said to heck with it, we ignored them. The week after, Congress increased U.S. aid to the contras by another hundred million dollars.[43] Again, the commentary across the board in the U.S.—the *New York Times*, the *Washington Post*, big international law experts—was unanimous: the World Court has discredited itself by passing this judgment, so obviously we don't have to pay any attention to it.[44] It just discredits the World Court to criticize the United States—that's like a truism here. Then right after that, when the U.N. Security Council called on all states to observe international law—not referring to the United States, but obliquely referring to this World Court decision—and it was vetoed by the United States (11 to 1, with 3 abstentions); and when the General Assembly also passed the same resolution, the first time 94 to 3 (Israel, El Salvador, and the United States), the next time 94 to 2 (Israel and the United States)—the press wouldn't even report it.[45] Well, that's what it means to be a great power: you do whatever you feel like.

And by now, the United States is practically strangling the U.N.—we're by far its biggest debtor nation. In fact, the U.N. can barely function because the United States won't pay its bills.[46] And parts of the U.N. that we don't like, like U.N.E.S.C.O. [the United Nations Educational, Scientific, and Cultural Organization]—because it's working for the Third World—we practically put them out of business.

The United States launched a huge propaganda campaign against U.N.E.S.C.O. in the 1970s and Eighties—it was full of outrageous lies, totally fabricated, but nevertheless it sufficed to essentially eliminate the Third World orientation of U.N.E.S.C.O. and make it stop doing things it was doing around the Third World, like improving literacy and health care and so on.[47] But that's just the reality of what the U.N. is going to face when it pursues policies that are not in the interests of the great powers—it can just go down the drain, the United States won't permit it.

WOMAN: *But why is it that the press won't report any of these things?*

Well, it's because the press has a job: its job is to keep people from understanding the world, and to keep them indoctrinated. Therefore it won't report things like this—and again, that follows pretty logically from the nature of the press institutions themselves. In fact, the way that the U.S. press covers United Nations votes gives a very good illustration of how it works. So for example, when the U.N. has a vote denouncing the ongoing Russian invasion of Afghanistan in November 1987, *that* they put on the front page. But when the U.N. has a vote in the same session, in fact within a few days, calling on all states to observe international law—this very muted resolution after the World Court decision, it didn't even mention the United States directly—then they won't put it on the front page, in fact they won't put it *anywhere*.[48]

Or take the summit when the Soviet Union and the United States signed the I.N.F. [Intermediate-range Nuclear Forces] treaty, in December 1987. Right at that time, there was a tremendous amount of media attention focused on arms treaties. Well, the line that the U.S. media constantly presented was, "Reagan the Peacemaker"—you know, "Reagan leading us to a new age," "First arms control treaty [to abolish a class of weapons systems]," and so on. That was the standard picture across the whole American press. Okay, that very month, the U.N. General Assembly had passed a series of disarmament resolutions—but if you want to know the details of them, you'll have to look them up in my book *Necessary Illusions*, because it's about the only place you can find them in print in the United States. The General Assembly passed a resolution calling for the banning of all weapons in outer space, Star Wars—it went through 154 to 1, the U.S. was the 1. They passed a resolution against the development of new weapons of mass destruction; it was 135 to 1. They passed one calling for a nuclear test freeze; it was 137 to 3, the United States picked up England and France on that one. And so it went.

Do you think any of that made the newspapers in the United States? No, because that's just the wrong story.[49] The story is "Reagan the Peacemaker," not "The United States is alone in the world, isolated in the world in attempting to maintain the arms race"—that's not the story. And in fact, when the *New York Times* did its summary report on what had happened at the U.N. that year, you can bet your life that none of this stuff was included—there wasn't one word.[50]

And the point is, if you want to be a "responsible" journalist, you have to understand what's important, and what's important is things that work for the cause—U.S. corporate power, that's the cause. And you will not stay in the press very long unless you've internalized and come to understand these values virtually intuitively—because there's a whole elaborate process of filtering and selection in the institutions to eliminate people who *don't* understand them and to help advance people who do. That's how you can get commentators in the *New York Times* asking questions like "What's wrong with the world?" when the U.S. is standing alone against every other country, and not even batting an eyelash. And of course, it's also part of the way the propaganda system keeps everyone else from understanding the elementary realities too.

## Business, Apartheid, and Racism

WOMAN: *Professor Chomsky, one issue where I've noticed that activists get kind of a good press in the United States—and it seems out of synch with what we usually see—is coverage of people protesting South African apartheid [official system of racial segregation and white supremacy, the legal basis for which was largely repealed in 1990–91]. I'm wondering if you have any ideas why coverage of that might be a bit more positive.*

I think you're right: anti-apartheid movements in the United States *do* get a pretty good press—so when some mayor or something demonstrates against South Africa, there's usually kind of a favorable report on it. And I think the main reason is that Western corporations themselves are basically anti-apartheid by this point, so that's going to tend to be reflected in the media coverage.

See, South Africa has been going through an internal economic transformation, from a society based on extractive industry to one based on industrial production—and that transformation has changed the nature of international interests in South Africa. As long as South Africa was primarily a society whose wealth was based on extracting diamonds, gold, uranium and so on, what you needed were large numbers of slaves, basically—people who would go down into the mines and work for a couple years, then die and be replaced by others. So you needed an illiterate, subdued population of workers, with families getting just enough income to produce more slaves, but not much more than that—then either you sent them down into the mines, or you turned them into mercenaries in the army and so on to help control the others. That was traditional South Africa. But as South Africa changes to an industrial society, those needs also are beginning to change: now you don't need slaves primarily, what you need is a docile, partially educated workforce.

Something similar happened in the United States during our industrial revolution, actually. Mass public education first was introduced in the United States in the nineteenth century as a way of training the largely rural workforce here for industry—in fact, the general population in the United States largely was opposed to public education, because it meant taking kids off the farms where they belonged and where they worked with their families, and forcing them into this setting in which they were basically being trained to become industrial workers.[51] That was part of the whole transformation of American society in the nineteenth century, and that transformation now is taking place for the black population in South Africa—which means for about 85 percent of the people there. So the white South African elites, and international investors generally, now need a workforce that is trained for industry, not just slaves for the mines. And that means they need people who can follow instructions, and read diagrams, and be managers and foremen, things like that—so slavery just is not the right system for the country anymore, they need to move towards something more like what we have in the United States. And it's pretty much for that reason that the West has become anti-apartheid, and that the media will therefore tend to give anti-apartheid movements a decent press.

I mean, usually political demonstrations get very negative reporting in the United States, no matter what they're for, because they show people they can do things, that they don't just have to be passive and isolated—and you're not supposed to have that lesson, you're supposed to think that you're powerless and can't do anything. So any kind of public protest typically won't be covered here, except maybe locally, and usually it will get very negative reporting; when it's protest against the policies of a favored U.S. ally, it always will. But in the case of South Africa, the reporting is quite supportive: so if people go into corporate shareholder meetings or something and make a fuss about disinvestment [withdrawing investments from South Africa to pressure its government], generally they'll get a favorable press these days.

Of course, it's not that what they're doing is *wrong*—what they're doing is right. But they should understand that the reason they're getting a reasonably favorable press right now is that, by this point, business regards them as its troops—corporate executives don't really *want* apartheid in South Africa anymore. It's like the reason that business was willing to support the Civil Rights Movement in the United States: American business had no use for Southern apartheid, in fact it was bad for business.

See, capitalism is not fundamentally racist—it can exploit racism for its purposes, but racism isn't built into it. Capitalism basically wants people to be interchangeable cogs, and differences among them, such as on the basis of race, usually are not functional. I mean, they may be functional for a period, like if you want a super-exploited workforce or something, but those situations are kind of anomalous. Over the long term, you can expect capitalism to be anti-racist—just because it's anti-human. And race is in fact a human characteristic—there's no reason why it should be a *negative* characteristic, but it is a human characteristic. So therefore identifications based on race interfere with the basic ideal that people should be available just as consumers and producers, interchangeable cogs who will purchase all of the junk that's produced—that's their ultimate function, and any other properties they might have are kind of irrelevant, and usually a nuisance.

So in this respect, I think you can expect that anti-apartheid moves will be reasonably well supported by the mainstream institutions in the United States. And over the long term, I suspect that apartheid in South Africa will break down—just for functional reasons. Of course, it's going to be really rough, because white privilege in South Africa is extreme, and the situation of blacks is grotesque. But over time, I assume that the apartheid system will erode—and I think we should press very hard to make that happen: like, one doesn't turn against the Civil Rights Movement because you realize that business interests are in favor of it. That's kind of not the point.

## Winning the Vietnam War

WOMAN: *Mr. Chomsky, what's really going on in Vietnam—is it just the horrible dictatorship it's portrayed to be, and do you see any prospects at all for social or economic recovery there?*

Well, Vietnam's a pretty tight and autocratic place—but it was obvious that it was going to be that way. Don't forget, what we did to that country practically wiped it out. You have to bear in mind what *happened* there. Nobody here cares, so nobody studies it carefully, but over the course of the Indochina wars the number of people killed was maybe four million or more. ["Indochina" was the French colony comprising the area of Vietnam, Cambodia, and Laos; the United States attacked each of those countries in the 1960s and Seventies.] Tens of millions of others were displaced from their homes. Large parts of the country were simply destroyed. There are still thousands and thousands of deaths every year because of our use of chemical weapons—children are born with birth defects, and cancers, and tumors, deformities. I mean, Vietnam suffered the kind of fate there's nothing to compare to in European history back to the Black Plague. It'll be a century before they can recover—if then.[52]

In fact, by about 1970, my own view, and I wrote this at the time, was that either nothing in the region would survive—which was a possibility— or else the only thing that would survive would be North Vietnam, which is a harsh, orthodox Marxist-Leninist regime. And the reason why only North Vietnam would have survived is because under conditions of tremendous violence, the only thing that survives is the toughest people.[53]

See, libertarian structures are not very resilient—they can easily be wiped out by violence, whereas tough authoritarian structures can often survive that violence; in fact, one of the *effects* of violence is to magnify the power of authoritarian groups. For example, suppose we came under physical attack here—suppose a bunch of gangsters came and wanted to kill us, and we had to find a way to survive. I suspect that what we would do (at least what I would do) is to look for whoever around here is the toughest bastard, and put them in charge—because they'd be the most likely to help us survive. That's what you do if you want to survive a hostile attack: you subject yourself to power and authority, and to people who know how to fight. That's in fact the *result* of a hostile attack: the ones left in command at the end are the elements who were capable of surviving, and usually they survived because they're very violent. Well, our attack on Vietnam was extraordinarily violent, and the more constructive National Liberation Front in South Vietnam just couldn't survive it, but the tough authoritarian regime of the North could—so it took over.

And because the pressures on them have never let up since the war, if there ever *were* any possibilities for recovery afterwards, the United States has ensured that Vietnam could never do anything with them. Because U.S.

policy since the war has been to make Vietnam suffer as much as possible, and to keep them isolated from the rest of the world: it's what's called "bleeding Vietnam." [54] The Chinese leadership is much more frank about it than we are—for example, Deng Xiaoping [China's dominant political figure until the 1990s] says straight out that the reason for supporting Pol Pot in Cambodia is that he's Vietnam's enemy, and he'll help us make Vietnam suffer as much as possible. We're not quite as open about it, but we take basically the same position—and for only slightly different reasons. China wants Vietnam to suffer because they're an ideological competitor, and they don't like having an independent state like that their border; the United States wants them to suffer because we're trying to increase the difficulty of economic reconstruction in Southeast Asia—so we'll support Pol Pot through allies like China and Thailand, in order to "bleed" Vietnam more effectively. [55] [Pol Pot was the Cambodian Khmer Rouge Party leader responsible for a mass slaughter in that country in the mid-1970s.]

I mean, remember what the Vietnam War was fought for, after all. The Vietnam War was fought to prevent Vietnam from becoming a successful model of economic and social development for the Third World. And we don't want to lose the war, Washington doesn't want to lose the war. So far we've won: Vietnam is no model for development, it's a model for destruction. But if the Vietnamese could ever pull themselves together somehow, Vietnam could again become such a model—and that's no good, we always have to prevent that. [56]

The extent of the sadism on this is extraordinary, in fact. For example, India tried to send a hundred buffalo to Vietnam, because the buffalo herds there had been virtually wiped out—Vietnam's a peasant society, remember, so buffalo mean tractors, fertilizer, and so on; the United States threatened to cut off "Food for Peace" aid to India if they did it. We tried to block Mennonites from sending wheat to Vietnam. We've effectively cut off all foreign aid to them over the past twenty years, by pressuring other countries not to give them anything. [57] And the only purpose of all these things has been to make Vietnam suffer as much as possible, and to prevent them from ever developing—and they've just been unable to deal with it. Whatever minuscule hopes they might have had have been eliminated, because they've made error after error in terms of economic reconstruction. I mean, in the last couple years, they've tried to fool around with liberalizing markets to attract foreign investors and so on, but it's pretty hard to envision any positive scenario for them.

Look, to try to deal with economic problems in general is not so simple—the United States is doing a rotten job of it, with all the advantages in the world. And to deal with problems of economic reconstruction under conditions of total devastation, and lack of resources, and imposed isolation from the world—that's very, very hard. I mean, economic development in the West was a very brutal process, and that was under pretty good conditions. For example, the American colonies in the eighteenth century were objectively better off than most Third World countries today—that's in *absolute* terms, not relative terms, meaning you had to work less to feed yourself, things like that.[58] And economic development here still was very brutal, even with those enormous advantages. And remember, that was with all of the resources in the world still around to be robbed—nobody has that anymore, they've all been robbed already. So there are just real, qualitative differences in the problems of Third World development today—and the Vietnamese have problems far beyond that, problems they simply cannot overcome at this point, as far as I can see.

[Editors' Note: Official U.S. relations with Vietnam changed in February 1994, as American businesses pressured the government to allow them to join foreign-based corporations that were violating the embargo and making profits off Vietnam.[59]]

## "Genocide": the United States and Pol Pot

MAN: *You said that we support Pol Pot in Cambodia through our allies. Isn't there a chance that there could be another genocide there if the Khmer Rouge gets back in power? I'm terrified of that possibility.*

Yeah, it's dangerous. What will happen there depends on whether the West continues to support them . . .

MAN: *But we may be heading for another genocide.*

Well, look, the business about "genocide" you've got to be a little careful about. Pol Pot was obviously a major mass murderer, but it's not clear that Pol Pot killed very many more people—or even *more* people—than the *United States* killed in Cambodia in the first half of the 1970s. We only talk about "genocide" when other people do the killing. [The U.S. bombed and invaded Cambodia beginning in 1969, and supported anti-Parliamentary right-wing forces in a civil war there which lasted until 1975; Pol Pot ruled the country between 1975 and '78.]

So there's a lot of uncertainty about just what the scale was of the Pol Pot massacre, but the best scholarly work in existence today estimates the deaths in Cambodia from all causes during the Pol Pot period in the hundreds of thousands, maybe as much as a million.[60] Well, just take a look at the killing in Cambodia that happened in the first half of the decade from 1970 to 1975—which is the period that *we're* responsible for: it was also in the hundreds of thousands.[61]

Furthermore, if you really want to be serious about it—let's say a million people died in the Pol Pot years, let's take a higher number—it's worth bearing in mind that when the United States stopped its attacks on inner Cambodia in 1975, American and other Western officials predicted that in the aftermath, about a million more Cambodians would die just from the *effects* of the American war.[62] At the time that the United States withdrew from Cambodia, people were dying from starvation in the city of Phnom Penh alone—forget the rest of the country—at the rate of 100,000 a year.[63] The last U.S. A.I.D. [Agency for International Development] mission in Cambodia predicted that there would have to be two years of slave labor and starvation before the country could even begin to get moving again.[64] So while the number of deaths you should attribute to the United States during the Pol Pot period isn't a simple calculation to make, obviously it's a lot—when you wipe out a country's agricultural system and drive a million people out of their homes and into a city as refugees, yeah, a lot of people are going to die. And the responsibility for their deaths is not with the regime that took over afterwards, it's with the people who *made* it that way.

And in fact, there's an even more subtle point to be made—but not an insignificant one. That is: why did Pol Pot and the Khmer Rouge carry out their massacre in the first place? Well, there's pretty good evidence that the Khmer Rouge forces took power primarily because they were the only ones who were tough enough bastards to survive the U.S. attacks. And given the destructive psychological effects of the American bombings on the peasant population there, some sort of violent outpouring was fairly predictable— and there was a big element of just plain peasant revenge in what happened.[65] So the U.S. bombings hit a real peak of ferocity in around 1973, and that's the same period in which the Pol Pot group started gaining power. The American bombardment was certainly a significant factor, possibly the critical factor, in building up peasant support for the Khmer Rouge in the first place; before that, they had been a pretty marginal element. Okay, if we were honest about the term "genocide," we would divide up the deaths in the Pol Pot period into a major part which is *our* responsibility, which is the responsibility of the United States.

### Heroes and Anti-Heroes

MAN: *Noam, I have to say, I'm getting a little depressed by all of this negative information—we need it, there's no question about it, but we also need a certain degree of empowerment. So let me just ask you, who are your heroes?*

Well, let me first just make a remark about the "empowerment" point, which comes up again and again. I never know exactly how to respond to it—because it's just the wrong question. The point is, there are lots of opportunities to do things, and if people do something with them, changes will happen. No matter how you look at it, it seems to me that's always what it comes down to.

MAN: *Well, I guess I'm asking about your heroes so that you'll be a little bit more specific about some of these "opportunities." For example, who do you really admire when it comes to activism?*

Well, my heroes are people who were working with S.N.C.C. [the Student Nonviolent Coordinating Committee, a Civil Rights Movement organization] in the South—people who day after day faced very harsh conditions and suffered badly, some of them were even killed. They'll never enter into history, but I knew some of them, I saw some of them—they're heroes. Draft resisters during the Vietnam War I think are heroes. Plenty of people in the Third World are heroes: if you ever have the chance to go to a place where people are really struggling—like the West Bank, Nicaragua, Laos—there's an awful lot of heroism, just an awful lot of heroism. Among sort of middle-class organizers, there are three or four people I know who would get the Nobel Peace Prize if it meant anything, which of course it doesn't, in fact it's kind of an insult to get it—take a look at who it goes to.[66] If you look around, there are people like that: if you want heroes, you can find them. You're not going to find them among anybody whose name is mentioned in the newspapers—if they're there, you know probably they're not heroes, they're anti-heroes.

I mean, there are plenty of people who when some popular movement gets going are willing to stand up and say, "I'm your leader"—the Eugene McCarthy phenomenon. Eugene McCarthy [a contender for the Democratic Party Presidential nomination in 1968] is a perfect example of it. I remember John Kenneth Galbraith [American economist] once saying, "McCarthy's the real hero of the Vietnam War opposition," and American liberalism always writes about him as a great hero.[67] Well, if you take a look at McCarthy's history, you can understand why. During the *hard* years of building up the anti-war movement, nobody ever heard of Eugene McCarthy. There were some people in Congress involved in opposing the war, but it wasn't McCarthy; in fact, it wasn't even McGovern, if you want to know the truth—it was Wayne Morse, Ernest Gruening, Gaylord Nelson, maybe a couple of others, but certainly not McCarthy. In fact, you never even *heard* of Eugene McCarthy until around the time of the Tet Offensive [in January 1968]. Around the time of the Tet Offensive, corporate America turned against the war, there was a huge mass popular movement out there, and Eugene McCarthy figured that he could get some personal power out of it, so he announced himself as "Your Leader." He didn't really say anything—if you look back, you don't even know which side he was on, if you read the words—but somehow he managed to put across the impression that he was this big anti-war leader.

He won the New Hampshire primary in '68 and went to the Democratic National Convention. At the Democratic Convention, lots and lots of young people showed up to work on his campaign—you know, "Clean for Gene" and so on—and they got battered bloody by the Chicago police [in a police riot with anti-war demonstrators]. McCarthy didn't bat an eyelash, he never even came down to talk to them. He didn't win at the 1968 Convention, so he disappeared. He had a lot of prestige at that point—totally undeserved—but he had a lot of prestige as the self-elected spokesman of the anti-war movement, and if he'd cared even marginally about anything he was saying, he would have used that undeserved status to work against the war. But he quit: the power game was over, it was more fun to write poetry and talk about baseball, so that's what he did. And that's why he's a liberal hero—because he's a total fraud. I mean, you couldn't have a more clear example of a total fraud.

Well, those are the kind of "heroes" that the culture is going to set up for you—the kind who show up when there are points to be gotten and power to be gotten, and who try to exploit popular movements for their own personal power-trips, and therefore marginalize the popular movements. Then if things don't work out for them, they go on and do something else: that's a "hero." Or you know, after you get shot, after you're killed, like Martin Luther King, then you can become a hero—but not while you're alive. Remember, despite all of the mythology today, Martin Luther King was strongly opposed while he was alive: the Kennedy administration really disliked him, they tried to block him in every possible way. I mean, eventually the Civil Rights Movement became powerful enough that they had to *pretend* that they liked him, so there was sort of a period of popularity for King when he was seen to be focusing on extremely narrow issues, like racist sheriffs in the South and so on. But as soon as he turned to broader issues, whether it was the Vietnam War, or planning the Poor People's Campaign [a 1968 encampment and protest march on Washington], or other things like that, he became a total pariah, and was actively opposed.[68]

I. F. Stone is another case like that. I. F. Stone is a great hero of the press—they all talk about, "Boy, if we only had more people like Izzy Stone" and so on. But if you take a look at the actual record, it's kind of revealing; I did it once. Up until 1971, Izzy Stone was a total outcast, his name wasn't even mentioned—and the reason is, he was publishing his radical news weekly [*I. F. Stone's Weekly*]. There were a lot of journalists ripping it off, but this guy was a Communist, so you don't ever want to mention him. Then in 1971, he couldn't continue putting out the *Weekly* anymore because he and his wife were getting too old, so they stopped publishing it—and within a year he won the George Polk Award, there were films being made about him, he was being hailed everywhere as the great maverick reporter who proved what a terrific press we had, "if only we had more people like him," and so on. Everybody just plays along with the farce, everybody plays along.

### "Anti-Intellectualism"

WOMAN: *Noam, I've noticed that in general there's a strong strain of anti-intellectualism in American society.*

When you say there's "anti-intellectualism," what exactly does that mean? Does it mean people think Henry Kissinger shouldn't be allowed to be National Security Advisor?

WOMAN: *Well, I feel there's a sense in which you're looked down on if you deal with ideas. Like, I'll go back and tell the people I work with that I spent the whole weekend listening to someone talk about foreign policy, and they won't look at that in a positive way.*

Yeah, because you should have been out making money, or watching sports or something. But see, I don't call that "anti-intellectual," that's just being de-politicized—what's especially "intellectual" about being concerned with the world? If we had functioning labor unions, the working class would be concerned with the world. In fact, they *are* in many places—Salvadoran peasants are concerned with the world, they're not "intellectuals."

These are funny words, actually. I mean, the way it's used, being an "intellectual" has virtually nothing to do with working with your mind: those are two different things. My suspicion is that plenty of people in the crafts, auto mechanics and so on, probably do as much or more intellectual work as plenty of people in universities. There are big areas in academia where what's called "scholarly" work is just clerical work, and I don't think clerical work's more challenging mentally than fixing an automobile engine—in fact, I think the opposite: I can *do* clerical work, I can never figure out how to fix an automobile engine.

So if by "intellectual" you mean people who are using their minds, then it's all over the society. If by "intellectual" you mean people who are a special class who are in the business of imposing thoughts, and framing ideas for people in power, and telling everyone what they should believe, and so on, well, yeah, that's different. Those people are called "intellectuals"—but they're really more a kind of secular priesthood, whose task is to uphold the doctrinal truths of the society. And the population *should* be anti-intellectual in that respect, I think that's a healthy reaction.

In fact, if you compare the United States with France—or with most of Europe, for that matter—I think one of the healthy things about the United States is precisely this: there's very little respect for intellectuals as such. And there shouldn't be. What's there to respect? I mean, in France if you're part of the intellectual elite and you cough, there's a front-page story in *Le Monde*. That's one of the reasons why French intellectual culture is so farcical—it's like Hollywood. You're in front of the television cameras all the time, and you've got to keep doing something new so they'll keep focusing on you and not on the guy at the next table, and people don't have ideas that are that good, so they have to come up with crazy stuff, and the intellectuals get all pompous and self-important. So I remember during the Vietnam War, there'd be these big international campaigns to protest the war, and a number of times I was asked to co-sign letters with, say, Jean-Paul Sartre [French philosopher]. Well, we'd co-sign some statement, and in France it was front-page news; here, nobody even mentioned it. And the French thought that was scandalous; I thought it was terrific—why the hell should anybody mention it? What difference does it make if two guys who happen to have some name recognition got together and signed a statement? Why should that be of any particular interest to anybody? So I think the American reaction is much healthier in this respect.

WOMAN: *But I want to point out that you've told us about a number of books this weekend which support some of the contentions you're making: you would not know a lot of these things if you hadn't read that material.*

That's right—but you see, that's a reflection of *privilege*, not a reflection of intellectual life. The fact is that if you're at a university, you're very privileged. For one thing, contrary to what a lot of people say, you don't have to work all that hard. And you control your own work—I mean, maybe you decide to work eighty hours a week, but *you* decide which eighty hours. That makes a tremendous difference: it's one of the few domains where you control your own work. And furthermore, you have a lot of resources—you've got training, you know how to use a library, you see the ads for books so you know which books are probably worth reading, you know there are declassified documents because you learned that in school somewhere, and you know how to find them because you know how to use a reference library. And that collection of skills and privileges gives you access to a lot of information. But it has nothing to do with being "intellectual": there are plenty of people in the universities who have all of this stuff, and use all of these things, and they do clerical work. Which is perfectly possible—you can get the declassified documents, and you can copy them, and compare them, and then make a notation about some footnote referring to something else. That's in fact most of the scholarship in these fields—take a look at the monographs sometime, there's not a thought in people's heads. I think there's less real intellectual work going on in a lot of university departments than there is in trying to figure out what's the matter with my car, which requires some creativity.

WOMAN: *Okay, let's accept that the auto mechanic is an intellectual—then I think on the other side, we also have to accept that those people who deal with books correctly, and aren't the clerical workers, are also intellectuals.*

Well, if by "intellectual" you just want to refer to people who use their minds, yeah, okay. But in that sense, I don't think that people *are* anti-intellectual. For example, if you take your car to a really hot-shot mechanic who's the only guy in your town who can ever figure out what's wrong—the guys in the car manufacturing place can never do it, but this guy's just got a real feel for automobiles; he looks at your car, and starts taking it apart . . .

WOMAN: *She . . .*

Or she, or whatever—you don't look down on that person. Nobody looks down on that person. You admire them.

WOMAN: *But people do look down on people who read books.*

But look, this guy may have read books—maybe he read the manual. Those manuals are not so easy to read; in fact, they're harder to read than most scholarly books, I think.

But I'm not trying to disagree, I just think that we should look at the thing a little differently. There's intellectual *work*, which plenty of people do; then there's what's called "intellectual *life*," which is a special craft which doesn't particularly require thought—in fact, you're probably better off if you don't think too much—and *that's* what's called being a respected intellectual. And people are right to look down on that, because there's nothing very special about it. It's just a not very interesting craft, not very well done usually.

In my own view, it's wrong if a society has these kinds of differentiations. My own early background was in a kind of Jewish working-class environment, where the people were not formally educated and they were workers—like somebody could be a shop-boy, or a seamstress or something like that—but they were very literate: I would call them intellectuals. They weren't "intellectuals" in the sense that people usually talk about, but they were very well-read, they thought about things, they argued about things—I don't see any reason why that can't be what you do when you're a seamstress.

## Spectator Sports

WOMAN: *Could you talk a bit more about the role that sports play in the society in de-politicizing people—it seems to me it's more significant than people usually assume.*

That's an interesting one, actually—I don't know all that much about it personally, but just looking at the phenomenon from the outside, it's obvious that professional sports, and non-participation sports generally, play a huge role. I mean, there's no doubt they take up just a tremendous amount of attention.

In fact, I have the habit when I'm driving of turning on these radio call-in programs, and it's striking when you listen to the ones about sports. They have these groups of sports reporters, or some kind of experts on a panel, and people call in and have discussions with them. First of all, the audience obviously is devoting an enormous amount of time to it all. But the more striking fact is, the callers have a tremendous amount of expertise, they have detailed knowledge of all kinds of things, they carry on these extremely complex discussions. And strikingly, they're not at all in awe of the experts—which is a little unusual. See, in most parts of the society, you're encouraged to defer to experts: we all do it more than we should. But in this area, people don't seem to do it—they're quite happy to have an argument with the coach of the Boston Celtics, and tell him what he should have done, and enter into big debates with him and so on. So the fact is that in this domain, people somehow feel quite confident, and they know a lot—there's obviously a great deal of intelligence going into it.

Actually, it reminds me in some ways of things that you find in non-literate or non-technological cultures—what are called "primitive" cultures—where for example, you get extremely elaborate kinship systems. Some anthropologists believe these systems have to do with incest taboos and so on, but that's kind of unlikely, because they're just elaborated *way* beyond any functional utility. And when you look at the structure of them, they seem like a kind of mathematics. It's as though people want to work out mathematical problems, and if they don't have calculus and arithmetic, they work them out with other structures. And one of the structures everybody has is relationships of kinship—so you work out your elaborate structures around that, and you develop experts, and theories, and so on. Or another thing you sometimes find in non-literate cultures is developments of the most extraordinary linguistic systems: often there's tremendous sophistication about language, and people play all sorts of games with language. So there are puberty rites where people who go through the same initiation period develop their own language that's usually some modification of the actual language, but with quite complex mental operations differentiating it—then that's theirs for the rest of their lives, and not other people's. And what all these things look like is that people just want to use their intelligence somehow, and if you don't have a lot of technology and so on, you do other things.

Well, in our society, we have things that you might use your intelligence on, like politics, but people really can't get involved in them in a very serious way—so what they do is they put their minds into other things, such as sports. You're trained to be obedient; you don't have an interesting job; there's no work around for you that's creative; in the cultural environment you're a passive observer of usually pretty tawdry stuff; political and social life are out of your range, they're in the hands of the rich folk. So what's left? Well, one thing that's left is sports—so you put a lot of the intelligence and the thought and the self-confidence into that. And I suppose that's also one of the basic functions it serves in the society in general: it occupies the population, and keeps them from trying to get involved with things that really matter. In fact, I presume that's part of the reason why spectator sports are supported to the degree they are by the dominant institutions.

And spectator sports also have other useful functions too. For one thing, they're a great way to build up chauvinism—you start by developing these totally irrational loyalties early in life, and they translate very nicely to other areas. I mean, I remember very well in high school having a sudden kind of *Erlebnis*, you know, a sudden insight, and asking myself, why do I care if my high school football team wins? I don't know anybody on the team. They don't know me. I wouldn't know what to say to them if I met them. Why do I care? Why do I get all excited if the football team wins and all downcast if it loses? And it's true, you do: you're taught from childhood that you've got to worry about the Philadelphia Phillies, where I was. In fact, there's apparently a psychological phenomenon of lack of self-confidence or something which affected boys of approximately my age who grew up in Philadelphia, because every sports team was always in last place, and it's kind of a blow to your ego when that happens, people are always lording it over you.

But the point is, this sense of irrational loyalty to some sort of meaning-less community is training for subordination to power, and for chauvinism. And of course, you're looking at gladiators, you're looking at guys who can do things you couldn't possibly do—like, you couldn't pole-vault seventeen feet, or do all these crazy things these people do. But it's a model that you're supposed to try to emulate. And they're gladiators fighting for your cause, so you've got to cheer them on, and you've got to be happy when the opposing quarterback gets carted off the field a total wreck and so on. All of this stuff builds up extremely anti-social aspects of human psychology. I mean, they're there; there's no doubt that they're there. But they're empha-sized, and exaggerated, and brought out by spectator sports: irrational competition, irrational loyalty to power systems, passive acquiescence to quite awful values, really. In fact, it's hard to imagine anything that con-tributes more fundamentally to authoritarian attitudes than this does, in addition to the fact that it just engages a lot of intelligence and keeps people away from other things.

So if you look at the whole phenomenon, it seems to me that it plays quite a substantial social role. I don't think it's the only thing that has this kind of effect. Soap operas, for example, do it in another domain—they teach people other kinds of passivity and absurdity. As a matter of fact, if you really want to do a serious media critique right across the board, these are the types of things which occupy most of the media, after all—most of it isn't shaping the news about El Salvador for politically articulate people, it's diverting the general population from things that really matter. So this is one respect in which the work that Ed Herman and I have done on the media is really defective—we don't talk about it much. But this stuff is a major part of the whole indoctrination and propaganda system, and it's worth examining more closely. There are people who've written about it,

Neil Postman and others—I just don't feel enough acquaintance with it to say more.[69]

## Western European Activism and Canada

MAN: *Professor Chomsky, I'm wondering whether there are any lessons about activism that you think we should learn from Western Europe—they seem to be very far ahead of us in terms of political organizing and strategies.*

No, I don't agree—we're always looking for a savior somewhere, and there isn't any. I mean, there are a lot of things that have developed in the United States which have not developed in Western Europe, and the popular movements here are much healthier in many respects than the European ones—theirs are very ideology-ridden: they've got "texts," and "theories," and all kinds of stuff that we don't have, which we're lucky we don't have. There's really been a lot of very successful organizing here over the years.

MAN: *But there are mass demonstrations there.*

Yeah, but we've had mass demonstrations too—we just had one in Washington a couple days ago [in support of abortion rights]. We know how to do that stuff; it's not very hard. I mean, there are no big secrets about any of this: there are very few lessons to transmit, so far as I know. Look, people have been involved in very successful organizing in the United States: the Civil Rights Movement, the anti-war movement, the ecological movement, the feminist movement, all of these things have been very successful developments.

MAN: *What about all the West European social-welfare policies, though?*

It's true, they have a lot of social-welfare programs we don't have—but that's true of Canada too, you don't even have to go all the way to Europe. For instance, they have a functioning public health insurance program in Canada, which we don't have here in the United States. But see, that has to do with the extreme power of private capital here, and with the fact that the capitalist class in the United States is extraordinarily class-conscious, while the working class is very diffuse and weak. So the result is, we don't have a lot of things that by now are pretty much taken for granted in every other industrial country: we have more homeless and less health.

Now, you can look at the specific historical particularities in the United States that have made it that way—and that's worth doing—but really it's not a big secret how to go about getting those kinds of programs. And if you want to understand what a reasonably rational national health care program would look like, you don't have to go very far. There's a good start, at least, right across the border.

MAN: *Why does Canada have programs like that, though?*

Well, there you have to look at the history: you have to ask, how has the history of Canada been different from the history of the United States? And there have been a lot of differences. For instance, one difference had to do with the American Revolution—in the American Revolution, a large number of people fled to Canada, lots in fact. And a lot of them fled because they didn't like the doctrinaire, kind of fanatic environment that took hold in the colonies. The percentage of colonists who fled in the American Revolution was actually about 4 percent, it was probably higher than the percentage of Vietnamese who fled Vietnam after the Vietnam War. And remember, they were fleeing from one of the richest places in the world— these were boat-people who fled in terror from Boston Harbor in the middle of winter to Nova Scotia, where they died in the snow trying to get away from all of these crazies here. The numbers are supposed to have been in the neighborhood of maybe a hundred thousand out of a total population of about two and a half million—so it was a substantial part of the population. And among them were people from groups who knew they were going to get it in the neck if the colonists won—blacks and Native Americans, for example.[70] And they were right: in the case of the Native Americans, it was genocide; in the case of blacks, it was slavery.

And actually, that wasn't the only big migration to Canada which contributed to some of the differences—there was also another major one around the turn of the century, coming out of the American Midwest after the Populist movement collapsed [the Populists were a political movement that formed out of agrarian protest in the 1880s and broke apart after 1896]. The Populists were the last gasp of large-scale popular democratic politics in the United States, and they were mainly centered in the Midwest—radical Kansas farmers and that sort of thing. And when they were finally defeated and the Populist Party dissolved, a lot of them just left. I don't know the numbers in this case, but a fair number of them went to Canada, and in fact they became part of the basis for the Canadian social-democratic movement which developed after that, and was responsible for pushing through a lot of the social-welfare programs in Canada.[71]

Apart from that, there are a lot of other things that have made Canada different. For instance, the United States has always been a much more advanced capitalist country, by far—corporations in the modern sense were an American invention, and ever since the beginning of the industrial revolution, corporate America has always been much more powerful than its Canadian counterpart. This was a much richer country; we kept trying to invade Canada; Canada's much more sparsely settled and much less populous than the United States; it was part of the British Empire; they have the French-English split, with Quebec there; and so on. So there are a lot of historical and other differences between the two of them, and I think it's a good question to look into in more detail. But the fact is, there are advantages and disadvantages to the two countries. A lot of things have been won in the United States that are good, and are a model for other places—and as far as organizing is concerned, it's the kind of thing you can do relatively freely here, free of the fear of very much direct state repression. So there are things you can learn everywhere: you can learn things from Nicaragua, you can learn things from Vietnam, you can learn things from Western Europe, and you can learn things from Canada. But if you want to go somewhere for salvation, you're not going to find it.

## Dispelling Illusions

WOMAN: *Noam, in general, how would you say ordinary people should go about trying to dispel their illusions about the world—what's the best way to start?*

Well, you don't sit in your room somewhere and dispel illusions—very few people are capable of doing that. I mean, some people are capable of doing it, but most aren't. Usually you find out what you think by interaction with people, otherwise you don't know what you think—you just hear something, and maybe you accept it, or you don't pay any attention to it, or something like that. You learn about things because you're interested in the topic, and when it's the social world, your interest in it often involves—*ought* to involve, at least—trying to change it, it's in that context that you learn. And you learn by trying out ideas, and hearing reactions to them, and hearing what other people have to say about the topic, and formulating programs, and trying to pursue them, and seeing where they break down, and getting some experience, and so on and so forth.

So dispelling the illusions is just a part of organizing and acting. It's not something that you do in a seminar, or in your living room—not that you *can't* do it there, but it's just a different kind of activity. Like, if you have some illusions about classical Greece, let's say, then you can probably do it in the library, to some extent at least. But if you're trying to dispel illusions about a live, ongoing social process that's changing all the time, and that you only get to see little pieces of—that's really not the way to do it. You do it through interactions with other people, and by functioning in some kind of community of concern, and of commitment, and of activism.

MAN: *If I were to hold a meeting in my community and invite someone to speak about the kinds of things we've been discussing this weekend, though, I'd probably get a very small turnout.*

Yeah, that's okay. Look, the peace movement in the Sixties became a huge mass movement, with tens of millions of people involved: it began with people doing just what you said, inviting somebody to come and talk in their living rooms. I mean, I remember it, because I did that for a couple of years. The world has just changed tremendously since then. Now I'm booked up two or more years in advance, I get huge audiences, sophisticated audiences, people who've thought about things, they're active, I learn from them. It's not long ago that I was getting invited to somebody's living room to talk to two or three neighbors who were ready to lynch me, or to some church where there'd be four people, including some guy who sort of wandered in because he didn't know what to do, and two people who wanted to kill you, and the organizer—that's not long ago, that's 1964. And when you're talking about other issues, like large-scale social change, well, it's still like 1964 in that respect. But things can change—and sometimes they change very fast.

Take the Civil Rights Movement in the United States: over a ten-year period, it was just a sea-change. Or take the feminist movement, which a lot of you are involved in: the changes came very fast. It went from being virtually nothing, a little nit-picking about activist groups having the women licking the stamps, and within a couple years it was a major movement, swept the country. When the time is right, things happen fast. They don't happen without any basis—things have to have been happening for a long period. But then they can crystallize at the right time, and often become very significant.

WOMAN: *Although—I do a lot of political work in my community, and after a while it does begin to feel like preaching to the converted. It's very frustrating.*

It sure is. Activism is very frustrating. But you also do get achievements: you bring a couple people in, and they begin to do things, and sooner or later it can lead to very large-scale change. We know that.

I mean, the old American Communist Party—make any criticisms you want about it, Stalinist, anything else—the fact is, there were some very strong things about it. One thing is, there were a lot of people who were just committed: they were going to show up when you needed somebody to turn the mimeograph machine, because they were committed that that's the way to get somewhere. And they were willing to work, they were going to work for changes with other people in their communities, whose lives they wanted to improve and help. And don't forget, *they* were the people who were fighting for civil rights in the days when it was no joke, when it wasn't a matter of going down to Selma on a big march, it was a matter of being alone in the South in places where you could very easily get killed—that was mostly the American Communist Party. Everybody who dumps on the Communist Party might remember these things.

And also, don't forget, a lot of the destruction that you see in the world happens because people are constantly organizing, and advancing, and progressing, and taking things over, and struggling against their oppression. I mean, the fact that all of these atrocities have been going on in Central America in the 1980s is a sign of *progress*, you know. Up until around the late 1970s, nobody here even commented on Central America. Why? Because it was *all* under control, it was *pure* atrocities, nobody was fighting back—so therefore no one here even paid attention to it. It only became an issue in the 1980s because there was a great deal of very successful organizing there: they *did* overthrow the Somoza regime in Nicaragua, there were huge peasant unions being formed for the first time in El Salvador and Guatemala, there was just a lot of extremely effective organizing taking place. So then the death squads came, and the U.S. trainers came, and people like you and me had to pay our taxes to have those people murdered. But they still have not yet eradicated it. Despite all the terror in Guatemala—you could even call it something like genocide—the working-class unions are reconstituting, they're still there. And crucially, in the 1980s that activism induced a solidarity movement in the United States which has interacted very constructively with the people there: that's an extremely important change, a dramatic change. So when we talk about what governments are up to, of course everything looks bleak. But look around—there are all kinds of other things happening, and that's what *you* do.

# 4

# Colloquy

*Based primarily on discussions at Fort Collins,*
*Colorado, April 10, 1990.*

### The Totalitarian Strain

MAN: *There's been a plethora of books recently by dissidents critiquing the media—yours and Ed Herman's, and Ben Bagdikian's, Michael Parenti's, Mark Hertsgaard's—but as I heard Alexander Cockburn say a couple days ago, "It's still one nation under Time/Warner": there's all of this literature that's available, but there really hasn't been much of a dent in the structure.*[1]

Where would there be a dent? Suppose you had a thousand books: would that change the fact that Time and Warner Communications can form a conglomerate? All of this literature is not tied up with any form— *any* form, I mean, not five people—of social organization that is trying to undermine the corporate structure of the media. This work all is just an effort to educate people so they're better able to protect themselves from the propaganda system. And *there* I think there has been an effect: a lot of people are attuned to propaganda in a way they weren't before. But none of this can be conceived of as an attempt to change the corporate structure directly—there isn't even a *proposal* about that in any one of these books. Take Ben Bagdikian's book, or the first chapter of Ed's and my book: they don't suggest how we might *change* corporate capitalism, that's a completely different topic. They just say, as long as you have corporate capitalism, here's what the media are going to look like.

WOMAN: *Are you going to do an article on what happened in Central America recently—the Nicaraguan elections [of 1990, in which the Sandinista Party lost to the U.S.-supported candidate, Violeta Chamorro]?*

I am—not on the elections themselves, on the U.S. *reaction* to the elections.[2] Nicaragua's for *them* to write about, I write about the United States.

But the reaction of the media here was pretty astonishing. The most remarkable feature was the unanimity. I mean, there was an absolutely unanimous reaction across the entire mainstream spectrum, from Anthony Lewis and Mary McGrory over to George Will and whatever other right-wing lunatic there is. In fact, about the only difference between the so-called "liberals" and "conservatives" was that the liberals pointed to the fact that the Nicaraguan people essentially voted with a gun to their heads and *then* said, "The election was free and fair, uncoerced, a miracle of democracy," whereas the conservatives didn't bother saying the people voted with a gun to their heads, they just said it was a miracle of democracy.[3]

Some of it was comical. For instance, the *New York Times* had a column by David Shipler, a liberal journalist, which said, yeah, the embargo's killing them, the contras are killing them, they know we're going to continue the embargo unless they vote for our candidate. Headline: "Victory For U.S. Fair Play."[4] The *Boston Globe*, which is a very liberal newspaper—it's the outer limit in the mainstream—had a headline: "Rallying to Chamorro." The theme was, okay, now all the people who love Nicaraguans, like we've all done all these years, must rally to Chamorro.[5] Well, say it was 1964, after Goldwater lost the Presidential race here two to one—can you imagine anybody saying, "Okay, now every Goldwater voter must 'rally to Johnson' "? That's straight out of Stalinist Russia. You don't "rally to the leader" in a democracy—you do whatever you feel like doing. But the idea that you've got to rally behind *der Führer* is quite acceptable in the American liberal press.

In fact, it's interesting that the media themselves even recognized the unanimity. So for example, the *New York Times* had an article by Elaine Sciolino surveying the U.S. reaction, and the headline was, "Americans United in Joy, But Divided Over Policy."[6] And the division over policy turns out to be the question: who gets credit for having achieved this magnificent result? See, that's where you get a liberal/conservative split: "did the contras help or hurt?" Is it better to do it the way it's done in El Salvador—leave women hanging from trees with their skin flayed off and bleeding to death, leave thousands of corpses beheaded by the roadside so that everybody else will get the point—or should you do what Senator Alan Cranston suggested in 1986, to pick a dove: let them "fester in their own juices," through economic strangulation and other means?[7] Well, the fact is, the right wing wins on that one: the contras obviously helped. But the idea that everyone was "United in Joy" over the result, that was considered perfectly legitimate. In other words, we're straight totalitarians: everyone is united, we all march on command, there isn't one word of dissidence tolerated. Phrases like "United in Joy" are the kinds of things you might see in the North Korean press, maybe. But it's interesting, American elites *pride* themselves on being dedicated totalitarians, they think that's the way we *ought* to be—we *ought* to be the worst totalitarian culture in the world, in which everyone agrees.

Look, anyone can see, a ten-year-old could see, that an election carried out under conditions where a monstrous superpower is saying, "Vote for our candidate or starve to death," is obviously not free. I mean, if some unimaginable superpower were to threaten us, saying, "We're going to reduce you to the level of Ethiopia unless you vote for our candidate," and then people here voted for their candidate, you'd have to be some kind of crazy Nazi or something to say that it was a free election. But in the United States, *everyone* says it—we're all "United in Joy." That's an interesting fact about the United States, actually—what it shows is how deeply totalitarian the culture really is. In fact, it would be very hard to mimic this even in a well-run totalitarian state, but here it passes without anybody even noticing it, because it's all so deeply ingrained. In any country that had even a *memory* of what democracy means, if you saw that everyone was "United in Joy," the article would say, "There's something really wrong with this country." Nobody can be "United in Joy" over anything. Pick the topic, it just can't be that people are "United in Joy" about it—unless it's Albania, then yeah, sure, you've got the guns pointed at you, you're "United in Joy." But in the United States, nobody even sees that there's anything odd about it.

WOMAN: *There was a breakthrough, though—the* Wall Street Journal *on its front page ran an article written by a man from* The Nation *[a left-leaning magazine] saying that we ought to be ashamed of what happened in Nicaragua.*

That wasn't on the front page, that was on the Op-Ed page—and that was Alex Cockburn, who's the *Wall Street Journal*'s once-a-month gesture to "some other voice." Sure, I mean, when I say the unity was a hundred percent, I know of precisely two exceptions in the mainstream press in the United States. Obviously I haven't read *everything* in the mainstream press, but I've looked at quite a lot, and I've been in touch with people all around the country who've been looking, and I found only two exceptions: one was Alex Cockburn in the *Wall Street Journal*, and the other was an editor I know at the *Boston Globe*, Randolph Ryan, who managed to put something about this in an editorial.[8] So the two of them were able to say what any eight-year-old would see right off—and as far as I know, that's it for the American press.

As a matter of fact, it was the same in the coverage before the elections. I, and probably you, and a lot of other people were following the media very closely just to see if there would be *one phrase*, just a phrase, anywhere in the mainstream media, that said that a Sandinista Party victory might be the best thing for Nicaragua—I haven't found a phrase. I mean, even journalists who *believe* it couldn't say it. Now, obviously the issue is contentious—it was contentious in Nicaragua—but here it's not, here you have to have 100 percent unanimity.

Furthermore, it was also assumed automatically, across the board, that Chamorro was the democratic candidate—and nobody ever gave you a reason *why* she was the democratic candidate. I mean, what are her democratic credentials? That's not anything you even have to argue in the United States: Washington says she's the democratic candidate, and American business says she's the democratic candidate, so that settles it—for American intellectuals, there are no further questions to ask. And the interesting thing is, again, nobody even sees that there's anything odd about this. Like, nobody writes an Op-Ed saying, "Isn't it strange? Just because Washington and the business community tell us she's the democratic candidate, does that mean that we have to repeat it and not look for some reason, find out what her democratic credentials are?" It wouldn't occur to anybody: the intellectual community in the United States is so disciplined they simply don't ask those questions.

## A Lithuania Hypothetical

MAN: *Dr. Chomsky, I just want to ask a question on this topic: Daniel Ortega [Nicaraguan President, Sandinista Party] was in power for how long, a decade?*

Yes.

MAN: *And yet he lost the election.*

Why "And yet"?

MAN: *Well, he had control of that country for ten years.*

What does it mean, "He had control of it"?

MAN: *He controlled the press.*

He did not. In fact, Nicaragua is the only country I know of in history that allowed a major opposition press [*La Prensa*] to operate while it was being attacked—a press which was calling for the overthrow of the government by violence, which was identifying with the foreign-run mercenary army attacking the country, and which was funded, partly openly and partly covertly (though everybody knew), by the foreign power attacking the country [i.e. the U.S.]. That's never happened before in history—the United States would never tolerate anything like that for one second. Furthermore, and quite apart from that, large parts of Nicaragua were flooded, and in fact dominated, by U.S. propaganda. Remember, there are large areas of Nicaragua where what people know is what they hear over the radio, and the United States ran major radio and television stations in Honduras and Costa Rica which dominated the information flow in large sectors of the Nicaraguan countryside.[9]

In fact, the level of freedom of the press in Nicaragua in the last ten years just broke new libertarian standards: there's never been anything even remotely comparable to it in history. Try to find a case.

MAN: *But given ten years in power, it seemed rather remarkable that Ortega wasn't able to hold on to that mandate.*

Really? Well let me ask you how remarkable it is. Suppose the Soviet Union were to play the game the way we do. Lithuania just declared independence, right [in March 1990]? Let's suppose that the Soviet Union were capable of doing what we did in Nicaragua. So: it would organize a terrorist army to attack Lithuania; it would train it to attack "soft targets," civilian targets; it would try to kill large numbers of health workers, teachers, farmers, and so on.[10] Meanwhile, it would impose an embargo—suppose it were able to do this—and block trade, block export and import, it would pressure international institutions to stop providing any assistance.[11] Of course, to make the analogy accurate, we'd have to assume that Lithuania begins at a level much lower than what it actually is.

Okay, now suppose that after ten years of this, Lithuania has been reduced to the level of Ethiopia, alright? And suppose that then there's an election, and Moscow says: "Look, we're going to continue this, all of it, unless you vote for the Communist Party." And now suppose that the Lithuanians *do* vote for the Communist Party. Would you find that remarkable?

MAN: *I don't think Nicaragua was reduced to the level of Ethiopia.*

Oh yeah, they were. They were reduced to the level of—well, maybe Haiti.[12] But just answer my question: would you find that remarkable?

MAN: *Under those circumstances, I guess I wouldn't.*

Okay, but then why do you find it remarkable when it happened in Nicaragua?

MAN: *Well, I don't have access to all the facts you do.*

You have every fact I told you—every fact I told you, you knew. Every fact I told you you can find on the front pages of the *New York Times*. It's just that when you hear the White House announce, "We're going to continue with the embargo unless Chamorro wins," you have to be able to think enough so you conclude, well, these people are voting with a gun to their heads.[13] If you can't think that far, it doesn't matter what the newspapers say. And the beauty of a really well-indoctrinated intellectual class is they *can't* think that far. They can think that far *easily* in the case of Lithuania, but they can't think that far in the case of the United States, even though the actual situation is the hypothetical one that I described. So often the information is *there*, in a sense—it's just that it's *not* there, because people are so indoctrinated that they simply don't see it.

## Perpetuating Brainwashing Under Freedom

MAN: *Why is it that across the board in the media you can't find examples of people using their brains?*

You can find them, but typically they're not in the mainstream press.

MAN: *Why is that?*

Because if they have the capacity to think freely and understand these types of things, they're going to be kept out by a very complicated filtering system—which actually starts in kindergarten, I think. In fact, the whole educational and professional training system is a very elaborate filter, which just weeds out people who are too independent, and who think for themselves, and who don't know how to be submissive, and so on—because they're dysfunctional to the institutions. I mean, it would be highly dysfunctional to have people in the media who could ask questions like this. So by the time you've made it to Bureau Chief or Editor, or you've become a bigshot at C.B.S. or something, the chances are that you've just got all this stuff in your bones—you've internalized values that make it clear to you that there are certain things you just don't say, and in fact, you don't even think about them anymore.

This was actually discussed years ago in an interesting essay by George Orwell, which happens to be the introduction to *Animal Farm. Animal Farm* is a satire on Soviet totalitarianism, obviously, and it's a very famous book, everybody reads it. But what people *don't* usually read is its introduction, which talks about censorship in England—and the main reason people don't read it is because it was censored, nicely; it simply wasn't published with the book. It was finally rediscovered about thirty years later and somebody somewhere published it, and now it's available in some modern editions. But in this essay Orwell said, look, this book is obviously about Stalinist Russia, however it's not all that different in England. And then he described how things work in England. He said: in England there isn't any commissar around who beats you over the head if you say the wrong thing, but nevertheless the results are not all that different. And then he had a two-line description of how the press works in England, which is pretty accurate, in fact. One of the reasons why the results are similar, he said, is because the press is owned by wealthy men who have strong interests in not having certain things said. The other, which he said is equally pertinent, is that if you're a well-educated person in England—you went to the right prep schools, then to Oxford, and now you're a bigshot somewhere—you have simply learned that there are certain things that it is not proper to say.[14]

And that's a large part of education, in fact: just internalizing the understanding that there are certain things it is not proper to say, and it is not proper to think. And if you don't learn that, typically you'll be weeded out of the institutions somewhere along the line. Well, those two factors are very important ones, and there are others, but they go a long way towards explaining the uniformity of ideology in the intellectual culture here.[15]

Now, of course, it's not a hundred percent—so you'll get a few people filtering through who will do things differently. Like I say, in this "United in Joy" business, I was able to find two people in the United States who were not "United in Joy," and were able to say so in the mainstream press. But if the system is really working well, it's not going to do things which undermine itself. In fact, it's a bit like asking, "How come *Pravda* under Stalin didn't have journalists denouncing the Gulags [Soviet penal labor camps]?" Why not? Well, it would have been dysfunctional to the system. I suspect it's not that the journalists in *Pravda* were *lying*—I mean, that was a different system, they used the threat of force to silence dissidents, which we don't use much here. But even in the Soviet Union, chances are very strong that if you actually bothered to look, you'd find that most of the journalists actually believed the things they wrote. And that's because people who *didn't* believe that kind of thing would never have made it onto *Pravda* in the first place. It's very hard to live with cognitive dissonance: only a real cynic can believe one thing and say another. So whether it's a totalitarian system or a free system, the people who are most useful to the system of power are the ones who actually believe what they say, and they're the ones who will typically make it through.

So take Tom Wicker at the *New York Times*: when you talk to him about this kind of stuff, he gets very irate and says, "Nobody tells *me* what to write." And that's perfectly true, nobody tells *him* what to write—but if he didn't already *know* what to write, he wouldn't be a columnist for the *New York Times*. Like, nobody tells Alex Cockburn what to write, and therefore he's *not* a columnist for the *New York Times*, because he thinks different things. You think the wrong thoughts, you're not in the system.

Now, it's interesting that the *Wall Street Journal* allows this one opening, Alex Cockburn. I mean, the opening is so minuscule that it's not even worth discussing—but it so happens that once a month, there is one mainstream journal in the United States which allows a real dissident to write a free and open column. So that means, like, .0001 percent of the coverage is free and independent. And it's in the *Wall Street Journal*, which doesn't care: for their audience the *New York Times* is Communist, so here's a guy who's even more Communist.

And the result of all of this is that it's a very effective system of ideological control—much more effective than Soviet totalitarianism ever was. In fact, if you look at the entire range of media in the Soviet Union that people were actually exposed to, they had much more dissidence in the 1980s than we do, overtly, and people were in fact reading a much broader range of press, listening to foreign broadcasts, and so on—which is pretty much unheard of in the U.S.[16] Or just to give one other example, during the Soviet invasion of Afghanistan, there was even a newscaster [Vladimir Danchev] who made broadcasts over Moscow radio for five successive nights back in 1983, denouncing the Russian invasion of Afghanistan—he actually called it an "invasion"—and calling on the Afghans to resist, before he was finally taken off the air.[17] That's *unimaginable* in the United States. I mean, can you imagine Dan Rather or anybody else getting on the radio and denouncing the U.S. "invasion" of South Vietnam, and calling on the Vietnamese to resist? That's inconceivable. The United States couldn't *have* that amount of intellectual freedom.

MAN: *Well, I don't know if that's "intellectual freedom," for a journalist to say that.*

Sure it is. It's intellectual freedom when a journalist can understand that 2 + 2 = 4; that's what Orwell was writing about in *1984*. Everybody here applauds that book, but nobody is willing to think about what it means. What Winston Smith [the main character] was saying is, if we can still understand that 2 + 2 = 4, they haven't taken everything away. Okay? Well, in the United States, people can't even understand that 2 + 2 = 4.

MAN: *Couldn't an editorialist say it, though, even if a reporter can't?*

Have any of them done it, in thirty years?

MAN: *I don't know.*

Well, I'll tell you, nobody has; I've checked, actually.[18]

WOMAN: *You make it sound so uniform, though—like there's only one or two people in the entire U.S. media who aren't dishonest or blindly serving power.*

Well, that's really not my point: obviously in any complex institution, there are going to be a fair number of people who want to do their work with integrity, and are good at it, and don't just end up serving power—these systems aren't totally monolithic, after all. A lot of people go into journalism with a real commitment to professional integrity—they like the field, and they want to do it honestly. And some of them continue to do an admirable job of it—in fact, some of them even manage to do it at journals like the *New York Times*.

In fact, to a large degree I think you can tell when the *New York Times*'s editors want a story covered accurately just by looking at who they send to the place. For instance, when they send John Kifner, that means they want the story told—because he's an honest journalist, and he's going to tell the story. I mean, I don't know him personally, but you can just tell from his work that he's a journalist of real integrity, and he's going to dig, he's going to find out the truth, and he's going to write about it—and the editors must know that. So I don't know anything about how they assign stories at the *Times*, but I'm willing to make a bet that when there's a story the *Times*'s editors want told, they'll send Kifner, and when his job is done they'll probably send him back to the "Metro" desk or something.

On the other hand, most of the people at the *Times* who make it to be correspondent or editor or whatever tend to be either very obedient or very cynical. The obedient ones have adapted—they've internalized the values and believe what they're saying, otherwise they probably wouldn't have made it that far. But there are also some plain cynics. James LeMoyne at the *Times* is a perfect example: James LeMoyne is an absolute crook, he's one of the most dishonest journalists I've ever seen. The dishonesty of his reporting is so extreme, in fact, that it can't *just* be indoctrination in his case. Actually, LeMoyne's tenure as a correspondent in Central America ended up with an exposure so bad that even the *Times* had to publish an admission about it. Did you follow that?

In 1988 LeMoyne had written a story which talked about two people in El Salvador who he claimed were tortured by left-wing guerrillas trying to undermine the elections; it was one part of a whole effort in the American press at the time to maintain support for the U.S. client regime in El Salvador despite its atrocities.[19] Well, a freelance journalist in Central America, Chris Norton, saw LeMoyne's article and was surprised by it, because the atrocities LeMoyne described were supposed to have taken place in an area of the country reporters couldn't get to, because it was under military occupation. Norton wanted to figure out just how LeMoyne knew about these people being tortured, so he went up as close to that region as he could, and he talked to the mayor, and to the priest, and to people in the community—and he discovered that one of the alleged victims didn't exist, and the other was perfectly fine. He then went back to San Salvador and did some more checking—and he discovered that LeMoyne had simply taken the story straight from a San Salvadoran newspaper, where it had been attributed to an army officer. It was in fact just straight army disinformation of a standard sort, which LeMoyne then reported in the *New York Times* as if he knew something about it. Then the State Department picked it up from the *New York Times* and distributed it to Congress to show that the Salvadoran guerrillas were undermining the election.

Well, Norton uncovered this, then another freelance journalist, Mark Cooper, picked up Norton's story and published something about it in the *L.A. Weekly*, an alternative weekly in Los Angeles. The piece then appeared in the Fairness and Accuracy in Reporting journal, *Extra!*—F.A.I.R. is a very good media analysis group in New York. Still no reaction from the *Times*. Finally, Alex Cockburn got ahold of it, and mentioned it in his column in *The Nation*.[20] Well, by that time word was sort of getting around about this, so the *Times* figured they had to react, and they published a correction—I think it's the longest correction they've ever published, it's several paragraphs long. It said, our usual high standards were not met in this case, one thing or another like that.[21]

Well, that's kind of an extreme example—but it's by no means the only case like that. In fact, just let me mention one other one, which was even more important—here LeMoyne really plied his trade.

## Journalism LeMoyne-Style: A Sample of the Cynical Aspect

As you know, for years it was necessary for the U.S. government to maintain the pretense that the contras in Nicaragua were a guerrilla force, not a U.S. proxy army. Now, it's perfectly obvious that they were *not* a guerrilla force—there are no guerrillas in history that have had anything remotely like the degree of support we gave the contras: there are no guerrillas in history that had three supply flights a day bringing them food and supplies and weapons, and who complained that they didn't have enough airplanes, and that they needed more helicopters. I mean, the whole thing was completely ridiculous: these guys had armaments that some units of the American army didn't have, they had computer centers, they had communications equipment. And they needed all of that, because Nicaragua was under constant surveillance by high-performance American reconnaissance aircraft to determine where Sandinista troops were being deployed, and the contras had to have some way of receiving that information.[22]

But the point is, it was necessary for the propaganda system to pretend that the contras were like the F.M.L.N. in El Salvador—just a regular indigenous guerrilla force opposing the government. And part of the method for claiming that these two forces were equivalent was to say that the F.M.L.N. guerrillas also had outside support from a foreign government—in other words, from the government of Nicaragua—and that was the only reason they could survive. Well, it's *conceivable* that the F.M.L.N. was getting outside support, but if so, it would have been some kind of a miracle—because it was undetectable. I mean, it's not that the United States is a primitive, stone-age society: there are technological means around to discover evidence of such things, but they never were able to detect any support coming from Nicaragua at all.

According to the State Department propaganda, the main arms flow from Nicaragua to the F.M.L.N. was across the Gulf of Fonseca.[23] Well, David MacMichael, who was the C.I.A. analyst in charge of analyzing this material in the early 1980s and then quit the Agency, testified at the World Court and pointed out what this meant. He described the situation: the Gulf of Fonseca is thirty kilometers wide; it's completely patrolled by the U.S. Navy; there's an island in the middle of it which had a super-sophisticated U.S. radar system that could pick up boats up and down the Pacific Coast; there were U.S. Navy S.E.A.L. teams running all around the place—yet they never even picked up a canoe. So if Nicaragua were sending arms across the Gulf of Fonseca, they had to have had some super-sophisticated methods.[24] I mean, the *Nicaraguans* had no problem whatsoever detecting the U.S. arms flow to the contras—they told reporters exactly where it was coming from; it was unreported in the United States, because the reporters chose not to report it, but the Nicaraguans had no problem detecting it.[25] Anyway, that was the propaganda line that had to be maintained in the American press, that was the official story. Now we come back to James LeMoyne.

The United States government opposed the Central American peace accords that were signed in 1987 [Esquipulas II, the so-called "Arias plan"], so it was therefore necessary to demolish them. And one of the ways of demolishing them was to increase aid to the contras. The press committed itself with great passion to helping this effort along; LeMoyne was right up front. Right after the accords were signed, LeMoyne published an article in which he wrote: there is "ample evidence" that the Salvadoran guerrillas are being supplied with arms by Nicaragua in violation of the peace accords, and without that support the guerrillas couldn't survive.[26] Alright, that had always been the necessary story, but just then it was especially important to drive it home—because right then the United States was tripling its supply flights to the contras in response to the accords, and of course in violation of the accords.[27] So the press wouldn't report that we were escalating our support for the contras, but they kept reporting that the Nicaraguans were illegally arming the F.M.L.N. in El Salvador—and now James LeMoyne says that there is "ample evidence" of it.

Well, when that story appeared, F.A.I.R. wrote a letter to the *New York Times*, asking them to please have James LeMoyne enlighten their readers about the "ample evidence" of this arms flow to the F.M.L.N.—since the World Court couldn't find it, and no independent investigator's been able to find it, and the guys who worked on it in the C.I.A. didn't know about it: could they please do that? Well, the *Times* didn't publish their letter, but F.A.I.R. did get a personal response back from the Foreign Editor, Joseph Lelyveld, who said, yes, maybe LeMoyne's report was a bit imprecise this time, it didn't meet his usual high standards, and so on.[28]

Then followed a period in which the *Times* had plenty of time to correct the "imprecision"—but instead article after article appeared by LeMoyne, George Volsky, Steven Engelberg and others, repeating exactly the same falsehood: that there was ample evidence of an arms flow from Nicaragua.[29] But F.A.I.R. just kept after them, and finally they got another letter back from Lelyveld, the Foreign Editor—this was around March now, their first letter was in August. Lelyveld said he had recently assigned LeMoyne to do a major story on the arms flow to the F.M.L.N., to really nail the thing down once and for all, and that they should wait for that story. Okay, they waited. Nothing happened. Six months later, they figured nothing was *going* to happen, so they published this interchange of letters with Lelyveld in the F.A.I.R. newsletter, and said: we don't see the story, what's going on?[30]

Two months after that, a story did finally appear in the *Times*—I think it was LeMoyne's last story before he left the *Times*, or whatever he did, took a leave or something. This is now fifteen months after his original story about the "ample evidence," nine months after he was assigned to do the follow-up. And if you take a look at the article the *Times* finally published, you'll discover that the "ample evidence" had turned into *no* evidence. LeMoyne said: well, there really is no direct evidence of any supply of arms from Nicaragua; some people say this, some people say that, but there's nothing concrete, there's nothing to point to. So that's the end of the story: it turns out the "ample evidence" is no evidence.[31]

Now, that's no joke—this is fabrication in the service of the state that has led to tens of thousands of people being killed, because maintaining this pretense over the years has been one of the ways in which the U.S. government has supported the terror in El Salvador and extended the war against Nicaragua. It's not a small point. This is serious lying, very serious. And it's just one of thousands of cases demonstrating that the media in the United States serve the interests of state-corporate power, they are organs of propaganda, as in fact one would expect them to be.[32]

### Rethinking Watergate

MAN: *But how do you explain Watergate, then? Those reporters weren't very sympathetic to power—they toppled a President.*

And just ask yourself *why* he was toppled—he was toppled because he had made a very bad mistake: he had antagonized people with power.

See, one of the serious illusions we live under in the United States, which is a major part of the whole system of indoctrination, is the idea that the *government* is the power—and the government's *not* the power, the government is one segment of power. Real power is in the hands of the people who own the society; the state-managers are usually just servants. And Watergate is actually a perfect illustration of the point—because right at the time of Watergate, history actually ran a controlled experiment for us. The Watergate exposures, it turns out, came at exactly the same time as the COINTELPRO exposures—I don't know if you know what I mean.

MAN: *COINTELPRO?*

See, you probably don't—but that already makes my point, because the COINTELPRO exposures were a thousand times more significant than Watergate. Remember what Watergate *was*, after all: Watergate was a matter of a bunch of guys from the Republican National Committee breaking into a Democratic Party office for essentially unknown reasons and doing no damage. Okay, that's petty burglary, it's not a big deal. Well, at the exact same time that Watergate was discovered, there were exposures in the courts and through the Freedom of Information Act of massive F.B.I. operations to undermine political freedom in the United States, running through every administration back to Roosevelt, but really picking up under Kennedy. It was called "COINTELPRO" [short for "Counterintelligence Program"], and it included a vast range of things.

It included the straight Gestapo-style assassination of a Black Panther leader; it included organizing race riots in an effort to destroy the black movements; it included attacks on the American Indian Movement, on the women's movement, you name it. It included fifteen years of F.B.I. disruption of the Socialist Workers Party—that meant regular F.B.I. burglaries, stealing membership lists and using them to threaten people, going to businesses and getting members fired from their jobs, and so on.[33] Well, that fact alone—the fact that for fifteen years the F.B.I. had been burglarizing and trying to undermine a legal political party—is already vastly more important than the fact that a bunch of Keystone Kops broke into the Democratic National Committee headquarters one time. The Socialist Workers Party is a legal political party, after all—the fact that they're a *weak* political party doesn't mean they have less rights than the Democrats. And this wasn't a bunch of gangsters, this was the national political police: that's very serious. And it didn't happen once in the Watergate office complex, it was going on for fifteen years, under every administration. And keep in mind, the Socialist Workers Party episode is just some tiny footnote to COINTELPRO. In comparison to this, Watergate is a tea party.

Well, look at the comparison in treatment—I mean, you're aware of the comparison in treatment, that's why you know about Watergate and you don't know about COINTELPRO. So what does that tell you? What it tells you is, people in power will defend themselves. The Democratic Party represents about half of corporate power, and those people are able to defend themselves; the Socialist Workers Party represents no power, the Black Panthers don't represent any power, the American Indian Movement doesn't represent any power—so you can do anything you want to them.

Or take a look at the Nixon administration's famous "Enemies List," which came out in the course of Watergate [exposed in 1973, the document named 208 Americans from various professions under the title "Opponents list and political enemies project"]. You've heard of that, but did you hear about the assassination of Fred Hampton? No. Nothing ever happened to any of the people who were on the Enemies List, which I know perfectly well, because I was on it—and it wasn't because *I* was on it that it made the front pages. But the F.B.I. and the Chicago police *assassinated* a Black Panther leader as he lay in his bed one night during the Nixon administration [on December 4, 1969]. Well, if the press had any integrity at all, if the *Washington Post* had any integrity, what they would have said is, "Watergate is totally insignificant and innocuous, who cares about any of that in comparison with these other things." But that's not what happened, obviously. And that just shows again, very dramatically, how the press is lined up with power.

The real lesson of Nixon's fall is that the President shouldn't call Thomas Watson [Chairman of I.B.M.] and McGeorge Bundy [former Democratic official] bad names—that means the Republic's collapsing. And the press prides itself on having exposed this fact. On the other hand, if you want to send the F.B.I. to organize the assassination of a Black Panther leader, that's fine by us; it's fine by the *Washington Post* too.

Incidentally, I think there is another reason why a lot of powerful people were out to get Nixon at that time—and it had to do with something a lot more profound than the Enemies List and the Watergate burglary. I suspect it had to do with the events of the summer of 1971, when the Nixon administration basically broke up the international economic arrangement that had existed for the previous twenty-five years [i.e. the so-called "Bretton Woods" system, established in 1944 at the United Nations Monetary and Financial Conference at Bretton Woods, New Hampshire]. See, by 1971 the Vietnam War had already badly weakened the United States economically relative to its industrial rivals, and one of the ways the Nixon administration reacted to that was by simply tearing apart the Bretton Woods system, which had been set up to organize the world economy after World War II. The Bretton Woods system had made the United States the world's banker, basically—it had established the U.S. dollar as a global reserve currency fixed to gold, and it imposed conditions about no import quotas, and so on. And Nixon just tore the whole thing to shreds: he went off the gold standard, he stopped the convertibility of the dollar, he raised import duties. No other country would have had the power to do that, but Nixon did it, and that made him a lot of powerful enemies—because multinational corporations and international banks relied on that system, and they did not like it being broken down. So if you look back, you'll find that Nixon was being attacked in places like the *Wall Street Journal* at the time, and I suspect that from that point on there were plenty of powerful people out to get him. Watergate just offered an opportunity.

In fact, in this respect I think Nixon was treated extremely unfairly. I mean, there were real crimes of the Nixon administration, and he should have been tried—but not for any of the Watergate business. Take the bombing of Cambodia, for instance: the bombing of Cambodia was *infinitely* worse than anything that came up in the Watergate hearings—this thing they call the "secret bombing" of Cambodia, which was "secret" because the press didn't talk about what they knew.[34] The U.S. killed maybe a couple hundred thousand people in Cambodia, they devastated a peasant society.[35] The bombing of Cambodia did not even appear in Nixon's Articles of Impeachment. It was raised in the Senate hearings, but only in one interesting respect—the question that was raised was, why hadn't Nixon informed Congress? It wasn't, why did you carry out one of the most intense bombings in history in densely populated areas of a peasant country, killing maybe 150,000 people? That never came up. The only question was, why didn't you tell Congress? In other words, were people with power granted their prerogatives? And once again, notice that what it means is, infringing on the rights of powerful people is unacceptable: "We're powerful, so you've got to tell us—then we'll tell you, 'Fine, go bomb Cambodia.'" In fact, that whole thing was a gag—because there was no reason for Congress not to have known about the bombing, just as there was no reason for the media not to have known: it was completely public.

So in terms of all the horrifying atrocities the Nixon government carried out, Watergate isn't even worth laughing about. It was a triviality. Watergate is a very clear example of what happens to servants when they forget their role and go after the people who own the place: they are very quickly put back into their box, and somebody else takes over. You couldn't ask for a better illustration of it than that—and it's even more dramatic because *this* is the great exposure that's supposed to demonstrate what a free and critical press we have. What Watergate really shows is what a submissive and obedient press we have, as the comparisons to COINTELPRO and Cambodia illustrate very clearly.

### Escaping Indoctrination

MAN: *But do you think things are ever going to change? Aren't we always going to have people entrenched in power, left or right, who want to preserve that power, and will use all of the means at their disposal to do it— and all we can really do is just sit back and complain about it?*

That's the attitude of people who thought that there was nothing you could do about feudalism and slavery. And there *was* something you could do about feudalism and slavery, but not by sitting and complaining about it. John Brown didn't sit and complain about it.

MAN: *He didn't get very far.*

He did. They overthrew slavery, and the Abolitionists played a big role in that.

[Brown's 1859 attempt to set off a slave revolt by seizing a federal armory in Harpers Ferry, Virginia, electrified the country and intensified the Abolitionist movement.]

MAN: *So as long as we criticize, try to offer constructive criticism, there's hope of changing the system?*

If the constructive criticism leads to the point where mass popular movements form that *do something* to change the system, sure, then there's hope. I mean, there wouldn't have been an American Revolution if people had been writing pamphlets but not doing anything more than that.

WOMAN: *Then what's the trick to holding on and not giving up—because it seems like a lot of people need it.*

The trick is not to be isolated—if you're isolated, like Winston Smith in *1984*, then sooner or later you're going to break, as he finally broke. That was the point of Orwell's story. In fact, the whole tradition of popular control has been exactly that: to keep people isolated, because if you can keep them isolated enough, you can get them to believe anything. But when people get together, all sorts of things are possible.

MAN: *It just seems so hopeless, though, because you make it sound like the entire press organization is locking dissidents out.*

That's largely true—but like I say, there's a lot of flexibility possible. I mean, it's true that the ideological barrier in the U.S. media is extreme— other countries have more openings for dissidence in the mainstream than we do, even though their economic systems are basically the same. But still there is quite a range of possibility for opening up the press here, even as it now stands: it doesn't have to be .0001 percent open to dissident perspectives, it could be .1 percent or something. So I actually think there are plenty of changes possible in the United States, even from within the institutions.

Remember that the media have two basic functions. One is to indoctrinate the elites, to make sure they have the right ideas and know how to serve power. In fact, typically the elites are the *most* indoctrinated segment of a society, because they are the ones who are exposed to the most propaganda and actually take part in the decision-making process. For them you have the *New York Times,* and the *Washington Post,* and the *Wall Street Journal,* and so on. But there's also a mass media, whose main function is just to get rid of the rest of the population—to marginalize and eliminate them, so they don't interfere with decision-making. And the press that's designed for that purpose isn't the *New York Times* and the *Washington Post,* it's sitcoms on television, and the *National Enquirer,* and sex and violence, and babies with three heads, and football, all that kind of stuff. But the approximately 85 percent of the population that is the main target of that media, they don't have it in their *genes* that they're not interested in the way the world works. And if they can escape from the effects of the de-education and indoctrination system, and the whole class system it's a part of—it's after all not *just* indoctrination that keeps people from getting involved in political life, by any means—if they can do that, then yeah, they're a big audience for an alternative, and there's some hope.

In fact, there's a very interesting history about this in England. For a long time in England, there was a mass, popular, daily labor press of quite good newspapers, with a huge readership—a much bigger readership than all the elite press in England combined, actually. It was the *Daily Herald* and the *News Chronicle* and the *Sunday Citizen*. And this was not just Alex Cockburn once a month in the *Wall Street Journal*, but *every day* there were newspapers giving a picture of the world and expressing a set of values radically different from those of the business community. And not only did they have a big circulation, but their audience was also very much involved—for instance, there were surveys showing that people actually *read* those newspapers much more than subscribers to things like the *Guardian* and the *London Times*. But they disappeared in the 1960s, and they disappeared due to market pressures—it didn't have anything to do with the number of readers they had, it had to do with the amount of capital they could attract. Could you get advertisers, could you get capital for investment? In short, could you appeal to the business community, which happens to hold the real power? And over time, they couldn't.[36]

It's the same thing here: for instance, in the United States there isn't even any such thing as a "labor reporter" anymore (except in the business press, actually)—but there are plenty of "business reporters." And again, that doesn't reflect *people's* interests: a lot more people are interested in the problems of workers than are interested in the bond market, if you count their numbers—but if you multiply their numbers by their power in the society, then yeah, it's true, the market for news about money and stocks is much greater than the market for news about issues which matter to working people.

But that's just the fact about an inegalitarian system: when you have a serious disproportion of power, independent forces are likely to collapse—just because they can't get access to enough capital in the end. Like in England, some media corporation didn't come along and try to offer this huge mass audience another paper with a social-democratic line. Business doesn't work that way—it's not trying to educate people to overthrow it, even if you could make a profit off it. I mean, if you could convince Rupert Murdoch that he can make a ton of money by publishing a newspaper which has a social-democratic or even more radical line, something calling for workers' management of corporations for instance, he wouldn't do it—because there are some things that are more important than profits, like maintaining the entire system of power.

In fact, this is also pretty much the same reason why American elites want military spending instead of social spending: if it turned out, as is likely, that using taxpayers' money for socially useful purposes was even more profitable than sending it through the military system, that still wouldn't change the decision to prefer military spending—because social spending is going to interfere with the basic prerogatives of power, it's going to organize popular constituencies, and have all these other negative side effects that you want to avoid.

WOMAN: *So what you're saying is, even if there were a major cultural change, with people at the grassroots level actually demanding a much more open press, there still wouldn't be the capital to support that press?*

No, people would have to take control of that capital. I mean, for one thing, if there really were a mass of people demanding that kind of press, they would *have* the capital—not at the level of big corporations, but like unions, say. When unions are a mass organization, they can accumulate strike funds, even though they can't compete with management and ownership in terms of total resources. But for another thing, there's no law of nature which says that control over capital has to be in a few hands—that's like saying that political power has to be in a few hands. Why? There wasn't a law that said that the king and the nobles had to run everything, and there isn't a law that says that corporate owners and managers have to run everything either. These are social arrangements. They developed historically, they can be changed historically.

## Understanding the Middle East Conflict

MAN: *If I can just change the topic a little, Professor—I'd like you to talk a bit about the situation in the Middle East these days. People say the Palestinians are utilizing the media more than they ever have before to draw attention to Israeli repression [i.e. during the Palestinian uprising of the late 1980s]. I'm wondering whether you think that will have any effect on Israel's occupation of the Palestinian territories on the West Bank and the Gaza Strip in the future?*
*[Editors' Note: The following discussion of the Israeli/Palestinian conflict forms the foundation of Chomsky's analysis of the so-called "peace process" that began in the early 1990s, which is discussed in chapters 5 and 8.]*

Well, this business about the Palestinians "using the media" is mostly racist garbage, in my view. The fact of the matter is that the Intifada is a big, mass, popular revolution in reaction to the absolutely brutal treatment the Palestinians have been living under—and it's going on in places where there are no television cameras, and places where there are.
See, there's a whole racist line which is very common in the United

States. One of my favorite versions of it appeared in the journal *Commentary,* in an article written by some professor in Canada. It said: the Palestinians are "people who breed, and bleed, and advertise their misery."[37] Straight Nazi propaganda. I mean, imagine if somebody said that about Jews: "Jews are people who breed, and bleed, and advertise their misery." But that's the kind of thing you hear—it's a particularly vulgar version of it, but the line is: look, the Palestinians are just doing it for the cameras because they're trying to discredit the Jews.

They do exactly the same thing when there are no cameras.

The real point is, Israel is having a lot of trouble putting down this popular revolution. I mean, the repression of the Palestinians in the West Bank is not qualitatively different right now from what it's been for the last twenty years—it's just that it's escalated in scale since the Palestinians started fighting back in the Intifada. So the brutality you see occasionally now on television has in fact been going on for the last twenty years, and it's just the nature of a military occupation: military occupations are harsh and brutal, there is no other kind [Israel seized the West Bank, Gaza Strip, and Golan Heights from Jordan, Egypt, and Syria during the Six Day War in 1967, and has controlled them ever since]. There's been home-destruction, collective punishments, expulsion, plenty of humiliation, censorship—I mean, you'd have to go back to the worst days of the American South to know what it's been like for the Palestinians in the Occupied Territories. They are not supposed to raise their heads—that's what they say in Israel, "They're raising their heads, we've got to do something about it." And that's the way the Palestinians have been living.[38]

Well, the United States has been quite happy supporting that—so long as it worked. But in the last few years, it hasn't worked. See, people with power understand exactly one thing: violence. If violence is effective, everything's okay; but if violence loses its effectiveness, then they start worrying and have to try something else. So right now you can see U.S. planners reassessing their policies towards the Occupied Territories, just as you can see the Israeli leadership reassessing them—because violence isn't working as well anymore. In fact, the occupation's beginning to be rather harmful for Israel. So it's entirely possible that there could be some tactical changes coming with respect to how Israel goes about controlling the Territories—but none of this has anything to do with "using the media."

WOMAN: *What do you think a solution might be for resolving the conflict in the region, then?*

Well, outside of the United States, everybody would know the answer to that question. I mean, for years there's been a very broad consensus in the world over the basic framework of a solution in the Middle East, with the exception of two countries: the United States and Israel.[39] It's going to have to be some variety of two-state settlement.

Look, there are two groups claiming the right of national self-determination in the same territory; they both have a claim, they're competing claims. There are various ways in which such competing claims could be reconciled—you could do it through a federation, one thing or another—but given the present state of conflict, it's just going to have to be done through some form of two-state settlement.[40] Now, you could talk about the modalities—should it be a confederation, how do you deal with economic integration, and so on—but the principle's quite clear: there has to be some settlement that recognizes the right of self-determination of Jews in something like the state of Israel, and the right of self-determination of Palestinians in something like a Palestinian state. And everybody knows where that Palestinian state would be—in the West Bank and Gaza Strip, along roughly the borders that existed before the Six Day War in 1967. And everybody knows who the representative of the Palestinians is: it's the Palestine Liberation Organization [P.L.O.].

All of this has been obvious for years—why hasn't it happened? Well, of course Israel's opposed to it. But the main reason it hasn't happened is because the United States has blocked it: the United States has been blocking the peace process in the Middle East for the last twenty years—*we're* the leaders of the rejectionist camp, not the Arabs or anybody else. See, the United States supports a policy which Henry Kissinger called "stalemate"; that was his word for it back in 1970.[41] At that time, there was kind of a split in the American government as to whether we should *join* the broad international consensus on a political settlement, or *block* a political settlement. And in that internal struggle, the hard-liners prevailed; Kissinger was the main spokesman. The policy that won out was what he called "stalemate": keep things the way they are, maintain the system of Israeli oppression. And there was a good reason for that, it wasn't just out of the blue: having an embattled, militaristic Israel is an important part of how we rule the world.

Basically the United States doesn't give a damn about Israel: if it goes down the drain, U.S. planners don't care one way or another, there's no moral obligation or anything else. But what they *do* care about is control of the enormous oil resources of the Middle East. I mean, a big part of the way you run the planet is by controlling Middle East oil, and in the late 1950s, the United States began to recognize that Israel would be a very useful ally in this respect. So for example, there's a National Security Council Memorandum in 1958 which points out that the main enemy of the United States in the Middle East (as everywhere) is nationalism, what they call "radical Arab nationalism"—which means independence, countries pursuing a course other than submission to the needs of American power. Well, that's always the enemy: the people there don't always see why the enormous wealth and resources of the region have to be in the control of American and British investors while they starve, they've never really gotten that into their heads—and sometimes they try to do something about it. Alright, that's unacceptable to the United States, and one of the things they pointed out is that a useful weapon against that sort of "radical Arab nationalism" would be a highly militarized Israel, which would then be a reliable base for U.S. power in the region.[42]

Now, that insight was not really acted upon extensively until the Six Day War in 1967, when, with U.S. support, Israel essentially destroyed Nasser [the Egyptian President]—who was regarded as the main Arab nationalist force in the Middle East—and virtually all the other Arab armies in the region too. That won Israel a lot of points, it established them as what's called a "strategic asset"—that is, a military force that can be used as an outlet for U.S. power. In fact, at the time, Israel and Iran under the Shah (which were allies, tacit allies) came to be regarded by American planners as two parts of a tripartite U.S. system for controlling the Middle East. This consisted first of all of Saudi Arabia, which is where most of the oil is, and then its two gendarmes, pre-revolutionary Iran and Israel—the "Guardians of the Gulf," as they were called, who were supposed to protect Saudi Arabia from indigenous nationalist forces in the area. Of course, when the Shah fell in the Iranian Revolution in 1979, Israel's role became even more important to the United States, it was the last "Guardian."[43]

Meanwhile, Israel began to pick up secondary functions: it started to serve as a mercenary state for the United States around the world. So in the 1960s, Israel started to be used as a conduit for intervening in the affairs of black African countries, under a big C.I.A. subsidy. And in the 1970s and Eighties, the United States increasingly turned to Israel as kind of a weapon against other parts of the Third World—Israel would provide armaments and training and computers and all sorts of other things to Third World dictatorships at times when it was hard for the U.S. government to give that support directly. For instance, Israel acted as the main U.S. contact with the South African military for years, right through the embargo [the U.N. Security Council imposed a mandatory arms embargo on South Africa in 1977 after the U.S. and Britain had vetoed even stronger resolutions].[44] Well, that's a very useful alliance, and that's another reason why Israel gets such extraordinary amounts of U.S. aid.[45]

## The Threat of Peace

But notice that this whole system only works as long as Israel remains embattled. So suppose there was a real peace settlement in the Middle East, and Israel was just integrated into the region as its most technologically advanced country, kind of like Switzerland or Luxembourg or something. Well, at that point its value to the United States is essentially over—we already have Luxembourg, we don't need another one. Israel's value to the United States depends on the fact that it is threatened with destruction: that makes them completely dependent on the United States for survival, and therefore extremely reliable—because if the rug ever is pulled out from under them in a situation of real conflict, they *will* get destroyed.

And that reasoning has held right up to the present. I mean, it's easy to show that the United States has blocked every move towards a political settlement that has come along in the Middle East—often we've just vetoed them at the U.N. Security Council.[46] In fact, up until very recently, it's been impossible in the United States even to *talk* about a political settlement. The official line in the United States has been, "The Arabs want to kill all the Jews and throw them into the sea"—with only two exceptions. One is King Hussein of Jordan, who's a "moderate," because he's on our side. And the other was President Sadat of Egypt, who in 1977 realized the error of his ways, so he flew to Jerusalem and became a man of peace—and that's why the Arabs killed him, because the Arabs'll kill anybody who's for peace [Sadat was assassinated in 1981]. That has been the official line in the United States, and you simply cannot deviate from it in the press or scholarship.

It's total lies from beginning to end. Take Sadat: Sadat made a peace offer to Israel in February 1971, a better offer from Israel's point of view than the one he later initiated in 1977 [which led to the Camp David peace talks]. It was a full peace treaty exactly in accord with U.N. Resolution 242 [which had called for a return to pre-June 1967 borders in the region with security guarantees, but made no mention of Palestinian rights]—the United States and Israel turned it down, therefore it's out of history.[47] In January 1976, Syria, Jordan and Egypt proposed a two-state peace settlement at the U.N. Security Council on the basis of U.N. 242, and the P.L.O. supported the proposal—it called for territorial guarantees, the whole business: the United States vetoed it, so it's out of history, it didn't happen.[48] And it just goes on from there: the United States was unwilling to support any of these peace offers, so they're out of history, they're down Orwell's memory hole.[49]

In fact, it's even at the point where journals in the United States will not permit *letters* referring to these proposals; the degree of control on this is startling, actually. For example, a few years ago George Will wrote a column in *Newsweek* called "Mideast Truth and Falsehood," about how peace activists are lying about the Middle East, everything they say is a lie. And in the article, there was one statement that had a vague relation to fact: he said that Sadat had refused to deal with Israel until 1977.[50] So I wrote them a letter, the kind of letter you write to *Newsweek*—you know, four lines—in which I said, "Will has one statement of fact, it's false; Sadat made a peace offer in 1971, and Israel and the United States turned it down." Well, a couple days later I got a call from a research editor who checks facts for the *Newsweek* "Letters" column. She said: "We're kind of interested in your letter, where did you get those facts?" So I told her, "Well, they're published in *Newsweek*, on February 8, 1971"—which is true, because it was a big proposal, it just happened to go down the memory hole in the United

States because it was the wrong story.[51] So she looked it up and called me back, and said, "Yeah, you're right, we found it there; okay, we'll run your letter." An hour later she called again and said, "Gee, I'm sorry, but we can't run the letter." I said, "What's the problem?" She said, "Well, the editor mentioned it to Will and he's having a tantrum; they decided they can't run it." Well, okay.

But the point is, in *Newsweek* and the *New York Times* and the *Washington Post* and so on, you simply cannot state these facts—it's like belief in divinity or something, the lies have become immutable truth.

WOMAN: *Then what happened with the Camp David Accords—why did the United States and Israel agree to deal with Egypt at that point?*

Well, if you look back to around 1971 or so, you'll find that all the American ambassadors in the Middle East were warning Kissinger that there was going to be a war if the United States kept blocking every diplomatic option for resolving the conflict.[52] Even the big oil companies were in favor of a political settlement, they were telling the White House: "Look, if you block every diplomatic option, the Arabs are going to go to war, they've got no choice."[53] But in the White House they were just laughing, it was all a big joke—just like they were laughing in Israel. And on purely racist grounds.

See, intelligence systems are very flawed institutions: they're highly ideological, they're fanatic, they're racist, and as a result the information that comes through them is usually grossly distorted. Well, in this case the intelligence information was, "Arabs don't know how to fight." The chief of Israeli military intelligence, Yehosifat Harkabi, his line was, "War is not the Arab's game"—you know, these gooks don't know which end of the gun to hold, you don't have to worry about them. And the American military, the C.I.A., everyone obviously was producing the same information: if Sadat mobilizes an army in the Sinai, you kind of laugh, "What do these guys think they're doing? We'll leave seven hundred men on the Bar-Lev Line and that'll stop them."[54] So the United States refused to pursue a diplomatic settlement, and that refusal then brought on the 1973 war—where suddenly it turned out that war *was* the Arab's game: the Egyptians won a major victory in the Sinai, it was quite a military operation, in fact. And it just shocked U.S. and Israeli intelligence, it really frightened them—because like I say, state planners usually understand violence, even if they can't understand anything else. So in the '73 war, it suddenly became clear that the assumption that "war is not the Arab's game" was false: Egypt *wasn't* a military basket-case.

Okay, as long as Egypt was a basket-case, the United States had been content to let them be a Russian ally—if the Russians want to sink money into this morass, that's fine, we don't mind, we just laugh at them. But in the 1973 war, it suddenly became clear that Egypt wasn't just a basket-case, they knew how to shoot and do all these other things that matter, so Kissinger decided to accept what had in fact been long-standing Egyptian offers to become an American client-state. Well, that's what Egypt had wanted all along, so they immediately kicked out the Russians and got on the American gravy-train. And now they're the second-biggest recipient of U.S. aid, though still way behind Israel—and at that point Sadat became a "moderate," because he had switched to our side. And since Egypt was considered the major Arab deterrent to hawkish Israeli policies, the obvious back-up position was just to remove them from the conflict, so Israel would be free to solidify its control in the region—as it has done, in fact. See, before the 1973 war, U.S. planners thought that Israel didn't have to worry about any Arab forces at all. Now they saw that that was wrong—so they moved to extract Egypt from the conflict. And that was the great achievement of the Camp David peace process: it enabled Israel to integrate the Occupied Territories and attack Lebanon without any Egyptian deterrent. Alright, try to say *that* in the U.S. media.

Incidentally, by now you are beginning to be able to say it in the strategic analysis literature. So if you read articles by strategic analysts, they're starting to say, yeah, that's the way it worked.[55] Of course that's the way it worked, that's the way it was *designed*. That's the way it was obviously going to work right at the time of Camp David—I mean, I was writing about this in 1977.[56] If you eliminate the major Arab deterrent force and increase U.S. aid to Israel to the level of 50 percent of total U.S. aid world-wide, and Israel is committed to integrating the Occupied Territories and attacking and disrupting Lebanon, if you get that configuration of events, what do you *think* is going to happen? It's transparent, a child could figure it out. But you can't say it, because to say it would imply that the United States is not the leader of the world peace forces, and is not interested in justice and freedom and human rights around the world. Therefore you can't say any of these things here, and by now you probably can't even *see* them.

## Water and the Occupied Territories

MAN: *But doesn't Israel need the Occupied Territories for defense purposes, with respect to the other Arab states on its borders—isn't that the main reason for holding on to them?*

Well, there I can only talk about the way that *they* look at it—the way the top Israeli decision-makers look at it. So there's a very interesting book published in Hebrew, called *Mechiro shel Ihud*, which is a detailed documentary record of the period from 1967 to 1977, when the Labor Party was in power in Israel [the Occupied Territories were originally seized by Israel in 1967]. It's by a guy named Yossi Beilin, who was the top advisor to Shimon Peres and is kind of a Labor Party dove, and he had access to all sorts of Labor Party documents. And the book is almost a daily record of cabinet meetings in Israel between 1967 and '77—right in the period when they were trying to figure out just what to do with the Occupied Territories.[57]

Well, there's virtually no mention of security, barely a mention of it. One thing that does get mentioned a lot is what they call the "demographic problem"—the problem of what do you do about too many Arabs in a Jewish state. Okay, that's called the "demographic problem" in Israel, and in fact, people here refer to it that way too.[58] The purpose of that term, which sounds like kind of a neutral sociological term, is to disguise the fact that it's a deeply racist notion—we would see that right off if we applied it here. Like, suppose some group in New York City started talking about the "demographic problem"—there are too many Jews and blacks. There are too many Jews and blacks in New York City, and we've got to do something about it, because they're taking over—so we've got to deal with the "demographic problem." It wouldn't be very hard to decode this. But in Israel and in this book of cabinet records, there's a lot of talk about the "demographic problem," and it's easy to see what that means.

Another thing they talk about a lot is water—and that's a very crucial thing, which is not discussed very much in the United States but it's probably the main reason why Israel is never going to give up the West Bank. See, this is a very arid region, so water is more important than oil, and there are very limited water resources in Israel. In fact, a lot of the wars in the Middle East have been about water—for instance, the wars involving Israel and Syria have usually been about the headwaters of the Jordan, which come from Syria, Jordan, and Lebanon. And as a matter of fact, one of the main reasons why Israel is holding on to the so-called "Security Zone" it seized in southern Lebanon [in the 1982 invasion] is that that area includes a mountain, Mount Hermon, which is a big part of the watershed that brings water to the region. Actually, the invasion of Lebanon was probably an attempt, among other things, to get ahold of the Litani River, a little farther to the north—but they were driven back by Shiite resistance and couldn't hold on to it, so they had to pull back.

Well, economic facts are classified in Israel, so you can't be sure of the exact numbers, but most of the studies on this, including some American studies, indicate that Israel is getting about a third of its water from the West Bank. And there really is no alternative to that, short of some sort of technological innovation—like, maybe someday someone will invent a technique of desalination, so they could use seawater. But at the moment, there is no other alternative: there are no underground water sources except the West Bank sources, Israel didn't get the Litani River, they obviously aren't going to get the Nile—so there just is no other water source for them, except the West Bank sources.

And in fact, one of the occupation policies that the Arabs in the West Bank have found most onerous is that Israel forbids them to dig deep wells.

Well, that's very hard on Arab agriculture—I mean, an Arab farmer on the West Bank has the same water allotment for farming that a Jewish city-dweller in Tel Aviv has just for drinking. Think about that: the drinking-water for a Jewish city resident is the same as the *total* water for an Arab farmer, who's got to do irrigation, and take care of livestock, and do everything else you do on a farm. And the Arabs are not allowed to sink deep wells, they're only allowed to sink shallow wells that you do without equipment—the deep wells are Jewish wells, only for Jewish settlers, and they get something like twelve times as much water, or some huge amount more water.[59]

Okay, so water's a big issue that comes up in the documents, there's the "demographic problem," there are historical reasons, and some other things too—but the fact is, there is very little talk about security concerns.

## Imperial Ambitions and the Arab Threat

MAN: *Well, I don't know about these cabinet records—but the fact is that when Israel was originally conceived in 1948, it was immediately lunged upon by virtually everybody on its borders: all of the Arab countries immediately tried to destroy it, and prevent its very existence. Wouldn't you say the Israeli people are justified in remembering that history still, as they set national policies today?*

Well, you're right that that's the standard line about what happened. But it's not true. Keep in mind the background facts. In November 1947, the U.N. General Assembly made a recommendation for a three-way partition of Palestine into a Jewish state, an Arab state, and a small internationally-administered zone that would have included Jerusalem [the area was under British imperial control].[60] Now, I should stress that this was a General Assembly *recommendation*, and General Assembly recommendations have no force: they are only recommendations. Israel *insists* that they have no force, I should say—Israel is by far the greatest violator of General Assembly recommendations, beginning in December 1948, when Israel rejected the General Assembly call for allowing Palestinian refugees the right of return [they had fled violence that broke out in Palestine beginning in November 1947]. In fact, Israel was accepted into the United Nations on *condition* that it accept that requirement, and it claimed that it would accept it—but then it immediately refused to carry through on that promise.[61] And it goes on right until today: I don't know how many, but probably hundreds of General Assembly recommendations have been rejected by Israel.

Anyway, such a recommendation was made by the General Assembly in November 1947, and at that point war broke out in Palestine among the Palestinians and the Zionists [Jewish nationalists]. The Zionists were by far the more powerful and better organized force, and by May 1948, when the state of Israel was formally established, about 300,000 Palestinians already had been expelled from their homes or had fled the fighting, and the Zionists controlled a region well beyond the area of the original Jewish state that had been proposed by the U.N.[62] Now, it's *then* that Israel was attacked by its neighbors—in May 1948; it's *then,* after the Zionists had taken control of this much larger part of the region and hundreds of thousands of civilians had been forced out, not before.

And furthermore, there's very good scholarship on this that's come out in Israel now which shows, I think pretty conclusively, that the intervention of the Arab states was very reluctant, and that it was to a large extent directed not against Israel, but against King Abdullah of Transjordan (what's now Jordan), who was basically a client ruler for the British. And the Arab states in fact did it because they felt that Abdullah was just a pawn of Britain, and they had good reason to believe that he was assisting the British in reconstructing their imperial system in the region in various ways [Britain had arranged to turn formal administration of Palestine over to the United Nations in May 1948]. It'll be a hundred years before any of this material enters mainstream American scholarship, I should say—but it's very good scholarship, and it's important.[63]

So anyway, the area that's now Jordan was being ruled by a British client, and the other Arab states in the region regarded the Jordanian military, quite correctly, as just a British army with kind of a guy with Arab headgear leading them. And they were very much concerned about the fact (which they knew at some level, even if they didn't know all of the details) that Abdullah and the Zionists were cooperating in a plan to prevent the establishment of a Palestinian state—which in fact did happen, Abdullah and the Zionists *did* carry out that plan of partitioning the area that was to be the Palestinian state between them.[64] And furthermore, Abdullah also had much greater plans of his own: he wanted to take over Syria, and become the king of "Greater Syria." And there was apparently a plan in which Israel was going to attack Syria, and then Abdullah was going to move into Syria to defend the Syrians and end up afterwards holding the whole pie, by pre-arrangement. Well, that plan never quite got worked out, as history shows—but the other Arab states had wind of it, so then they moved in against Israel to try to block Abdullah's goals.[65]

And there were powerful reasons for that, remember: this was the period of decolonization, and the major concern of the people of the region at the time was to get the British out—and Abdullah was just a pawn of the British, and they didn't want to see British imperialism reestablished. Of course, they didn't want the state of Israel around either, and they opposed it—but that was probably a minor consideration in the attack; really a minor consideration, actually. In fact, in 1949 both Syria and Egypt made very explicit proposals for a peace treaty with Israel, and Israel rejected them—Israel didn't want such a peace treaty.[66]

Alright, the reason all of this material is only coming out recently is there are rules in Israel about not releasing archives until several decades later—so the history is usually written about thirty or forty years late (and then of course, it's also very distorted for other reasons). But there's really nothing in any of the things I've said that should be a great surprise to anyone who *really* knows the history—yes, now there are archival records and new scholarship to back it up, and I think it's very convincing scholarship and will come to be recognized as the right story. But it's really no great surprise: something like that was always understood. For example, the agreement between Ben-Gurion [first Israeli Prime Minister] and Abdullah to partition Palestine has been known for years—that's come out in memoirs, everybody's talked about it, and so on.[67] But you're right, it's not part of the standard line in the United States—it just happens to be the correct story.

*MAN: But just to challenge you on some of this—I thought that what Israel was trying to preserve in the agreement to partition Palestine was the idea that Jordan would not send troops into Israel. That's why they were really cooperating with Abdullah—Ben-Gurion and the rest of the Israeli leadership at the time were very concerned about the fact that there were huge trained armies in Jordan, which were a big threat to them.*

No, on the contrary—they weren't much concerned about that. In fact, Ben-Gurion actually had to intervene to prevent his armies from taking over part of what's now the West Bank [in October 1948], because the Jordanian Legion had already been essentially destroyed and was out of arms, and the Israeli military command thought they could easily take over more territory. See, Yigal Allon, who was the commander of the Israeli army, didn't know about this agreement with Abdullah to prevent the establishment of a Palestinian state—and there was a bitter battle between Ben-Gurion and the army, in which Ben-Gurion had to hold the army back in order to honor this secret agreement he had entered into.[68] So really there was no military threat from Jordan, not at all.

*MAN: But the Israeli army held back at that point because Ben-Gurion still had some hope that perhaps peace would prevail if they held back.*

No—in fact we know very well what Ben-Gurion wanted, because he left ample diaries and so on. And his position, which he was very clear and explicit about—and there's a lot of documentation about this in my book *The Fateful Triangle*—was that Israel should not accept *any* boundaries, regardless of whether there was peace or not, because the limits of what he called "Zionist aspiration" are much broader: they include southern Syria, Transjordan, big areas which he laid out. And he said, we'll kind of hold off now, but somehow we'll ultimately get them all—in fact, with regard to Lebanon, Ben-Gurion was proposing that Israel take over Southern

Lebanon on some pretext as late as the mid-1950s.[69] So we know all about what he wanted, and like the rest, it's very different from the stories you always hear.

## Prospects for the Palestinians

WOMAN: *Then is there any hope at all for justice for the hundreds and hundreds of thousands of Palestinians who have been displaced from their homeland over the years—as well as for those who are still in Israel and the Territories?*

Well, the objective reality is that most of the Palestinian refugees will never go back to Palestine—that's just a fact of life, just like the American Indians will never get back what they had on the American continent. So in that respect, there'll never be justice. And there's just no way out of that: if there was ever any prospect of Palestinians in any large number going back to what was formerly Palestine, Israel would probably blow up the world, which they're capable of doing.[70] And that's never going to happen.

So the only question is, what kind of limited form of justice can be achieved? And that's tricky. I mean, if Israel can't suppress the Intifada at a reasonable cost, the United States and Israel might shift from their rejectionist stance and become willing to accept some variety of Palestinian self-determination. And if that happens, then you'll have to look seriously at what you mean by a "two-state settlement"—and the reality is, it's not very easy to envision, for some of the reasons I've mentioned: there are resource problems, there are problems of integration of the areas, there are border-setting issues. Remember that the U.N. resolution partitioning Palestine [in 1947] did not strictly speaking call for two states, it called for an economic confederation—and that was quite realistic.[71] Anybody who's been there knows that two states don't make much sense—because the regions are just too closely integrated, and the borders are too crazy, and when you look even more seriously you see even further that it wouldn't work. So the only thing that makes any sense is some sort of confederation. But you can pretty well predict what will happen: there will be two states, except only one of the states will really exist, the other one will just collect garbage.

In fact, I suspect that'll be the next proposal, and it'll all come under the banner of a "two state" settlement—and that's going to be a lot harder to argue about, because then people will really have to think behind the headlines to see what's going on. But achieving some kind of meaningful federation between the Israelis and the Palestinians, with really divided sovereignty—that's going to be extremely hard, we just have to face that. And that's about the only kind of solution that makes any sense, I think—it's the only limited form of justice I can see.

MAN: *There's also the different mentality between the Arabs and Jews that figures into it too, don't you think—isn't that always going to get in the way of peace?*

They're the same kind of people, they have the same kind of mentality. They bleed when they're cut, they mourn when their children are killed. I'm not aware of any difference between them.

## Legitimacy in History

WOMAN: *Do you think the passage of time can give legitimacy to Israel, even if maybe it was started out on the wrong sort of basis, displacing the indigenous population in a racist manner and so on?*

Well, yeah—the general answer to your question just has to be yes. If not, we'd have to go back to the days of hunter-gatherer societies, because all of history has been illegitimate.

I mean, take a case close to the Palestinians, which we as Americans ought to think about—take the United States. Now, I think the treatment of the Palestinians by Israel has been bad, but in comparison to the treatment of the native population here by our forefathers, it's been a paradise.

Here in the United States, we just committed genocide. Period. Pure genocide. And it wasn't just in the United States, it was all up and down the Hemisphere. Current estimates are that north of the Rio Grande, there were about twelve to fifteen million Native Americans at the time Columbus landed, something like that. By the time Europeans reached the continental borders of the United States, there were about 200,000. Okay: mass genocide. Across the whole Western Hemisphere, the population decline was probably on the order of from a hundred million people to about five million.[72] That's pretty serious stuff—it was horrifying right from the beginning in the early seventeenth century, then it got worse after the United States was established, and it just continued until finally the native populations were basically stuck away in little enclaves. The history of treaty violations by the United States is just grotesque: treaties with the Indian nations by law have a status the same as that of treaties among sovereign states, but throughout our history nobody ever paid the slightest attention to them—as soon as you wanted more land, you just forgot the treaty and robbed it; it's a very ugly and vicious history.[73] Hitler in fact used the treatment of the Native Americans as a model, explicitly—he said, that's what we're going to do with the Jews.[74]

In fact, a book came out in Germany recently called, in German, *The Five Hundred Year Reich*—actually, it's part of a big effort that's beginning to develop around the world to try to turn 1992 into a year of memory of genocide, instead of a year of celebration of the 500th anniversary of what's called Columbus's "discovery" of America. And in Germany, people under-stand that title: Hitler was going to establish a "Thousand Year Reich," and the point of the book is that the colonization of the Western Hemi-sphere was essentially Hitlerian—and it's lasted for five hundred years.[75]

I should add, actually, that throughout American history this genocide has been accepted as perfectly legitimate. So for example, there were people who spoke up for blacks and opposed slavery—there were the Abolitionists and there was the Civil Rights Movement. But you won't find much support for the American Indians. And the same was true of scholarship: for in-stance, in Samuel Eliot Morison's history of Columbus—you know, big Harvard historian—he talks about what a great man Columbus was, terrific person and so on, and then he has this little line saying, of course Columbus did set off a program of what he calls "complete genocide," and he was a major mass-murderer himself. But then he says, that was only a minor flaw, he was really a terrific seaman, this and that and the other thing.[76]

In fact, let me tell you a personal story to indicate just how far out of his-tory all of this really is. A few Thanksgivings ago I took a walk with some friends and family in a National Park, and we came across a tombstone which had just been put in along the path. It said: "Here lies an Indian woman, a Wampanoag, whose family and tribe gave of themselves and their land that this great nation might be born and grow." Okay, "gave of themselves and their land"—in fact, were murdered, scattered, dispersed, and we stole their land, that's what we're sitting on. You know, there can't be anything more illegitimate: the whole history of this country is illegiti-mate. Our forefathers stole about a third of Mexico in a war in which they claimed that Mexico attacked us, but if you look back it turns out that that "attack" took place inside of Mexican territory [the U.S. acquired the area from Texas to California after the Mexican War in 1848].[77] And it goes on and on. So you know, what can be legitimate?

Take the development of the state system in Europe. The state system in Europe, which was finally sort of established in 1945, is the result of savage wars and murders and atrocities going back hundreds and hundreds of years. In fact, the main reason why the plague of European civilization was able to spread all over the world in the past five hundred years is that the Europeans were just a lot more vicious and savage than anyone else, because they'd had a lot more practice murdering one another—so when they came to other places, they knew how to do it, and were very good at it. Well, the European state system has continued to be an extremely bloody and brutal arrangement, right to today. I mean, there are wars all over the Third World just because the national boundaries the European invaders imposed on these places have nothing to do with anything, except where one European power could expand at the expense of other European powers.

Okay, if anything has no legitimacy, it's this. But that's our nation-state system, and we just have to begin with it. I mean, it's there, and it has what-ever legitimacy—I wouldn't *say* that it's "legitimate," I'd just say that it exists, we have to recognize that it exists, and states have to be given whatever rights they are accorded in the international system. But the indigenous populations have to be given comparable rights too, I think—at least. So when I denounce apologetics for Israel's oppression, remember, it's not in any particular criticism of Israel. In fact, I think Israel is just as ugly a state as every other state. The only difference is that Israel has a fabricated image in the United States—it's regarded as having some unique moral quality, and there's all sorts of imagery about purity of arms, and high noble intent and so on.[78] It's complete mythology, just pure fabrication: Israel's a country like every other country, and we should recognize that and stop the nonsense. To talk about legitimacy is ridiculous—the word doesn't apply, to their history or anyone else's.

## Qualifications to Speak on World Affairs; A Presidential Campaign

MAN: *Mr. Chomsky, I'm wondering what specific qualifications you have to be able to speak all around the country about world affairs?*

None whatsoever. I mean, the qualifications that I have to speak on world affairs are exactly the same ones Henry Kissinger has, and Walt Rostow has, or anybody in the Political Science Department, professional historians—none, none that you don't have. The only difference is, I don't *pretend* to have qualifications, nor do I pretend that qualifications are needed. I mean, if somebody were to ask me to give a talk on quantum physics, I'd refuse—because I don't understand enough. But world affairs are trivial: there's nothing in the social sciences or history or whatever that is beyond the intellectual capacities of an ordinary fifteen-year-old. You have to do a little work, you have to do some reading, you have to be able to think, but there's nothing deep—if there are any theories around that require some special kind of training to understand, then they've been kept a carefully guarded secret.

In fact, I think the idea that you're supposed to have special qualifications to talk about world affairs is just another scam—it's kind of like Leninism [position that socialist revolution should be led by a "vanguard" party]: it's just another technique for making the population feel that they don't know anything, and they'd better just stay out of it and let us smart guys run it. In order to do that, what you pretend is that there's some esoteric discipline, and you've got to have some letters after your name before you can say anything about it. The fact is, that's a joke.

MAN: *But don't you also use that system too, because of your name-recognition and the fact that you're a famous linguist? I mean, would I be invited to go somewhere and give talks?*

You think I was invited here because people know me as a linguist? Okay, if *that* was the reason, then it was a bad mistake. But there are plenty of other linguists around, and they aren't getting invited to places like this—so I don't really think that can be the reason. I assumed that the reason is that these are topics that I've written a lot about, and I've spoken a lot about, and I've demonstrated a lot about, and I've gone to jail about, and so on and so forth—I assumed that's the reason. If it's not, well, then it's a bad mistake. If anybody thinks that you should listen to me because I'm a professor at M.I.T., that's nonsense. You should decide whether something makes sense by its *content*, not by the letters after the name of the person who says it. And the idea that you're supposed to have special qualifications to talk about things that are common sense, that's just another scam—it's another way to try to marginalize people, and you shouldn't fall for it.

WOMAN: *Seeing as you're such a big draw with audiences, though, and since you do have some name-recognition—I'm wondering, what would you think about running a Presidential campaign? I mean, huge crowds come out to listen to your talks all around the country, those people might support something like that and want to begin getting involved with it.*

Well, it's true about the audiences—but I don't think that has to do with name-recognition or anything like that. See, there are only about ten people in the country, literally, who do this kind of thing—John Stockwell, Alex Cockburn, Dan Ellsberg, Howard Zinn, Holly Sklar, only a couple others—and we all get the same reaction. I think it's just a matter of people all over the country being hungry to hear a different viewpoint. And what's more, we all get the same reaction wherever we go—it's the same in towns where nobody's ever heard of me. Like, I was in central Michigan last week, they didn't know who I was from Adam, but it was the same kind of crowd.

WOMAN: *But seeing as you do get all this draw, why not run a Presidential campaign?*

First of all, there's nobody around to run for President, and if there were . . .

WOMAN: *You, Stockwell . . .*

Anybody who wants to be President, you should right away say, "I don't want to hear that guy anymore."

WOMAN: *I'm sorry?*

You should say, "I don't want to listen to that person anymore." Anybody who wants to become your leader, you should say, "I don't want to follow." That's like a rule of thumb which almost never fails.

WOMAN: *But what about just to create a forum where more of the population would hear this different point of view?*

Well, if you want to use it kind of instrumentally, like jujitsu or something—use the properties of the system against it—okay. But I don't really think that makes any sense, frankly.

WOMAN: *The form of government we have just has to be overthrown, in your view? There's no way of doing it through reform?*

It's not a relevant distinction: if you could ever get to the point where a reformist candidate had a chance, you'd already have won, you'd already have done the main thing. The main thing is to develop the kind of mass support which would make a revolution meaningful. At that point, some crook will come along and say, "I'm your leader, I'll do it for you."

MAN: *What do you think could have that effect, though? Just like Noam Chomsky, say, going and talking to five hundred people here and there? Just keep plugging away?*

Yeah, you keep plugging away—that's the way social change takes place. That's the way every social change in history has taken place: by a lot of people, who nobody ever heard of, doing work.

MAN: *Did you go through a phase of hopelessness, or . . .*

Yeah, every evening.

MAN: *I feel like I'm kind of stuck in one.*

Every evening. I mean, look: if you want to feel hopeless, there are a lot of things you could feel hopeless about. If you want to sort of work out objectively what's the chance that the human species will survive for another century, probably not very high. But I mean, what's the point?

MAN: *You've just got to work at it.*

Yeah, what's the point? First of all, those predictions don't mean anything—they're more just a reflection of your mood or your personality than anything else. And if you act on that assumption, then you're guaranteeing that that'll happen. If you act on the assumption that things can change, well, maybe they will. Okay, the only rational choice, given those alternatives, is to forget the pessimism.

# 5

# Ruling the World

*Based on discussions in New York, Massachusetts, Maryland, Colorado, Illinois, and Ontario in 1990 and between 1993 and 1996.*

## Soviet Versus Western Economic Development

WOMAN: *In a best-case scenario for the future, how do you envision an economic system that works?*

Well, our economic system "works," it just works in the interests of the masters, and I'd like to see one that works in the interests of the general population. And that will only happen when *they* are the "principal architects" of policy, to borrow Adam Smith's phrase.[1] I mean, as long as power is narrowly concentrated, whether in the economic or the political system, you know who's going to benefit from the policies—you don't have to be a genius to figure that out. That's why democracy would be a *good* thing for the general public. But of course, achieving real democracy will require that the whole system of corporate capitalism be completely dismantled—because it's radically *anti*-democratic. And that can't be done by a stroke of the pen, you know: you have to build up alternative popular institutions, which could allow control over society's investment decisions to be moved into the hands of working people and communities. That's a long job, it requires building up an entire cultural and institutional basis for the changes, it's not something that's just going to happen on its own. There are people who have written about what such a system might look like—kind of a "participatory economy," it's sometimes called.[2] But sure, that's the way to go, I think.

MAN: *But Mr. Chomsky, we just went through a long experience with anticapitalism like the kind you're advocating—and it didn't work out very well. It was tried, and the experiment failed. Why are you now advocating the same old thing again?*

I'm not. On the contrary—I presume you're talking about the Soviet Union?

MAN: *Exactly.*

Well, there are really two points that ought to be made. First of all, the Soviet Union was basically a capitalist system. The first thing that Lenin and Trotsky did when they took power in October 1917, remember, was to destroy all of the forms of socialist initiative that had developed in Russia since the start of the Russian Revolution in February 1917 [the Russian Tsar was overthrown by popular revolution in February 1917; Lenin's Bolshevik Party took over eight months later in a military coup]. Just now I was talking about workers and communities participating in decision-making—the first thing the Bolsheviks did was to destroy that, totally. They destroyed the factory councils, they undermined the soviets [elected local governing bodies], they eliminated the Constituent Assembly [democratically elected parliament initially dominated by a rival socialist group, which was to govern Russia but was dispersed by Bolshevik troops in January 1918]. In fact, they dismantled every form of popular organization in Russia and set up a command economy with wages and profits, on sort of a centralized state-capitalist model.[3] So on the one hand, the example you're referring to is just the extreme *opposite* of what I was talking about, not the same.

Secondly comes another question. Whatever you think of the Soviet economic system, did it work or did it fail? Well, in a culture with deeply totalitarian strains, like ours, we always ask an idiotic question about that: we ask, how does Russia compare economically with Western Europe, or with the United States? And the answer is, it looks pretty bad. But an eight-year-old would know the problem with that question: these economies haven't been alike for six hundred years—you'd have to go back to the pre-Columbian period before East and West Europe were anything more or less alike economically. Eastern Europe had started becoming sort of a Third World service-area for Western Europe even before the time of Columbus, providing resources and raw materials for the emerging textile and metal industries of the West. And for centuries, Russia remained a deeply impoverished Third World country.[4] I mean, there were a few small pockets of development there and also a rich sector of elites, writers and so on—but that's like every Third World country: Latin American literature is some of the richest in the world, for example, even though its people are some of the most miserable in the world. And if you just look at the Soviet Union's economic development in the twentieth century, it's extremely revealing. For instance, the proportion of Eastern European to Western European income was declining until around 1913, then it started rising very fast until around 1950, when it kind of leveled off. Then in the mid-1960s, as the Soviet economy began to stagnate, the proportion started to decline a bit, then it declined a bit more into the late 1980s. After 1989, when the Soviet Empire finally broke up, it went into free-fall—and it is now again approximately what it was in 1913.[5] Okay, that tells you something about whether the Soviet economic model was successful or not.

Now, suppose we asked a rational question, instead of asking an insane question like "how did the Soviet Union compare with Western Europe?" If you want to evaluate alternative modes of economic development—whether you like them or not—what you ought to ask is, how did societies that were *like* the Soviet Union in 1910 compare with it in 1990? Well, history doesn't offer precise analogs, but there are good choices. So we could compare Russia and Brazil, say, or Bulgaria and Guatemala—those are reasonable comparisons. Brazil, for example, ought to be a super-rich country: it has unbelievable natural resources, it has no enemies, it hasn't been practically destroyed three times by invasions in this century [i.e. the Soviet Union suffered massive losses in both World Wars and the 1918 Western intervention in its Civil War]. In fact, it's a lot better equipped to develop than the Soviet Union ever was. Okay, just compare Brazil and Russia—that's a sane comparison.

Well, there's a good reason why nobody undertakes it, and we only make idiotic comparisons—because if you compare Brazil and Russia, or Guatemala and Hungary, you get the wrong answer. Brazil, for maybe 5 or 10 percent of its population, is indeed like Western Europe—and for around 80 percent of its population, it's kind of like Central Africa. In fact, for probably 80 percent of the Brazilian population, Soviet Russia would have looked like heaven. If a Guatemalan peasant suddenly landed in Bulgaria, he'd probably think he'd gone to paradise or something. So therefore we don't make those comparisons, we only make crazy comparisons, which anybody who thinks for a second would see are preposterous. And everybody here *does* make them: all the academics make them, all the development economists make them, the newspaper commentators make them. But just think for a second: if you want to know how successful the Soviet economic system was, compare Russia in 1990 with someplace that was *like* it in 1910. Is that such a brilliant insight?

In fact, the World Bank gave its own analysis of the success of the Soviet development model. The World Bank is not a radical outfit, as I'm sure you realize, but in 1990 it described Russia and China as "relatively successful societies that developed by extricating themselves from the international market," although finally they ran into trouble and had to return to the fold.[6] But "relatively successful"—and as compared with countries they were like before their revolutions, *very* successful.

In fact, that's exactly what the U.S. was worried about in the Cold War in the first place, if you want to know the truth—that Soviet economic development just looked too *good* to poor Third World countries, it was a model they wanted to follow. I mean, in part the Cold War went on because it turned out to be a very good way for the two superpowers to keep control over their respective empires—each using fear of the other to mobilize its own population, and at the same time kind of tacitly agreeing not to interfere with the other's domains. But for the U.S., the *origin* of the Cold War—and in fact the stated concern of American planners throughout—was that a huge area of the traditional Third World had extricated itself from exploitation by the West, and was now starting to pursue an independent course.[7] So if you read the declassified internal government record—of which we have plenty by now—you'll see that the main concern of top Western planners right into the 1960s was that the example of Soviet development was threatening to break apart the whole American world system, because Russia was in fact doing so *well*. For example, guys like John Foster Dulles [American Secretary of State] and Harold Macmillan [British Prime Minister] were frightened out of their wits by Russia's developmental success—and it *was* successful.[8] I mean, notice that Russia is not referred to as a "Third World" country today, it's called a "failed developed country" or something like that—in other words, it did develop, although ultimately it failed, and now we can go ahead and start reintegrating it back into the traditional Third World again.

And in fact, you can see that process taking place ever since the Soviet Empire dissolved—and with the standard effects. The so-called "economic reforms" we've been instituting in the former Soviet-bloc countries have been an absolute catastrophe for most of their populations—but Western investors and a standard Third World elite of super-rich are making huge fortunes, in part by skimming off most of the "aid" that gets sent there, in various ways.[9] In fact, U.N.I.C.E.F. [United Nations International Children's Emergency Fund] put out a study a little while ago estimating just the simple human cost, like deaths, of what they call the "capitalist reforms" in Russia and Poland and the others (and incidentally, they *approved* of the reforms)—and for Russia, they calculated that there have been about a half-million extra deaths a year just as a result of them. Poland's a smaller country, so it was a smaller number, but the results were proportional throughout the region. In the Czech Republic, the percentage of the population living in poverty has gone from 5.7 percent in 1989 to 18.2 percent in 1992; in Poland, the figures are something like from 20 percent to 40 percent. So if you walk down the streets of Warsaw now, sure, you'll find a lot of nice stuff in the shop windows—but that's the same as in any Third World country: plenty of wealth, very narrowly concentrated; and poverty, starvation, death, and huge inequality for the vast majority.[10]

And actually, that's the reason the so-called "Communist" Parties in Eastern Europe and Russia are getting votes these days. I mean, when they describe that here, they say, "it's nostalgia, they forget how bad it was in the old days"—but there's no nostalgia.[11] I don't think anybody there actually *wants* to go back to the Stalinist dungeon again—it's not that they're nostalgic about the *past*, it's that they're apprehensive about the *future*. They can see what's coming very well, namely Brazil and Guatemala, and as bad as their system was, that's worse. Much worse.

## Supporting Terror

So the fact that Russia had pulled itself out of the West's traditional Third World service-area and was developing on an independent course was really one of the major motivations behind the Cold War. I mean, the standard line you always hear about it is that we were opposing Stalin's terror—but that's total bullshit. First of all, we shouldn't even be able to *repeat* that line without a sense of self-mockery, given our record. Do we oppose anybody else's terror? Do we oppose Indonesia's terror in East Timor? Do we oppose terror in Guatemala and El Salvador? Do we oppose what we did to South Vietnam? No, we support terror all the time—in fact, we put it in power.

Just take a look at U.S. aid, for instance. There have been a lot of studies of it, including studies by people who write in the mainstream, and what they show is that there is in fact a very high correlation between U.S. foreign aid and human rights abuses. For example, Lars Schoultz at the University of North Carolina—who's the major academic specialist on human rights in Latin America and a highly respected mainstream scholar—published a study on U.S. aid to Latin America almost fifteen years ago, in which he identified an extremely close correlation between U.S. aid and torture: as he put it, the more a country tortures its citizens and the more egregious are the violations of human rights, the higher is U.S. aid.[12]

In fact, it's true at this very moment. The leading human rights violator in the Western Hemisphere by a good margin is Colombia, which has just an atrocious record—they have "social cleansing" programs, before every election members of the opposition parties get murdered, labor union leaders are murdered, students, dissidents are murdered, there are death squads all around. Okay, more than half of U.S. aid to the entire Hemisphere goes to Colombia, and the figure's increasing under Clinton.[13] Well, that's just normal, and like I say, similar results have been shown world-wide.[14] So claims about our concern for human rights are extremely difficult to support: in precisely the regions of the world where we've had the most control, the most hideous things you can imagine happen systematically—people have to sell their organs for money in order to survive, police death squads leave flayed bodies hanging by the roadsides with their genitals stuffed in their mouths, children are enslaved, and worse, those aren't the worst stories.[15]

As for Stalin, leaders in the West *admired* him, they didn't give a damn about his terror. President Truman, for example, described Stalin as "smart as hell," "honest," "we can get along with him," "it'll be a real catastrophe if he dies." He said, what goes on in Russia I don't really care about, it's not my business, so long as "we get our way 85 percent of the time."[16] We get our way 85 percent of the time with this nice, smart, decent, honest guy, we can do business with him fine; he wants to murder 40 million people, what do we care? Winston Churchill was the same: the British documents are now being declassified, and after the Yalta Conference in February 1945, Churchill was praising Stalin in internal cabinet meetings as a man of honor we can trust, who can help lead us forward to a new world, a "champion of peace," "illustrious," and so on.[17] He was particularly impressed with the fact that Stalin didn't lift a finger while British troops occupied Greece [beginning in November 1944] and under Churchill's order treated Athens like "a conquered city where a local rebellion is in progress," carrying out a big massacre to destroy the Greek anti-Nazi resistance and restore the Nazi collaborators to power. Stalin just stood there quietly and let the British do it, so Churchill said he's a really nice guy.[18]

None of these guys had anything against Stalin's crimes. What's more, they had nothing against *Hitler's* crimes—all this talk about Western leaders' principled opposition to atrocities is just a complete fabrication, totally undermined by a look at the documentary record.[19] It's just that if you've been properly educated, you can't understand facts like these: even if the information is right in front of your eyes, you can't comprehend it.

## *"People's Democratic Socialist Republics"*

Well, let me just end with one last point to do with your question. One of the issues which has devastated a substantial portion of the left in recent years, and caused enormous triumphalism elsewhere, is the alleged fact that there's been this great battle between socialism and capitalism in the twentieth century, and in the end capitalism won and socialism lost—and the reason we know that socialism lost is because the Soviet Union disintegrated. So you have big cover stories in *The Nation* about "The End of Socialism," and you have socialists who all their lives considered themselves anti-Stalinist saying, "Yes, it's true, socialism has lost because Russia failed."[20] I mean, even to raise questions about this is something you're not supposed to do in our culture, but let's try it. Suppose you ask a simple question: namely, why do people like the editors at *The Nation* say that "socialism" failed, why don't they say that "democracy" failed?—and the proof that "democracy" failed is, look what happened to Eastern Europe. After all, those countries also called themselves "democratic"—in fact, they called themselves "People's Democracies," real advanced forms of democracy. So why don't we conclude that "democracy" failed, not just that "socialism" failed? Well, I haven't seen any articles anywhere saying, "Look, democracy failed, let's forget about democracy." And it's obvious why: the fact that they *called* themselves democratic doesn't mean that they *were* democratic. Pretty obvious, right?

Okay, then in what sense did socialism fail? I mean, it's true that the Soviet Union and its satellites in Eastern Europe *called* themselves "socialist"—but they also called themselves "democratic." Were they socialist? Well, you can argue about what socialism is, but there are some ideas that are sort of at the core of it, like workers' control over production, elimination of wage labor, things like that. Did those countries have any of those things? They weren't even a *thought* there. Again, in the pre-Bolshevik part of the Russian Revolution, there *were* socialist initiatives—but they were crushed instantly after the Bolsheviks took power, like within months. In fact, just as the moves towards democracy in Russia were instantly destroyed, the moves towards socialism were equally instantly destroyed. The Bolshevik takeover was a coup—and that was perfectly well understood at the time, in fact. So if you look in the mainstream of the Marxist movement, Lenin's takeover was regarded as counter-revolutionary; if you look at independent leftists like Bertrand Russell, it was instantly obvious to them; to the libertarian left, it was a truism.[21]

But that truism has been driven out of people's heads over the years, as part of a whole prolonged effort to discredit the very idea of socialism by associating it with Soviet totalitarianism. And obviously that effort has been extremely successful—that's why people can tell themselves that socialism failed when they look at what happened to the Soviet Union, and not even see the slightest thing odd about it. And that's been a very valuable propaganda triumph for elites in the West—because it's made it very easy to undercut moves towards real changes in the social system here by saying, "Well, that's socialism—and look what it leads to."

Okay, hopefully with the fall of the Soviet Union we can at least begin to get past that barrier, and start recovering an understanding of what socialism could really stand for.

## The Organ Trade

WOMAN: *You mentioned "social cleansing" and people in the Third World selling their body parts for money. I don't know if you saw the recent Barbara Walters program . . .*

The answer is, "No by definition."

WOMAN: *Well, I have to admit I watched it. She had a segment on some American women who were attacked by villagers in Guatemala and put in jail for allegedly stealing babies for the organ trade. The gist of the story was that the Guatemalan people are totally out of their minds for supposing that babies are being taken out of the country and used for black market sale of organs.[22] What I'd like to know is, do you know of any evidence that this black market trade in children's organs does in fact exist, and do you think the U.S. might be playing a role in it?*

Well, look: suppose you started a rumor in Boston that children from the Boston suburbs are being kidnapped by Guatemalans and taken to Guatemala so their bodies could be used for organ transplants. How far off the ground do you think that rumor would get?

WOMAN: *Not far.*

Okay, but in Guatemalan peasant societies it does get off the ground. Do they have different genes than we do?

WOMAN: *No.*

Alright, so there's got to be some reason why the story spreads there and it wouldn't spread here. And the reason is very clear. Though the specific stories are doubtless false in this case, there's a background which is true—that's why nobody would believe it here, and they do believe it there: because they know about other things that go on.

For one thing, in Latin America there is plenty of kidnapping of children. Now, what the children are used for, you can argue. Some of them are kidnapped for adoption, some of them are used for prostitution—and that goes on throughout the U.S. domains. I mean, you take a look at the U.S. domains—Thailand, Brazil, practically everywhere you go—there are young children being kidnapped for sex-slavery, or just plain slavery.[23] So kidnapping of children unquestionably takes place. And there is strong evidence—I don't think anybody doubts it very much—that people in these regions are killed for organ transplants.[24] Now, whether it's children or not, I don't know. But if you take a look at the recent Amnesty International report on Colombia, for example, they say almost casually—just because it's so routine—that in Colombia they carry out what's called "social cleansing": the army and the paramilitary forces go through the cities and pick up "undesirables," like homeless people, or homosexuals, or prostitutes, or drug addicts, anybody they don't like, and they just take them and murder them, then chop them up and mutilate their bodies for organ transplants. That's called "social cleansing," and everybody thinks it's a great idea.[25] And again, this goes on throughout the U.S. domains.

In fact, it's even beginning now in Eastern Europe as they're being turned back into another sector of the Third World—people are starting to sell organs to survive, like you sell a cornea or a kidney or something.[26]

WOMAN: *Your own?*

Yeah, your own. You just sell it because you're totally desperate—so you sell your eyes, or your kidney, something that can be taken out without killing you. That goes on, and it's been going on for a long time.

Well, you know, that's a background, and against that background these stories, which have been rampant, are believable—and they are in fact believed. And it's not just by peasants in the highlands: the chief official in the

Salvadoran government in charge of children [Victoria de Aviles], the "Procurator for the Defense of Children," she's called, recently stated that children in El Salvador are being kidnapped for adoption, crime, and organ transplants. Well, I don't know if that's true or not, but it's not an authority you just dismiss. In Brazil too there's been a lot of testimony about these things from very respectable sources: church sources, medical investigators, legal sources, and others.[27]

Now, it's interesting: I didn't see the Barbara Walters program you mentioned, but I've read the State Department reports on which she probably based her stuff—and they're very selective in their coverage. They say, "Oh, it's all nonsense and lies, and it was all started by the Communists," and they trace it back to sort of Communist sources—which doubtless picked it up, but *they* are not the sources. The State Department carefully excluded all the other sources, like the church sources, the government sources, the mainstream legal investigators, the human rights groups—they didn't mention them, they just said, "Yeah, the stories were picked up by the Russian propaganda apparatus back in the bad old days." But that's not where it comes from. Like I say, the Russians couldn't start these stories in the Boston suburbs—and there's a reason why they couldn't start them in the Boston suburbs and somebody *could* start them in Guatemala. And the reason is, there's a background in Guatemala against which these things are not implausible—which is not to say these women are being correctly charged; undoubtedly they're not, these women are just women who happened to be in Guatemala. But the point is, that background makes it easy for people there to be frightened, and in that sort of context it's quite understandable how these attacks can have happened.

## The Real Crime of Cuba

WOMAN: *Mr. Chomsky, I'm wondering, how do you explain our embargo on Cuba—why is it still going on, and can you talk a bit about the policies that have been behind it over the years?*

Well, Cuba is a country the United States has considered that it *owns* ever since the 1820s. In fact, one of the earliest parts of U.S. foreign relations history was the decision by Thomas Jefferson, John Quincy Adams and others to try to annex Cuba. At the time the British navy was in the way, and they were a real deterrent, so the plan, in Adams's words, was to wait until Cuba falls into our hands like a ripe fruit, by the laws of political gravitation.[28] Well, finally it did, and the U.S. ran it—with the usual effects—all the way up until 1959.

In January 1959, Cuba had a popular nationalist revolution. We now know from declassified U.S. government documents that the formal decision to overthrow Castro was made by the American government in March

1960—that's very important, because at that point there were no Russians around, and Castro was in fact considered anti-Communist by the U.S. [Castro did not align with the Soviet Union until May 1961, after the U.S. had severed diplomatic relations with Cuba in January and had sponsored an invasion attempt in April.][29] So the reason for deciding to overthrow the Castro government can't have had anything to do with Cuba being a Russian outpost in the Cold War—Cuba was just taking an independent path, which has always been unacceptable to powerful interests in the United States.

Strafing and sabotage operations began as early as October 1959. Then, soon after his inauguration in 1961, John F. Kennedy launched a terrorist campaign against them which is without even remote comparison in the history of international terrorism [Operation MONGOOSE].[30] And in February 1962, we instituted the embargo—which has had absolutely *devastating* effects on the Cuban population.

Remember, Cuba's a tiny country right in the U.S. sphere of influence—it's not going to be able to survive on its own for very long against a monster. But over the years, it was able to survive—barely—thanks to Soviet support: the Soviet Union was the one place Cuba could turn to to try to resist the United States, and the Soviets did provide them with sort of a margin for survival. And we should be realistic about what happened there: many important and impressive things have been achieved, but it's also been pretty tyrannical, so there's been an upside and a downside. However, the country certainly was succeeding in terms that are meaningful to other populations in the region—I mean, just compare Cuba with Haiti or the Dominican Republic right next door, or with any other place in Latin America which the United States has controlled: the difference is obvious, and that's exactly what the United States has always been concerned about.

Look, the real crime of Cuba was never the repression, which, whatever you think about it, doesn't even come *close* to the kind of repression we have traditionally supported, and in fact implemented, in nearby countries: not even close. The real crime of Cuba was the *successes,* in terms of things like health care and feeding people, and the general threat of a "demonstration effect" that follows from that—that is, the threat that people in other countries might try to do the same things. That's what they call a rotten apple that might spoil the barrel, or a virus that might infect the region—and then our whole imperial system begins to fall apart. I mean, for thirty years, Cuba has been doing things which are simply intolerable—such as sending tens of thousands of doctors to support suffering people around the Third World, or developing biotechnology in a poor country with no options, or having health services roughly at the level of the advanced countries and way out of line with the rest of Latin America.[31] These things are not tolerable to American power—they'd be intolerable anywhere in the Third World, and they're multiply intolerable in a country which is expected to be a U.S. colony. That's Cuba's real crime.[32]

In fact, when the Soviet Empire was disintegrating and the supposed Soviet threat in Cuba had evaporated beyond the point that anyone could possibly take it seriously, an interesting event took place, though nobody in the U.S. media seemed to notice it. For the last thirty years the story had always been, "We have to defend ourselves against Cuba because it's an outpost of the Russians." Okay, all of a sudden the Russians weren't there anymore—so what happens? All of a sudden it turned out that we really had Cuba under an embargo because of our love for democracy and human rights, not because they're an outpost of Communism about to destroy us—now it turns out *that's* why we have to keep torturing them—and nobody in the American press even questions this development. The propaganda system didn't skip a beat: check back and try to find anybody who even noticed this little curiosity.

Then in 1992, a liberal Democrat, Robert Torricelli, pushed a bill through Congress called the Cuban Democracy Act, which made the embargo still *tighter*—it forbids foreign-based U.S. subsidiaries from trading with Cuba, it allows seizure of cargo from foreign ships that trade with Cuba if they enter U.S. waters, and so on. In fact, this proposal by the liberal Democrat Torricelli was so obviously in conflict with international law that George Bush himself even vetoed it—until he was out-flanked from the right during the Presidential campaign by Bill Clinton, and finally agreed to accept it. Well, the so-called "Cuban Democracy Act" was immediately denounced by I think every major U.S. ally. At the U.N., the entire world condemned it, with the exception of two countries—the United States and Israel; the *New York Times* apparently never discovered that fact. The preceding year, there had been a U.N. vote on the embargo in which the United States managed to get three votes for its side—itself, Israel, and Romania. But Romania apparently dropped off this year.

But the U.S. makes its own rules—we don't care what happens at the U.N., or what international law requires. As our U.N. ambassador, Madeleine Albright, put it in a debate: "if possible we will act multilaterally, if necessary we will act unilaterally"—violently, she meant.[33] And that's the way it goes when you're the chief Mafia Don: if you can get support from others, fine, otherwise you just do it yourself—because you don't follow any rules. Well, that's us, and the Cuba case illustrates it about as well as you could.

The enhanced embargo has been quite effective: about 90 percent of the aid and trade it's cut off has been food and medicine—and that's had the predictable consequences. In fact, there have been several articles in leading medical journals recently which describe some of the effects: the health system, which was extremely good, is collapsing; there's a tremendous shortage of medicines; malnutrition is increasing; rare diseases that haven't been seen since Japanese prison camps in the Second World War are reappearing; infant mortality is going up; general health conditions are going down.[34] In other words, it's working fine—we're "enhancing democracy." Maybe we'll ultimately make them as well off as Haiti or Nicaragua, or one of these other countries we've been taking care of all these years.

I mean, putting sanctions on a country in general is a very questionable operation—particularly when those sanctions are not being supported by the population that's supposedly being helped. But this embargo is a particularly brutal one, a really major crime in my opinion. And there's a lot that can be done to stop it, if enough people in the United States actually get together and start doing something about it. In fact, by now even sectors of the U.S. business community are beginning to have second thoughts about the embargo—they're getting a little concerned that they might be cut out of potentially lucrative business operations if the other rich countries of the world stop obeying our rules and just begin violating it.[35] So there's a lot of room for change on this issue—it's certainly something that ought to be pressed very strongly right now.

## Panama and Popular Invasions

WOMAN: *Noam, I'm wondering how you explain the very high popular approval ratings in the United States for the government's attacks on Grenada, Libya, Panama and so on. You often talk about the population becoming more dissident—but in the polls after the Panama invasion, about 80 percent of the American people said that they supported it. My Congressman told us the results of a poll he sent out—81 percent of 23,000 respondents to the question "Do you support the Panama invasion?" said yes, they did support it.*

Well, I think there's been approval mostly because the interventions you mentioned were all quick and successful. I mean, if you can do something where you have an overwhelming advantage, the other side can't fight back, you can't lose, you'll win in a couple days and then people can just forget about it, sure, you'll get a high approval rating. That's just standard jingoism—but I do not think that kind of support can be sustained for very long the way it could a couple decades ago.

The approval ratings are also high because people don't get any information about what really *happens* in these operations. For instance, I don't think anybody here actually knows what happened in Panama. After the first couple days of the invasion, the news coverage in the U.S. just stopped. So there were big round-ups of union leaders, the political opposition was all rounded up and jailed, and so on and so forth—but none of that stuff was even reported in the United States.[36] Or for example, when Quayle [American Vice-President] went down to Panama in December 1989, if you watched the news coverage on television all you saw was everybody cheering—but if you looked carefully, you'd have noticed that everybody in the crowd was white. In fact, the *New York Times* claimed that Quayle had not even gone to the black neighborhood in Panama City, El Chorrillo, at all on his trip—but that was a flat-out lie.[37] He did go, the motorcade went through there, and there was an accurate Associated Press report about it by a good journalist, Rita Beamish. She said that in the church Quayle went to where all the television crews were, everybody was cheering, but they were all rich white folk. She said that as the motorcade went by in the black neighborhood, people were silent, stolid, looking out the windows of what was left of their homes, no clapping, no nothing.[38] Okay, so that story didn't appear in the *New York Times*, what appeared was "We're heroes in Panama."

Or another thing nobody here knows is that every year since the U.S. invasion—as the Panamanians themselves call it—Panama commemorates it with a national day of mourning. Nobody here knows that, obviously, because the press doesn't report it.[39] I mean, the government George Bush installed in Panama *itself* described the country as "a country under military occupation."[40] There's a group of eight Latin American democracies called the "Group of Eight," and Panama was expelled from it in March 1990, because, as they pointed out, a country under military occupation cannot possibly be considered "democratic."[41] Well, none of this has appeared in the American press either.

And if you just look at how the U.S. media presented the *reasons* for the invasion at the time, it becomes even more obvious why people in the United States generally supported it. What were supposed to be the reasons for invading Panama and getting rid of Noriega?

MAN: *Drug trafficking.*

Drug trafficking? Noriega was much more of a drug trafficker in 1985 than in 1989—why didn't we have to go and invade Panama and get rid of him in 1985? I mean, if we actually had newspapers in the United States, which we don't, the first thing they would have asked is, "Why did we have to get rid of Noriega in 1989, but not in 1985?" Well, take a look: what was the difference between 1989 and 1985?

MAN: *He was on the C.I.A. payroll in '85.*

Yeah, he was on the payroll—he was *our* thug in 1985, so therefore we didn't have to get rid of him. But in the intervening years he was getting too independent, too big for his britches: he wasn't following orders, he was supporting the Contadora treaty [a plan for peace in Central America], and other bad stuff like that.[42] Well, the United States doesn't want anything like that in its domains, so at that point we had to get rid of him. But again, none of this was presented in the U.S. media at the time of these polls— what was presented was: he's the narco-trafficker that's destroying the United States, he's getting your kid hooked on cocaine. Alright, with that kind of media presentation, it's not surprising that 80 percent of the population would want us to invade Panama and throw him in jail. So frankly, I would interpret the poll results you mention quite differently.

In fact, there are still other things which go into explaining them, I think. For example, take George McGovern [1972 Presidential candidate who campaigned on an anti-war platform]. George McGovern did not support the invasion of Panama—in fact, about two months afterwards he wrote an Op-Ed piece in the *Washington Post* saying he had opposed it from the very moment Bush did it. But he also said that he had *refrained from saying so at the time*.[43] So if he'd been asked about it in a poll, he probably would have answered that he *did* support the invasion. And the reason is, if you're a red-blooded patriotic American, then when the government is conducting a violent act you're supposed to rally around the flag. That's part of our brainwashing, you know—to have that concept of patriotism drilled into our heads. And people really do feel it, even people like George McGovern, somebody who surely would have been in the 20 percent, but if he'd been polled about it would have voted with the 80 percent. We don't want to be "anti-American," to use the standard term—which in itself is a pretty startling propaganda triumph, actually. Like, go to Italy and try using the word "anti-Italianism," call somebody there "anti-Italian" and just see what happens—they'd crack up in ridicule. But here those totalitarian values really do mean something to people, because there have been very extensive and systematic efforts to control the population in ways like that, and they have been highly successful. I mean, there's a huge public relations industry in the United States, and it doesn't spend billions of dollars a year for nothing, you know.[44] So you really have to be a little bit more careful and nuanced when you interpret these kinds of poll results, in my view.

And the fact is, in the 1980s and Nineties, U.S. interventions in the Third World have been of quite a different character than ever before in the past. Direct U.S. military interventions in the last twenty years have been guided by a very simple principle, which was not true before in our history: never attack anybody who can fight back—and that's not accidental. So take a look at who we attacked directly in the 1980s. Grenada: a hundred thousand people, the nutmeg capital of the world, defended by 43 Cuban paramilitaries and a couple Grenadan militiamen. Libya: it's totally defenseless, you can bomb them, you can knock their ships out of the water, you can do anything you want to them, because there's no way for them to react. Or look at Panama: Panama was already under U.S. military occupation at the time of the invasion—literally. I mean, American forces were able to try dry runs on their targets a couple days before the "invasion" to make sure everything would go smoothly, and the whole thing was over and done with in a day or two.[45] Well, as long as you can carry out an attack against a completely defenseless target like that, sure, then you can get up and strut around with manly poses and talk about how brave you are. But you don't ever attack anybody who can fight back anymore—if there's anybody who can fight back, you've got to resort to other methods: subversion, mercenary states, things like that.

Okay, that's just a major shift in U.S. policy. It's not a constraint that Kennedy and Johnson labored under—when they wanted to attack some country, they just attacked it, didn't give it a second thought. Johnson sent 23,000 U.S. Marines to invade and wreck the Dominican Republic in 1965—where people *did* fight back, incidentally. And the two of them sent a huge expeditionary force of over half a million men to invade Vietnam, which went on for years and years without any popular response here. Well, that's the sign of a big change—and I think the change is that the American population simply won't tolerate the traditional kind of intervention any longer, they'll only accept the kind of invasion we carried out in Panama.[46] That's my understanding of the political scene, at least.

## Muslims and U.S. Foreign Policy

MAN: *Dr. Chomsky, I have a question. Would you agree that in this attack on the less powerful people of the world generally, there is also a secret, vicious war being waged on the Muslim people? And what do you think is in store for Muslims in general in the world?*

Well, it does happen to be the case that plenty of Muslims have been getting it in the neck from the United States—but that's not because they're Muslims, it's because they're not sufficiently under control. There are plenty of white Christian people who are also getting it in the neck. In the 1980s, the United States fought a vicious war in Central America primarily against the Catholic Church—and that means European priests, not just priests from indigenous origins—because the Church had started working for what they called "the preferential option for the poor," therefore they had to go.[47] In fact, when Americas Watch [a human rights organization focused on North and South America] did their wrap-up study on the 1980s, they pointed out that it was a decade framed by the murder of the Archbishop in 1980 and the murder of six Jesuit intellectuals in 1989, both in El Salvador—yeah, that wasn't accidental.[48]

See, the Catholic Church became the main target of the U.S. attacks in Central America because there was a radical and very conscious change in critically important sectors of the Church (including dominant elements among the Latin American bishops) who recognized that for hundreds of years it had been a Church of the rich and the oppressors, which was telling the poor, "This is your fate, accept it." And so they decided to finally become a Church in part devoted to the liberation of the poor—and they immediately fell under attack.

So you're right, it *is* true that the U.S. is attacking a substantial part of the world that happens to be Muslim, but we're not attacking it *because* they're Muslim—we don't care if they're Martians. The question is, are they obedient?

This is very easy to prove, actually. For instance, there's a lot of talk in the U.S. about "Islamic fundamentalism," as if that's some bad thing we're trying to fight. But the most extreme Islamic fundamentalist state in the world is Saudi Arabia: are we going after the leaders of Saudi Arabia? No, they're great guys—they torture and murder and kill and all that stuff, but they also send the oil profits from their country to the West and not to the people of the region, so they're just fine.[49] Or take non-state agents: I suppose the most extreme fanatic Islamic fundamentalist in the world is Gulbuddin Hekmatyar in Afghanistan, who got over a billion dollars of aid from the United States and Saudi Arabia and is now tearing what's left of Afghanistan to pieces. Yeah, he's a good guy, he's been fighting on our side—narco-trafficker, terrorist, all those things, but doing what we wanted.[50]

On the other hand, if Islamic fundamentalists are organizing clinics in the slums of Cairo, they're going to have to go, just as the liberation theologians in Latin America who happened to be Basques—you know, blue eyes, blond hair and so on—had to go. I mean, there *is* a racist element to U.S. policy, of course, but the basic motivation is not that, I think. The real goal is just maintaining obedience—as in Cuba, as in Panama, and so on.

## Haiti: Disturbance at an Export Platform

MAN: *Mr. Chomsky, Haiti and Jean-Bertrand Aristide [populist Haitian priest elected president in 1990] have been all over the news in recent years, and it seems to me our present policies towards Haiti don't quite fit the overall picture you describe. In that country at least, it does seem that the United States is trying to institute democracy of some sort—after all, we ousted the coup leaders [who deposed Aristide in 1991] and restored the popularly-elected leader to power in 1994. It appears to me your thesis might be breaking down a little on this one, and I'm interested if you have an analysis of that: what's been happening in Haiti?*

Well, I'll start with the context, and we can see how different things are. The United States has been supporting the Haitian military and dictators for two hundred years—it's not a new policy. And for the last twenty or thirty years, the U.S. has basically been trying to turn Haiti into kind of an export platform with super-cheap labor and lucrative returns for U.S. investors. And for a long time it seemed to be working: there was a lot of repression, the population was under control, American investors were making big profits, and so on. Then in 1990, something happened which really surprised the hell out of everyone. There was this free election in Haiti, which everyone here assumed would be won by the former World

Bank official we were backing [Marc Bazin], who had all the resources, and foreign support, and so on—but meanwhile something had been going on in the slums and peasant communities of Haiti that nobody here was paying any attention to: a lively and vibrant civil society was forming, with big grassroots organizations, and people getting involved in all kinds of activities. There was in fact a *huge* amount of popular organizing and activism—but who here was paying any attention? The C.I.A. doesn't look at stuff like that, certainly American journalists don't. So nobody here knew. Well, all of a sudden, in December 1990, these grassroots organizations came out of the woodwork and won the election. Catastrophe.

At that point, the only question for people who know anything about American history should have been, "how are they going to get rid of this guy?"—because something like the Aristide victory simply is not tolerable in our sphere: a populist movement based on grassroots support, and a priest infected with liberation theology? That won't last. And of course, the U.S. instantly started to undermine the Aristide government: investment and aid were cut off, except to the Haitian business community so it could start forming counter-Aristide forces; the National Endowment for Democracy went in to try to set up counter-institutions to subvert the new government, which by an odd accident are exactly the institutions that survived intact after the 1991 coup, though nobody here happened to notice that little coincidence; and so on.[51]

But nevertheless, despite all this, within a couple months of the election the Aristide regime was in fact proving itself to be very successful—which of course made it even more dangerous from the perspective of U.S. power. It was getting support from international lending institutions, because it was cutting down on bureaucracy; it was finally starting to put the country in order after decades of corruption and abuses by the U.S.-backed Duvalier family dictatorship; drug trafficking was being cut back; atrocities were reduced far below the normal level; the flow of refugees to the U.S. virtually stopped.[52]

Okay, September, there's a military coup, and Aristide is overthrown. Theoretically the United States announced an embargo and sanctions on the new junta—but that was pure fraud: the Bush administration made it very clear, instantly, that it was not going to pay any attention to the sanctions (meaning nobody else in the world had to pay any attention to them either). Bush established what they called an "exemption" to the embargo—in other words, about eight hundred U.S.-owned firms were made "exempt" from it. The *New York Times* really had to do a little work on that one. They described this as "fine-tuning" the embargo—you know, to direct it more exactly against the coup leaders, since we don't want the Haitian people to suffer, as we've demonstrated so clearly over the years.[53] Meanwhile, total U.S. trade with Haiti stayed not very much below the norm during the course of this "embargo," and in fact, in 1993 under Bill Clinton it went up by 50 percent.[54] Somehow the free press seemed to miss this completely. Nobody thought enough to do what I did: give a call to the Commerce Department and ask for the trade figures; it takes approximately two minutes, and you discover exactly what happened. But I guess that's beyond the resources of the press here, because they never managed to find it out.

Well, as this was all going on, the Haitian generals in effect were being told: "Look, murder the leaders of the popular organizations, intimidate the whole population, destroy anyone who looks like they might get in the way after you're gone. We'll give you a certain amount of time to do it, then when your job is done, we'll let you know and you can go off to the south of France and be very nicely treated; and don't worry, you'll have plenty of money when you retire, you'll be rich and comfortable for the rest of your lives." And that's exactly what Cédras [the coup leader] and those guys did, that's precisely what happened—and of course they were given total amnesty when they finally did agree to step down [after a diplomatic mission by former U.S. President Jimmy Carter in October 1994].[55]

Alright, the day before the U.S. troops were sent into Haiti, a big story to do with this came across the Associated Press news-wires—meaning every newsroom in the country knew about it. What it said was that a Justice Department investigation had just revealed that American oil companies were supplying oil directly to the Haitian coup leaders in violation of the embargo, which everybody knew, but also with the official authorization of the U.S. government at the highest level, which not everybody knew. I mean, you could have guessed as much, but you didn't know for certain that the administration in Washington was openly permitting American corporations to support the Haitian junta until this story broke. And what this Justice Department investigation had found was that the Secretary of the Treasury under Bush essentially had just told the big American oil companies, yeah it's illegal, but don't worry about it, we won't pursue it—and the same exact thing was going on under Clinton too.

Okay, the following day I did a Nexis [news media database] search on this, just out of curiosity, and it turns out that that story *did* in fact appear in the American press—in something called *Platt's Oilgram*, a journal for the oil industry. Somehow *they* discovered it. It was also in a bunch of local papers, like the Dayton Ohio Whatever and so on—just because local editors aren't always sophisticated enough to know the things you're not supposed to publish. But it never hit the national press, save for a couple lines buried in the *Wall Street Journal* somewhere, which didn't give the full picture.[56]

And remember, this was at precisely the time when everybody in the country was focusing on Haiti: there were American troops being sent there, supposedly to throw out the coup leaders, there were thousands of stories about Haiti and the embargo, but the media completely silenced this report of the Justice Department investigation. And keep in mind, that was the biggest story of the week—what it said was, there never were any sanctions, never: not under Bush, not under Clinton. Well, that would have given the whole thing away, of course, so therefore it simply did not appear in the major American media.

So the American troops moved in, and the generals who led the coup basically were told, "You did your job, now you can go away and be rich and happy." Aristide was finally allowed to return to office for a few months to finish out his term—with the popular organizations that had elected him now massacred. And do you remember Bill Clinton's big speech about this on T.V. [in September 1994], when he said that President Aristide has shown what a true democrat he is because he's agreed to step down in early 1996, when the Haitian constitution says he has to step down? You remember that? Well, the Haitian constitution didn't say he had to step down in early 1996—Bill Clinton said that. The Haitian constitution says that the president is supposed to be in office for a term of five years, it doesn't deal with the question of what happens if three of those five years are spent in forced exile, while U.S.-trained terrorists have stolen his office and are murdering the population as he sits in Washington. That's *Bill Clinton's* interpretation, it's the United States's interpretation.[57] I mean, people who hate democracy as much as we do will say, "Okay, that counts." But if you actually *believe* in demgcracy, that means that the people who voted for Aristide—which was the overwhelming majority of the Haitian population—have a right to five years with him as president. But just try to find anyone in the United States who even notices the *possibility* of this. Actually, it *has* been mentioned in Canada—but I haven't been able to find a word suggesting it in the United States, again reflecting just how profound is the contempt for democracy here.[58]

So Aristide was allowed in for a few months with his hands tied, and with a national economic plan being rammed down his throat by the World Bank, a standard structural adjustment package.[59] I mean, it was referred to in the press as "the program that Aristide is offering the donor nations"—offering it with a gun to his head—and it has lots of nice rhetoric around in it for the benefit of Western journalists. But when you get right down to the core part of it, what it says is the following.

It says: "The renovated government," meaning Aristide, "must focus its energies and efforts on civil society," particularly export industries and foreign investors.[60] Okay, *that's* Haitian civil society—foreign investors in New York City are Haitian civil society, not grassroots organizations in Haiti, they're *not* Haitian civil society. And what that means is, under these World Bank economic conditions, whatever foreign resources do come into Haiti will have to be used to turn the country back into what we've always wanted it to be in the first place: an export platform with super-cheap manufacturing labor and agricultural exports to the United States that keep the peasants there from subsistence farming as the population starves.

So the upshot is, things in Haiti have been returned to 1990 again—but with one important difference: the popular movements have been decimated. I mean, people in Haiti were extremely happy when the coup leaders were finally kicked out—and boy, if I'd been living there, I'd have been happy too: at least there weren't murderers in control torturing and killing them anymore. But that's basically the choice between water-torture and electric-torture, really. I guess water-torture's better, or so people say. But the hope for Haitian democracy is finished, at least for the moment—it'll just go back to being a U.S. export platform again. Meanwhile, there'll be more rousing speeches here about our love for democracy and free elections, and just how far we'll go to uphold our democratic ideals around the world. Maybe in fifty years they'll even discover the business about the oil.

## Texaco and the Spanish Revolution

Incidentally, there's a little historical footnote here, if you're interested. The oil company that was authorized by the Treasury Department under Bush and Clinton to ship oil to the Haitian coup leaders happened to be Texaco. And people of about my age who were attuned to these sorts of things might remember back to the 1930s, when the Roosevelt administration was trying to undermine the Spanish Republic at the time of the Spanish Revolution in 1936 and '37—you'll remember that Texaco also played a role.

See, the Western powers were strongly opposed to the Spanish Republican forces at that point during the Spanish Civil War—because the Republican side was aligned with a popular revolution, the anarcho-syndicalist revolution that was breaking out in Spain, and there was a danger that that revolution might take root and spread to other countries. After the anarcho-syndicalist organizations were put down by force, the Western powers didn't care so much anymore [anarcho-syndicalism is a sort of non-Leninist or libertarian socialism]. But while the revolution was still going on in Spain and the Republican forces were at war with General Franco and his Fascist army—who were being actively supported by Hitler and Mussolini, remember—the Western countries and Stalinist Russia all wanted to see the Republican forces just gotten rid of. And one of the ways in which the Roosevelt administration helped to see that they *were* gotten rid of was through what was called the "Neutrality Act"—you know, we're going to be neutral, we're not going to send any support to either the Republican side or the Fascist side, we're just going to let them fight their own war.[61] Except the "Neutrality Act" was only 50 percent applied in this case.

You see, the Fascists were getting all the guns they needed from Germany, but they didn't have enough oil. So therefore the Texaco Oil Company—which happened to be run by an outright Nazi at the time [Captain Thorkild Rieber], something that wasn't so unusual in those days, actually—simply terminated its existing oil contracts with the Spanish Republic and redirected its tankers in mid-ocean to start sending the Fascists the oil they needed, in July 1936.[62] It was all totally illegal, of course, but the Roosevelt administration never pushed the issue.

And again, the entire American press at the time was never able to discover it—except the small left-wing press: somehow *they* were able to find out about it. So if you read the small left-wing press in the United States back in 1937, they were reporting this all the time, but the big American newspapers just have never had the resources to find out about things like this, so they never said a word.[63] I mean, years later people writing diplomatic history sort of mention these facts in the margins—but at the time there was nothing in the mainstream.[64] And that's exactly what we just saw in Haiti: the American press would not tell people that the U.S. was actively undermining the sanctions, that there never *were* any sanctions, and that the U.S. was simply trying to get back the old pre-Aristide business climate once again—which was pretty much achieved.

### Averting Democracy in Italy

MAN: *Noam, since you mentioned the U.S. opposing popular democracy and supporting fascist-type structures in Spain and Haiti—I just want to point out that that also happened in Italy, France, Greece, and other allied Western countries after World War II. I mean, there's a big history of the U.S. undermining democracy and supporting fascist elements in the past half century or so, even in the rich European societies.*

That's right—in fact, that was the first major post-war operation by the United States: to destroy the anti-fascist resistance all over the world and restore more or less fascist structures to power, and also many Fascist collaborators. That happened everywhere, actually: from European countries like Italy and France and Greece, to places like Korea and Thailand. It's the first chapter of post-war history, really—how we broke up the Italian unions, and the French unions, and the Japanese unions, and avoided the very real threat of popular democracy that had arisen around the world by the end of World War II.[65]

The first big American intervention was in Italy in 1948, and the point was to disrupt the Italian election—and it was a huge operation. See, U.S. planners were afraid there was going to be a democratic election in Italy which would result in a victory for the Italian anti-fascist movement. That prospect had to be avoided for the same reason it always has to be avoided: powerful interests in the United States do not want people with the wrong sort of priorities in charge of any government. And in the case of Italy, there was a major effort to prevent the popular-democratic forces that had comprised the anti-fascist resistance from winning the election after the war.[66] In fact, U.S. opposition to Italian democracy reached the point of almost sponsoring a military coup around the late 1960s, just to keep the Communists (meaning the working-class parties) out of the government.[67] And it's probable that when the rest of the internal U.S. records are declassified, we'll find that Italy was actually the major target of C.I.A. operations in the world for years after that—that seems to be the case up until around 1975, when the declassified record sort of runs dry.[68]

It was the same story in France—and the same throughout Europe. In fact, if you look back, the main reason for the partition of Germany into Eastern and Western countries—which was Western-initiated, remember—was put rather nicely by George Kennan [of the U.S. State Department], who was one of the main architects of the post-war world. Back in 1946, he said: we have to "wall off" Western Germany (nice phrase) from the Eastern Zone, because of the danger that a German Communist movement might develop—which would just be too powerful; Germany's an important, powerful country, you know, and since the world was kind of social-democratic at that time, a unified socialist movement in a place like Germany or Japan would have been totally intolerable. So therefore we had to wall off Western Germany from the Eastern Zone in order to prevent that possibility from taking place.[69]

In Italy, it was an especially serious problem—because the anti-fascist resistance there was huge, and it was extremely popular and prestigious. See, France has a much better propaganda system than Italy, so we know a lot more about the French resistance than the Italian resistance. But the fact of the matter is the Italian resistance was *way* more significant than the French resistance—I mean, the people who were involved in the French resistance were very courageous and honorable, but it was a very small sector of the society: France as a whole was mostly collaborationist during the Nazi occupation.[70] But Italy was quite different: the Italian resistance was so significant that it basically liberated Northern Italy, and it was holding down maybe six or seven German divisions, and the Italian working-class part of it was very organized, and had widespread support in the population. In fact, when the American and British armies made it up to Northern Italy, they had to throw out a government that had already been established by the Italian resistance in the region, and they had to dismantle various steps towards workers' control over industry that were being set up. And what they did was to restore the old industrial owners, on the grounds that removal of these Fascist collaborators had been "arbitrary dismissal" of legitimate owners—that's the term that was used.[71] And then we also undermined the democratic processes, because it was obvious that the resistance and not the discredited conservative order was going to win the upcoming elections. So there was a threat of real democracy breaking out in Italy—what's technically referred to by the U.S. government as "Communism"—and as usual, that had to be stopped.

Well, as you say, the same thing also happened elsewhere at the time—and in other countries it was much more violent, actually. So to destroy the anti-Nazi resistance in Greece and restore the Nazi collaborators to power there, it took a war in which maybe 160,000 people were killed and 800,000 became refugees—the country still hasn't recovered from it.[72] In Korea, it meant killing 100,000 people in the late 1940s, before what we call the "Korean War" even started.[73] But in Italy it was enough just to carry out subversion—and the United States took that very seriously. So we funded ultra-right Masonic Lodges and terrorist paramilitary groups in Italy, the Fascist police and strikebreakers were brought back, we withheld food, we made sure their economy couldn't function.[74] In fact, the first National Security Council Memorandum, N.S.C. 1, is about Italy and the Italian elections. And what it says is that if the Communists come to power in the election through legitimate democratic means, the United States must declare a national emergency: the Sixth Fleet in the Mediterranean should be put on alert, the United States should start subversive activities in Italy to overthrow the Italian government, and we should begin contingency planning for direct military intervention—that's if the resistance wins a legitimate democratic election.[75]

And this was not taken as a joke, not at all—in fact, there were people at the top levels of the U.S. government who took even more extreme positions than that. For instance, George Kennan again, who's considered a great humanist, thought that we ought to invade Italy even *before* the election and not allow anything like that to happen in the first place—but he was kind of held down by other people who said, look, we can probably buy off the election by the threat of starvation and extensive terrorism and subversion, which in the end turned out to be correct.[76]

And these sorts of policies were still being followed by the United States right into the 1970s, when the declassified records dry up. The end of the documentation that we have at this point is around 1975—that's when the House Pike Committee Report released a lot of information about U.S. subversive activities—and who knows whether it went on after that.[77] Most of the literature about this is in Italian, but there's some in English—for example, Ed Herman and Frank Brodhead have a good book on the so-called "plot to kill the Pope" disinformation story, which includes an interesting discussion of some of the more recent material on Italy—and there are others.[78] And as I say, the same sorts of policies also were carried out in France, Germany, Japan, and so on.

Actually, the U.S. also reconstructed the Mafia as part of this whole effort to split the European labor movement after the war. I mean, the Mafia had mostly been wiped out by the Fascists—Fascists tend to run a pretty tight ship, they don't like competition. So Hitler and Mussolini had essentially wiped out the Mafia, and as the American liberating armies moved into Sicily and then through Southern Italy and into France, they reconstituted it as a tool to break strikes. See, the U.S. needed goons to break strikers' knees on the waterfront and that kind of thing, and where are you going to find guys like that? Well, the answer was, in the Mafia. So in France, the C.I.A.—working together with the leadership of the American labor movement, incidentally—resurrected the Corsican Mafia. And the Mafia don't just do it for fun, you know—I mean, maybe they also enjoy it, but they want a payoff. And as kind of a quid pro quo for smashing up the French labor movement, they were allowed to reconstitute the heroin trade, which had been reduced to virtually zero under the Fascists—that's the origin of the famous "French Connection," the main source of the post-war heroin racket.[79]

And there were also covert activities in this period involving the Vatican, the U.S. State Department, and British and American intelligence to save and employ many of the worst Nazi war criminals, and use them in exactly the same sorts of operations the Nazis used them for, against the popular resistance forces in the West and then in Eastern Europe. For example, the guy who invented the gas chambers, Walter Rauff, was secreted off to work on counterinsurgency in Chile. The head of Nazi intelligence on the Eastern Front, Reinhard Gehlen, joined American intelligence doing the same kind of work for us in Eastern Europe. The "Butcher of Lyon," Klaus Barbie, worked for the Americans spying on the French until finally they had to move him out through the Vatican-run "ratline" to Latin America, where then he finished out his career.[80] That was another part of the whole post-war effort of the United States to destroy the prospects for independent democracy—and certainly it's something which took place.

## P.R. in Somalia

MAN: *Professor Chomsky, in light of all this I'm wondering, do you think there has ever been such a thing as a humanitarian intervention by the U.S.? Take what we were supposed to have been doing in Somalia, for example: that was framed as a humanitarian action here—do you think that was all image, or was there also some reality to it too?*

Well, states are not moral agents; they are vehicles of power, which operate in the interests of the particular internal power structures of their societies. So anybody who intervenes in another country, except maybe Luxembourg or something, is going to be intervening for their own purposes—that's always been true in history. And the Somalia operation, to take the case you mention, certainly was not humanitarian.

I mean, the U.S. waited very carefully until the famine there was pretty much over and the major international aid organizations, like the Red Cross and Save the Children and so on, were getting about eighty percent of their aid into the country (using Somalis to do most of the work, it turns out) before it decided to move in.[81] So if the U.S. government had had any humanitarian feelings with regard to Somalia, it had plenty of time to show it—in fact, it could have shown it from 1978 through 1990, when the U.S. was the chief supporter of Siad Barre, the Somali warlord who destroyed the country and killed maybe fifty or sixty thousand people with U.S. assistance, long before the famine.[82] But when our favorite tyrant collapsed, the U.S. pulled out, a civil war then erupted, there was mass starvation—and the U.S. did nothing. When the famine and fighting were at their peak, in the first half of 1992, the U.S. still did nothing.

By around the time of the November 1992 Presidential election here, it was clear that Somalia could provide some good photo op's—if we send thirty thousand Marines in when the famine is declining and the fighting is calming down, we'll get really nice shots of Marine colonels handing out cookies to starving children; that'll look good, it'll be a real shot in the arm for the Pentagon budget. And in fact, it was even described that way by people like Colin Powell [then Chairman of the Joint Chiefs of Staff] and others—they were saying, well, you know, it'll look good for the Pentagon.[83]

Of course, it should have been obvious to them that pretty soon it was going to turn into a nightmare: when you put a foreign military force into a country, it won't be long before they're fighting the local population. That's almost automatic, even if the population had welcomed them. Take Northern Ireland, for example: the British were *called in* by the Catholic population [in August 1969]; a couple months later, they were *murdering* the Catholic population.[84] That's what foreign armies are like, the dynamics are clear—and in the case of Somalia, it was only a question of time before the shooting started.[85]

MAN: *Then you were opposed to the whole U.S. operation?*

By that point I was sort of, like, neutral. I mean, you couldn't really tell whether it would cause more good than harm, though it was certainly not a humanitarian intervention. But the more important point is, there was always a much better alternative.

Look: the U.S. should have given aid right away, and the U.N. should have remained there throughout the famine. But by the time you got to mid-1992, things were already beginning to improve—and they were beginning to improve partly under the leadership of a U.N. negotiator, an Algerian named Mohammed Sahnoun, who was doing extremely well by all accounts: he was starting to bring local groups together, he had a lot of respect from all sides in the conflict, he was working with traditional elders and women's groups and so on. And they were starting to rehabilitate Somalian society, and to address some of its problems—he was just extremely effective by the testimony of all the international aid agencies, and a lot of others. But he was thrown out, because he publicly opposed the incompetence and corruption of the U.N. operation. They simply got rid of him—and that means the U.S. supported it.[86]

So you see, you really didn't *need* an intervention at that time: the best thing would have been just to continue giving support to Sahnoun and others like him, who were trying to bring together the various parts of Somalian civil society. I mean, *that's* the way you've got to do it, or else there isn't really going to be any lasting progress—you have to help the civil society reconstruct itself, because *they're* the only ones who can ultimately solve their own problems. And Sahnoun and others were doing that, so it would have been very efficient just to help them continue doing it. But of course, that was never a thought here: you don't get any P.R. for the Pentagon that way.

So you can ask whether in the end the Somalis benefited or were harmed by what we did, and I'm not certain what the answer is. But whatever happened, *they* were secondary: they were just props for photo opportunities. Maybe they were helped by it—I hope so—but if so it was purely incidental.

## The Gulf War

MAN: *Probably the major U.S. foreign policy event of recent years was the Gulf War. What would you say was the media's contribution to that? As I remember it, the coverage in the United States was all "rah-rah" support as we bombed Iraq.*

It's true there was a lot of that—but in my view, the much more significant period for reviewing the media on the Gulf War is not what people usually concentrate on, and what the media themselves are willing to talk about: that is, the six weeks of the actual bombing [January 16 to February 27, 1991], when the constraints on reporting were naturally pretty tight and there was the predictable patriotic jingoism. The most important period was between August 1990 and January 1991—the period when a decision had to be made about how to respond to Saddam Hussein's invasion of Kuwait [on August 2, 1990].

The decision to use violence is always a very serious one. In a functioning democratic society—I don't mean one with democratic forms, but I stress "functioning"—that decision would only be taken after a lot of public discussion of the issues, and consideration of the alternatives, and weighing of the consequences. Then, after appropriate public debate, maybe a decision would be made to resort to violence. Well, that never happened in the case of the Gulf War—and it was the fault of the American media that it never happened.

Look: the fundamental question throughout the pre-war period was whether the U.S. would pursue the peaceful means that were available—and which are in fact *required* to be pursued by international law—for a diplomatic settlement and negotiated Iraqi withdrawal from Kuwait, or whether on the other hand we would *undercut* any possibility for a diplomatic settlement, and move straight to the arena of violence.[87] Well, we don't know whether diplomatic means actually *were* available in this case, but we don't know that for a very simple reason: Iraq put them on the table, but they were rejected, and they were rejected *at once* by the Bush administration starting in mid-August 1990, and running right through to the start of the bombing in mid-January.[88]

What was the media's role in this? Well, they suppressed the story, basically. I mean, you'd have to be a real media addict to know that Iraq had made proposals in mid-August 1990 that frightened the State Department enough so that they were worried they would have to try to—as the *New York Times* correspondent put it in a moment of carelessness—"reject the diplomatic track."[89] And that suppression continued right up until the bombing started in January 1991: there were diplomatic offers on the table, whether serious or not we don't know, for Iraqi withdrawal in the context of a conference on regional issues, and other things which certainly sounded negotiable—and indeed were *regarded* by U.S. Middle East specialists in the government as, as they put it, "serious" and "negotiable" proposals.[90] But barely anybody knew about this. In Europe, I think virtually no one knew. In the United States, you could have known it if you read the one newspaper in the country that actually followed the story, namely *Newsday* in Long Island. And *Newsday* followed it in part I suspect—although I can't prove this—because they were being leaked material from somebody in the government who was trying to smoke out the *New York Times*, which had failed to publish it. See, *Newsday* is a very funny publication to see information being leaked to—it's good, but it's a small suburban newspaper. However, it does happen to be on sale at every newsstand in New York, so when their whole front page has a big headline saying "Iraq Sent Pullout Deal to U.S.," the *New York Times* can't pretend not to see it, and they'll have to publish some sort of back-page acknowledgment and dismissal the next day—which is indeed what happened.[91]

But the point is, by refusing to allow the discussion and debate—and even the information—that would be the basis for sane decision-making about the need for war in a democratic society, the media set the stage for what turned out to be, predictably, a very destructive and murderous conflict. People don't want a war unless you absolutely have to have one, but the media would not present the possibility that there were alternatives—so therefore we went to war very much in the manner of a totalitarian society.[92] That's really the main point about the media and the Gulf War, in my view.

Of course, it didn't stop there—there were also plenty of the things that you referred to as well. So before and during the war, the Bush administration had to build up an image in people's minds of Iraq as a monstrous military superpower, in order to mobilize enough popular hysteria so that people here would go along with their policies. And again, the media did their job 100 percent. So I don't know how well you remember what was going on around the country back then, but people were literally quaking in their boots about the extraordinary might of Iraq—it was a superpower with artillery we'd never dreamt of, all this kind of stuff.[93] I mean, this was a defenseless Third World country that was so weak it had been unable to defeat post-revolutionary Iran in eight years of warfare [from 1980 to '88]—and that was with the support of the United States, the Soviet Union, all of Europe, the Arab oil countries: not an inconsiderable segment of world power. Yet with all those allies, Iraq had been unable to defeat post-revolutionary Iran, which had killed off its own officers' corps and barely had an army left: all of a sudden this was the superpower that was going to conquer the world? You really had to be a deeply brainwashed Western intellectual even to look at this image—a defenseless Third World country threatening the two most advanced military forces in the world, the United States and Britain—and not completely collapse in ridicule. But as you recall, that's what all of them were saying—and people here really believed it.

In fact, during the Gulf War I dropped my scheduled speaking engagements and accepted invitations to talk in the most reactionary parts of the country I could find—just because I was curious what I'd see. So I went to some place in Georgia which is surrounded by military bases; I went to Lehigh, Pennsylvania, a jingoist working-class town; to some conservative towns in Massachusetts, to Appalachia, places like that. And everywhere I went, people were terrified out of their wits. Sometimes it was pretty amazing.

For instance, there's a college in northern California called Chico State, which is where guys like Reagan and Shultz [Reagan's Secretary of State] send their kids so they won't be infected by "lefties" at Berkeley. The place is right in the middle of four hundred miles of cornfields, or whatever it is they grow out there, a million miles from nowhere, and when you fly in you land at an airport that's about half the size of a house. Well, when I landed there, a student and a faculty member who were like the two local radicals at the school came out to meet me. And as we were walking to the car, I noticed we had to go a pretty long distance, because the airport was all surrounded with yellow police tape. So I asked these guys, "What's going on, are they rebuilding the landing strip or something?" You know what they said? "No, that's to protect the airport from Arab terrorists." I said, "Arab terrorists in northern California?" But they thought so. And when I got into the town, everybody was walking around in army fatigues and wearing yellow ribbons, saying "If Saddam comes, we're going to fight to the death," and so on.

And in a sense, people really believed it. I should say, though, that in every one of these towns I went to, the propaganda line was so thin that as soon as you started discussing the situation and you made a few jokes about what the reality was, the whole thing just totally collapsed, and by the end of the talk you'd get a huge standing ovation. Friends of mine who spoke around the country at the time found exactly the same thing, incidentally—Alexander Cockburn, for instance. But that was the image of Iraq that the media presented right on cue—and with the help of that propaganda cover, Bush was able to carry out his bombardment for six weeks, and kill a few hundred thousand people, and leave Iraq in total ruins, and put on a huge show of force and violence.[94]

And notice that contrary to the line that's constantly presented about what the Gulf War was fought for, in reality it had nothing to do with not liking Saddam Hussein—as can very easily be demonstrated. So just take a look at what happened right after the U.S. bombardment ended. A week after the war, Saddam Hussein turned to crushing the Shiite population in the south of Iraq and the Kurdish population in the north: what did the United States do? It watched. In fact, rebelling Iraqi generals pleaded with the United States to let them use captured Iraqi equipment to try to over-throw Saddam Hussein. The U.S. refused. Saudi Arabia, our leading ally in the region, approached the United States with a plan to support the rebel generals in their attempt to overthrow Saddam after the war; the Bush ad-ministration blocked the plan, and it was immediately dropped.[95]

Furthermore, there was no secret about the American decision to leave Saddam Hussein in power after the Gulf War—and there was even a reason given for it. The reason was explained by a spokesman for the State De-partment at the *New York Times*, Thomas Friedman. What he said was, it is necessary that Saddam Hussein remain in control of Iraq for what's called "stability." He said: "The best of all worlds" would be "an iron-fisted Iraqi junta" that would rule Iraq the way Saddam Hussein did—much to the approval of Turkey and Saudi Arabia, and of course the boss in Washington. But since they couldn't get the "best of all worlds" right then, they were going to have to settle for second best—namely, Saddam Hussein himself, so he could rule Iraq, as Friedman put it, with an "iron fist."[96]

Therefore the United States did nothing to prevent Saddam from mas-sacring the Shiite rebels as U.S. troops were stationed all over the region—and that's been going on ever since, with his attack on the marsh dwellers and others. And the only reason why any barriers were ever put up to his at-tack on the Kurds in the north was that a huge international outcry devel-oped in the West, as people here watched Iraqi forces massacring people who this time happened to have blue eyes and Western features—it was just pure racism that no similar public response ever developed to his assault on the Shiites.

But sure, Saddam Hussein stayed in power after the war—and he was supported by George Bush again, just like before the war. Meanwhile, the real victim of the bombing and the U.S.-imposed embargo has been the gen-eral population of Iraq. In fact, literally hundreds of thousands of children have died in Iraq since the end of the war, just as a result of American in-sistence on maintaining sanctions—and by now the United States and England are alone at the U.N. Security Council in insisting that the sanc-tions against Iraq still remain in effect, even though the formal U.N. condi-tions for them have by this point been satisfied.[97] But again, that's another story you won't see pursued very far in the U.S. press.

Also, it's widely agreed that Saddam Hussein's hold on power has not been *weakened* by all of this—it's actually been *strengthened*. For instance, there was an article not too long ago in *Foreign Affairs*, the main foreign policy journal, which pointed out that Saddam Hussein now can at least appeal to nationalism in the Iraqi population to tighten his rule—while the sanctions have turned what was previously a relatively wealthy country into a deeply impoverished one, with literally more than a million people dying of malnutrition and disease.[98]

And this is all being done by the United States for its own reasons. It has nothing much to do with disliking Saddam Hussein—as you can see from the fact that he was George Bush's great friend and trading partner right up until the moment of the Kuwait invasion.[99] Or as you can see from the fact that the Bush White House intervened repeatedly well into 1990 to prevent the Treasury Department and others who thought Iraq wasn't credit-worthy from cutting back on U.S. loan guarantees to their dear friend Saddam Hussein.[100] Or as you can see from the fact that we supported him again immediately after the war ended, as he was decimating internal resistance to his rule with "Stormin' Norman" Schwarzkopf [the U.S. general] sitting nearby and refusing even to lift a finger.[101]

WOMAN: *So you think in the end the U.S. just wanted to regain control of the Kuwaiti oil fields that Saddam had captured—it was just a war fought for oil?*

Well, a good place to start if you want to know what something was about is to look to see what changes it introduced. And particularly in the case of a war planned in advance where the outcome was never in any doubt, I think you have solid reason to believe the result was what the thing was really for in the first place. Well, what changes did the Gulf War introduce? The one big thing that happened right as soon as the war ended was that the U.S. arranged the Madrid Conference on the Middle East [in October 1991], which set off what was called the "peace process" that culminated in Israel and the P.L.O. signing the Oslo Agreement in 1994—and with that, the U.S. and Israel won their twenty-year campaign of rejecting the possibility of Palestinian national rights, flat out.[102] The Palestinians were basically destroyed. [Editors' Note: The Oslo Agreement is discussed in more detail at the end of this chapter and in chapter 8.]

In fact, you didn't even need hindsight to figure this out, it was perfectly obvious right at the time of the Gulf War that this was going to happen—like, I had an article in Z *Magazine* saying, okay, now that the Gulf War is over, the U.S. will try to ram through its rejectionist program for a settlement of the Palestinian question.[103] And that's exactly what happened.

So look at what took place. The last of the annual U.N. votes on the Palestinians was held in December 1990, and the result was the same as always: 144 to 2, the U.S. and Israel standing alone against the rest of the world in rejecting any sort of recognition of Palestinian national rights.[104] Then came the U.S. bombardment of Iraq in January 1991. After the war, the U.S. set up the Madrid Conference and the U.N. didn't hold any more votes on the Palestinian question after that. The Madrid Conference was run completely by the U.S.—it was based totally on American programs, there was nothing for the Palestinians at all. The agenda was, Israel takes what it wants from the Occupied Territories; the relationships between Israel and the U.S.-client oil monarchies in the region, like Saudi Arabia and Oman and Qatar and so on (which have always existed, even though they were officially at war), now kind of rise above the surface and become more overt—and the Palestinians get it in the neck, they're offered nothing. And that was the big effect of the Gulf War: it sort of intimidated everyone, it was a big show of American power that demonstrated that the U.S. will use force to get its way wherever it feels like it, now that the Soviet Union is out of the game. So the Soviet Union was gone—there was no longer that space left for Third World countries to be independent and "non-aligned." And also, the entire Third World just had been devastated by the huge crisis of capitalism that swept the world in the 1980s. Arab nationalism had been dealt yet another blow by Saddam's aggression and P.L.O. tactics of more than the usual ineptitude; so the rulers of the Arab states had less need than before to respond to popular pressures and make pro-Palestinian gestures. Well, after all that, it really was no longer necessary for the U.S. to undermine all diplomatic initiatives in the Middle East, as we'd been doing for the past twenty years. Now we could just use force. The Gulf War was the first demonstration of that.

So everybody was scared shitless by it, and Europe finally backed off on the question of Palestinian national rights: they don't even make any proposals about that anymore. In fact, it was kind of interesting that even Norway agreed to be the intermediary in 1993, and to help implement U.S. and Israeli rejectionism in the Oslo Agreement—they wouldn't have done that a couple years earlier.

And that's primarily what the Gulf War was about, I think. It wasn't about fear of losing oil. It wasn't about international law, or principled opposition to aggression or anything like that. It wasn't that they didn't like Saddam Hussein—they didn't care about Saddam Hussein one way or the other. It was that after the Gulf War was over, the U.S. was in a perfect position to ram through its rejectionist program and fully extend the Monroe Doctrine to the Middle East [the Monroe Doctrine was proclaimed by the U.S. in 1823 and stated that Latin America was the exclusive domain of the United States, not the European colonial powers]. It was our way of saying: "Look, this is our turf, we'll do what we feel like here." As George Bush in fact put it: "What we say goes." [105] Now the world understands that; the Gulf War helped them understand it.

## Bosnia: Intervention Questions

MAN: *Noam, do you recall any major issues on which your views have to-tally flip-flopped at some point, perhaps by thinking them out more or something like that? It strikes me that your positions have remained ex-tremely consistent over the years. Or are there issues that you wish you'd written and talked about, but haven't yet?*

Well, there are a lot of major issues on which I simply haven't taken any position—just because I don't really know what to say. For example, take the conflict in the former Yugoslavia in the early 1990s [i.e. after the break-up of the Soviet bloc in 1991 and '92, Bosnia and Herzegovina began the process of seceding from Yugoslavia and several years of civil war between the Croat, Muslim, and Serb populations followed]. I didn't really have any opinion on what to do about that, actually. I never heard a good proposal about how to resolve it, and I didn't have one myself—so when people asked me to comment on it, I just talked about the general problems and gave no proposal. And in fact, there are plenty of major issues like that in the world, where I just don't know what to say—I don't see any good solutions, or even anything very helpful that could be done. Fortunately there are hundreds of other cases where there are obvious things that can be done, and I think those are the ones where we really ought to focus our at-tention.

But Bosnia was a striking example—just because everybody was talking so much about it—of an issue where if anyone had a good idea about how to stop the atrocities, I missed it. I mean, lots of people said, "Let's bomb everybody"—okay, great. And there were a lot of people posturing and preening their feathers about how they were the only moral ones because they were opposed to what was happening in Sarajevo [the Bosnian capital, where ethnic warfare raged in the early 1990s]. Yeah, sure, we all were op-posed to what was happening in Sarajevo—but what did you propose to do about it? That's where it got a lot less obvious. Kill the Serbs? They're human beings too, you know, and it's not like the position of these Serb peasants up in the hills is zero. I mean, maybe their lifestyle's not as much like ours as all those nice Europeans in Sarajevo, but they're people too. In fact, I should say that there's been a lot of class bias in general in the West-ern reactions to what's been going on there, and in the media coverage in particular. But even if you did decide that it was the Serb peasants who were the killers and the people in Sarajevo were like Gandhi, still the question re-mained: what should you do? Okay, that's where it got very hard.

And there are plenty of other issues like that too. Take Rwanda [where more than half a million people were killed in a civil war in 1994]—you can see plenty of things people shouldn't have done, but once the massacres got started, I don't know of a lot that anybody could do about them. They were horrendous, certainly, but what exactly could you do?

## Toying With India

MAN: *Professor Chomsky, India is refusing to sign the Nuclear Non-Proliferation Treaty unless the countries that already have nuclear weapons agree to give them up. That seems to me to be a pretty brazen contravention of U.S. authority, especially for a poor Third World country like India. Why do you think they're saying that, and what is the U.S. reaction going to be to that kind of disobedience?*

Well, India is basically just saying what everybody else in the Third World *thinks* but is afraid to say publicly: that the Nuclear Non-Proliferation Treaty is a ridiculous joke. I mean, the Nuclear Non-Proliferation Treaty is just a way of ensuring that the rich powerful countries have a monopoly of nuclear weapons—not much else. Now, obviously nuclear proliferation is a bad thing—but you know, is it better for the *United States* to have them? Do we have a better record in international affairs than India? Well, everybody in the Third World can appreciate that hypocrisy, but not a lot of them are willing to get up and say it. In India they do say it—and actually that's not so surprising.

You see, India is a fairly independent country. It was the head of the Non-Aligned Movement [a coalition of Third World nations at the U.N.], and it's a big country—in fact, within a small number of years India will probably be larger than China, if you project the current population growth rates.[106] India was also one of the first countries to be colonized, and it was destroyed by colonialism—and however brainwashed Indian intellectuals may be (and they are), an understanding of that history is not very deep below the surface. And it does show up in independence. For example, take Nehru [the first Indian Prime Minister]: although he was very pro-Western and very anglophile, he was absolutely *despised* by American leaders. You should see the stuff that's coming out about him these days in declassified American documents, they just hated him with a passion. And the reason was, he was standing up for some level of Indian independence.[107] And that streak of independence in India has remained.

In fact, if you look over the history of U.S. attitudes towards India since British decolonization [in 1947], they've in general been kind of ambivalent. On the one hand, the U.S. was opposed to India because it was fairly independent—it was trying to develop an independent economy and an independent foreign policy. But on the other hand, the U.S. was extremely worried about *China* right next door—they were worried about Chinese economic success in the years after their revolution [in 1949], because they were very much afraid that China would be a development model that other Third World countries would want to follow. So we have extensive declassified documents on this stretching until roughly the early 1960s, and right into the time of the Kennedy administration the documentary record is very explicit: the big fear was that China was starting to look too successful. And therefore, much as they disliked it, U.S. planners determined that they had to support India as sort of the democratic alternative to China, so then they could say to other countries: the Indian way is better than the Chinese way, be capitalist, have a parliament and so on. And if you look over the history, that ambivalence did lead to policy conflicts.[108]

For instance, the U.S. gave very little aid to India. In fact, sometimes it was absolutely scandalous—like, right after Indian independence, in around 1950, India had its last massive famine (under the British there were famines all the time), and while there aren't very good statistics, probably something on the order of maybe 13 to 15 million people died from starvation. Well, we have the U.S. internal records from that period, and at first there wasn't even any *question* of giving them aid—I mean, we had food coming out our ears, just huge food surpluses, but there was no aid going to India because we did not like Nehru's independence and his moves towards non-alignment and neutrality. But then there was a discussion about whether the U.S. should give India food aid as a *weapon*—that is, we give them some food aid as a way of forcing them to accept U.S. policies on various issues. And after that, a little bit of aid was trickled out—but it was delayed and conditioned on India's accepting American positions on things like the Korean War and so on. Nobody knows exactly how many millions of people died because of that.[109]

By the 1960s under Kennedy, the U.S. was shifting towards giving some aid to India to make it sort of a counterweight to China, so they'd look good as compared with Communist China—but again, the aid was with strings attached. For instance, India badly needed fertilizers, and they wanted to develop their own fertilizer industry using hydrocarbon resources—which they had plenty of, along with a lot of other energy resources—but they needed U.S. aid to do it. And after a big discussion in the United States, which you can read about in the pages of the *New York Times* if you look back, a decision was made here to help them do it—but only if they would use *Western*-based hydrocarbons. So India was not allowed to develop its own hydrocarbon resources, instead they had to buy them from the American oil companies, and in addition they had to allow dominant U.S. control over the fertilizer and any other industries which developed. Well, India resisted those conditions very strongly—but in the end, they had to give in. And you can read *New York Times* articles in the 1960s recognizing this situation, and basically saying: well, the Indians don't like it, but there's nothing they can do about it, because we've got them by the throat—they'll just have to do what we want.[110]

Well, alright, that sort of ambivalent dynamic continued through the 1970s and Eighties. In the 1980s, India had a very fast growth rate, but it also adopted extremely bad fiscal policies which got them deeply into debt—and the debt crisis led them into accepting structural adjustment "reforms," as throughout the Third World. In India's case, the reforms have actually been fairly moderate, though they've still had the usual effects: for most of the population there's been a decline, and for an elite sector it's meant wealth. The country shot into a deep depression right away, but recently it's been pulling out of it, though still it hasn't recovered the 1980s growth rates—and of course, the recovery is extremely inegalitarian in terms of who actually "recovers." But right now the U.S. is very supportive of India, because the country has opened itself even more to Western control. Still, there's also this history of independence which doesn't go away so easily. And sometimes it does show up in India doing things like speaking up against the hypocrisy of the Nuclear Non-Proliferation Treaty, when most other Third World countries would be too afraid to step out of line like that.

## The Oslo Agreement and Imperialist Revival

MAN: *Noam, you said that the Oslo Agreement in the Middle East was sort of a consequence of the Gulf War—I'm wondering, what do you think are the prospects for the Palestinians now that they've signed it? And do you see them still being able to organize resistance to the Israeli occupation, even without pressure from international solidarity movements in the West?*

Well, first of all, it's not the *Palestinians* who signed anything. It was the group around Arafat—and they simply made a decision to capitulate. And as far as the prospects go for the Palestinian people right now, in the absence of serious international solidarity movements, their hopes are dead—because this agreement was a complete sellout, it was a total capitulation.

A couple nights ago I was reading an article in the Israeli press by a friend of mine at Tel Aviv University, who summarized what's been going on very nicely. She said: people in Israel are comparing this agreement with the end of apartheid in South Africa, but the true comparison is with the *onset* of apartheid—with the enactment of the 1950s laws in South Africa which set up the Bantustans [partially self-governing black districts].[111] And that's right, that's more or less what the Oslo Agreement is: it's enslavement, it's a plan for enslavement, with about as much independence for the Territories—less maybe—as the Bantustans had. So that means that the whole struggle against apartheid is just *beginning* right now, not ending.

Israel and the United States essentially got the settlement they'd been holding out for for more than twenty years, and for which the U.S. has blocked every international diplomatic initiative without exception for well over twenty years.[112] In 1994 they finally won, the world capitulated—it's not that the *Palestinians* capitulated, the whole world capitulated on this one. In fact, it capitulated so profoundly that it doesn't even remember what it stood for for so long.

It's amazing in Europe: Europe has become extraordinarily colonized culturally by the United States, to an extent that is almost unbelievable—Europeans aren't aware of it apparently, but if you go there it's kind of like a pale United States at this point, yet they still have this feeling of great independence, so it's even more dramatic. I mean, Western European intellectuals like to think of themselves as very sophisticated and sort of laughing about these dumb Americans—but they are so brainwashed by the United States that it's a joke. Their perceptions of the world and their misunderstandings and so on are all filtered through American television and movies and newspapers, but somehow by this point they just don't recognize it. And one of the issues where this is most clearly demonstrated is with respect to the Middle East. I mean, it's not ancient history, but on the issue of the right of self-determination for the Palestinians, the Europeans have just forgotten what they stood for, at least on paper, until around the time of the Gulf War—because anything like self-determination is completely *out* of the Oslo Agreement.[113]

The long-term arrangement between Israel and the Palestinians now will be in terms of U.N. 242 alone. [U.N. 242 was a November 1967 United Nations Security Council Resolution calling for Israel to withdraw from the territory it had just seized and for a regional peace treaty.] Well, the whole battle all along has been about whether a settlement in the Middle East is going to be *just* in terms of U.N. 242, which doesn't say anything about the Palestinians, or U.N. 242 plus *other* U.N. Resolutions which also call for Palestinian rights. Well, now it turns out that the answer is just 242—so Israel does whatever it feels like.

Right now there are huge construction projects going up all over the Occupied Territories (with, as always, U.S. funding), and Israel will just continue with its settlement program [the idea is to "settle" Jewish citizens in the Palestinian territories, which are not officially part of the state of Israel, to solidify Israel's claim to them]. And what they've pretty much been doing is creating a large bulge of Jewish settlers around this big area they call "Greater Jerusalem," in order to break the West Bank into two separate parts and enclose Jerusalem—they're basically breaking the West Bank into two cantons, where they'll then gladly cede authority to the local cops to do the dirty business of keeping order. It would be like asking the New York City police force whether they would like to turn Harlem over to local mercenaries to patrol, while they hold on to Wall Street, the Upper East Side, Madison Avenue, and so on—if you asked the New York City police force that, I'm sure they'd be delighted. Who wants to patrol Harlem?

Well, that's in effect what's happening in the Occupied Territories right now: the idea is, see if you can get local mercenaries, who are still always under your whip, to run the place for you, while you continue integrating the area into Israel. Actually, some Israeli commentators have used the term "neocolonialism" to describe what's being done with the Territories, and that's essentially correct, I think.[114]

In fact, I think what's been taking place in the Middle East is really just a part of something much broader that's happened throughout the West in recent years, particularly since the Gulf War: there's been a real revival of traditional European racism and imperialism, in a very dramatic way. I mean, people often talk about neo-fascists being on the rise, but I think that's really missing the point: they're just the froth on the surface. In my view, what we're seeing now is a profound revival of pure old-fashioned racist imperialism, with regard to the entire Third World. You see it in articles by British journalists in the *New York Times Magazine* about how the best thing we can do for Africa is to recolonize it; it shows up at the economic level in structural adjustment programs, which are a big part of how we siphon off the wealth of the Third World to the rich countries; the anti-immigrant campaigns in the U.S. and Europe are a part of it; this program for the Palestinians is another part of it—and one could go on and on.[115] The idea is, "We smashed up the world and stole everything from it—now we're not going to let anyone come and take any piece of it back." That's an attitude I see right on the surface all over the place in the West these days.

So to go back to your question, the Oslo Agreement was just a complete capitulation. I mean, I'm not saying it shouldn't have been signed—like, maybe that's the best that the Palestinians could do given the state they were in. But we shouldn't have any illusions about it: all of their problems are exactly the same, maybe worse. And unless there's support from the West . . . I don't know what to say. Without support from inside the imperial countries, no group in the Third World has any hope. The Palestinians certainly don't.

# 6

# Community Activists

*Based on discussions in British Columbia, Massachusetts, Illinois,
Maryland, and Wyoming in 1989 and between 1993 and 1996.*

### Discussion Circle

. . . I hardly know what to say. What all of you said reflects, I think very
accurately, the state that we're in. Any place I go to, there are people like
you. They're all interested in significant, important problems—problems of
personal empowerment, of understanding the world, of working with others, of just finding out what your values are; of trying to figure out how people can control their own lives, and helping each other to do it. We're all
facing essentially the same fact: there's no structure of popular institutions
around within which we can work.

You don't have to go back very far in history to find that in past days, a
group like us wouldn't have been meeting in a place like this: we would
have been meeting in the labor union headquarters. There's still a residue of
that in parts of the world. For instance, I was in England last week giving
political talks, and talks in England are not in churches or on college campuses, they're in a guild hall—because in England there's still a residue of
the period when there was a popular movement, a workers' movement,
with its own media, its own places of gathering, its own ways of bringing
people together. There was a time when we had a working-class culture
here too. I mean, I can remember it—barely, because I was a child—but
there was a live working-class culture in the United States not that long ago.
My family was in it, that's how I got my political education. A lot of it was
centered around the Communist Party [U.S.A.], which for the people who
were involved in it didn't mean supporting Stalin's crimes, it meant saving
people's lives in the South, and unionizing industry, and being at the front
of every civil rights struggle, doing everything that was important.

I mean, the American Communist Party had a lot of terrible things about
it, but it also had a lot of very good things too. And one of them was this—

177

I mean, that was a *life*. The Communist Party wasn't something you voted for, it was something where if you were an unemployed seamstress in New York and you wanted to get away for the summer, they had a summer camp where you could go and be with your friends, get into the Catskill Mountains, that sort of thing. And it was picnics, and meetings, and concerts, fighting on picket lines, demonstrations, the whole business. That was all just normal life, it was very organic.

And they had their own media. In fact, you don't have to go back too far in the United States, a little earlier than that, to find working-class and community-based newspapers that were roughly at the scale of the mainstream capitalist press. So a journal like *Appeal to Reason*, which was sort of a socialist journal in the early part of the century, had I think about three quarters of a million subscribers—meaning who knows how many people actually read it.[1] And that was in a much smaller population than today of course, much smaller.

Now, we're not in anything like that situation: we don't have parties, we don't have media, we don't have stable institutions—so, this group isn't meeting in a union hall, because there isn't any such thing. On the other hand, we have other advantages. There's a tremendous diversity and range of interests and concerns now, and an awful lot of people are involved. And that gives us a kind of strength: an organized, centralized movement can easily be crushed; a very diverse movement that's rooted all over the society—well, you can get rid of this piece and that piece and the other piece, but it'll just come back up somewhere else. So there are both strengths and weaknesses, and I think we should recognize that.

My own feeling is that the right approach is to build on the strengths: to recognize what's healthy and solid about having not hundreds, but thousands of flowers blooming all over the place—people with parallel concerns, maybe differently focused, but at the core sort of similar values and a similar interest in empowerment, in learning, in helping people understand how to defend themselves against external power and take control of their own lives, in reaching out your hand to people who need it. All the things that you people have talked about—that's a common array of concerns. And the fact that there's a tremendous diversity can be a real advantage—it can be a real way of learning, of learning about yourself, and what you care about, and what you want to do, and so on. But of course, if it's going to bring about real change, that broad array of concerns is going to require some form of integration and inter-communication and collaboration among its various sub-parts.

Now, we're not going to develop that sort of integration through the mainstream institutions—that would be crazy. I mean, you should not expect an institution to say, "Help me destroy myself," that's not the way institutions function. And if anybody *inside* the institution tried to do that, they wouldn't be inside it much longer. Now, that's not to say that you can do nothing if you're already in something like the mass media. People who have seeped in from the popular movements can have effects—and people outside them can also have effects, just by barraging the editors and so on. I mean, the editors don't like people coming to their doors and causing trouble any more than politicians do, or businessmen do. And if you come and you bother them, and give them material, and pressure them, you can sometimes get results. But in the end, there really are only small changes that can be made within the existing institutions—because they've got their own commitments, which are basically to private power. In the case of the media, they have a commitment to indoctrination in the interests of power, and that imposes pretty strict limits on what they can do.

So the answer is, we've got to create alternatives, and the alternatives have got to integrate these lots and lots of different interests and concerns into a movement—or maybe not *one* necessarily, which somebody could then cut the head off of, but a series of interconnected ones: lots of associations of people with similar concerns, who've got in mind the other people next door who have related concerns, and who can get together with them to work for changes. Maybe then we can ultimately construct serious alternative media—I mean, not "serious" in the sense that the *concerns* of existing alternative media aren't serious, but serious in scale, at the point where they can consistently present people with a different picture of the world, a picture different than the one you get from an indoctrination system based on private control over resources. And as to how you can do that, well, I don't think there's any big secret about it—if there's any big secret about getting social change, I've never heard of it.

WOMAN: *Just keep organizing.*

Yes—large-scale social change in the past and major social revolutions in the past, so far as I know, have come about just because lots of people, working wherever they are, have worked hard, and have looked around to find other people who are working hard, and have tried to work together with them when they find them. I think every social change in history, from the democratic revolutions to things like the Civil Rights Movement, has worked that way. It's mostly just a question of scale and dedication. There are plenty of resources around that people can use; they're very scattered—but part of the way the institutions protect themselves is to *keep* them scattered. It's very important for institutions of concentrated power to keep people alone and isolated: that way they're ineffective, they can't defend themselves against indoctrination, they can't even figure out what they think.

So I think it makes sense to look at what the institutions are doing and to take that almost as a key: what they're trying to do is what we're trying to combat. If they're keeping people isolated and separate, well, we're trying to do the opposite, we're trying to bring them together. So in your local community, you want to have "unity groups" or whatever they're called, I don't know, " 'left' unity groups"—I don't even like the word. But you want to turn them into sources of alternative action that people can get involved with, and can join in together to fight the effects of atomization. There are plenty of resources around, enormous numbers of people are interested—and if you don't see organizations that are doing things, well, figure out what you can do, and do it yourself. I don't think there are any secrets.

MAN: *The greatest source of information for me in these past couple years has been our co-op radio. And I trust everyone here supports co-op radio— if not, well, you should. Because we have to cultivate and develop any form of alternate media that is working, or that we can think of that will work. So I just want to say, hats off to co-op radio: I'm glad you're here.*

It's certainly true—when you go to towns or communities that have alternative radio or other media that involve community participation, the general mood is strikingly different. And the reason is, people there are constantly challenged with a different point of view, and they can participate in the debates, they're not just passive spectators. That's the way you learn, that's the way you discover who you are, and what you really want, it's how you figure out your own values and gain understanding. You have to be able to knock ideas off other people and hear them get beaten down in order to find out what you actually think. That's learning, as distinct from indoctrination—and listener-supported radio is very good in that respect. But the same is true of the whole tremendous network of alternative media that exists by now on just about every imaginable issue, all over Canada and the United States.

For instance, I don't know how many of you know the journal Z *Magazine*, but it's a political journal that's an offshoot of South End Press, which brings together interests of essentially the sort that you've all been raising here. And it's national, and you read it in one place and see that people are thinking about the same things somewhere else, and you write a letter in, or propose an article and so on—that's the type of serious intercommunication that we want to foster. After all, we're living in a world where you don't have to talk just to the person who lives next door, we have the same interests as people all across the world, and these days we can communicate with them. In fact, as they develop, things like this could really help to unify the popular movements, and they should be pressed as far as they can go, I think.[2]

## The Early Peace Movement and a Change in the 1970s

MAN: *Noam, there are two contradictory strains that I can identify in your work on the question of "hope." On the one hand, you speak about the ef-*

*forts organizing on behalf of Central America and East Timor and other activist causes—some of the successes that people like us have had. But on the other hand, I hear you always talking about the destructions the U.S. and other powers are causing all over the world, and it seems to me that you draw a picture of an overall global trend which is very despairing. I'm wondering, how do you deal with that tension personally—do you just keep doing what you do because it's the right thing to do, or do you actually have a sense of hope in it?*

Do I personally? Well, first of all, I don't think that matters very much—because that's only a reflection of *my* personality and mood, and who gives a damn? But if I try to be realistic about it and ask myself what I could say that would mean something to someone else—well, you know, twenty-five years ago I did it because I thought you just have to do it, you can't look yourself in the mirror if you don't do it. I didn't think that there was any hope at all at the time. I mean, when I got involved in the anti-Vietnam War movement, it seemed to me *impossible* that it would ever have any effect. In fact, the few of us who got involved in the early Sixties confidently expected that the only consequence of what we were doing would be that we'd spend years and years in jail and destroy our lives; I came very close to that, incidentally.

I mean, just to tell you personally, when I got started actively in the peace movement my wife went back to college, because we figured that somebody was going to have to support the kids, I wasn't going to be able to. And in fact, there were only two reasons why that didn't happen. One was, the F.B.I. was too incompetent and ideologically fanatic to figure out what I was doing—that's not a joke actually, and it's something to bear in mind. And the other was, the Tet Offensive happened in 1968, and it changed U.S. government policy towards the war, so they began to cancel the prosecutions of activists that were under way. In fact, the Tet Offensive even changed people's heads—you know who was prosecuting those trials? Ramsey Clark, just to illustrate how things have changed. [Clark was President Johnson's Attorney General and is now a radical political activist.]

But those were pretty difficult days: it was real confrontation with state power, and it was getting ugly, especially if you were involved in resistance, helping deserters, that sort of thing. And it was just *impossible* at that time to imagine that anything would come out of it. And that was wrong, a lot came out of it—not out of what I did, but out of what lots and lots of people were doing all over the country. A lot came out of it. So looking back, I think my evaluation of the "hope" was much too pessimistic: it was based on a complete misunderstanding. I was sort of believing what I read. And the immediate experience supported it—like, right off, you found that when you tried to give a talk you needed two hundred cops to save you from being lynched. But it didn't take too long for that to change, and in a couple years it had changed very significantly.

Now, I don't think what happened with the movements in the 1960s led to very much sophistication and insight, frankly—but I think what happened in the later years did. And exactly how that worked I don't really understand at all. But something happened in the 1970s that just changed things—people were looking at things differently. It wasn't just, "I hate that they're dropping napalm on babies," it was, "I really want to change the world, and I don't like coercion and control," and that kind of thing. That happened in the Seventies, and you can certainly see the consequences. I mean, in the 1960s, I never even talked about the nature of the institutions or capitalism—it was just too exotic. Now I don't cut corners: I can be giving a talk in eastern Kentucky or in central Iowa or something, and I say exactly what I think. And people understand it—they may not agree, they may be surprised, but they want to listen and think about it, and they take it seriously. So I think there's reason to be hopeful.

But on the other hand, don't forget, the people with power in the society are watching all these things too, and *they* have institutions. They can learn, they can see what didn't work the last time and do it better the next time—and they have plenty of resources to try out different strategies. On our side what happens is, people forget. I mean, it *does* take skills to organize, it's not that simple. You want to organize a demonstration or a letter-writing campaign or do fundraising, it does take skills—and those skills tend to get lost. You can see it happening over and over. The people who do it the first time around work hard and learn how to do things, then get burnt out and drift off to something else. Then another issue comes up, and others with a roughly similar understanding, but maybe a little younger or less experienced, have to start over again and learn all the skills from the beginning. How do you organize a meeting? How do you get leaflets out? Is it worth approaching the press? In what way do you approach them? Well, since we don't have stable popular institutions, all these things that you kind of get in your bones after a while if you do a lot of organizing do not become part of the common lore that the movements could call on and improve upon, if we only had more integration and more continuity. But for people with power, there *is* a common lore, and they *do* improve upon it.

In fact, this is part of an ongoing battle that stretches back to the seventeenth century. If you go back to the beginnings of the modern version of democracy, it's the same conflict: people are trying to figure out ways to control their own lives, and people with power are trying to stop them. Now, until we dissolve the centers of private power and really get popular control over how the most crucial decisions in the society get made—like the decisions about what's produced and what's invested and so on—this battle is always going to go on. But yes, there have been both victories and defeats: you can look at the course of events and see many significant victories by gangsters and murderers and thugs, and you can also see many respects in which people have been able to stop them, and limit their victories, and offer people an opportunity to keep living and to improve their lives. So it doesn't make sense to be either optimistic or pessimistic, I think. You just look at what's happening and try to do the best you can under those circumstances.

WOMAN: *Can I give it a whack? For years I've been working with people who are doing twenty-five years in prison and never getting out, that sort of thing. To answer the question, "How do you keep going?"—I figure, the most pessimistic way to look at it is, it's really bad: fifty thousand nuclear bombs floating around, we don't need some dumb American President to put his finger on the wrong button. I figure, it's a miracle that we're here, realistically, let's face it.*

It is.

WOMAN: *Okay, so if you accept that, you have two choices: you can cut your throat and forget about it, or you can keep fighting. If you're going to keep fighting, then you've got to fight to win, and to survive. So what you do is, you find yourself a corner that you can fight really well from, and that you like, and that you fit in—and you give it the works, have a good time. That way you can keep your sanity, you don't get overwhelmed with the whole enormous situation, and you can accomplish something. And as I say, you have a good time while you're doing it—that's the way I keep going.*

MAN: *But do you ever succeed, or do you just keep fighting?*

Well, see, you *have* succeeded—things are better than they would have been if you hadn't done it.

ANOTHER WOMAN: *And we should remember that the mainstream media obviously won't publicize and draw attention to the successes—so we have to keep reminding ourselves of just how much we have achieved. I think we get burned out when we stop reminding ourselves of that.*

That's right, we should always bear that in mind—that they're *not* going to tell us we're succeeding, it would be against their interests to tell us that. The media's part of what popular organizing has to oppose, remember. And they're not going to function in a way so as to self-destruct.

For instance, take this supposed big phenomenon that swept the country in the 1970s, the "Culture of Narcissism," and the "Me Generation" and so on. I'm just convinced that that whole thing was crafted by the public relations industry to tell mainly young people, "Look, this is who you are—you don't care about all this solidarity and sympathy and helping people" that had started to break out. And of course, that's what they *would* do. In fact, they shouldn't get their salaries if they don't do things like that. We should *expect* them to do it, we should expect them to tell us: "You guys can't do anything, you're all alone, you're each separate; you've never achieved anything, and you never *will* achieve anything." *Of course* they should tell us that—and they should even tell us, "You don't *want* to achieve anything, all you want to do is consume more."

As long as power's concentrated, that's what it's going to tell us— "There's no point in working to help other people, you don't care about them, you're just out for yourself." Sure it's going to tell us that, because that's what's in its interests. There's no point in telling ourselves, "They're lying to us" over and over again. Of course they are; it's like saying the sun's setting or something like that. Obviously they are.

So what we want to try to do is develop stable enough structures so that we can learn these kinds of things and not keep getting beaten down by the indoctrination—so we don't have to keep fighting the same battles over and over again, we can go on to new ones, and bigger ones, better ones. I think that could be done; slowly, over time.

MAN: *Do you see any of those sorts of continuing progressive structures developing these days in the United States?*

There isn't a lot, it's mostly local. So I'll go to some place like Detroit, say, and there'll be a meeting like this with people from different parts of the city who are working on different things—but many of them don't even know about the others. Everything is pretty much fractionated. Now, if you go to a small town which has listener-supported radio—like Boulder, Colorado, for instance—it's different, it's unified. And part of the reason it's unified is because of one community radio station and a couple of journals and so on that everybody can be a part of. Or I remember going to some town in New Hampshire which happened to have a movement bookstore, and everybody went to the bookstore to find out what was going on, you'd go there and look at what's on the wall and stick together that way. You do find things like that around the country.

But take Boston, where there's nothing central to bring people together—there's no community radio, there's no community newspaper. I mean, there are lots of people doing all sorts of activist work, but they don't even know about each other: there's a group in one section working on Bikes for Nicaragua, there's a group in another section of the city working on a Sister Cities program for Central America, they don't even know of each other's existence.

## The Nuclear Freeze Movement

WOMAN: *What else do you feel we can learn from organizations you don't think are going about it the right way?*

Well, there are plenty of groups around that are doing things I don't think are very constructive, even though I'm often a member of them and give them support and so on. Take the nuclear freeze campaign, for example: I really thought they were going about it the wrong way. The nuclear freeze campaign was in a way one of the most successful popular organizing movements in history: they managed to get 75 percent of the American population in favor of a nuclear freeze at a time when there was no articulate public support for that position—there wasn't a newspaper, a political figure, anybody who came out publicly for it.[3] Now, in a way that's a tremendous achievement. But frankly I didn't think it was an achievement, I thought the disarmament movement was going to collapse—and in fact, it did collapse. And the reason it collapsed is, it wasn't based on anything: it was based on nothing except people signing a petition.

I mean, if you sign a petition it's kind of nice—but that's the end of it, you just go back home and do whatever you were doing: there's no continuity, there's no real engagement, it's not sustained activity that builds up a community of activism. Well, an awful lot of the political work I see in the United States is of that type.

Now, if we had stable popular institutions, we'd be able to remember how we failed the last time, instead of somebody else doing it all over again and making the same mistakes—we'd know that's not the way to do anything. The nuclear freeze movement amounted to a public opinion poll, basically: they found out that three times as many people want the government to spend the money on Medicare and things like that as want it spent on nuclear weapons. So what? What are they going to do about it? Nothing. So all these nuclear freeze people did was answer a poll question—that's not organizing.

I think an awful lot of movement activity goes into things like that, and it doesn't get anywhere—in fact, that's what leads to burn-out. I mean, you had all these people collecting all these signatures, and they worked hard, they got so many signatures you could show that almost all of the country wants a nuclear freeze. Then they went to the Democratic Party Convention [in 1984] and presented their results, and everybody there said, "Gee, that's really nice that you did that, we're going to support you all the way"—then the Democrats went off to the election and never mentioned it again, unless they were talking in some town where they figured they could score some easy points by referring to it: you know, "We've got to remember in this town you want to say so on and so forth." That's the kind of thing that gets people frustrated, and makes them give up. But that's because they started with illusions about how power operates and how you effect change—and we shouldn't have those illusions, any more than we should have illusions about whether the media's telling you the truth. If you don't have the illusions, then you don't get burnt out by the failure—and the way we overcome the illusions is by developing our own institutions, where we can learn from experiences like this.

For instance, if we see a big organizing effort where everybody signs the petitions and some people try to introduce the issue into the '84 Democratic Party platform, and it has absolutely no effect, and a year later Mikhail

Gorbachev [Soviet leader] declares a unilateral nuclear test freeze and *still* there's no effect—well, we should be learning something.[4] Then we should be carrying on to the next step. But that wasn't the reaction of the nuclear freeze organizers. The reaction among the organizers wasn't, "Well, we obviously misunderstood the way things work"—it was, "We did the right thing, but we partially failed: we convinced the population, but we didn't manage to convince the elites, so now let's convince the elites." You know, "We'll go talk to the strategic analysts, who are confused—they don't understand what we understand—and we'll explain to them why a nuclear freeze would be a good thing." And in fact, that's the direction a lot of the disarmament movement took after that: the people went off and got themselves MacArthur Fellowships and so on, and then they went around "convincing" the strategic analysts.[5]

Well, that's one of the ways in which you can kid yourself into believing that you're still doing your work, when really you're being bought off—because there's nothing that elites like better than saying, "Oh, come convince me." That stops you from organizing, and getting people involved, and causing disruption, because now you're talking to some elite smart guy—and you can do that forever: any argument you can give in favor of it, he can give an argument against it, and it just keeps going. And also, you get respectable, and you're invited to lunch at the Harvard Faculty Club, and everybody pays attention to you and loves you, and it's all great. That's in fact the direction in which the nuclear freeze movement went—and that's a mistake. And we ought to be aware of those mistakes and learn from them: if you're getting accepted in elite circles, chances are very strong that you're doing something wrong—I mean, for very simple reasons. Why should they have any respect for people who are trying to undermine their power? It doesn't make any sense.

## Awareness and Actions

MAN: *A lot of the activists I work with operate under the assumption that if we can just make people aware, everything's going to work out and there'll be a change. Even with c.d. [civil disobedience] actions protesting nuclear weapons, that's been my assumption too: get people to see us doing it, hold up our signs. But it seems like that's not all that is needed, really— what more, would you say, besides education?*

Education is just the beginning—and furthermore, there are situations where you can get everybody aware and on your side, and they still won't be able to do anything. Like, take a look at Haiti. I don't think there's much doubt about what 90 percent of the population there wants, and they're aware of it—they just can't do anything about it without getting slaughtered. So there's a whole series of things which have to happen, and they *begin* with awareness; you don't do anything without awareness, obviously—you don't do anything unless you're aware that there's something that ought to be done, so that's the beginning almost by definition. But real awareness in fact comes about through practice and experience with the world. It's not, first you become aware and *then* you start doing things; you become aware *through* doing things.

For instance, you become aware of the limits of reformist politics by trying it. In my view, you should always push all of the opportunities to their limits—partly because sometimes you can get some useful results that help people, but primarily because pretty soon you'll find out what those limits *are*, and you'll understand *why* there are limits; you'll gain awareness you can't gain from a lecture. I mean, you can hear all the lectures you like about the way that power works, but you learn it very fast when you actually confront it, without the lectures. So there's an interaction between awareness and action—and sometimes the steps you have to take to make changes require taking things to the level of violent revolutionary struggle. Like, if people in Haiti were in a position to overthrow the military there by force, in my opinion they ought to do it. Sometimes it comes to that.

As to the c.d. demonstrations about nuclear weapons, just personally speaking, I had a lot of disagreements with some of my friends on that, people I really respect a lot, like the people in Plowshares [a group active on disarmament issues]. I mean, I think these are all tactical questions—like, I don't think there's any question of principle involved in whether you should smash a missile nose-cone or not, it's not like a contract between you and God or something. The question is, what are the effects? And there I thought the effects were negative. It seemed to me that the effects of what they were doing were, first of all, to remove *them* from political action, because they were going to be in jail for twenty years, and also to tie up tons of money and effort in courts, which is absolutely the worst place to be. I mean, the worst waste of time and effort and money in the world is a court—so any time you can stay out of courts, you're well off. But the second thing is, I don't think that they reached people—because they didn't prepare the ground for it. Like, if you smash up a missile nose-cone in some town where people are working at the missile plant and there's no other way they can make a living, and they haven't heard of any reason why we shouldn't have missiles, that doesn't educate anybody, it just gets them mad at you.

So I think these tactical questions have to be very carefully thought through—you can't really predict with much certainty, but as well as you can, you have to make a guess as to what the effect of the tactic is going to be. If the effect is going to be to build up awareness, that's good. But of course, awareness is only the beginning, because people can be aware and still not do anything—for instance, maybe they're afraid they'll lose their jobs. And obviously you can't criticize people for worrying about that; they've got kids, they've got to live. That's fair enough. It's hard to struggle for your rights—you usually suffer.

## Leaders and Movements

*WOMAN: As an activist, I think we also have an obligation to get across the fact that we have fun doing this—that we get nurtured by working on these issues which are close to our essence. If we're looking to the long term, and building up the types of institutions you're talking about, we have to project that a lot more than we do, almost as a way of recruitment. Too often, people's image of "the activist" is of someone who's always burned out. We have to create a culture that is engaging to people and exciting, so that it doesn't just seem like we're putting in the hours and chanting radical slogans.*

See, I think the people who've really made social movements successful have been the ones who *did* those things. They're gone from history of course: none of the books mention them, nobody knows the names of the people who really made the social movements in history work—but that's the way it's always happened, I think.

And this is even true of the recent ones, like the anti-war movement in the 1960s. So there are a lot of books coming out these days that tell you what went on in the S.D.S. [Students for a Democratic Society] office, or what one smart guy said to some other smart guy—but none of that had anything to do with why the peace movement in the Sixties became a huge mass movement. From my own personal experience in it, and that's only a little piece of it obviously, I know who was doing the *really* important things, and I remember them—like, I remember that this student worked hard to set up that demonstration, and that's why I had a chance to talk there; and they were bringing other people in to get involved; they were enjoying what they were doing, and communicating that to others somehow. That's what makes popular movements work—but of course, that's all going to be gone from history: what will be left in history is just the fluff on the top.

*MAN: I'm curious what you think about some of the more famous leaders of change—like Martin Luther King or Mahatma Gandhi, for instance. You don't ever seem to mention them when you speak. Why is that?*

Well, let's take Martin Luther King. See, I think Martin Luther King was an important person, but I do not think that he was a big agent of change. In fact, I think Martin Luther King was able to play a role in bringing about change only because the *real* agents of change were doing a lot of work. And the real agents of change were people working at the grassroots level, like S.N.C.C. [Student Nonviolent Coordinating Committee] activists, for example.

Look, part of the whole technique of disempowering people is to make sure that the real agents of change fall out of history, and are never recognized in the culture for what they are. So it's necessary to distort history and make it look as if Great Men did everything—that's part of how you teach people they can't do anything, they're helpless, they just have to wait for some Great Man to come along and do it for them.

But just take a look at the Civil Rights Movement in the United States, for example—take, say, Rosa Parks [who triggered the 1955 Montgomery Bus Boycott protesting racial segregation]. I mean, the *story* about Rosa Parks is, this courageous black woman suddenly decided, "I've had enough, I'm not going to sit in the back of the bus." Well, that's sort of half true—but only half. Rosa Parks came out of a community, a well-organized community, which in fact had Communist Party roots if you trace it back, things like Highlander School [a Tennessee school for educating political organizers] and so on.[6] But it was a community of people who were working together and had decided on a plan for breaking through the system of segregation—Rosa Parks was just an agent of that plan.

Okay, that's all out of history. What's in history is, one person had the courage to do something—which she did. But not on her own. Nobody does anything on their own. Rosa Parks came out of an organized community of committed people, people who'd been working together for change for a very long time. And that's how it always works.

The same was true of Martin Luther King: he was able to appear and give public speeches because S.N.C.C. workers and Freedom Riders and others had prepared the ground—and taken a brutal beating for it. And a lot of those people were pretty privileged kids, remember: they *chose* it, they didn't have to do it. *They're* the Civil Rights Movement. Martin Luther King was important because he could stand up there and get the cameras, but these other people were the real Civil Rights Movement. I'm sure he would have said the same thing too, incidentally—or at least, he should have.

As for Gandhi, again it's the same story. He had a very mixed record, actually—but the point is, it was the people on the ground who did the work that prepared the basis for Gandhi to become prominent, and sort of articulate things. And when you look at any other popular movement, I think it's always like that.

## Levels of Change

MAN: *Noam, as we work to build up that kind of movement, what do you think are the best methods we should be using as pressure tactics right now? Should we be doing the traditional reformist kind of steps—lobbying legislators, writing letters, trying to get Democrats into office—or should we go with more of a direct action kind of approach, demonstrations and civil disobedience and so on?*

Well, those are tactical decisions *you* have to make—the only people qualified to make that kind of decision are the ones who live in a place, and can see what's going on. So really it would be ridiculous for me to have an opinion on it.

Demonstrations are often the right thing to do, you just have to make tactical decisions—but keep in mind, they're just as reformist as lobbying your legislature. And there's nothing wrong with that. I mean, even if you're the most extreme revolutionary in the world, you're going to use whatever methods are available to try to ameliorate things, and then if ultimately you run into limits where powerful institutions will not permit more reform, well, then you go beyond it. But first you have to reach those limits—and there are many ways of reaching them. One way is lobbying your legislator, one may be another political party, others are demonstrations—which simply change the conditions under which powerful people make decisions. But that does have an effect.

Let me just give you an example. There's a part of the *Pentagon Papers* [the leaked official Defense Department planning record of U.S. involvement in Vietnam] which is considered politically incorrect—it doesn't appear in big histories and nobody discusses it, because it's just too revealing. It's the part that deals with the time right after the Tet Offensive. Right after the Tet Offensive in 1968, everyone recognized that the Vietnam War was going to take a long time, it wasn't going to be possible to win it quickly—so major decisions had to be made about strategy and policy. Well, the Joint Chiefs of Staff were asked by General Westmoreland, the top American commander in Vietnam, to send 200,000 more troops over to the war—and they refused, they didn't want to do it. And the reason is, they said they were afraid they might have to use the troops here in the United States to put down a civil war: they said they were going to need the troops at home for "civil disorder control," as they put it, and therefore they didn't want to send them to Vietnam.[7] These guys thought the society was going to crack up in 1968, because people here were just too opposed to what they were doing.

In fact, the "civil disorder" was also one of the reasons why a group called the "Wise Men" came to Washington with a lot of money in their pockets, and shortly after, in an unusually blatant power-play, essentially told President Johnson, "You're through: you're not running for reelection."[8] And he didn't. We started withdrawing from Vietnam, and we entered into peace negotiations, and so on. Well, a lot of public protest here and huge demonstrations and direct actions were a big part of the reason behind that.

So, yes, demonstrations and resistance can have effects—but they're no more revolutionary than talking to your legislator. They don't affect power, they don't change the institutions of power, they just change the decisions that will be made *within* those institutions. And that's a fine thing to do. There's nothing wrong with that, it helps a lot of people. I mean, I don't think the institutions of power should exist either, but that's another question for right now.

MAN: *What would you say are the most important causes for us to be focusing on, then—I mean, what do you think can actually be done by activists working today?*

Well, everything can be done—everything can be done up to the point of eliminating all structures of authority and repression: they're human institutions, they can be dismantled. If you ask what's most important at this point—well, you know, that's not the kind of thing you just decide right on the spot, those are decisions that come by serious thought and discussion in groups like this, among people who are really trying to institute change.

I mean, you have to start with where the world is. Like, you don't start by saying, "Okay, let's overthrow transnational corporations"—because right now it's just not within range. So you start by saying, "Look, here's where the world is, what can we begin to do?" Well, you can begin to do things which will get people to understand better what the real source of power is, and just how much they can achieve if they get involved in political activism. And once you've broken through the pretense, you just construct organizations—that's it. You work on the things that are worth working on. If it's taking control of your community, it's that. If it's gaining control of your workplace, it's that. If it's working on solidarity, it's that. If it's taking care of the homeless, it's that.

With regard to the domestic scene, take the fact that the criminal justice system increasingly is becoming a system for targeting the poor and minorities, who are being turned into people under military occupation. Look, that's an easy one to change—you really just have to change public opinion on that one. You aren't striking at the core of private power when you begin to have a civilized criminal justice system instead of a brutal, barbaric one. So that's an example of something I think is changeable. Or you could start by getting us to stop torturing people in the Third World, right? Easy things to do are, stop killing children in Cuba, stop massacring people in East Timor, get people in the United States to realize that Palestinians are human beings—those are easy things. So let's do those, first do the easy things.

On things like what's taking place in the international economy, you're getting into harder territory—because there, crucial interests of authoritarian institutions are at stake. And at that point, you're going to have to face the fact, which sooner or later we're going to have to face after all, that maybe the most totalitarian institution in human history—or certainly close to it—is a corporation: it's a centrally-managed institution in which authority is structured strictly from top to bottom, control is in the hands of owners and investors, if you're inside the organization you take orders from above and transmit them down, if you're outside it there are only extremely weak popular controls, which indeed are fast eroding. And this isn't some new insight of mine, incidentally—for example, it was pointed out by Thomas Jefferson in his later years, which were only the early days of corporations. Jefferson warned that if power was going to shift into the hands of what he called "banking institutions and moneyed incorporations," then the democratic experiment would be over: we'd have a form of absolutism worse than what the colonists had struggled against.[9]

Okay, Thomas Jefferson is not exactly a figure who's off the mainstream spectrum in American history, so this is not some new off-the-wall insight—it's as American as apple pie, and we should recognize what Thomas Jefferson could see. But when you do recognize it, you realize it's a hard nut to crack—because these are *enormous* agglomerations of power, indeed concentrating, and indeed transnational, which are almost totally protected from public scrutiny and popular participation. And that's just got to change.

After all, why do corporations have the rights they do? Why are they treated as "immortal persons," contrary to the warnings of people like Adam Smith and others?[10] It's not by nature—in fact, these rights weren't even granted by Congress, this happened because of decisions made in courts by judges and lawyers, which simply changed the world totally.[11]

So, if you ask what should be done: well, I don't think any sane human being can look around at the world and not figure out things that have to be done—take a walk through the streets, you'll find plenty of things that have to be done. So you know, you get started doing them. But you're not going to be able to do them alone. Like, if you take a walk down the streets and say, "That ought to be done," nothing's going to happen. On the other hand, if people become organized enough to act together, yeah, then you can achieve things. And there's no particular limit to what you can achieve. I mean, that's why we don't still have slavery.

MAN: *Could you mention some specific organizations that we could try to link up with and network with, which are doing a good job of working on these problems?*

Well, a lot of organizations are involved, from a lot of different points of view. For example, at one level—which is important, though of course superficial—Ralph Nader's Public Citizen is involved [the group works primarily on consumer issues]. That's important, like I say, but not really touching the basic structure of power.

Beyond that, if the American labor movement ever recovers the insights that ordinary working people had a hundred years ago, then it will be working on them too. So if you look back a hundred years—and even much more recently than that, in fact—you'll find that the major goal of the labor movement in the United States was achieving industrial democracy: placing the workplace under democratic control.[12] And it wasn't because they'd read Marx—people figured that out for themselves long before Marx: it was just the natural response to industrial capitalism. And in fact, Marx didn't say much about it anyway. So it could be the labor movement that's doing it.

But there's a ton of activism going on around the country apart from that—and though right now it's focused on pretty narrow issues, ultimately the people are all talking about the same thing: illegitimate authority of one form or another. I mean, if you want a list of organizations to contact, it's easy to find—just write to any of the major progressive funding organizations, like Resist in Boston, for example, and they'll be delighted to give you a list of the couple hundred groups they've funded in the last few years: you'll find among them groups involved in any political cause you can imagine.[13] Also, in any major city there's typically some church which is a coordinating center for all kinds of peace and justice activities—and you'll find anything in the world there. That happens everywhere, and they'll be thrilled if you help direct people to them.

## Non-Violence

MAN: *Mr. Chomsky, I've always hoped we could disassemble corporate capitalism through non-violent yet very determined and organized resistance, and the creation of alternative institutions that could someday take over and diffuse power peacefully. I'm wondering, do you think that kind of hope for non-violence is at all realistic—and how do you feel about the use of violence in general?*

Well, like I say, nobody really knows anything much about tactics—at least I don't. But I think you have to think through the non-violence question in detail. I mean, anybody is going to try to do things non-violently if possible: what's the point of violence? But when you begin to encroach on power, you may find that it's necessary to defend your rights—and defense of your rights sometimes does require violence, then either you use it or you don't, depending on your moral values.

So take a look at American labor history. Around the first half of this century, hundreds of American workers were simply killed by security forces, just for trying to organize.[14] The United States has an unusually violent labor history, so violent in fact that if you read the right-wing British press in the 1890s—the *right-wing* British press, like the London *Times*—they just couldn't understand the brutality of the treatment of American workers and their lack of rights.[15] And it's not because the *workers* were trying to be violent—it's because people with power were violently protecting their power against people trying to get elementary rights.

Alright, if you're a pacifist or something, you have to ask yourself some questions at that point: are people allowed to defend themselves by force when they're attacked by force? Well, okay, people's values may differ on that, but those are at least the questions.

My own opinion is that popular movements should try a lot of tactics, but even things that are non-violent on their face could *become* violent. For example, one thing that I think is important is the building of a political party which could enter the political arena and represent the population, not just business interests—I mean, it's certainly conceivable that there could be a party like that in the United States. But if such a party ever got any power, people with power in the society would defend themselves against it. And at that point everyone's got to decide: do you use violence to protect your rights or don't you? Look, violence usually comes from the powerful—people may talk about it coming from the revolutionaries, but that's typically because they're attacked and they then defend themselves with violence.

The same question also arises with another thing that I think has to go on now—the building up of alternative media, and of networks of activist organizations which could help bring people together to fight the effects of indoctrination, like we've been talking about. Again, that's non-violent—but only up to the point where it starts to have the effect of undermining corporate power, when then you may discover that it's not going to be non-violent anymore, because the rich may find ways of defending themselves with violence. So talking about non-violence is easy, but personally I can't really see taking it as an absolute principle.

Now, of course, there are also ways of *transcending* violence. Like, if enough people got together and took over a factory, let's say, the police would try to stop them—but ultimately the police and soldiers are just other people, and if understanding and solidarity were to spread enough, they *wouldn't* stop them. So in a sense, one answer to your question just has to be more solidarity, broader solidarity—so they can't bring in soldiers from someplace else to smash people up. But that's going to be hard, we simply have to face that—it's not just going to happen on its own. The fact that societies today are so stratified and divided by hatreds means that elites don't have to go very far away to bring in people who are willing to repress you.

But that can change—in fact, it *has* to change, because there's a real limit to how much popular movements can defend themselves with violence and still maintain a popular-democratic character, in my opinion. To the extent that the defense would require guns and warfare, I think that any revolutionary developments would probably decline, and the chance of real changes would likely be destroyed. So the hope ultimately lies in more international solidarity, I think, and in the political appeal of what you're doing to other people in this country, and elsewhere around the world as well.

## Transcending Capitalism

MAN: *Referring back to your comments about escaping from or doing away with capitalism, I'm wondering what workable scheme you would put in its place?*

Me?

MAN: *Or what would you suggest to others who might be in a position to set it up and get it going?*

Well, I think that what used to be called, centuries ago, "wage slavery" is intolerable. I mean, I do not think that people ought to be forced to rent themselves in order to survive. I think that the economic institutions ought to be run democratically—by their participants, and by the communities in which they live. And I think that through various forms of free association and federalism, it's possible to imagine a society working like that. I mean, I don't think you can lay it out in *detail*—nobody's smart enough to design a society; you've got to experiment. But reasonable principles on which to build such a society are quite clear.

MAN: *Most efforts at planned economies kind of go against the grain of democratic ideals, and founder on those rocks.*

Well, it depends which planned economies you mean. There are lots of planned economies—the United States is a planned economy, for example. I mean, we talk about ourselves as a "free market," but that's baloney. The only parts of the U.S. economy that are internationally competitive are the planned parts, the state-subsidized parts—like capital-intensive agriculture (which has a state-guaranteed market as a cushion in case there are excesses); or high-technology industry (which is dependent on the Pentagon system); or pharmaceuticals (which is massively subsidized by publicly-funded research). Those are the parts of the U.S. economy that are functioning well.[16]

And if you go to the East Asian countries that are supposed to be the big economic successes—you know, what everybody talks about as a triumph of free-market democracy—they don't even have the most remote relation to free-market democracy: formally speaking they're fascist, they're state-organized economies run in cooperation with big conglomerates. That's precisely fascism, it's not the free market.

Now, that kind of planned economy "works," in a way—it produces at least. Other kinds of command economies don't work, or work differently: for example, the Eastern European planned economies in the Soviet era were highly centralized, over-bureaucratized, and they worked very inefficiently, although they did provide a kind of minimal safety-net for people.

But all of these systems have been very anti-democratic—like, in the Soviet Union, there were virtually no peasants or workers involved in any decision-making process.

MAN: *It would be hard to find a working model of an ideal.*

Yes, but in the eighteenth century it would have been hard to find a working model of a political democracy—that didn't prove it couldn't exist. By the nineteenth century, it did exist. Unless you think that human history is over, it's not an argument to say "it's not around." You go back two hundred years, it was hard to imagine slavery being abolished.

## The Kibbutz Experiment

ANOTHER MAN: *How could you make decisions democratically without a bureaucracy? I don't see how a large mass of people could actively participate in all of the decisions that need to be made in a complex modern society.*

No, I don't think they can—I think you've got to delegate some of those responsibilities. But the question is, where does authority ultimately lie? I mean, since the very beginnings of the modern democratic revolutions in the seventeenth and eighteenth centuries, it's always been recognized that people have to be represented—the question is, are we represented by, as they put it, "countrymen like ourselves," or are we represented by "our betters"?[17]

For example, suppose this was our community, and we wanted to enter into some kind of arrangement with the community down the road—if we were fairly big in scale, we couldn't *all* do it and get them *all* to do it, we'd have to delegate the right to negotiate things to representatives. But then the question is, who has the power to ultimately authorize those decisions? Well, if it's a democracy, that power ought to lie not just *formally* in the population, but *actually* in the population—meaning the representatives can be recalled, they're answerable back to their community, they can be replaced. In fact, there should be as much as possible in the way of constant replacement, so that political participation just becomes a part of everybody's life.

But I agree, I don't think it's possible to have large masses of people get together to decide every topic—it would be unfeasible and pointless. You're going to want to pick committees to look into things and report back, and so on and so forth.[18] But the real question is, where does authority lie?

MAN: *It sounds like the model you're looking to is similar to that of the kibbutzim [collective farming communities in Israel].*

Yeah, the kibbutz is actually as close to a full democracy as there is, I think. In fact, I lived on one for a while, and had planned to stay there, for precisely these reasons. On the other hand, life is full of all kinds of ironies, and the fact is—as I have come to understand over the years even more than I did at one time—although the kibbutzim are very authentic democracies internally, there are a lot of very ugly features about them.

For one thing, they're extremely racist: I don't think there's a single Arab on any kibbutz in Israel, and it turns out that a fair number of them have been turned down. Like, if a couple forms between a Jewish member of a kibbutz and an Arab, they generally end up living in an Arab village. The other thing about them is, they have an extremely unpleasant relationship with the state—which I didn't really know about until fairly recently, even though it's been that way for a long time.

See, part of the reason why the kibbutzim are economically successful is that they get a substantial state subsidy, and in return for that state subsidy they essentially provide the officers' corps for the elite military units in Israel. So if you look at who goes into the pilot training schools and the rangers and all that kind of stuff, it's kibbutz kids—that's the trade-off: the government subsidizes them as long as they provide the Praetorian Guard. Furthermore, I think they end up providing the Praetorian Guard in part as a result of kibbutz education. And here there are things that people who believe in libertarian ideas, as I do, really have to worry about.

You see, there's something very authoritarian about the libertarian structure of the kibbutz—I could see it when I lived in it, in fact. There's tremendous group pressure to conform. I mean, there's no force that *makes* you conform, but the group pressures are very powerful. The dynamics of how this worked were never very clear to me, but you could just see it in operation: the fear of exclusion is very great—not exclusion in the sense of not being allowed into the dining room or something, but just that you won't be a part of things somehow. It's like being excluded from a family: if you're a kid and your family excludes you—like maybe they let you sit at the table, but they don't talk to you—that's devastating, you just can't survive it. And something like that carries over into these communities.

I've never heard of anybody studying it, but if you watch the kids growing up, you can understand *why* they're going to go into the rangers and the pilot programs and the commandos. There's a tremendous macho pressure, right from the very beginning—you're just no good unless you can go through Marine Corps training and become a really tough bastard. And that starts pretty early, and I think the kids go through real traumas if they can't do it: it's psychologically very difficult.

And the results are striking. For example, there's a movement of resisters in Israel [Yesh G'vul], people who won't serve in the Occupied Territories— but it doesn't have any kibbutz kids in it: the movement just doesn't exist there. Kibbutz kids also have a reputation for being what are called "good soldiers"—which means, you know, not nice people: do what you gotta do.

All of these things are other aspects of it, and the whole phenomenon comes pretty much without force or authority, but because of a dynamics of conformism that's extremely powerful.

Like, the kibbutz I lived in was made up of pretty educated people—they were German refugees, and a lot of them had university degrees and so on—but every single person in the whole kibbutz read the same newspaper. And the idea that you might read a different newspaper—well, it's not that there was a law against it, it was just that it couldn't be done: you're a member of *this* branch of the kibbutz movement, that's the newspaper you read.

MAN: *Then how can we build a social contract which is cooperative in nature, but at the same time recognizes individual humanity? It seems to me that there's always going to be a very tense polar pull there.*

Where's the polar pull—between what and what?

MAN: *Between a collective value and an individual value.*

I guess I don't see why there has to be any contradiction there at all. It seems to me that a crucial aspect of humanity is being a part of functioning communities—so if we can create social bonds in which people find satisfaction, we've done it: there's no contradiction.

Look, you can't really figure out what problems are going to arise in group situations unless you experiment with them—it's like physics: you can't just sit around and think what the world would be like under such and such conditions, you've got to experiment and learn how things actually work out. And one of the things I think you learn from the kibbutz experiment is that you can in fact construct quite viable and successful democratic structures—but there are still going to be problems that come along. And one of the problems that people just have to face is the effect of group pressures to conform.

I think everybody knows about this from families. Living in a family is a crucial part of human life, you don't want to give it up. On the other hand, there plainly are problems that go along with it—nobody has to be told that. And a serious problem, which becomes almost pathological when it arises in a close-knit group, is exclusion—and to avoid exclusion often means doing things you wouldn't want to do if you had your own way. But that's just a part of living, to be faced with human problems like that.

Actually, I'm not a great enthusiast of Marx, but one comment he made seems appropriate here. I'm quoting, so pardon the sexist language, but somewhere or other he said: socialism is an effort to try to solve man's *animal* problems, and after having solved the animal problems, then we can face the *human* problems—but it's not a part of socialism to solve the human problems; socialism is an effort to get you to the point where you can *face* the human problems. And I think the kind of thing you're concerned about is a human problem—and those are going to be there. Humans are very complicated creatures, and have lots of ways of torturing themselves in their inter-personal relations. Everybody knows that, without soap operas.

## "Anarchism" and "Libertarianism"

WOMAN: *Professor Chomsky, on a slightly different topic, there's a separate meaning of the word "anarchy" different from the one you often talk about—namely, "chaos."*

Yeah, it's a bum rap, basically—it's like referring to Soviet-style bureaucracy as "socialism," or any other term of discourse that's been given a second meaning for the purpose of ideological warfare. I mean, "chaos" is a meaning of the word, but it's not a meaning that has any relevance to social thought. Anarchy as a social philosophy has never meant "chaos"—in fact, anarchists have typically believed in a highly organized society, just one that's organized democratically from below.

WOMAN: *It seems to me that as a social system, anarchism makes such bottom-line sense that it was necessary to discredit the word, and take it out of people's whole vocabulary and thinking—so you just have a reflex of fear when you hear it.*

Yeah, anarchism has always been regarded as the ultimate evil by people with power. So in Woodrow Wilson's Red Scare [a 1919 campaign against "subversives" in the U.S.], they were harsh on socialists, but they murdered anarchists—they were really bad news.

See, the idea that people could be free is extremely frightening to anybody with power. That's why the 1960s have such a bad reputation. I mean, there's a big literature about the Sixties, and it's mostly written by intellectuals, because they're the people who write books, so naturally it has a very bad name—because they *hated* it. You could see it in the faculty clubs at the time: people were just traumatized by the idea that students were suddenly asking questions and not just copying things down. In fact, when people like Allan Bloom [author of *The Closing of the American Mind*] write as if the foundations of civilization were collapsing in the Sixties, from their point of view that's exactly right: they were. Because the foundations of civilization are, "I'm a big professor, and I tell you what to say, and what to think, and you write it down in your notebooks, and you repeat it." If you get up and say, "I don't understand why I should read Plato, I think it's nonsense," that's destroying the foundations of civilization. But maybe it's a perfectly sensible question—plenty of philosophers have said it, so why isn't it a sensible question?

As with any mass popular movement, there was a lot of crazy stuff going on in the Sixties—but that's the only thing that makes it into history: the crazy stuff around the periphery. The main things that were going on are out of history—and that's because they had a kind of libertarian character, and there is nothing more frightening to people with power.

MAN: *What's the difference between "libertarian" and "anarchist," exactly?*

There's no difference, really. I think they're the same thing. But you see, "libertarian" has a special meaning in the United States. The United States is off the spectrum of the main tradition in this respect: what's called "libertarianism" here is unbridled capitalism. Now, that's always been opposed in the European libertarian tradition, where every anarchist has been a socialist—because the point is, if you have unbridled capitalism, you have all kinds of authority: you have *extreme* authority.

If capital is privately controlled, then people are going to have to rent themselves in order to survive. Now, you can say, "they rent themselves freely, it's a free contract"—but that's a joke. If your choice is, "do what I tell you or starve," that's not a choice—it's in fact what was commonly referred to as wage slavery in more civilized times, like the eighteenth and nineteenth centuries, for example.

The American version of "libertarianism" is an aberration, though—nobody really takes it seriously. I mean, everybody knows that a society that worked by American libertarian principles would self-destruct in three seconds. The only reason people pretend to take it seriously is because you can use it as a weapon. Like, when somebody comes out in favor of a tax, you can say: "No, I'm a libertarian, I'm against that tax"—but of course, I'm still in favor of the government building roads, and having schools, and killing Libyans, and all that sort of stuff.

Now, there *are* consistent libertarians, people like Murray Rothbard [American academic]—and if you just read the world that they describe, it's a world so full of hate that no human being would want to live in it. This is a world where you don't have roads because you don't see any reason why you should cooperate in building a road that you're not going to use: if you want a road, you get together with a bunch of other people who are going to use that road and you build it, then you charge people to ride on it. If you don't like the pollution from somebody's automobile, you take them to court and you litigate it. Who would want to live in a world like that? It's a world built on hatred.[19]

The whole thing's not even worth talking about, though. First of all, it couldn't function for a second—and if it could, all you'd want to do is get out, or commit suicide or something. But this is a special American aberration, it's not really serious.

## Articulating Visions

MAN: *You often seem reluctant to get very specific in spelling out your vision of an anarchist society and how we could get there. Don't you think it's important for activists to do that, though—to try to communicate to people a workable plan for the future, which then can help give them the hope and energy to continue struggling? I'm curious why you don't do that more often.*

Well, I suppose I *don't* feel that in order to work hard for social change you need to be able to spell out a plan for a future society in any kind of detail. What I feel should drive a person to work for change are certain *principles* you'd like to see achieved. Now, you may not know in detail—and I don't think that any of us *do* know in detail—how those principles can best be realized at this point in complex systems like human societies. But I don't really see why that should make any difference: what you try to do is advance the principles. Now, that may be what some people call "reformism"—but that's kind of like a put-down: reforms can be quite revolutionary if they lead in a certain direction. And to push in that direction, I don't think you have to know precisely how a future society would work: I think what you have to be able to do is spell out the principles you want to see such a society realize—and I think we can imagine *many* different ways in which a future society could realize them. Well, work to help people start trying them.

So for example, in the case of workers taking control of the workplace, there are a lot of different ways in which you can think of workplaces being controlled—and since nobody knows enough about what all the effects are going to be of large-scale social changes, I think what we should do is try them piecemeal. In fact, I have a rather conservative attitude towards social change: since we're dealing with complex systems which nobody understands very much, the sensible move I think is to make changes and then see what happens—and if they work, make further changes. That's true across the board, actually.

So, I don't feel in a position—and even if I felt I was, I wouldn't say it—to know what the long-term results are going to look like in any kind of detail: those are things that will have to be discovered, in my view. Instead, the basic principle I would like to see communicated to people is the idea that every form of authority and domination and hierarchy, every authoritarian structure, has to prove that it's justified—it has no prior justification. For instance, when you stop your five-year-old kid from trying to cross the street, that's an authoritarian situation: it's got to be justified. Well, in that case, I think you *can* give a justification. But the burden of proof for any exercise of authority is always on the person exercising it—invariably. And when you look, most of the time these authority structures have no justification: they have no moral justification, they have no justification in the interests of the person lower in the hierarchy, or in the interests of other people, or the environment, or the future, or the society, or anything else—they're just there in order to preserve certain structures of power and domination, and the people at the top.

So I think that whenever you find situations of power, these questions should be asked—and the person who claims the legitimacy of the authority always bears the burden of justifying it. And if they can't justify it, it's illegitimate and should be dismantled. To tell you the truth, I don't really understand anarchism as being much more than that. As far as I can see, it's just the point of view that says that people have the right to be free, and if there are constraints on that freedom then you've got to justify them. Sometimes you can—but of course, anarchism or anything else doesn't give you the answers about when that is. You just have to look at the specific cases.

MAN: *But if we ever had a society with no wage incentive and no authority, where would the drive come from to advance and grow?*

Well, the drive to "advance"—I think you have to ask exactly what that means. If you mean a drive to *produce more,* well, who wants it? Is that necessarily the right thing to do? It's not obvious. In fact, in many areas it's probably the wrong thing to do—maybe it's a good thing that there wouldn't be the same drive to produce. People have to be *driven* to have certain wants in our system—why? Why not leave them alone so they can just be happy, do other things?

Whatever "drive" there is ought to be internal. So take a look at kids: they're creative, they explore, they want to try new things. I mean, why does a kid start to walk? You take a one-year-old kid, he's crawling fine, he can get anywhere across the room he likes really fast, so fast his parents have to run after him to keep him from knocking everything down—all of a sudden he gets up and starts walking. He's terrible at walking: he walks one step and he falls on his face, and if he wants to really get somewhere he's going to crawl. So why do kids start walking? Well, they just want to do new things, that's the way people are built. We're built to want to do new things, even if they're not efficient, even if they're harmful, even if you get hurt—and I don't think that ever stops.

People want to explore, we want to press our capacities to their limits, we want to appreciate what we can. But the joy of creation is something very few people get the opportunity to have in our society: artists get to have it, craftspeople have it, scientists. And if you've been lucky enough to have had that opportunity, you know it's quite an experience—and it doesn't have to be discovering Einstein's theory of relativity: anybody can have that pleasure, even by seeing what *other* people have done. For instance, if you read even a simple mathematical proof like the Pythagorean Theorem, what you study in tenth grade, and you finally figure out what it's all about, that's exciting—"My God, I never understood that before." Okay, that's creativity, even though somebody else proved it two thousand years ago.

You just keep being struck by the marvels of what you're discovering, and you're "discovering" it, even though somebody else did it already. Then if you can ever add a little bit to what's already known—alright, that's very exciting. And I think the same thing is true of a person who builds a boat: I don't see why it's fundamentally any different—I mean, I wish *I* could do that; I can't, I can't imagine doing it.

Well, I think people should be able to live in a society where they can exercise these kinds of internal drives and develop their capacities freely—instead of being forced into the narrow range of options that are available to most people in the world now. And by that, I mean not only options that are *objectively* available, but also options that are *subjectively* available—like, how are people allowed to think, how are they able to think? Remember, there are all kinds of ways of thinking that are cut off from us in our society—not because we're incapable of them, but because various blockages have been developed and imposed to prevent people from thinking in those ways. That's what indoctrination is *about* in the first place, in fact—and I don't mean somebody giving you lectures: sitcoms on television, sports that you watch, every aspect of the culture implicitly involves an expression of what a "proper" life and a "proper" set of values are, and that's all indoctrination.

So I think what has to happen is, other options have to be opened up to people—both subjectively, and in fact concretely: meaning you can do something about them without great suffering. And that's one of the main purposes of socialism, I think: to reach a point where people have the opportunity to decide freely for *themselves* what their needs are, and not just have the "choices" forced on them by some arbitrary system of power.

## "Want" Creation

MAN: *But you could say that "to truck and barter" is human nature—that people are fundamentally materialist, and will always want to accumulate more and more under any social structure.*

You could *say* it, but there's no reason to *believe* it. You look at peasant societies, they go on for thousands of years without it—do those people have a different human nature? Or just look inside a family: do people "truck and barter" over how much you're going to eat for dinner? Well, certainly a family is a normal social structure, and you don't see people accumulating more and more for themselves regardless of the needs of the other people.

In fact, just take a look at the history of "trucking and bartering" itself: look at the history of modern capitalism, about which we know a lot. The first thing you'll notice is, peasants had to be driven by force and violence into a wage-labor system they did not want; then major efforts were undertaken—conscious efforts—to create wants. In fact, if you look back, there's a whole interesting literature of conscious discussion of the need to manufacture wants in the general population. It's happened over the whole long stretch of capitalism of course, but one place where you can see it very nicely encapsulated is around the time when slavery was terminated. It's very dramatic to look at cases like these.

For example, in 1831 there was a big slave revolt in Jamaica—which was one of the things that led the British to decide to give up slavery in their colonies: after some slave revolts, they basically said, "It's not paying anymore." So within a couple years the British wanted to move from a slave economy to a so-called "free" economy, but they still wanted the basic structure to remain exactly the same—and if you take a look back at the parliamentary debates in England at the time, they were talking very consciously about all this. They were saying: look, we've got to keep it the way it is, the masters have to become the owners, the slaves have to become the happy workers—somehow we've got to work it all out.

Well, there was a little problem in Jamaica: since there was a lot of open land there, when the British let the slaves go free they just wanted to move out onto the land and be perfectly happy, they didn't want to work for the British sugar plantations anymore. So what everyone was asking in Parliament in London was, "How can we force them to keep working for us, even when they're no longer enslaved into it?" Alright, two things were decided upon: first, they would use state force to close off the open land and prevent people from going and surviving on their own. And secondly, they realized that since all these workers didn't really *want* a lot of things—they just wanted to satisfy their basic needs, which they could easily do in that tropical climate—the British capitalists would have to start creating a whole set of wants for them, and make them start desiring things they didn't then desire, so then the only way they'd be able to satisfy their new material desires would be by working for wages in the British sugar plantations.[20]

There was very conscious discussion of the need to create wants—and in fact, extensive efforts were then undertaken to do exactly what they do on T.V. today: to create wants, to make you want the latest pair of sneakers you don't really need, so then people will be driven into a wage-labor society. And that pattern has been repeated over and over again through the whole entire history of capitalism.[21] In fact, what the whole history of capitalism shows is that people have had to be *driven* into situations which are then claimed to be their nature. But if the history of capitalism shows anything, it shows it's *not* their nature, that they've had to be forced into it, and that that effort has had to be maintained right until this day.

## Dissidents: Ignored or Vilified

MAN: *Noam, if I can just change the topic a bit. You've been called a neo-Nazi, your books have been burned, you've been called anti-Israeli—don't you get a bit upset by the way that your views are always distorted by the media and by intellectuals?*

No, why should I? I get called anything, I'm accused of everything you can dream of: being a Communist propagandist, a Nazi propagandist, a pawn of freedom of speech, an anti-Semite, liar, whatever you want.[22] Actually, I think that's all a good sign. I mean, if you're a dissident, typically you're ignored. If you can't be ignored, and you can't be answered, you're vilified—that's obvious: no institution is going to help people undermine it. So I would only regard the kinds of things you're talking about as signs of progress.

And in fact, it's gotten a lot better since the 1960s. Again, we don't re-member—younger people, in particular, don't appreciate—just how much it's changed. Let me just give you an illustration. Boston's a pretty liberal city, and the first major anti-Vietnam War action there was in October 1965, the "International Days of Protest," it was called. There was a public demonstration on the Boston Common—which is like Hyde Park, Union Square, it's where you give talks—and I was supposed to be one of the speakers. Well, the meeting was completely broken up: we never said one word. There were thousands of counter-demonstrators, mostly students marching over from the universities—and I was very pleased that there were hundreds of cops there, otherwise we would have been lynched.

The media were just irate about the demonstration. The front page of the *Boston Globe* had a big picture of a wounded war veteran on it, and the rest of the page was all condemnations of these people who dared to get up and say that we shouldn't bomb North Vietnam. All of the radio programs were deluged with denunciations of these Communists and traitors. The liberals in Congress denounced the "utter irresponsibility" of the demonstrators, who were questioning the right of the United States to bomb North Viet-nam—this was in 1965.[23] Incidentally, I should say that those demonstra-tions were so tepid it's embarrassing even to think about them—we weren't even criticizing the attack on *South* Vietnam, which was much worse, we were only talking about the extension of the bombing to the North.

The next big demonstration was in March '66, that was the second In-ternational Days of Protest. We figured there was no point in having a pub-lic demonstration, because we'd get killed, and we didn't want to have it at a university because the university would probably get smashed to dust, so we decided to have it in a church. So there was a march from Harvard Square down to the Arlington Street Church in downtown Boston, the Uni-tarian Church which was kind of the center of the movement activities, and the march was pretty well protected—guys on motorcycles were driving up and back trying to keep people from getting slaughtered and so on. Finally we got down to the church and went in: the church was attacked—there were big mobs outside throwing projectiles, tomatoes, cans. I mean, the po-lice were *there*, and they were preventing people from getting killed, but they weren't doing much more than that. That was in 1966.

There's been a big change since then—a big, big change. All of that stuff is *inconceivable* today, absolutely inconceivable.

MAN: *What I'm struck with in each of the three major misunderstandings that are used against you—the Faurisson affair [Chomsky made public statements in 1979 and '80 that a French professor who denied the Holocaust should not be jailed for his writings by the French government, and was denounced as a defender of the man's views*[24]*], your statements about Cambodia [Chomsky compared the genocide in Cambodia to that in East Timor, corrected numerous statistical falsifications about Cambodia, and was labeled an apologist for Pol Pot*[25]*], and your stance on the Israeli/ Palestinian conflict*[26]*—is how much your views have been distorted and oversimplified by the press. I don't understand why you'd want to keep bringing these ideas to the mass media when they always insist on misrepresenting them.*

But why is that surprising? First of all, this is not happening in the mass media, this is happening in the intellectual journals. And intellectuals are specialists in defamation, they're basically commissars [Soviet officials responsible for political indoctrination]—they're the ideological managers, so they are the ones who feel the most threatened by dissidence. The mass media don't care that much, they just ignore it, or say it's crazy or something like that. In fact, this stuff barely enters the national media; sure, you'll get a throwaway line saying, "this guy's an apologist for this that and the other thing," but that's just feeding off the intellectual culture. The place where it's really done is inside the intellectual journals—because that's their specialty. They're commissars: it's not fundamentally different from the Communist Party.

And also, I'm a particular target for other reasons—a lot of what I write is a critique of the American liberal intellectual establishment, and they don't like that particularly.

WOMAN: *You also criticize Israel, right?*

Yeah, the most sensitive of these issues has to do with the Middle East. In fact, there are organizations which are just dedicated to defamation on that issue. I mean, I didn't even get involved in writing about the Middle East at first, although that was always my main interest since childhood, partially for this reason—because they're very Stalinist-like, and I knew how they worked from the inside. In fact, I was one of the people who was doing it when I was a kid; you sort of get absorbed in this stuff, you know. And they're just *desperate* to prevent discussion of the issues.

So for example, the Anti-Defamation League [of B'nai B'rith], which masquerades as a civil rights organization, is in fact just a defamation organization. The office in Boston happens to be a rather leaky place, and I've been leaked a lot of stuff from there by people working in the office who are just outraged by what goes on. For instance, they leaked me my file a couple years ago—it had hundreds of pages of material, because whenever I speak anywhere, they've got a spy working for them who's taking notes and sending them back to some central office. So somebody will be here, say, taking notes on what I'm saying, and some version of it will get into my file and then be circulated around to their offices in the rest of the country: there are intercepted communications, and fevered inter-office memos, "he said so-and-so at such-and-such"—all kinds of *schmutz,* as they call it in my culture ["*schmutz*" means "dirt" in Yiddish].[27]

But if any of you have ever looked at your F.B.I. file through a Freedom of Information Act release, you've probably discovered that intelligence agencies are in general extremely incompetent—that's one of the reasons why there are so many intelligence failures: they just never get anything straight, for all kinds of reasons. And part of it is because the information they get typically is being transmitted to them by agents and informants who are ideological fanatics, and they always misunderstand things in their own crazy ways. So if you look at an F.B.I. file where you actually know what the facts are, you'll usually see that the information has some relation to reality—you can sort of figure out what they're talking about—but by the time it's worked its way through the ideological fanaticism of the intelligence system, there's been all sorts of weird distortion. And that's true of the Anti-Defamation League's intelligence too.

But this stuff certainly is circulated around—like, probably somebody in this area received it from the regional office, and there'll be some article in the local newspaper tomorrow that'll pull a lot of junk out of the file, that's what usually happens when I go places. And the point is that it's used to close off the discussion: since they can't deal with the issues, they've got to close off the discussion—and the best way to do it is by throwing enough slime so that maybe people will figure, where there's smoke there's fire, so we'd better not listen.

Well, the A.D.L. is an organized group where that's their main job.[28] But there are plenty of others who do the same sort of thing—because this is really the institutional task of the whole intellectual community. I mean, the job of mainstream intellectuals is to serve as a kind of secular priesthood, to ensure that the doctrinal faith is maintained. So if you go back to a period when the Church was dominant, the priesthood did it: they were the ones who watched out for heresy and went after it. And as societies became more secular in the eighteenth and nineteenth centuries, the same controls were needed: the institutions still had to defend themselves, after all, and if they couldn't do it by burning people at the stake or sending them to inquisitions anymore, they had to find other ways. Well, over time that responsibility was transferred to the intellectual class—to be guardians of the sacred political truths, hatchet-men of one sort or another.

So you see, as a dissident, you shouldn't be surprised to get all of this stuff done to you, it's in fact a positive sign—it means that you can't just be ignored anymore.

WOMAN: *You're really not discouraged by the fact that your work almost never gets portrayed accurately to the public or reviewed in a serious way by the press?*

No, not at all—and we really *shouldn't* get discouraged by that kind of thing. Look, I am not expecting to be applauded by people in editorial offices and at Faculty Clubs—that's not my audience. I mean, I was in India a little while ago and visited rural self-governing villages, and the people there were happy to see me. I was in Australia at the invitation of Timorese refugees, and they were glad that I was trying to help them. Recently I gave talks at a labor federation in Canada, and I've done that in the United States often—those are the people that I want to talk to, they're the audience I'd like to address.

Now, it's interesting and worth pointing out that the media in the United States are different in this respect—I do get pretty easy access to national media in other countries. In fact, it's only in the United States and the old Soviet Empire that I haven't had any real access to the major media over the years. And it's not just *me*, of course: the major media in the U.S., as was the case in the former Soviet Empire, pretty much exclude *anybody* with a dissident voice. So I can have interviews and articles in major journals and newspapers in Western Europe, and in Australia, and all up and down the Western Hemisphere. And often I get invitations from leading journals in other countries to write for them—like, recently I had an article in Israel's most important newspaper, *Ha'aretz*, which is kind of the equivalent of the *New York Times*: it was an invited critique of their foreign policy, and of the so-called "peace process."[29] Or in Australia, I gave a talk at the National Press Club in the Parliament Building, which was nationally televised twice on Australian World Services, their version of the B.B.C.—they wanted me to speak about *Australia's* foreign policy, so I gave a very critical talk to a national audience, and I spoke to Parliamentarians and journalists and so on, and was all over the press and papers there. And the same thing is true in Europe; I'm often on the C.B.C. nationally in Canada; and so on. Well, as you say, that's all unheard of in the United States—and the main reason, I think, is just that what people think, and are allowed to think, is much more important here, so the controls are much greater.[30]

MAN: *I heard something vaguely about your books being burned in Canada once. Were you there? What was that like for you?*

That was in Toronto. Yeah, I was there. I mean, I think people have a right to burn books if they want. I was in fact interviewed about it, I said the obvious thing—I'd rather they read them than burn them, but if they want to burn them, I don't care. Actually, you don't really have to worry about burning books—burning books is virtually impossible. Books are like bricks: they're very hard to burn.

MAN: *Was that a popular rabble or something? How did it happen?*

It was actually Vietnamese refugees. There's a Vietnamese refugee community that heard, or decided, or whatever, that I was . . . I don't know what. It was impossible to find out what they'd heard. They obviously knew that I was against the Vietnam War, and they were obviously very pro-war—you know, they thought the Americans should have stayed in and won it, that's why they're Vietnamese refugees. So they burned the books—which is fine, it's a reasonable form of protest. Now, if the *government* burns books, that's a different story, or if a *corporation* burns books, that's a different story.

In fact, just as an aside, I should say that I've had much worse destruction of books than that. You know how there's been all this business all over the front pages recently about big media mega-mergers, and there's all kinds of thoughtful discussion about whether this is going to harm the freedom of the press and so on? I really have to laugh. The first book that Ed Herman and I wrote together was published in 1974 by a rather profitable textbook publisher which happened to be owned by Warner Communications. Well, one of the executives at the corporation [William Sarnoff] didn't like the advertising copy that he saw about it, and he asked to see the book—and he was horrified by the book, and wouldn't let the publisher distribute it. Then came a long hassle, in which the people who ran the publishing company tried to insist on their right to publish, and in the end Warner Communications just put the publisher out of business, they decided that the easiest way to deal with the situation was just to terminate them. That meant that not only was *our* book destroyed, but *everybody's* books were destroyed. That does the Ayatollah one better: that's way beyond burning a book, that's destroying every book by this publisher to prevent one particular book, which had already been printed, from being distributed.[31] Now, *that* I would regard as much more serious than a number of people burning a book for symbolic reasons. If they want to do that, fine.

WOMAN: *How significant do you think these media mega-mergers really are in the end?*

Well, the first chapter of our book *Manufacturing Consent* does talk a bit about the corporate concentration of the media—and that part actually was written by Ed Herman, who's a specialist in corporate control; I didn't have anything to do with it. But my own feeling is that that particular issue is not quite as important as it's sometimes made out to be. I mean, if there were fifty media corporations instead of three, for example, I think they'd do about the same thing they do now—just because they all have basically the same interests. Maybe there'd be a little bit more competition, but probably not much. That's my view of the question, at least.

MAN: *Have you ever had your linguistics work censored or impeded in publication because of your politics?*

Never in the United States—but in the rest of the world, sure. For instance, I'll never forget one week, it must have been around 1979 or so, when I was sent two newspapers: one from Argentina and one from the Soviet Union. Argentina was then under the rule of these neo-Nazi generals, and I was sent *La Prensa* from Buenos Aires, the big newspaper in Argentina—there was a big article saying, "You can't read this guy's linguistics work because it's Marxist and subversive." The same week I got an article from *Izvestia* in the Soviet Union which said, "You can't read this guy's linguistics work because he's idealist and counter-revolutionary." I thought that was pretty nice.

MAN: *Noam, aren't you at all afraid of being silenced by the establishment for being so prominent and vocal in speaking out against U.S. power and its abuses?*

No, not really—and for a very simple reason, actually: if you look at me, you'll see what it is. I'm white, I'm privileged, and that means I'm basically immune from punishment by power. I mean, I don't want to say that it's a hundred percent immunity—but the fact of the matter is that these two things mean that you can buy a lot of freedom.

Look, there isn't any true capitalist society in the world, it couldn't survive for ten minutes, but there are variations on capitalism, and the U.S. is towards the capitalist end of the world spectrum—not very far towards it, I should say, but towards it at least in values. And if you had a truly capitalist society, everything would be a commodity, including freedom: there would be as much of it as you can buy. Well, since the U.S. is towards that end of the spectrum, it means there's an awful lot of freedom around if you can afford it. So if you're a black organizer in the ghetto, you don't have much of it, and you're in trouble—they can send the Chicago police in to murder you, like they did with Fred Hampton [a Black Panther assassinated by the F.B.I. in 1969]. But if you're a white professional like me, you can buy a lot of freedom.

And beyond that, I also happen to belong to a sector of the society where those who have real power are going to want to protect me—I mean, they may hate everything about me and want to see me disappear, but they don't want the state to be powerful enough to go after people *like* me, because then it could go after people like *them*. So the fact of the matter is that in societies like ours, privileged people like me are pretty well protected. It's not a hundred percent, but there's a lot of leeway around.

## Teaching About Resistance

WOMAN: *Do you have any thoughts about how best to begin helping people understand some of these ideas—like about the media institutions and how they prevent people from thinking freely for themselves?*

Well, I don't think any of it's very hard, to tell you the honest truth—I mean, intellectuals make a career of trying to make simple things look hard, because that's part of the way you get your salary paid and so on. But the fact of the matter is, the social world—to the extent that we understand it at all—is more or less right there in front of you after you sort of peel away the blinders a little. It's an extremely hard thing to understand if you're all alone trying to do it, but through the kinds of interactions and groups we've been talking about, you can do it pretty easily.

So when you have a chance to meet with people or talk with them, I think the thing to do is to try to get them to learn how to explore things for themselves—for example, to help them learn for *themselves* the way that the media shape and frame issues for the purpose of manipulation and control. Now, there's not much point in doing it abstractly—you know, like some theory of how it works. What you have to do is look at cases. So take cases that people are interested in, and just teach them how to do research projects—research projects are very easy to do, you don't need a Ph.D.; maybe in physics you do, but not in these topics. You just have to have common sense. You have to have common sense, you have to look carefully at the facts; it may be a little bit of work to *find* the facts—like usually you're not just going to find them right there in the headlines or something. But if you do a little work, you can find out what the facts are, you can find out the way they're being distorted and modified by the institutions. And then the purposes of those distortions quickly become clear.

MAN: *It's hard to know the best way to stimulate people's interest as a teacher or an organizer, but certainly there are ways of* not *doing it, even while* appearing *to do it. Earlier, in response to the question about civil disobedience, you mentioned people lecturing on resistance—that would seem to me to be an example of not doing it, while pretending to do it.*

Well, I'm not so convinced that that's *not* a way to do it, actually. Like, I think there are things to teach people about resistance—I've personally liked to listen to people who have had experiences with it, and who may have ideas about it that I don't have. If you want to call that "lecturing," okay—but it's not necessarily wrong: there are lots of things you can learn from other people who have thought about subjects and had experiences.

MAN: *But what I'm wondering is, what else do you think would go into teaching people about resistance, and activism in general?*

First of all I don't think you should mislead people: you should get them to understand that if they're going to be independent thinkers, they are probably going to pay a cost. I mean, one has to begin with an understanding of the way the world works: the world does not reward honesty and independence, it rewards obedience and service. It's a world of concentrated power, and those who have power are not going to reward people who question that power. So to begin with, I don't think anybody should be misled about that.

After you understand that, okay, then you make your own choices. If your choice is that you want to be independent anyhow, even though you recognize what's involved, then you should just go ahead and try to do it—but those can be extremely hard choices sometimes. For instance, I know that as an older person who often gets approached by younger people for advice, I'm always very hesitant to give it on these sorts of decisions (even though sometimes the circumstances are such that I have to)—because I'm in no position to tell anybody else what to decide. But what I think one can do is to help people understand what the objective realities are.

Look, you can gain a lot by activism, like all of you were saying earlier—but there are also many things that you can lose. And some of those things are not unimportant, like security for example—that's not unimportant. And people just have to make their own choices about that when they decide what they're going to do.

## Isolation

WOMAN: *To stay on a personal level for a moment, Noam, I've always been kind of fascinated by how you find the time to write books and articles, and teach, give talks all over the country, have a family life, be the leading figure in linguistics, you document your work very thoroughly—are you in some kind of a time warp, where you experience something other than a 24-hour day like the rest of us?*

No, it's just pure, ordinary fanaticism—and in fact, a lot of things go. Anybody who's pretty seriously involved in political activity or organizing knows that a lot of other things just go, like personal lives sometimes. I mean, yeah, I try to keep my personal life going—so my grandkids and children were over a few nights ago, and I played with them, that sort of thing. But personal relationships do suffer. For instance, if I see my closest personal friends, whom I've known for fifty years, we're extremely close and so on, once or twice a year, it's a good year. But that's the way it goes: you can't do everything, so you just have to make choices.

Actually, it was kind of striking to watch it during the Sixties—all of a sudden a lot of people really threw themselves into activism, and when I think about it, very few of the couples made it through. Very few. Not because they hated each other or anything—it was just that it was too much of an emotional burden, even if both of them were involved, and something snaps. In fact, it was like a tidal wave right through that period, particularly after some of the big political trials. So couples would stick together for as long as the trial was going on, and immediately afterwards get divorced—it was just too much. And that's a reflection of what tends to happen in general when you get really seriously involved.

I mean, it's extremely hard to lead a deeply committed life in several different areas and have them all work. Some of them give, and one of the ones that gives often is personal life—and that's hard to deal with, because you just can't go on that way. I don't really know what the answer is to that, actually; people have found different answers.

MAN: *It's comforting for me that you experience the same thing.*

Oh, everybody does.

MAN: *I feel very isolated when I get so involved in activism that my personal life becomes nonexistent—I really feel a void, not connecting with people.*

Oh yeah, it's a terrible void—and it then makes it impossible for you to work. After all, we're not automata: we function as part of a matrix of human relations, and need to connect with other people.

MAN: *And the personal isolation then reinforces the political isolation.*

It's tough, yeah. I mean, partly the problem is a result of the fact that we're all so isolated: if we had live, ongoing popular organizations, this wouldn't be so true. The history of the labor movement in the United States is interesting in this respect, actually: when people were really working together organizing, that overcame the isolation. In fact, it even overcame things like racism and sexism to a great extent. And this goes way back.

I mean, about a century ago in the United States, the labor movement was getting smashed all over the place: they were only defeated, there were no victories. But in the course of those defeats—things like, say, the Homestead strike [an 1892 strike at a Carnegie Steel plant in Pennsylvania]—it's amazing what happened. Homestead's an interesting case, actually, because it was a working-class town, and the strikers simply took the place over:

they took over the town and ran everything. And this was during a very racist period, remember—there weren't a lot of blacks around right there, but there was real racism directed at Eastern Europeans. So, what were called "Huns" (which could be Slovaks or anybody, it didn't have to be Hungarians) were treated sort of the way blacks are treated—and the racism was very vicious. But it all collapsed in the middle of the Homestead strike. And also, women were running all sorts of things too, a lot of the sexism was broken down as well. And that's what tends to happen when people join together in common struggles.[32]

It also happened in the formation of the C.I.O. [a union for mass-production industries formed in 1935]—black and white workers worked together to create the C.I.O. And it happened in the Civil Rights Movement—S.N.C.C., for example, was very open, it was white, black, anything. A lot of the unpleasant aspects of life disappear, and you can compensate for them, in the course of some kind of common struggle. In fact, an old friend of mine who was in the Polish resistance in Warsaw during the Nazi occupation—and lived through that time and survived—always used to say that it was the best period of his life. I mean, it was extremely dangerous—you could end up in a gas chamber and everybody knew it—but there was a sense of community that he'd never felt before, and never had after.

So the best answer, I suspect, is just the same as for everything else—we have to develop stable popular organizations, and a culture of concern, and commitment, and activism, and solidarity, which can help to sustain us in these struggles, and which can help break down some of the barriers that have been set up to divide and distract us.

### Science and Human Nature

MAN: *Noam, could you elaborate a little more on what your own opinions are about human nature—for instance, do you see humans as more destructive than constructive, or is it maybe the other way around?*

Well, first of all, my opinion about it is no better than yours: it's just pure intuition, nobody really understands anything about human nature. Look, people don't understand much about big molecules—when you get beyond that to things like human nature, anybody's guess is as good as anyone else's.

MAN: *But you've studied a lot of the results of human nature.*

Yeah, but if you look at the results of human nature, you see everything: you see enormous self-sacrifice, you see tremendous courage, you see integrity, you see destructiveness, you see anything you want. That doesn't tell you much.

MAN: *It seems like a great deal of your research documents the destructive nature of humans, though.*

Well, but a lot of it documents other things too. I mean, my general feeling is that over time, there's measurable progress: it's not huge, but it's significant. And sometimes it's been pretty dramatic. For instance, take the sort of "original sin" of American history—what happened to the native population here. It's a remarkable fact that until the 1960s, the culture simply could not come to terms with that at all. Until the 1960s, with very rare exceptions, academic scholarship was grossly falsifying the history, and suppressing the reality of what happened—even the number of people killed was radically falsified. I mean, as late as 1969, in one of the leading diplomatic histories of the United States, the author Thomas Bailey could write that after the American Revolution, the former colonists turned to the task of "felling trees and Indians."[33] *Nobody* could say that now—you couldn't even say that in a *Wall Street Journal* editorial now. Well, those are important changes, and it's part of a lot of other significant progress too. Slavery was considered a fine thing not long ago.

MAN: *So you think that human nature is individually kind of destructive, but overall it's constructive?*

I don't know—like, they didn't have gas chambers in the nineteenth century, so you can find all kinds of things. And if you want to look for scientific answers, it's zilch, nobody knows a thing: the answers mostly come from history or intuition or something. I mean, science can only answer very simple questions—when things get complicated, you just guess.

ANOTHER MAN: *People often ask you about the connections between your scientific work in linguistics and your politics, and you tend to say something about, "Yes, there are a few tenuous connections." Would you amplify on that? I myself have been thinking that maybe part of our political problem is that the human brain is very good at seeing things in competitive terms like "more" and "less," and it's not very good at conceptualizing "enough."*

Well, that may be true—but these are topics where the scientific study of language has nothing to say. I mean, you know as much about it as the fanciest linguist around.

MAN: *Where are they, then—even the tenuous connections?*

Not there; the tenuous connections are somewhere else.

First of all, we should remember that the kinds of things that any sort of science can shed light on are pretty narrow: when you start moving to complicated systems, scientific knowledge declines very fast. And when you get to the nature of human beings, the sciences have nothing to say. There are a few areas where you can get a lot of insight and understanding, and certain aspects of language happen to be one of those areas, for some reason—but that insight still doesn't bear on questions of real human concern, at least not at a level which has any consequences for human life.

The connections are quite different—and they *are* tenuous. The only reason for stressing them is because they've been pointed out many times through the course of modern intellectual history, and in fact they lie right at the core of classical liberalism. I mean, contrary to the contemporary version of it, classical liberalism (which remember was pre-capitalist, and in fact, anti-capitalist) focused on the right of people to control their own work, and the need for free creative work under your own control—for human freedom and creativity. So to a classical liberal, wage labor under capitalism would have been considered totally immoral, because it frustrates the fundamental need of people to control their own work: you're a slave to someone else.

Well, in trying to locate sort of a core in human nature for a right to free, creative work and control over it, some classical liberal philosophers looked at other aspects of human intelligence, and one aspect that had indeed been studied since the seventeenth century, and had a lot to do with Cartesian thought as well [i.e. after the French philosopher Descartes], was language—where it was recognized, quite accurately, that sort of an identifying criterion of possession of a mind in the human sense (as distinct from an animal or an automaton) is the free creative aspect of the normal use of language.

So for example, a central part of Descartes' argument for a sharp, even ontological distinction between humans and everything else in the world was that if you pose a question to a human being about a new topic using phrases that the person has never heard before, they can give you a new response relevant to what you said, which is not caused by their internal state and not caused by any external circumstances, but which somehow comes out of some creative capacity of their mind. But the same thing won't be true of an automaton or an animal or anything else—like, if you take a machine and set it in a certain environment and push a button, what will come out is predetermined; or if you give a pigeon a certain stimulus, its actions also are going to be predetermined. But in human language, the product that comes out is *not* predetermined—it's undetermined, but still somehow appropriate to situations.

Well, to Descartes, that was the crucial aspect of the human mind. And there was an attempt right through the classical liberal period, by Rousseau, and Humboldt, and others, to link up these elements and identify sort of a need and a right to freedom, an "instinct for freedom," it was sometimes called, something at the cognitive core of human nature: free creative thought and its expression.

Now, that's pretty metaphoric—like I say, nobody really knows anything about human nature, so certainly you don't know whether there's an instinct for freedom or not. I mean, if somebody wants to say that humans are born to be slaves, they can give as much of a scientific argument as Rousseau could when he said they're born to be free—it's like where your hopes are, it's not that there's any scientific knowledge.

And the same thing is true today: like, you can read any book you want about sociobiology [theory that specific social behaviors and not just physical characteristics result from evolution], and it's mostly just fairy tales—I mean, it's all fine when it's talking about ants; when it goes up to the level of mammals, it starts being guesswork; and when it gets to humans, it's like, say anything that comes to your head. But I think you can see a possible connection of that sort—a potential connection. Whether that connection can actually be made substantive, who knows? It's all so far beyond scientific understanding at this point that you can't even dream about it. So that's the main reason why I don't talk about these things much. I just think they're interesting ideas, which are maybe worth thinking about in the back of your mind, or maybe writing poems about or something. But they're simply not topics for scientific inquiry at this point.

## Charlatans in the Sciences

WOMAN: *Noam, there's an idea in behavioral science, tied in with Piaget's theory of cognitive development, that human compassion is a learned quality [the Swiss psychologist Piaget believed that mental development in children progresses through four genetically-determined stages]. Some politicians have seized upon this idea to promote the death penalty being used more often: like, either you catch the boat or you don't, either you learn human compassion or you don't—so if these murderers haven't learned it, well, then it's impossible to teach it to them now. I'm sure you're familiar with these arguments?*

This stuff doesn't even rise to the level of idiocy—literally. I mean, if people want to have a fraudulent reason for defending the death penalty, fine, but there is no scientific basis. Take Piaget: Piaget's work on developmental psychology was interesting, he had some interesting experiments and so on—the whole edifice has totally collapsed, nobody believes a word of it anymore. It turned out that all of the developmental "stages" are false: as you got better experiments, you could show that tiny infants could do all the things he postulated they couldn't do at that stage. I mean, it was an interesting set of ideas, it wasn't stupid—and people learned from the experimental work. But there's nothing left of the picture. Zero.

As far as compassion being learned, any one of you knows as much as the fanciest scientist—and what you know is what you know by intuition and experience: you've seen children, maybe you've had children, you've played with them, you see the way they grow up. That's what anybody knows, nobody knows any more than that. And the sciences have nothing more to tell you—and furthermore, there's no indication that they ever will: it's just way too far away. I mean, they may give you some statistical evidence, or maybe someday somebody will be able to show that this kind of background leads to more compassionate people than some other kind of background, that's entirely possible. But that doesn't mean there's ever going to be an understanding of it.

Look, as science progresses, there will be attempts to draw political conclusions from it—but they're going to be like this Piaget and the death penalty thing: that is, people who have some political agenda will find some total charlatan in the sciences who will tell them, "this is the basis for it." But in terms of actual scientific knowledge, we aren't even within super-telescope distance of touching any of these questions—there's just nothing there. I mean, it's not that you can't do research on them: you can do descriptive research, you can do therapy, you can try to extend insights by making them a little bit more careful and controlled—but that's about it.

It's kind of like psychotherapy: some people say they get something out of psychotherapy, and maybe they do and maybe they don't—but if they do, it's not because there's any science behind it: there's no science behind it, any more than there is behind faith-healing. It's just that somehow, various kinds of human interactions sometimes seem to work.

I remember an anthropologist friend of mine who's worked in Southwest American Indian communities once described to me people being healed in tribal healing ceremonies: he said that if he didn't see it with his own eyes, he wouldn't have believed it. So some person will be really ill—I mean, very serious problems, physical symptoms, he's not making it up—and they will go through some community-type ritual which involves dancing, and singing, this and that and the other thing, and the person just gets better: you see it happening, nobody knows why it's happening; maybe it's something about empathy, or being part of a community, whatever it might be. Well, there's about as much scientific understanding in that as there is in psychotherapy.

Or even just take narrow questions of medicine. You know how they decide what kinds of drugs are worth giving to you, say for heart problems? It's not because the *science* of it is understood—they just do epidemiological studies with controlled populations, to see if one of the sample populations takes this drug and the other sample population takes that drug, which one lives a little bit longer. I mean, you can call that "science" if you like—but it's the kind of science that can be done by anybody who can count basically, or who knows something about studying samples and things like that. It's not because anyone understands the *biology* of these things—usually that's barely understood, if at all.

So I think that whenever you hear people talking about things like "learning of compassion" and so on, a big red flag should go up.

WOMAN: *You don't think science will ever have much to say about human behavior—there's just something spiritual at the human level that is undefinable by science?*

It's not just about *humans* that scientific insight is very limited—even simple physical things can't be dealt with either. For instance, there's a "three body problem" in physics: you can't really figure out what happens when three bodies are moving, the equations are just too complicated. In fact, a physicist I was talking to recently gave me another example—he said if you take a cup of coffee with cream swirling around in it, presumably all of the natural laws are known, but you can't solve the equations because they're just too complex. Alright, that's not human beings, that's cream swirling around in a cup of coffee: we can't figure out what's going on.

The point is, we may know the laws, but the possibility of applying them, or of solving the equations, or of working out the problems, or of understanding what's going on, declines very fast when we get past only the very simplest things.

Also, we probably *don't* know all the laws—I mean, it's very unlikely that we really do know the laws, even at the core of science. A physicist will tell you much more about this than I can, but take, say, the matter in the universe: more than 90 percent of the matter in the universe is what's called "dark matter"—and it's called "dark" because nobody knows what it is. It's just sort of postulated that it exists, because if you don't postulate it, everything blows up—so you have to assume that it's there. And that's over 90 percent of the matter in the universe: you don't even know what it is. In fact, a new branch of physics has developed around superconductivity ["superconductivity" refers to the complete disappearance of electrical resistance in various solids at ultra-low temperatures], and while I don't have the knowledge to evaluate the claims, what some of the physicists working on it say is that they can now virtually prove (I mean, not *quite* prove, but come quite close to proving) that in this domain of highly condensed matter, there are principles which are literally not deducible from the known laws of nature: so you can't reduce the principles of superconductivity to the known laws of nature. And again, that's talking about really simple things, nothing like a complex organism.

Then when you begin to talk about how organisms develop—well, people say it's "natural selection," and that's not false: undoubtedly Darwin was sort of right. But it could be that natural selection is only a very peripheral part of the development of organisms. So, there's a channel of physical possibilities that physical laws make available, and within that channel of physical possibilities only certain things can happen—and within the range of those things that can happen, you are going to get effects due to natural selection. But the structure of the channel is totally unknown: I mean, nobody knows what kinds of laws apply to complex organisms, there are just the bare beginnings these days of the studies of self-organizing systems—how systems develop structure and complexity just by virtue of their nature. These things are just barely beginning to be understood—and we're talking about things *way* simpler than human beings.

For instance, in neurophysiology, the organism that people study is a little worm called nematodes—and the reason they study nematodes is because they're tiny, for one thing: they have a thousand cells, a three-day gestation period, three hundred neurons, and the entire wiring diagram of the three hundred neurons is known, so we know exactly how they're all linked up together. But still, nobody can figure out why the stupid worm does what it does, whatever it does—I don't know, probably turn left or something. Whatever it does is so far unexplained on the basis of a three-hundred-neuron system, where the entire structure of it is known, and the whole gestation period is completely known. It's just too complicated, too many things are going on, there are too many chemical interactions. And this is three hundred neurons—it's not $10^{11}$ neurons, like in your head. So the difference is just so qualitatively huge that the fall-off in understanding when it comes to human beings is extremely dramatic.

And this is again why the study of language is so particularly interesting, because for some reason it seems like things in the inorganic world: there are aspects of it you can study by the methods of the sciences, which is curious—but still it's like a little laser beam of light that goes through human behavior, leaving most things about language out. Like, science has nothing to say about what you and I are doing now—only about the mechanisms that are *involved* in it, not about how we do it. About that, there's nothing to say, except again you can write poems. So the reach of scientific understanding is highly specific: very deep in the few areas where it goes, but they're limited areas.

Now, when you say that human behavior might be beyond our inquiry, that's possible—but I wouldn't say that's because of a "spiritual" property we have: the same thing might be true of large parts of nature. So there's some capacity of the brain, some faculty of the mind that nobody understands, which allows us to do scientific inquiry—and like any other part of biology, it's highly structured: it's very good at certain things, and consequently very bad at other things. I mean, you can't be good at something if you're not bad at something else, those two things necessarily go together—like, if you're a great weight-lifter, you're going to be a rotten butterfly. You can't be both, right? So if a human embryo can become a human being, it can't become a fly—it's too "weak" to become a fly, if you like, because it's "strong" enough to become a human being: by a matter of logic, those things go together. So if you have a great capacity in one area, you're going to have lousy capacities in another area. And if the human science-forming capacity is good enough to figure out quantum theory for some completely unexplained reason, it's also going to be so bad that it's not going to figure out lots of other things. And we don't know what those other things are—but they might very well be most everything that we're really interested in.

So when someone comes along claiming a scientific basis for some social policy or anything else having to do with human beings, I'd be very skeptical if I were you—because the knowledge just isn't there right now, and may never be, either.

## Adam Smith: Real and Fake

MAN: *You said that classical liberalism was "anti-capitalist." What did you mean by that?*

Well, the underlying, fundamental principles of Adam Smith and other classical liberals were that people should be free: they shouldn't be under the control of authoritarian institutions, they shouldn't be subjected to things like division of labor, which destroys them. So look at Smith: why was he in favor of markets? He gave kind of a complicated argument for them, but at the core of it was the idea that if you had perfect liberty, markets would lead to perfect equality—that's why Adam Smith was in favor of markets.[34] Adam Smith was in favor of markets because he thought that people ought to be completely equal—*completely equal*—and that was because, as a classical liberal, he believed that people's fundamental character involves notions like sympathy, and solidarity, the right to control their own work, and so on and so forth: all the exact opposite of capitalism.

In fact, there are no two points of view more antithetical than classical liberalism and capitalism—and that's why when the University of Chicago publishes a bicentennial edition of Smith, they have to distort the text (which they did): because as a true classical liberal, Smith was strongly opposed to all of the idiocy they now spout in his name.

So if you read George Stigler's introduction to the bicentennial edition of *The Wealth of Nations*—it's a big scholarly edition, University of Chicago Press, so it's kind of interesting to look at—it is diametrically opposed to Smith's text on point after point.[35] Smith is famous for what he wrote about division of labor: he's supposed to have thought that division of labor was a great thing. Well, he didn't: he thought division of labor was a *terrible* thing—in fact, he said that in any civilized society, the government is going to have to intervene to prevent division of labor from simply destroying people. Okay, now take a look at the University of Chicago's index (you know, a detailed scholarly index) under "division of labor": you won't find an entry for that passage—it's simply not there.[36]

Well, that's *real* scholarship: suppress the facts totally, present them as the opposite of what they are, and figure, "probably nobody's going to read to page 473 anyhow, because I didn't." I mean, ask the guys who edited it if *they* ever read to page 473—answer: well, they probably read the first paragraph, then sort of remembered what they'd been taught in some college course.

But the point is, for classical liberals in the eighteenth century, there was a certain conception of just what human beings are like—namely, that what kind of creatures they are depends on the kind of work they do, and the kind of control they have over it, and their ability to act creatively and according to their own decisions and choices. And there was in fact a lot of very insightful comment about this at the time.

So for example, one of the founders of classical liberalism, Wilhelm von Humboldt (who incidentally is very admired by so-called "conservatives" today, because they don't read him), pointed out that if a worker produces a beautiful object on command, you may "admire what the worker does, but you will despise what he is"—because that's not really behaving like a human being, it's just behaving like a machine.[37] And that conception runs right through classical liberalism. In fact, even half a century later, Alexis de Tocqueville [French politician and writer] pointed out that you can have systems in which "the art advances and the artisan recedes," but that's inhuman—because what you're really interested in is the artisan, you're interested in *people*, and for people to have the opportunity to live full and rewarding lives they have to be in control of what they do, even if that happens to be economically less efficient.[38]

Well, okay—obviously there's just been a dramatic change in intellectual and cultural attitudes over the past couple centuries. But I think those classical liberal conceptions now have to be recovered, and the ideas at the heart of them should take root on a mass scale.

Now, the sources of power and authority that people could see in front of their eyes in the eighteenth century were quite different from the ones that we have today—back then it was the feudal system, and the Church, and the absolutist state that they were focused on; they couldn't see the industrial corporation, because it didn't exist yet. But if you take the basic classical liberal principles and apply them to the modern period, I think you actually come pretty close to the principles that animated revolutionary Barcelona in the late 1930s—to what's called "anarcho-syndicalism." [Anarcho-syndicalism is a form of libertarian socialism that was practiced briefly in regions of Spain during its revolution and civil war of 1936, until it was destroyed by the simultaneous efforts of the Soviet Union, the Western powers, and the Fascists.] I think that's about as high a level as humans have yet achieved in trying to realize these libertarian principles, which in my view are the right ones. I mean, I'm not saying that everything that was done in that revolution was right, but in its general spirit and character, in the idea of developing the kind of society that Orwell saw and described in I think his greatest work, *Homage to Catalonia*—with popular control over all the institutions of society—okay, that's the right direction in which to move, I think.[39]

# The Computer and the Crowbar

MAN: *Noam, given what you were saying before about our limited under-standing of human nature and social change, don't you think there's a cau-tion there in general for people intervening in social patterns involving human beings?*

Yes—any kind of drastic intervention in a human being, or a human soci-ety, is very dubious. Like, suppose you've got a personal computer and it isn't working—it's a bad idea to hit it with a crowbar. Maybe hitting it with a crowbar will by accident fix it, but it's by and large not a good tactic—and human societies are much more complex than computers, as are human be-ings. So you really never understand what you're doing. People have to carry out changes for themselves: they can't be imposed upon them from above.

Take the Spanish Revolution again. I mean, that was just one year in a rather undeveloped country (though it had industry and so on), so it's not like a model for the future. But a lot of interesting things happened in the course of it, and they didn't just happen out of the blue—they happened out of maybe fifty years of serious organizing and experimentation, and at-tempts to try it, and failures, and being smashed up by the army, and then trying again. So when people say it was spontaneous, that's just not true: it came from a lot of experience, and thinking, and working, and so on, and then when the revolutionary moment came and the existing system sort of collapsed, people had in their heads a picture of what to do, and had even tried it, and they then tried to implement it on a mass scale. And it was im-plemented in many different ways—there wasn't any single pattern that was followed, the various collectives were experimenting on their own under different conditions, and finding out for themselves what worked.[40] And that's a good example of how I think constructive change has to happen.

On the other hand, if an economist from, say, Harvard, goes to some Eastern European country today and tells them, "Here's the way to de-velop," that's worse than hitting a computer with a crowbar: there are a million different social and cultural and economic factors they don't understand, and any big change that's pressed on people is very likely to be disastrous, no matter what it is—and of course, it always *is* disastrous. Inci-dentally, it's disastrous for the *victims*—it's usually very good for the people who are carrying out the experiments, which is why these experiments have been carried out for the last couple hundred years, since the British started them in India. I mean, every one of them is a disaster for the victims and they're invariably good for the guys carrying out the experiments.[41] Well, as far as people who are interested in social reform are concerned, what that suggests is, people better do it themselves, and a step at a time, under their own control. That's in fact what was being attempted on a fairly local scale in Barcelona, and I think it's the kind of thing we have to work towards now.

# 7

# Intellectuals and Social Change

*Based primarily on discussions at Woods Hole and Rowe, Massachusetts, in 1989, 1993 and 1994.*

## The Leninist/Capitalist Intelligentsia

MAN: *Your vision of a libertarian socialism is a very appealing one—I'm wondering, what's gone wrong?*

First of all, maybe nothing's gone wrong. You could argue that we haven't been ready for it yet—but there was also a period when we weren't ready for ending slavery either; when conditions, including subjective conditions, were such that abolition just wasn't in the cards. So one could argue that conditions today are such that we need the degree of hierarchy and domination that exists in totalitarian institutions like capitalist enterprises, just in order to satisfy our needs—or else a "dictatorship of the proletariat," or some other authoritarian structure like that. I mean, I don't believe a word of it—but the point is, the justification for any kind of power system has to be *argued* and proven to people before it has any claim to legitimacy. And those arguments haven't been made out in this case.

If you look at what's actually *happened* to the various efforts at libertarian socialism that have taken place around the world, the concentration of force and violence present in those situations has just been such that certain outcomes were virtually guaranteed, and consequently all incipient efforts at cooperative workers' control, say, have simply been crushed. There have in fact been efforts in this direction for hundreds of years—the problem is, they regularly get destroyed. And often they're destroyed by force.

The Bolsheviks [political party that seized power during the Russian Revolution and later became the Communist Party] are a perfect example. In the stages leading up to the Bolshevik coup in October 1917, there *were* incipient socialist institutions developing in Russia—workers' councils, collectives, things like that [i.e. after a popular revolution first toppled the

Tsar in February 1917]. And they survived to an extent once the Bolsheviks took over—but not for very long; Lenin and Trotsky pretty much eliminated them as they consolidated their power. I mean, you can argue about the *justification* for eliminating them, but the fact is that the socialist initiatives were pretty quickly eliminated.

Now, people who want to justify it say, "The Bolsheviks had to do it"—that's the standard justification: Lenin and Trotsky had to do it, because of the contingencies of the civil war, for survival, there wouldn't have been food otherwise, this and that. Well, obviously the question there is, was that true? To answer that, you've got to look at the historical facts: I don't think it was true. In fact, I think the incipient socialist structures in Russia were dismantled *before* the really dire conditions arose. Alright, here you get into a question where you don't want to be too cavalier about it—it's a question of historical fact, and of what the people were like, what they were thinking and so on, and you've got to find out what the answer is, you can't just guess. But from reading their own writings, my feeling is that Lenin and Trotsky knew what they were doing, it was conscious and understandable, and they even had a theory behind it, both a moral theory and a socio-economic theory.[1]

First of all, as orthodox Marxists, they didn't really believe that a socialist revolution was *possible* in Russia, because Russia was just a peasant backwater: it wasn't the kind of advanced industrial society where in their view the coming socialist revolution was supposed to happen. So when the Bolsheviks got power, they were hoping to carry out kind of a holding action and wait for "the iron laws of history" to grind out the revolution in Germany, where it was supposed to happen by historical necessity, and then Russia would continue to be a backwater, but it would then develop with German help.[2]

Well, it didn't end up happening in Germany: there *was* a revolution, in January 1919, but it was wiped out, and the German working class was suppressed. So at that point, Lenin and Trotsky were stuck holding the bag—and they basically ended up trying to run a peasant society by violence: since Russia was such a deeply impoverished Third World society, they thought it was necessary just to beat the people into development. So they took steps to turn the workers into what they called a "labor army," under control of a "maximal leader," who was going to force the country to industrialize under what they themselves referred to as "state-capitalism."[3] Their hope was that this would carry Russia over the early stages of capitalism and industrialization, until it reached a point of material development where then the iron laws of history would start to work as the Master said they were going to, and socialism would finally be achieved [i.e. Karl Marx theorized that history progresses according to natural "laws," and that the advanced stages of capitalism will inevitably lead to socialism].

So there was a theory behind their actions, and in fact a moral principle—namely, it will be better for people in the long run if we do this. But what they did, I think, was to set the framework for a totalitarian system, which of course Stalin then accelerated.

MAN: *Would you describe the authoritarian result of the Bolsheviks' actions as an honest mistake, a "historical accident" maybe—or was it just the natural outgrowth of the Leninist worldview: the idea that only a few people are smart and knowledgeable enough to be the leaders, and they should run the show?*

Yeah, in my opinion the heart of the problem is Marxism-Leninism itself—the very idea that a "vanguard party" can, or has any right to, or has any capacity to lead the stupid masses towards some future they're too dumb to understand for themselves. I think what it's going to lead them towards is "I rule you with a whip." Institutions of domination have a nice way of reproducing themselves—I think that's kind of like an obvious sociological truism.

And actually, if you look back, that was in fact Bakunin's prediction half a century before—he said this was exactly what was going to happen. [Bakunin was a nineteenth-century Russian anarchist, and with Marx a leading figure in the main socialist labor organization of the time, the First International.] I mean, Bakunin was talking about the people around Marx, this was before Lenin was born, but his prediction was that the nature of the intelligentsia as a formation in modern industrial society is that they are going to try to become the social managers. Now, they're not going to become the social managers because they own capital, and they're not going to become the social managers because they've got a lot of guns. They are going to become the social managers because they can control, organize, and direct what's called "knowledge"—they have the skills to process information, and to mobilize support for decision-making, and so on and so forth. And Bakunin predicted that these people would fall into two categories. On the one hand, there would be the "left" intellectuals, who would try to rise to power on the backs of mass popular movements, and if they could gain power, they would then beat the people into submission and try to control them. On the other hand, if they found that they couldn't get power that way themselves, they would become the servants of what we would nowadays call "state-capitalism," though Bakunin didn't use the term. And either of these two categories of intellectuals, he said, would be "beating the people with the people's stick"—that is, they'd be presenting themselves as representatives of the people, so they'd be holding the people's stick, but they would be beating the people with it.[4]

Well, Bakunin didn't go on with this, but I think it follows from his analysis that it's extremely easy to shift from one position to the other—it's extremely easy to undergo what's called the "God That Failed" syndrome. You start off as basically a Leninist, someone who's going to become part of what Bakunin called the "Red Bureaucracy," you see that power doesn't lie that way, and then you very easily become an ideologist of the right, and devote your life to exposing the sins of your former comrades, who haven't yet seen the light and shifted to where power really lies. And you barely have to change at all, really, you're just operating under a different formal power structure. In fact, we're seeing it right now in the former Soviet Union: the same guys who were Communist thugs, Stalinist thugs two years back are now running banks, they're enthusiastic free-marketeers, praising America and so on. And this has been going on for forty years—it's become kind of a joke.

Now, Bakunin didn't say it's the *nature* of people that this will happen. I mean, I don't know how much he thought it through, but what we should say is that a Red Bureaucracy or its state-capitalist commissar-class equivalent is not going to take over because that's the nature of people—it's that the ones who *don't* do it will be cast by the wayside, the ones who do do it will make out. The ones who are ruthless and brutal and harsh enough to seize power are the ones who are going to survive. The ones who try to associate themselves with popular organizations and help the general population *itself* become organized, who try to assist popular movements in that kind of way, they're just not going to survive under these situations of concentrated power.

## Marxist "Theory" and Intellectual Fakery

WOMAN: *Noam, apart from the idea of the "vanguard," I'm interested why you're so critical of the whole broader category of Marxist analysis in general—like people in the universities and so on who refer to themselves as "Marxists." I've noticed you're never very happy with it.*

Well, I guess one thing that's unattractive to me about "Marxism" is the very idea that there *is* such a thing. It's a rather striking fact that you don't find things like "Marxism" in the sciences—like, there isn't any part of physics which is "Einsteinianism," let's say, or "Planckianism" or something like that. It doesn't make any sense—because people aren't gods: they just discover things, and they make mistakes, and their graduate students tell them why they're wrong, and then they go on and do things better the next time. But there are no gods around. I mean, scientists do use the terms "Newtonianism" and "Darwinism," but nobody thinks of those as doctrines that you've got to somehow be loyal to, and figure out what the Master thought, and what he would have said in this new circumstance and so on. That sort of thing is just completely alien to rational existence, it only shows up in irrational domains.

So Marxism, Freudianism: any one of these things I think is an irrational cult. They're theology, so they're whatever you think of theology; I don't think much of it. In fact, in my view that's exactly the right analogy: notions like Marxism and Freudianism belong to the history of organized religion.

So part of my problem is just its existence: it seems to me that even to *dis-*

*cuss* something like "Marxism" is already making a mistake. Like, we don't discuss "Planckism." Why not? Because it would be crazy. Planck [German physicist] had some things to say, and some of them are right, and those were absorbed into later science, and some of them are wrong, and they were improved on. It's not that Planck wasn't a great man—all kinds of great discoveries, very smart, mistakes, this and that. That's really the way we ought to look at it, I think. As soon as you set up the idea of "Marxism" or "Freudianism" or something, you've already abandoned rationality.

It seems to me the question a rational person ought to ask is, what is there in Marx's work that's worth saving and modifying, and what is there that ought to be abandoned? Okay, then you look and you find things. I think Marx did some very interesting descriptive work on nineteenth-century history. He was a very good journalist. When he describes the British in India, or the Paris Commune [70-day French workers' revolution in 1871], or the parts of *Capital* that talk about industrial London, a lot of that is kind of interesting—I think later scholarship has improved it and changed it, but it's quite interesting.[5]

He had an abstract model of capitalism which—I'm not sure how valuable it is, to tell you the truth. It was an abstract model, and like any abstract model, it's not really intended to be descriptively accurate in detail, it's intended to sort of pull out some crucial features and study those. And you have to ask in the case of an abstract model, how much of the complex reality does it really capture? That's questionable in this case—first of all, it's questionable how much of nineteenth-century capitalism it captured, and I think it's even more questionable how much of late-twentieth-century capitalism it captures.

There are supposed to be *laws* [i.e. of history and economics]. I can't understand them, that's all I can say; it doesn't seem to me that there are any laws that follow from it. Not that I know of any *better* laws, I just don't think we know about "laws" in history.

There's nothing about socialism in Marx, he wasn't a socialist philosopher—there are about five sentences in Marx's whole work that refer to socialism.[6] He was a theorist of capitalism. I think he introduced some interesting concepts at least, which every sensible person ought to have mastered and employ, notions like class, and relations of production . . .

WOMAN: *Dialectics?*

Dialectics is one that I've never understood, actually—I've just never understood what the word means. Marx doesn't use it, incidentally, it's used by Engels.[7] And if anybody can tell me what it is, I'll be happy. I mean, I've read all kinds of things which talk about "dialectics"—I haven't the foggiest idea what it is. It seems to mean something about complexity, or alternative positions, or change, or something. I don't know.

I'll tell you the honest truth: I'm kind of simple-minded when it comes to these things. Whenever I hear a four-syllable word I get skeptical, because I want to make sure you can't say it in monosyllables. Don't forget, part of the whole intellectual vocation is creating a niche for yourself, and if everybody can understand what you're talking about, you've sort of lost, because then what makes you special? What makes you special has got to be something that you had to work really hard to understand, and you mastered it, and all those guys out there don't understand it, and then that becomes the basis for your privilege and your power.

So take what's called "literary theory"—I mean, I don't think there's any such thing as literary "theory," any more than there's cultural "theory" or historical "theory." If you're just reading books and talking about them and getting people to understand them, okay, you can be terrific at that, like Edmund Wilson was terrific at it—but he didn't have a literary *theory*. On the other hand, if you want to mingle in the same room with that physicist over there who's talking about quarks, you'd better have a complicated theory too that nobody can understand: *he* has a complicated theory that nobody can understand, why shouldn't *I* have a complicated theory that nobody can understand? If someone came along with a theory of history, it would be the same: either it would be truisms, or maybe some smart ideas, like somebody could say, "Why not look at economic factors lying behind the Constitution?" or something like that—but there'd be nothing there that couldn't be said in monosyllables.

In fact, it's extremely rare, outside of the natural sciences, to find things that *can't* be said in monosyllables: there are just interesting, simple ideas, which are often extremely difficult to come up with and hard to work out. Like, if you want to try to understand how the modern industrial economy developed, let's say, that can take a lot of work. But the "theory" will be extremely thin, if by "theory" we mean something with principles which are not obvious when you first look at them, and from which you can deduce surprising consequences and try to confirm the principles—you're not going to find anything like that in the social world.

Incidentally, I should say that my own political writing is often denounced from both the left and the right for being non-theoretical—and that's completely correct. But it's exactly as theoretical as anyone else's, I just don't call it "theoretical," I call it "trivial"—which is in fact what it is. I mean, it's not that some of these people whose stuff is considered "deep theory" and so on don't have some interesting things to say. Often they have very interesting things to say. But it's nothing that you couldn't say at the level of a high school student, or that a high school student couldn't figure out if they had the time and support and a little bit of training.

I think people should be extremely skeptical when intellectual life constructs structures which aren't transparent—because the fact of the matter is that in most areas of life, we just don't understand anything very much. There are some areas, like say, quantum physics, where they're not faking. But most of the time it's just fakery, I think: anything that's at all understood can probably be described pretty simply. And when words like "dialectics" come along, or "hermeneutics," and all this kind of stuff that's supposed to be very profound, like Goering, "I reach for my revolver."

MAN: *I find it very reinforcing that you don't understand the word "dialectics," it sort of validates me.*

I'm not saying that it doesn't have any meaning—you observe people using the term and they look like they're communicating. But it's like when I watch people talking Turkish: something's going on, but I'm not part of it.

Actually, occasionally in interviews I've said this about not understanding "dialectics," and I get long letters back from people saying, "You don't understand, here's what 'dialectical' is"—and either it's incomprehensible, or else it's trivial. So maybe I've got a gene missing or something—like people can be tone-deaf, they just can't hear the music. But everything I encounter in these fields either seems to be sort of interesting, but pretty obvious once you see it—maybe you didn't see it at first, and somebody had to point it out to you—or else just incomprehensible.

I'm skeptical: I think one has a right to be skeptical when you don't understand something. I mean, when I look at a page of, say, quantum electrodynamics, I don't understand a word of it. But I know what I would have to do to *get* to understand it, and I'm pretty confident that I *could* get to understand it—I've understood other complicated things. So I figure if I bothered to put myself through the discipline, and I studied the early stuff and the later stuff, I'd finally get to the point where I understood it. Or I could go to someone in the Physics Department and say, "Tell me why everybody's excited about this stuff," and they could adapt it to my level and tell me how to pursue it further. Maybe I wouldn't understand it very deeply, or I couldn't have invented it or something, but I'd at least begin to understand it. On the other hand, when I look at a page of Marxist philosophy or literary theory, I have the feeling that I could stare at it for the rest of my life and I'd never understand it—and I don't know how to proceed to *get* to understand it any better, I don't even know what steps I could take.

I mean, it's possible that these fields are beyond me, maybe I'm not smart enough or something. But that would have kind of a funny conclusion—it's nothing to do with me. That would mean that somehow in these domains people have been able to create something that's more complex than physics and mathematics—because those are subjects I think I could get to understand. And I just don't believe that, frankly: I don't believe that literary theorists or Marxian philosophers have advanced to some new intellectual level that transcends century after century of hard intellectual work.

MAN: *Do you think the same thing about philosophy in general?*

There are parts of philosophy which I think I understand, and it's most of classical philosophy. And there are things that I don't understand, because they don't make any sense—and that's okay too, these are hard questions. I mean, it's not necessarily a criticism to say that something doesn't make sense: there are subjects that it's hard to talk sensibly about. But if I read, say, Russell, or analytic philosophy, or Wittgenstein and so on, I think I can come to understand what they're saying, and I can see why I think it's wrong, as I often do. But when I read, you know, Derrida, or Lacan, or Althusser, or any of these—I just don't understand it. It's like words passing in front of my eyes: I can't follow the arguments, I don't see the arguments, anything that looks like a description of a fact looks wrong to me. So maybe I'm missing a gene or something, it's possible. But my honest opinion is, I think it's all fraud.

MAN: *I think you may be glorifying the scientists a bit by projecting them as somehow kind of pure. For example, take Newtonian mechanics: Einstein came along and showed how it was wrong, but over the years the scientific community did refer to it as "Newtonian" mechanics.*

That's an interesting case, because Newtonian mechanics *was* treated as kind of holy—because it was such a revolutionary development. I mean, it was really the first time in human history that people ever had an explanation of things in any deep sense: it was so comprehensive, and so simple, and so far-reaching in its consequences that it almost looked like it was *necessary.* And in fact, it was treated that way for a long time—so much so that Kant, for example, regarded it as the task of philosophy to derive Newtonian physics from *a priori* principles, and to show that it was certain truth, on a par with mathematics. And it really wasn't until the late-nineteenth and early-twentieth century that the fallacy of those conceptions became quite clear, and with that realization there was a real advance in our conception of what "science" is. So science did have kind of a religious character for a period, you're right—and that was something we had to get ourselves out of, I think. It doesn't happen anymore.

## Ideological Control in the Sciences and Humanities

MAN: *Would you say that as academic disciplines, the sciences are fundamentally different from the humanities and social sciences in terms of ideological control? There don't seem to be the same kinds of barriers to inquiry or the same commitment to indoctrination in the scientific fields as there are in other areas, like in economics or political science, for instance.*

Well, I think there *was* an ideological control problem in the sciences, it's just that we transcended it—Galileo faced it, for example [the Italian astronomer and scientist was arrested by the Roman Catholic Church in 1633 and compelled to renounce his conclusion that the earth revolves around the sun]. You go back a couple centuries in the West and the ideological control problem in the sciences was severe: Descartes is alleged to have destroyed the final volume of his treatise on the world, the one that was supposed to deal with the human mind, because he learned of the fate of Galileo. That's the analog to death squads—the Inquisition was doing precisely that. Okay, that's passed in the West at least, but not everywhere.

MAN: *But why has it passed?*

Well, I think there are a few reasons. One is just a general increase in freedom and enlightenment, won through popular struggles over centuries— we've become a much freer society than we were in absolutist times. And intellectuals have often played a role in that, breaking down ideological barriers and creating kind of a space for greater freedom of thought, for instance during the Enlightenment [in the eighteenth century]. That often took a lot of courage and quite a struggle, and it goes on until today.

There are also utilitarian reasons. It turns out that, especially since the mid-nineteenth century, the ability to gain a deeper understanding of the physical world through modern science has interacted critically with modern industrial development: progress in the sciences has contributed materially to private profit-making, private power. So there are utilitarian reasons for allowing freedom of scientific inquiry, but I wouldn't over-exaggerate them—I think what's happened with the sciences is a lot like the process that's led to freedom in other domains, like why we don't have slavery, let's say, or why after 150 years of American history women won the right to vote [in 1920].

And also, remember, after the great scientific revolutions that led to the Enlightenment, it got to the point where you couldn't *do* science anymore if you were subjected to the kinds of doctrinal controls that remain quite effective in other fields. I mean, if you're a physicist after Newton trying to spin off ideological fanaticism, you're just out of the game—progress has been too much. That's very different from the social sciences and the humanities—you can tell falsehoods forever in those fields and nothing will ever stop you, like you don't have Mother Nature around keeping you honest. And the result is, there's a real difference in the two cultures.

So when you go to graduate school in the natural sciences, you're immediately brought into critical inquiry—and in fact, what you're learning is kind of a craft; you don't really *teach* science, people sort of get the idea how to do it as apprentices, hopefully by working with good people. But the goal is to learn how to do creative work, and to challenge everything. That's very different from the humanities and the social sciences, where what you're supposed to do is absorb a body of knowledge, and then pick yourself a little area in it and for the rest of your life work on that. I mean, the way you become a highly respected scholar in the humanities, say, is to pick some arcane area, like English novels from 1720 to 1790, and get to know more of the *data* about that than any other human being in history.

So you know who copied this word from that, and so on. A lot of it is kind of mindless, but that's the sort of thing you're supposed to know. And there's really very little intellectual challenge: the only way you could be wrong is if you got a comma out of place—and in fact, that's considered the worst crime. I'm kind of caricaturing it a bit—but frankly I think it works this way. And certainly the sciences are very different.

## The Function of the Schools

WOMAN: *But I guess I don't quite see how this ideological control mechanism actually* works *in the humanities and social sciences—I mean, how exactly is it that the schools end up being an indoctrination system? Can you describe the process in more detail?*

Well, the main point I think is that the entire school curriculum, from kindergarten through graduate school, will be tolerated only so long as it continues to perform its institutional role. So take the universities, which in many respects are not very different from the media in the way they function—though they're a much more complex system, so they're harder to study systematically. Universities do not generate nearly enough funds to support themselves from tuition money alone: they're parasitic institutions that need to be supported from the outside, and that means they're dependent on wealthy alumni, on corporations, and on the government, which are groups with the same basic interests. Well, as long as the universities *serve* those interests, they'll be funded. If they ever *stop* serving those interests, they'll start to get in trouble.

So for example, in the late 1960s it began to appear that the universities were *not* adequately performing that service—students were asking questions, they were thinking independently, they were rejecting a lot of the Establishment value-system, challenging all sorts of things—and the corporations began to react to that, they began to react in a number of ways. For one thing, they began to develop alternative programs, like I.B.M. began to set up kind of a vocational training program to produce engineers on their own: if M.I.T. wasn't going to do it for them the way they wanted, they'd do it themselves—and that would have meant they'd stop funding M.I.T. Well, of course things never really got out of hand in the Sixties, so the moves in that direction were very limited. But those are the kinds of pressures there are.[8]

And in fact, you can even see similar things right now. Take all this business about Allan Bloom and that book everybody's been talking about, *The Closing of the American Mind*.[9] It's this huge best-seller, I don't know if you've bothered looking at it—it's mind-bogglingly stupid. I read it once in the supermarket while my . . . I hate to say it, while my wife was shopping I stood there and read the damn thing; it takes about fifteen minutes to read.

MAN: *You read two thousand words a minute?*

I mean, "read"—you know, sort of turn the pages to see if there's anything there that isn't totally stupid. But what that book is basically saying is that education ought to be set up like some sort of variant of the Marine Corps, in which you just march the students through a canon of "great thoughts" that are picked out for everybody. So some group of people will say, "Here are the great thoughts, the great thoughts of Western civilization are in this corpus; you guys sit there and learn them, read them and learn them, and be able to repeat them." That's the kind of model Bloom is calling for.

Well, anybody who's ever thought about education or been involved in it, or even gone to school, knows that the effect of that is that students will end up knowing and understanding virtually nothing. It doesn't matter how great the thoughts are, if they are simply imposed upon you from the outside and you're forced through them step by step, after you're done you'll have forgotten what they are. I mean, I'm sure that every one of you has taken any number of courses in school in which you worked, and you did your homework, you passed the exam, maybe you even got an "A"— and a week later you couldn't even remember what the course was about. You only learn things and learn how to think if there's some purpose for learning, some motivation that's coming out of *you* somehow. In fact, all of the methodology in education isn't really much more than that—getting students to want to learn. Once they want to learn, they'll do it.

But the point is that this model Bloom and all these other people are calling for is just a part of the whole method of imposing discipline through the schools, and of preventing people from learning how to think for themselves. So what you do is make students go through and sort of memorize a canon of what are called "Good Books," which you force on them, and then somehow great things are supposed to happen. It's a completely stupid form of education, but I think that's part of why it's selected and supported, and why there's so much hysteria that it's been questioned in past years— just because it's very functional to train people and discipline them in ways like this. The popularity of the Bloom thing, I would imagine, is mostly a reaction to the sort of liberating effect that the student movement of the Sixties and other challenges to the schools and universities began to have.

WOMAN: *All of Allan Bloom's "great thoughts" are by elite white males.*

Yeah, okay—but it wouldn't even matter if he had some different array of material, it really wouldn't matter. The idea that there's some array of "the deep thoughts," and we smart people will pick them out and you dumb guys will learn them—or memorize them at least, because you don't really learn them if they're just forced on you—that's nonsense. If you're serious about, say, reading Plato,[10] it's fine to read Plato—but you try to figure out what's right, what's wrong, what's a better way of looking at it, why was he saying this when he should have been saying something else, what grotesque error of reasoning did he make over here, and so on and so forth. That's the way you would read serious work, just like you would in the sciences. But you're not supposed to read it that way here, you're supposed to read it because it's the truth, or it's the great thoughts or something. And that's kind of like the worst form of theology.

The point is, it doesn't matter *what* you read, what matters is *how* you read it. Now, I don't mean comic books, but there's a lot of cultural wealth out there from all over the place, and to learn what it means for something to be culturally rich, you can explore almost anywhere: there's no fixed subset that is the basis of truth and understanding. I mean, you can read the "Good Books," and memorize what they said, and forget them a week later—if it doesn't *mean* anything to you personally, you'd might as well not have read them. And it's very hard to know what's *going* to mean something to different people. But there's plenty of exciting literature around in the world, and there's absolutely no reason to believe that unless you've read the Greeks and Dante and so on, you've missed things—I mean, yeah, you've missed things, but you've also missed things if you haven't learned something about other cultural traditions too.

Just take a look at philosophy, for example, which is a field that I know something about: some of the best, most exciting, most active philosophers in the contemporary world, people who've made a real impact on the field, couldn't tell Plato from Aristotle, except for what they remember from some Freshman course they once took. Now, that's not to say you shouldn't read Plato and Aristotle—sure, there are millions of things you should read; nobody's ever going to read more than a tiny fraction of the things you wished you knew. But just reading them does you no good: you only learn if the material is integrated into your own creative processes somehow, otherwise it just passes through your mind and disappears. And there's nothing valuable about that—it has basically the effect of learning the catechism, or memorizing the Constitution or something like that.

Real education is about getting people involved in thinking for themselves—and that's a tricky business to know how to do well, but clearly it requires that whatever it is you're looking at has to somehow catch people's interest and make them *want* to think, and make them *want* to pursue and explore. And just regurgitating "Good Books" is absolutely the worst way to do it—that's just a way of turning people into automata. You may call that an education if you want, but it's really the opposite of an education, which is why people like William Bennett [Reagan's Secretary of Education] and Allan Bloom and these others are all so much in favor of it.

WOMAN: *Are you saying that the real purpose of the universities and the schools is just to indoctrinate people—and really not much else?*

Well, I'm not quite saying that. Like, I wouldn't say that *no* meaningful work takes place in the schools, or that they only exist to provide manpower for the corporate system or something like that—these are very complex systems, after all. But the basic institutional role and function of the schools, and why they're supported, is to provide an ideological service: there's a real selection for obedience and conformity. And I think that process starts in kindergarten, actually.

Let me just tell you a personal story. My oldest, closest friend is a guy who came to the United States from Latvia when he was fifteen, fleeing from Hitler. He escaped to New York with his parents and went to George Washington High School, which in those days at least was the school for bright Jewish kids in New York City. And he once told me that the first thing that struck him about American schools was the fact that if he got a "C" in a course, nobody cared, but if he came to school three minutes late he was sent to the principal's office—and that generalized. He realized that what it meant is, what's valued here is the ability to work on an assembly line, even if it's an intellectual assembly line. The important thing is to be able to obey orders, and to do what you're told, and to be where you're supposed to be. The values are, you're going to be a factory worker somewhere—maybe they'll call it a university—but you're going to be following somebody else's orders, and just doing your work in some prescribed way. And what matters is discipline, not figuring things out for yourself, or understanding things that interest you—those are kind of marginal: just make sure you meet the requirements of a factory.

Well, that's pretty much what the schools are like, I think: they reward discipline and obedience, and they punish independence of mind. If you happen to be a little innovative, or maybe you forgot to come to school one day because you were reading a book or something, that's a tragedy, that's a crime—because you're not supposed to think, you're supposed to obey, and just proceed through the material in whatever way they require.

And in fact, most of the people who make it through the education system and get into the elite universities are able to do it because they've been willing to obey a lot of stupid orders for years and years—that's the way I did it, for example. Like, you're told by some stupid teacher, "Do this," which you know makes no sense whatsoever, but you do it, and if you do it you get to the next rung, and then you obey the next order, and finally you work your way through and they give you your letters: an awful lot of education is like that, from the very beginning. Some people go along with it because they figure, "Okay, I'll do any stupid thing that asshole says because I want to get ahead"; others do it because they've just internalized the values—but after a while, those two things tend to get sort of blurred. But you do it, or else you're out: you ask too many questions and you're going to get in trouble.

Now, there are also people who *don't* go along—and they're called "behavior problems," or "unmotivated," or things like that. Well, you don't want to be too glib about it—there *are* children with behavior problems—but a lot of them are just independent-minded, or don't like to conform, or just want to go their own way. And they get into trouble right from the very beginning, and are typically weeded out. I mean, I've taught young kids too, and the fact is there are always some who just don't take your word for it. And the very unfortunate tendency is to try to beat them down, because they're a pain in the neck. But what they ought to be is encouraged. Yeah: why take my word for it? Who the heck am I? Figure it out for yourself. That's what real education would be *about*, in fact.

Actually, I happen to have been very lucky myself and gone to an experimental-progressive Deweyite school, from about the time I was age one-and-a-half to twelve [John Dewey was an American philosopher and educational reformer]. And there it was done routinely: children were encouraged to challenge everything, and you sort of worked on your own, you were supposed to think things through for yourself—it was a real experience. And it was quite a striking change when it ended and I had to go to the city high school, which was the pride of the city school system. It was the school for academically-oriented kids in Philadelphia—and it was the dumbest, most ridiculous place I've ever been, it was like falling into a black hole or something. For one thing, it was extremely competitive—because that's one of the best ways of controlling people. So everybody was ranked, and you always knew exactly where you were: are you third in the class, or maybe did you move down to fourth? All of this stuff is put into people's heads in various ways in the schools—that you've got to beat down the person next to you, and just look out for yourself. And there are all sorts of other things like that too.

But the point is, there's nothing *necessary* about them in education. I know, because I went through an alternative to it—so it can certainly be done. But given the external power structure of the society in which they function now, the institutional role of the schools for the most part is just to train people for obedience and conformity, and to make them controllable and indoctrinated—and as long as the schools fulfill that role, they'll be supported.

Now, of course, it doesn't work a hundred percent—so you do get some people all the way through who don't go along. And as I was saying, in the sciences at least, people have to be trained for creativity and disobedience—because there is no other way you can *do* science. But in the humanities and social sciences, and in fields like journalism and economics and so on, that's much less true—there people have to be trained to be managers, and controllers, and to accept things, and not to question too much. So you really do get a very different kind of education. And people who break out of line are weeded out or beaten back in all kinds of ways.

I mean, it's not very abstract: if you're, say, a young person in college, or in journalism, or for that matter a fourth grader, and you have too much of an independent mind, there's a whole variety of devices that will be used to deflect you from that error—and if you can't be controlled, to marginalize or just eliminate you. In fourth grade, you're a "behavior problem." In college, you may be "irresponsible," or "erratic," or "not the right kind of student." If you make it to the faculty, you'll fail in what's sometimes called "collegiality," getting along with your colleagues. If you're a young journalist and you're pursuing stories that the people at the managerial level above you understand, either intuitively or explicitly, are not to be pursued, you can be sent off to work at the Police desk, and advised that you don't have "proper standards of objectivity." There's a whole range of these techniques.

Now, we live in a free society, so you don't get sent to gas chambers and they don't send the death squads after you—as is commonly done, and not far from here, say in Mexico.[11] But there are nevertheless quite successful devices, both subtle and extreme, to ensure that doctrinal correctness is not seriously infringed upon.

## Subtler Methods of Control

Let me just start with some of the more subtle ways; I'll give you an example. After I finished college, I went to this program at Harvard called the "Society of Fellows"—which is kind of this elite finishing school, where they teach you to be a Harvard or Yale professor, and to drink the right wine, and say the right things, and so on and so forth. I mean, you had all of the resources of Harvard available to you and your only responsibility was to show up at a dinner once a week, so it was great for just doing your work if you wanted to. But the real point of the whole thing was socialization: teaching the right values.

For instance, I remember there was a lot of anglophilia at Harvard at the time—you were supposed to wear British clothes, and pretend you spoke with a British accent, that sort of stuff. In fact, there were actually guys there who I thought were British, who had never been outside of the United States. If any of you have studied literature or history or something, you might recognize some of this, those are the places you usually find it. Well, somehow I managed to survive that, I don't know how exactly—but most didn't. And what I discovered is that a large part of education at the really elite institutions is simply refinement, teaching the social graces: what kind of clothes you should wear, how to drink port the right way, how to have polite conversation without talking about serious topics, but of course indicating that you *could* talk about serious topics if you were so vulgar as to actually do it, all kinds of things which an intellectual is supposed to know how to do. And that was really the main point of the program, I think.

Actually, there are much more important cases too—and they're even more revealing about the role of the elite schools. For example, the 1930s were a period of major labor strife and labor struggle in the U.S., and it was scaring the daylights out of the whole business community here—because labor was finally winning the right to organize, and there were other legislative victories as well. And there were a lot of efforts to try to overcome this, but one of them was that Harvard introduced a "Trade Union Program." What it did was to bring in rising young people in the labor movement—you know, the guy who looks like he's going to be the Local president next year—and have them stay in dorms in the Business School, and put them through a whole socialization process, help them come to share some of the values and understandings of the elite, teach them that "Our job is to work together," "We're all in this together," and so on and so forth. I mean, there are always two lines: for the public it's, "We're all in this together, management and labor are cooperating, joint enterprise, harmony" and so on—meanwhile business is fighting a vicious class war on the side. And that effort to socialize and integrate union activists—well, I've never measured its success, but I'm sure it was very successful. And the process was similar to what I experienced and saw a Harvard education to be myself.

Or let me tell you another story I heard about twenty years ago from a black civil rights activist who came up to study at Harvard Law School—it kind of illustrates some of the other pressures that are around. This guy gave a talk in which he described how the kids starting off at Harvard Law School come in with long hair and backpacks and social ideals, they're all going to go into public service law to change the world and so on—that's the first year. Around springtime, the recruiters come for the cushy summer jobs in the Wall Street law firms, and these students figure, "What the heck, I can put on a tie and a jacket and shave for one day, just because I need that money and why shouldn't I have it?" So they put on the tie and the jacket for that one day, and they get the job, and then they go off for the summer—and when they come back in the fall, it's ties, and jackets, and obedience, a shift of ideology. Sometimes it takes two years.

Well, obviously he was over-drawing the point—but those sorts of factors also are very influential. I mean, I've felt it all my life: it's extremely easy to be sucked into the dominant culture, it can be very appealing. There are a lot of rewards. And what's more, the people you meet don't look like bad people—you don't want to sit there and insult them. Maybe they're perfectly nice people. So you try to be friends, maybe you even are friends. Well, you begin to conform, you begin to adapt, you begin to smooth off the harsher edges—and pretty soon it's just happened, it kind of seeps in. And education at a place like Harvard is largely geared to that, to a remarkable extent in fact.

And there are many other subtle mechanisms which contribute to ideological control as well, of course—including just the fact that the universities support and encourage people to occupy themselves with irrelevant and innocuous work.

Or just take the fact that certain topics are unstudiable in the schools—

because they don't fall anywhere: the disciplines are divided in such a way that they simply will not be studied. That's something that's extremely important. So for example, take a question that people were very worried about in the United States for years and years—the economic competitiveness of Japan. Now, I always thought the talk about "American declinism" and "Japan as Number 1" was vastly overblown, just as the later idea of a "Japanese decline" is wildly exaggerated. In fact, Japan retains a very considerable edge in crucial areas of manufacturing, especially in high tech. They did get in trouble because of a huge stock market and real estate boom that collapsed, but serious economists don't believe that Japan has really lost competitiveness in these areas.[12]

Well, why has Japan been so economically competitive? I mean, there are a lot of reasons why, but the major reason is very clear. Both Japan and the United States (and every other industrial country in the world, actually) have essentially state-coordinated economies—but our traditional system of state coordination is less efficient than theirs.

Remember, talk about "free trade" is fine in editorials, but nobody actually practices it in reality: in every modern economy, the taxpayers are made to subsidize the private corporations, who then keep the profits for themselves. But the point is, different countries have different ways of arranging those subsidies. So take a look at the competitive parts of the U.S. economy, the parts that are successful in international trade—they're all state-subsidized. Capital-intensive agriculture is a well-known case: American capital-intensive agriculture is able to compete internationally because the state purchases the excess products and stores them, and subsidizes the energy inputs, and so on.

Or look at high-technology industry: research and development for high technology is very costly, and corporations don't make any profits off it directly—so therefore the taxpayer is made to pay for it. And in the United States, that's traditionally been done largely through the Pentagon system: the Pentagon pays for high-tech research and development, then if something comes out of it which happens to be marketable, it's handed over to private corporations so they can make the profits. And the research mostly isn't weapons, incidentally—it's things like computers, which are the center of any contemporary industrial economy, and were developed through the Pentagon system in the United States. And the same is true of virtually all high tech, in fact. And furthermore, there's another important subsidy there: the Pentagon also purchases the *output* of high-technology industry, it serves as a state-guaranteed market for waste-production—that's what contracts for developing weapons systems are; I mean, you don't actually *use* the weapons you're paying for, you just destroy them in a couple years and replace them with the next array of even more advanced stuff you don't need. Well, all of that is just perfect for pouring continuous taxpayer subsidies into high-tech industry, and it's because of these enormous subsidies that American high tech is competitive internationally.

Well, Japan has run its economy pretty much the same way we do, except with one crucial difference. Instead of using the military system, the way they've worked their public subsidies in Japan is they have a government ministry, M.I.T.I. [the Ministry of International Trade and Industry], which sits down with the big corporations and conglomerates and banking firms, and plans their economic system for the next couple years—they plan how much consumption there's going to be, and how much investment there's going to be, and where the investment should go, and so on. Well, that's more efficient. And since Japan is a very disciplined and obedient society culturally, the population there just does what they tell them, and nobody ever asks any questions about it.

Alright, to see how this difference played out over the years, just look at the "Star Wars" program in the United States, for example. Star Wars [the Strategic Defense Initiative] is the pretext for a huge amount of research and development spending through the Pentagon system here—it's our way of funding the new generation of computer technology, lasers, new software, and so on. Well, if you look at the distribution of expenses for Star Wars, it turns out that it was virtually the same allocation of funding as was made through the Japanese state-directed economic system in the same time period: in those same years, M.I.T.I. made about the same judgments about how to distribute their resources as we did, they spent about the same proportion of money in lasers, and the same proportion in software, and so on.[13] And the reason is that all of these planners make approximately the same judgments about the likely new technologies.

Well, why was Japan so competitive with the U.S. economically, despite highly inauspicious conditions? There are a lot of reasons. But the main reason is that they directed their public subsidy straight to the commercial market. So to work on lasers, they tried to figure out ways of producing lasers for the commercial market, and they do it pretty well. But when we want to develop lasers for the commercial market, what we do is pour the money into the Pentagon, which then tries to work out a way to use a laser to shoot down a missile ten thousand miles away—and if they can work that out, then they hope there'll be some commercial spin-offs that come out of it all. Okay, that's less efficient. And since the Japanese are no dumber than we are, and they have an efficient system of state-coordination while we have an inefficient one, over the years they succeeded in the economic competition.

Well, these are major phenomena of modern life—but where do you go to study them in the universities or the academic profession? That's a very interesting question. You don't go to the economics department, because that's not what they look at: the real hot-shot economics departments are interested in abstract models of how a pure free-enterprise economy works—you know, generalizations to ten-dimensional space of some nonexistent free-market system. You don't go to the political science department, because they're concerned with electoral statistics, and voting patterns, and micro-bureaucracy—like the way one government bureaucrat talks to another in some detailed air. You don't go to the anthropology department, because they're studying hill tribesmen in New Guinea. You don't go to the sociology department, because they're studying crime in the ghettos. In fact, you don't go anywhere—there isn't any field that deals with these topics. There's no journal that deals with them. In fact, there is no academic profession that is concerned with the central problems of modern society. Now, you can go to the *business school*, and there they'll talk about them—because those people are in the real world. But not in the academic departments: nobody there is going to tell you what's really going on in the world.[14]

And it's extremely important that there *not* be a field that studies these questions—because if there ever were such a field, people might come to understand too much, and in a relatively free society like ours, they might start to do something with that understanding. Well, no institution is going to encourage *that*. I mean, there's nothing in what I just said that you couldn't explain to junior high school students, it's all pretty straightforward. But it's not what you study in a junior high Civics course—what you study there is propaganda about the way systems are supposed to work but don't.

Incidentally, part of the genius of this aspect of the higher education system is that it can get people to sell out even while they think they're doing exactly the right thing. So some young person going into academia will say to themselves, "Look, I'm going to be a real radical here"—and you *can* be, as long as you adapt yourself to these categories which guarantee that you'll never ask the right questions, and that you'll never even *look* at the right questions. But you don't *feel* like you're selling out, you're not saying "I'm working for the ruling class" or anything like that—you're not, you're being a Marxist economist or something. But the effect is, they've totally neutralized you.

Alright, all of these are subtle forms of control, with the effect of preventing serious insight into the way that power actually works in the society. And it makes very good sense for a system to be set up like that: powerful institutions don't want to be investigated, obviously. Why would they? They don't want the public to know how they work—maybe the people inside them understand how they work, but they don't want anybody else to know, because that would threaten and undermine their power. So one should *expect* the institutions to function in such a way as to protect themselves—and some of the ways in which they protect themselves are by various subtle techniques of ideological control like these.

## Cruder Methods of Control

Then aside from all that, there are also crude methods of control. So if some young political scientist or economist decides they *are* going to try to ask these kinds of questions, the chances are they're going to be marginalized in some fashion, or else be weeded out of the institution altogether. At the extreme end, there have been repeated university purges in the United States. During the 1950s, for example, the universities were just cleaned out of dissident thought—people were fired on all kinds of grounds, or not allowed to teach things. And the effects of that were very strong. Then during the late 1960s, when the political ferment really got going, the purges began again—and often they were just straight political firings, not even obscured.[15] For instance, a lot of the best Asia scholars from the United States are now teaching in Australia and Japan—because they couldn't keep jobs in the U.S., they had the wrong ideas. Australia has some of the best Southeast Asia scholars in the world, and they're mostly Americans who were young scholars in the Sixties and couldn't make it into the American academic system, because they thought the wrong things. So if you want to study Cambodia with a top American scholar, you basically have to go to Australia.[16] One of the best Japan historians in the world [Herbert Bix] is teaching in a Japanese university—he's American, but he can't get a job in the United States.

Or let me just tell you a story about M.I.T., which is pretty revealing. A young political science professor—who's by now one of the top people in the field, incidentally [Thomas Ferguson]—was appointed at M.I.T. as an assistant professor right after he got his Ph.D. from Princeton; he's very radical, but he's also extremely smart, so the department just needed him. Well, one day I was sitting in my office and he came over fuming. He told me that the chairman of his department had just come into his office and told him straight out: "If you ever want to get tenure in this department, keep away from anything after the New Deal; you can write all of your radical stuff up to the New Deal, but if you try and do it for the post-New Deal period, you're never going to get tenure in this department."[17] He just told him straight out. Usually you're not told it straight out, but you get to understand it—you get to understand it from the reactions you receive.

This kind of stuff also happens with graduate students. I'm what's called an "Institute Professor" at M.I.T., which means I can teach courses in any department of the university. And over the years I've taught all over the place—but if I even get *near* Political Science, you can feel the bad vibes starting. So in other departments, I'm often asked to be on students' Ph.D. committees, but in Political Science it's virtually never happened—and the few times it has happened, it's always been Third World women. And there's a reason for that: Third World women have a little bit of extra space to maneuver in, because the department doesn't want to appear *too* overtly racist or *too* overtly sexist, so there are some things they can do that other people can't.

Well, a few years ago, one very smart woman graduate student in the Political Science Department wanted to do her dissertation on the media and Southern Africa, and she wanted me to be on her Ph.D. committee. Okay, it's a topic that I'm interested in, and I've worked on it probably more than anybody else there, so there was just no way for them to say I couldn't do it. Then the routine started. The first stage in the doctoral process is that the candidate has a meeting with a couple of faculty members and presents her proposal. Usually two faculty members show up, that's about it. This time it was different: they circulated a notice through the department saying that every faculty member had to show up—and the reason was, *I* was going to be there, and they had to combat this baleful influence. So everybody showed up.

Well, the woman started presenting her dissertation proposal, and you could just see people turning pale. Somebody asked her, "What's your hypothesis?"—you're supposed to have a hypothesis—and it was that media coverage of Southern Africa is going to be influenced by corporate interests. People were practically passing out and falling out the windows. Then starts the critical analysis: "What's your methodology going to be? What tests are you going to use?" And gradually an apparatus was set up and a level of proof demanded that you just can't meet in the social sciences. It wasn't, "I'm going to read the editorials and figure out what they say"— you had to count the words, and do all sorts of statistical nonsense, and so on and so forth. But she fought it through, she just continued fighting. They ultimately required so much junk in her thesis, so much irrelevant, phony social-scientific junk, numbers and charts and meaningless business, that you could barely pick out the content from the morass of methodology. But she did finally make it through—just because she was willing to fight it out. Now, you know, you can do that—but it's tough. And some people really get killed.

## The Fate of an Honest Intellectual

I'll tell you another, last case—and there are many others like this. Here's a story which is really tragic. How many of you know about Joan Peters, the book by Joan Peters? There was this best-seller a few years ago [in 1984], it went through about ten printings, by a woman named Joan Peters—or at least, *signed* by Joan Peters—called *From Time Immemorial.*[18] It was a big scholarly-looking book with lots of footnotes, which purported to show that the Palestinians were all recent immigrants [i.e. to the Jewish-settled areas of the former Palestine, during the British mandate years of 1920 to 1948]. And it was *very* popular—it got literally hundreds of rave reviews, and no negative reviews: the *Washington Post*, the *New York Times*, everybody was just raving about it.[19] Here was this book which proved that there were really no Palestinians! Of course, the implicit message was, if Israel kicks them all out there's no moral issue, because they're just recent immigrants who came in because the Jews had built up the country. And there was all kinds of demographic analysis in it, and a big professor of demography at the University of Chicago [Philip M. Hauser] authenticated it.[20] That was the big intellectual hit for that year: Saul Bellow, Barbara Tuchman, everybody was talking about it as the greatest thing since chocolate cake.[21]

Well, one graduate student at Princeton, a guy named Norman Finkelstein, started reading through the book. He was interested in the history of Zionism, and as he read the book he was kind of surprised by some of the things it said. He's a very careful student, and he started checking the references—and it turned out that the whole thing was a hoax, it was completely faked: probably it had been put together by some intelligence agency or something like that. Well, Finkelstein wrote up a short paper of just preliminary findings, it was about twenty-five pages or so, and he sent it around to I think thirty people who were interested in the topic, scholars in the field and so on, saying: "Here's what I've found in this book, do you think it's worth pursuing?"

Well, he got back one answer, from me. I told him, yeah, I think it's an interesting topic, but I warned him, if you follow this, you're going to get in trouble—because you're going to expose the American intellectual community as a gang of frauds, and they are not going to like it, and they're going to destroy you. So I said: if you want to do it, go ahead, but be aware of what you're getting into. It's an important issue, it makes a big difference whether you eliminate the moral basis for driving out a population—it's preparing the basis for some real horrors—so a lot of people's lives could be at stake. But your life is at stake too, I told him, because if you pursue this, your career is going to be ruined.

Well, he didn't believe me. We became very close friends after this, I didn't know him before. He went ahead and wrote up an article, and he started submitting it to journals. Nothing: they didn't even bother responding. I finally managed to place a piece of it in *In These Times*, a tiny left-wing journal published in Illinois, where some of you may have seen it.[22] Otherwise nothing, no response. Meanwhile his professors—this is Princeton University, supposed to be a serious place—stopped talking to him: they wouldn't make appointments with him, they wouldn't read his papers, he basically had to quit the program.

By this time, he was getting kind of desperate, and he asked me what to do. I gave him what I thought was good advice, but what turned out to be bad advice: I suggested that he shift over to a different department, where I knew some people and figured he'd at least be treated decently. That turned out to be wrong. He switched over, and when he got to the point of writing his thesis he literally could not get the faculty to read it, he couldn't get them to come to his thesis defense. Finally, out of embarrassment, they granted him a Ph.D.—he's very smart, incidentally—but they will not even write a letter for him saying that he was a student at Princeton University. I mean, sometimes you have students for whom it's hard to write good letters of recommendation, because you really didn't think they were very good—

but you can write *something*, there are ways of doing these things. This guy was good, but he literally cannot get a letter.

He's now living in a little apartment somewhere in New York City, and he's a part-time social worker working with teenage drop-outs. Very promising scholar—if he'd done what he was told, he would have gone on and right now he'd be a professor somewhere at some big university. Instead he's working part-time with disturbed teenaged kids for a couple thousand dollars a year.[23] That's a lot better than a death squad, it's true—it's a whole lot better than a death squad. But those are the techniques of control that are around.

But let me just go on with the Joan Peters story. Finkelstein's very persistent: he took a summer off and sat in the New York Public Library, where he went through every single reference in the book—and he found a record of fraud that you cannot believe. Well, the New York intellectual community is a pretty small place, and pretty soon everybody knew about this, everybody knew the book was a fraud and it was going to be exposed sooner or later. The one journal that was smart enough to react intelligently was the *New York Review of Books*—they knew that the thing was a sham, but the editor didn't want to offend his friends, so he just didn't run a review at all. That was the one journal that *didn't* run a review.

Meanwhile, Finkelstein was being called in by big professors in the field who were telling him, "Look, call off your crusade; you drop this and we'll take care of you, we'll make sure you get a job," all this kind of stuff. But he kept doing it—he kept on and on. Every time there was a favorable review, he'd write a letter to the editor which wouldn't get printed; he was doing whatever he could do. We approached the publishers and asked them if they were going to respond to any of this, and they said no—and they were right. Why should they respond? They had the whole system buttoned up, there was never going to be a critical word about this in the United States. But then they made a technical error: they allowed the book to appear in England, where you can't control the intellectual community quite as easily.

Well, as soon as I heard that the book was going to come out in England, I immediately sent copies of Finkelstein's work to a number of British scholars and journalists who are interested in the Middle East—and they were ready. As soon as the book appeared, it was just demolished, it was blown out of the water. Every major journal, the *Times Literary Supplement,* the *London Review,* the *Observer,* everybody had a review saying, this doesn't even reach the level of nonsense, of idiocy. A lot of the criticism used Finkelstein's work without any acknowledgment, I should say—but about the kindest word anybody said about the book was "ludicrous," or "preposterous."[24]

Well, people here read British reviews—if you're in the American intellectual community, you read the *Times Literary Supplement* and the *London Review,* so it began to get a little embarrassing. You started getting back-tracking: people started saying, "Well, look, I didn't really say the book was good, I just said it's an interesting topic," things like that. At that point, the *New York Review* swung into action, and they did what they always do in these circumstances. See, there's like a routine that you go through—if a book gets blown out of the water in England in places people here will see, or if a book gets praised in England, you have to react. And if it's a book on Israel, there's a standard way of doing it: you get an Israeli scholar to review it. That's called covering your ass—because whatever an Israeli scholar says, you're pretty safe: no one can accuse the journal of anti-Semitism, none of the usual stuff works.

So after the Peters book got blown out of the water in England, the *New York Review* assigned it to a good person actually, in fact Israel's leading specialist on Palestinian nationalism [Yehoshua Porath], someone who knows a lot about the subject. And he wrote a review, which they then didn't publish—it went on for almost a year without the thing being published; nobody knows exactly what was going on, but you can guess that there must have been a lot of pressure not to publish it. Eventually it was even written up in the *New York Times* that this review wasn't getting published, so finally some version of it did appear.[25] It was critical, it said the book is nonsense and so on, but it cut corners, the guy didn't say what he knew.[26]

Actually, the Israeli reviews in general were extremely critical: the reaction of the Israeli press was that they hoped the book would not be widely read, because ultimately it would be harmful to the Jews—sooner or later it would get exposed, and then it would just look like a fraud and a hoax, and it would reflect badly on Israel.[27] They underestimated the American intellectual community, I should say.

Anyhow, by that point the American intellectual community realized that the Peters book was an embarrassment, and it sort of disappeared— nobody talks about it anymore. I mean, you still find it at newsstands in the airport and so on, but the best and the brightest know that they are not supposed to talk about it anymore: because it was exposed and they were exposed.

Well, the point is, what happened to Finkelstein is the kind of thing that can happen when you're an honest critic—and we could go on and on with other cases like that. [Editors' Note: Finkelstein has since published several books with independent presses.]

Still, in the universities or in any other institution, you can often find some dissidents hanging around in the woodwork—and they can survive in one fashion or another, particularly if they get community support. But if they become too disruptive or too obstreperous—or you know, too effective—they're likely to be kicked out. The standard thing, though, is that they won't make it within the institutions in the first place, particularly if they were that way when they were young—they'll simply be weeded out somewhere along the line. So in most cases, the people who make it through the institutions and are able to remain in them have already internalized the right kinds of beliefs: it's not a problem for them to be obedient, they already are obedient, that's how they got there. And that's pretty much how the ideological control system perpetuates itself in the schools—that's the basic story of how it operates, I think.

## Forging Working-Class Culture

MAN: *Noam, I want to turn for a moment to people who* weren't *sent through the ideological control system of the schools, to see what kind of independent minds people today should be struggling to foster. I've often heard you talk about the insights that guided the early labor movement in the United States at the beginning of the industrial revolution in the 1820s. You say that social movements today are going to have to start by regaining some of that understanding. My question is, who were those people exactly—was it mostly European immigrants to the United States?*

No, it's what were called at the time the "Lowell mill-girls"—meaning young women who came off the farms to work in factories. In fact, a good deal of the labor organizing in the nineteenth century in the United States was done by women, because just like today in the Third World, it was assumed that the most docile and controllable segment of the workforce was women—so therefore they were the most exploited.

Remember, the early industrial revolution was built on textiles. It took off around here—it was in Lowell and Lawrence [Massachusetts], places like that. And very extensively the labor force was made up of women. In fact, some of the main labor journals at the time were edited by women, and they were young women mostly. And they were people who wanted to read, they wanted to learn, they wanted to study—that was just considered normal by working people back then. And they wanted to have free lives. In fact, many of them didn't work in the mills for very long—they'd work there for a couple years, then go back to some other life. But in the early stages of the American labor movement, it was the Lowell mill-girls, or farmers who were being driven off their farms by industry, who were the ones who built up the early working-class culture.

When the big waves of European immigrants began to arrive in the United States, the story started to change a bit, actually. See, the major wave of immigration to the United States happened around the middle of the nineteenth century, and the immigrants who were arriving were fleeing from *extremely* impoverished parts of Europe—like Ireland, for example. That was at the time of the Irish famine [of 1846–51], and Ireland was being absolutely devastated by it, so a lot of people just escaped to North America if they could.

People often forget, Ireland's the oldest colony in the world: it could have been a rich place, just like England, but it's been a colony for 800 years, and it's one of the few parts of the world that was not only *underde-veloped*, like most colonies, but also *depopulated*—Ireland now has about half the population it had in the early nineteenth century, in fact. And the Irish famine was an economists' famine—Ireland was actually exporting food to England during the famine, because the sacred principles of Political Economy said that that's the way it has to be: if there's a better market for it in England, that's where the food has to go, and you certainly couldn't send food *to* Ireland, because that would have interfered with the market.[28]

So there was mass starvation taking place in Ireland, and the Irish immigrants who were coming to the United States were desperate for work, so they could be forced to work for essentially nothing—the same was also true of a lot of the people who were coming here from Southern and Eastern Europe. And that undercut the early labor movement to a significant extent—I mean, the Lowell mill-girls could not, or would not, work at the level of the millions of immigrants who were coming in. So it took a long time before you started to get the growth of labor organizing here again, because the domestic workforce could just be displaced whenever it started to protest.

And the poor immigrants who came here were treated like dogs—I mean, miserably treated. So for example, Irish women were used for experimentation in Mengele-style experiments in the United States in the nineteenth century [Mengele was a Nazi doctor who "experimented" on live human beings]. That's not a joke—gynecological surgery was literally developed by Mengeles, who used subjects like indigent Irish women or slaves, and just subjected them to experiment after experiment, like thirty experiments, to try to figure out how to make the procedures work. In fact, doctors exactly like Joseph Mengele were *honored* for that in the United States—you still see their pictures up on the walls in medical schools.[29]

So it wasn't a European input that brought about the American labor movement, quite the opposite. But I mean, these were just natural reactions: you didn't have to have any training to understand these things, you didn't have to read Marx or anything like that. It's just degrading to have to follow orders, and to be stuck in a place where you slave for twelve hours a day, then go to a dormitory where they watch your morals and so on—which is what it was like. People simply regarded that as degrading.

It was the same with craftsmen, people who had been self-employed and were now being forced into the factories—they wanted to be able to run their own lives. I mean, shoemakers would hire people to read to them while they were working—and that didn't mean read Stephen King or something, it meant read real stuff. These were people who had libraries, and they wanted to live lives, they wanted to control their own work—but they were being forced into shoe-manufacturing plants in places like Lowell where they were treated, not even like animals, like machines. And that was degrading, and demeaning—and they fought against it. And incidentally, they weren't fighting against it so much because it was reducing their economic level, which it wasn't (in fact it was probably raising it)—it was because it was taking power out of their hands, and subordinating them to others, and turning them into mindless tools of production. And they didn't want that.

In fact, if you want to do some really interesting reading, one book I would suggest is the first book of labor history that was written—ever, I think. It came out in 1924, and it was just republished in Chicago: it's called *The Industrial Worker*, by Norman Ware, and it's mostly excerpts from the independent labor press in the United States in the mid-nineteenth century.[30] See, there was a big independent workers' press in the United States at the time—it was about at the scale of the capitalist press, actually—and it was run by what were called "factory girls," or by craftsmen. And it's extremely interesting to look at.

Right through the nineteenth century, working people in the United States were struggling against the imposition of what they described as "degradation," "oppression," "wage slavery," "taking away our elementary rights," "turning us into tools of production," everything that we now call modern capitalism (which is in fact state-capitalism) they fought against for a full century—and very bitterly, it was an extremely hard struggle. And they were calling for "labor republicanism"—you know, "Let's go back to the days when we were free people." "Labor" just means "people," after all.

And in fact, they also were fighting against the imposition of the mass public education system—and rightly, because they understood exactly what it was: a technique to beat independence out of the heads of farmers and to turn them into docile and obedient factory workers.[31] That's ultimately why public education was instituted in the United States in the first place: to meet the needs of newly-emerging industry. See, part of the process of trying to develop a degraded and obedient labor force was to make the workers stupid and passive—and mass education was one of the ways that was achieved. And of course, there was also a much broader effort to destroy the independent working-class intellectual culture that had developed, which ranged from a huge amount of just outright force, to more subtle techniques like propaganda and public relations campaigns.

And those efforts have been sustained right to this day, in fact. So labor unions have by now been virtually wiped out in the United States, in part by a huge amount of business propaganda, running from cinema to almost everything, and through a lot of other techniques as well. But the whole process took a long time—I'm old enough to remember what the working-class culture was like in the United States: there was still a high level of it when I was growing up in the late 1930s. It took a long time to beat it out of workers' heads and turn them into passive tools; it took a long time to make people accept that this type of exploitation is the only alternative, so they'd better just forget about their rights and say, "Okay, I'm degraded."

So the first thing that has to happen, I think, is we have to recover some of that old understanding. I mean, it all starts with cultural changes. We have to dismantle all of this stuff culturally: we've got to change people's minds, their spirits, and help them recover what was common understanding in a more civilized period, like a century ago on the shop floors of Lowell. If that kind of understanding could be natural among a huge part of the general population in the nineteenth century, it can be natural again today. And it's something we've really got to work on now.

## The Fraud of Modern Economics

MAN: *Noam, you mentioned Ireland being forced to export food to England during the Irish famine because of the supposed demands of the free market. How exactly did that kind of "free market" economic thinking get instituted as legitimate in the universities and in the popular ideology as a whole over the years—for instance, the work of the Social Darwinists [who claimed that natural selection and "survival of the fittest" determine individual and societal wealth], and of Malthus [early-nineteenth-century economist who argued that poverty was inevitable and population growth should be checked by famine, war, and disease], and others who in various ways blamed the poor for being poor?*

Malthus gets kind of a bad press, actually: he's singled out as the guy who said that people should just be left to starve if they can't support themselves—but really that was pretty much the line of classical economics in general. In fact, Malthus was one of the founders of classical economics, right alongside of guys like David Ricardo.

Malthus's point was basically this: if you don't have independent wealth, and you can't sell your labor on the market at a level at which you can survive, then you have no right being here—go to the workhouse prison or go somewhere else. And in those days, "go somewhere else" meant go to North America, or to Australia, and so on. Now, he wasn't saying it was anyone's *fault* if they were poor and had to remove themselves; he was saying, it's a law of nature that this is the way it has to be.[32] Ricardo in fact said that it was true at the level of "the principle of gravitation"—and of course, to try to interfere with a law of nature like that only makes things worse.[33]

So what both Malthus and Ricardo were arguing, sort of in parallel, was that you only harm the poor by making them believe that they have rights other than what they can win on the market, like a basic right to live, because that kind of right interferes with the market, and with efficiency, and with growth and so on—so ultimately people will just be worse off if you try to recognize them. And as you suggest, those ideas are basically still taught today—I don't think the free-market ideology that's taught in university economics departments right now is very much different. Sure, you have more mathematical formulas and so on today, but really it's pretty much the same story.

MAN: *But how did that thinking get instituted?*

How did it get instituted? As a weapon of class warfare. Actually, the history of this is kind of intriguing—and as far as I know, there's only one book about it: it's by a good economic historian named Rajani Kanth, who was just rewarded for his efforts by being thrown out of the University of Utah. But he goes through it all, and it's very revealing.[34]

You see, during the early stages of the industrial revolution, as England was coming out of a feudal-type society and into what's basically a state-capitalist system, the rising bourgeoisie there had a problem. In a traditional society like the feudal system, people had a certain place, and they had certain rights—in fact, they had what was called at the time a "right to live." I mean, under feudalism it may have been a *lousy* right, but nevertheless people were assumed to have some natural entitlement for survival. But with the rise of what we call capitalism, that right had to be destroyed: people had to have it knocked out of their heads that they had any automatic "right to live" beyond what they could win for themselves on the labor market. And that was the main point of classical economics.[35]

Remember the context in which all of this was taking place: classical economics developed after a period in which a large part of the English population had been forcibly driven off the land they had been farming for centuries—that was *by force*, it wasn't a pretty picture [i.e. intensive enclosure of communal lands by acts of Parliament occurred between 1750 and 1860]. In fact, very likely one of the main reasons why England led the industrial revolution was just that they had been much more violent in driving people off the land than in other places. For instance, in France a lot of people were able to remain on the land, and therefore they resisted industrialization more.[36]

But even after the rising bourgeoisie in England had driven millions of peasants off the land, there was a period when the population's "right to live" still was preserved by what we would today call "welfare." There was a set of laws in England which gave people rights, called the "Poor Laws" [initially and most comprehensively codified in 1601]—which essentially kept you alive if you couldn't survive otherwise; they provided sort of a minimum level of subsistence, like subsidies on food and so on. And there was also something called the "Corn Laws" [dating in varying forms from the twelfth century], which gave landlords certain rights beyond those they could get on the market—they raised the price of corn, that sort of thing. And together, these laws were considered among the main impediments to the new rising British industrial class—so therefore they just had to go.

Well, those people needed an ideology to support their effort to knock out of people's heads the idea that they had this basic right to live, and that's what classical economics was about—classical economics said: no one has any right to live, you only have a right to what you can gain for yourself on the labor market. And the founders of classical economics in fact said they'd developed a "scientific theory" of it, with—as they put it—"the certainty of the principle of gravitation."

Alright, by the 1830s, political conditions in England had changed enough so that the rising bourgeoisie were able to kill the Poor Laws [they were significantly limited in 1832], and then later they managed to do away with the Corn Laws [in 1846]. And by around 1840 or 1845, they won the elections and took over the government. Then at that point, a very interesting thing happened. They gave up the theory, and Political Economy changed.

It changed for a number of reasons. For one thing, these guys had won, so they didn't need it so much as an ideological weapon anymore. For another, they recognized that they themselves needed a powerful interventionist state to defend industry from the hardships of competition in the open market—as they always *had* in fact. And beyond that, eliminating people's "right to live" was starting to have some negative side-effects. First of all, it was causing riots all over the place: for a long period, the British army was mostly preoccupied with putting down riots across England. Then something even worse happened—the population started to organize: you got the beginnings of an organized labor movement, and later the Chartist movement [an 1838–48 popular campaign for Parliamentary reform], and then a socialist movement developed. And at that point, the elites in England recognized that the game just had to be called off, or else they *really* would be in trouble—so by the time you get to the second half of the nineteenth century, things like John Stuart Mill's *Principles of Political Economy*, which gives kind of a social-democratic line, were becoming the reigning ideology.

See, the "science" happens to be a very flexible one: you can change it to do whatever you feel like, it's that kind of "science." So by the middle of the nineteenth century, the "science" had changed, and now it turned out that laissez faire [the idea that the economy functions best without government interference] was a bad thing after all—and what you got instead were the intellectual foundations for what's called the "welfare state." And in fact, for a century afterwards, "laissez faire" was basically a dirty word—nobody talked about it anymore. And what the "science" now said was that you had better give the population some way of surviving, or else they're going to challenge your right to rule. You can take away their right to live, but then they're going to take away your right to rule—and that's no good, so ways have to be found to accommodate them.

Well, it wasn't until recent years that laissez-faire ideology was revived again—and again, it was as a weapon of class warfare. I mean, as far as I can see, the principles of classical economics in effect are still taught: I don't think what's taught in the University of Chicago Economics Department today is all that different, what's called "neo-liberalism" [an economic stance stressing cutbacks in social services, stable currencies, and balanced budgets]. And it doesn't have any more validity than it had in the early nineteenth century—in fact, it has even *less*. At least in the early nineteenth century, Ricardo's and Malthus's assumptions had *some* relation to reality. Today those assumptions have *no* relation to reality.

Look: the basic assumption of the classical economists was that labor is highly mobile and capital is relatively immobile—that's required, that's crucial to proving all their nice theorems. That was the reason they could say, "If you can't get enough to survive on the labor market, go someplace else"—because you *could* go someplace else: after the native populations of places like the United States and Australia and Tasmania were exterminated or driven away, then yeah, poor Europeans could go someplace else. So in the early nineteenth century, labor was indeed mobile. And back then, capital was indeed *immobile*—first because "capital" primarily meant land, and you can't move land, and also because to the extent that there was investment, it was very local: like, you didn't have communications systems that allowed for easy transfers of money all around the world, like we do today.

So in the early nineteenth century, the assumption that labor is mobile and capital is immobile was more or less realistic—and on the basis of that assumption, you could try to prove things about comparative advantage and all this stuff you learn in school about Portugal and wine and so on [Ricardo's most famous hypothetical for demonstrating how free trade could be mutually advantageous to participating countries involved England concentrating on selling cloth and Portugal wine].

Incidentally, if you want to know how well those theorems actually work, just compare Portugal and England after a hundred years of trying them out—growing wine versus industrializing as possible modes of development. But let's put that aside . . .

Well, by now the assumptions underpinning these theories are not only *false*—they're the *opposite* of the truth. By now labor is *immobile*, through immigration restrictions and so on, and capital is highly *mobile*, primarily because of technological changes. So none of the results work anymore. But you're still taught them, you're still taught the theories exactly as before—even though the reality today is the exact opposite of what was assumed in the early nineteenth century. I mean, if you look at some of the fancier economists, Paul Krugman and so on, they've got all kinds of little tricks here and there to make the results not quite so grotesquely ridiculous as they'd otherwise be. But fundamentally, it all just is pretty ridiculous.

I mean, if capital is mobile and labor is immobile, there's no reason why mobile capital shouldn't seek *absolute* advantage and play one national workforce against another, go wherever the labor is cheapest and thereby drive *everybody's* standard of living down. In fact, that's exactly what we're seeing in N.A.F.T.A. [the North American Free Trade Agreement] and all these other international trade agreements which are being instituted right now. Nothing in these abstract economic models actually *works* in the real world. It doesn't matter how many footnotes they put in, or how many ways they tinker around the edges. The whole enterprise is totally rotten at the core: it has no relation to reality anymore—and furthermore, it never did.

## The <u>Real</u> Market

So take a look at one of the things you don't say if you're an economist within one of the ideological institutions, although surely every economist has to know it. Take the fact that there is not a single case on record in history of any country that has developed successfully through adherence to "free market" principles: none. Certainly not the United States. I mean, the United States has always had *extensive* state intervention in the economy, right from the earliest days—we would be exporting fur right now if we were following the principles of comparative advantage.

Look, the reason why the industrial revolution took off in places like Lowell and Lawrence is because of high protectionist tariffs the U.S. government set up to keep out British goods. And the same thing runs right up to today: like, we would not have successful high-tech industry in the United States today if it wasn't for a huge public subsidy to advanced industry, mostly through the Pentagon system and N.A.S.A. and so on—that doesn't have the vaguest relation to a "free market."

In fact, if you want a good illustration, just read today's *New York Times*. There's a story on the business page about how we've got a funny kind of economic recovery going on in the country right now: there's a lot of economic growth, but not many good new jobs—you know, big surprise. And they use one factory as an example, a stove factory that's being set up in Tulsa by the Whirlpool corporation. Well, the last paragraph of the article points out how the "free market" really works: the reason why Whirlpool decided to put the factory in Tulsa instead of, say, in Mexico, is that the taxpayers in Tulsa County are going to pay 25 percent of the corporation's capital costs.[37] Okay, that's how the free market *really* works— in fact, that's how it's *always* worked, from the early days of the industrial revolution right up until this morning, without any known exception.[38]

As a matter of fact, the United States has been the most economically protectionist country in history. We've traditionally had the highest protectionist tariffs in the world, so much so that one leading economic historian in a recent book (published by the University of Chicago Press, no less) describes us as "the mother country and bastion of modern protectionism."[39] So for example, in the late nineteenth century, when Europe was actually toying around with laissez faire for a brief period, American tariffs were five to ten times as high as theirs—and that was the fastest economic growth period in American history.[40]

And it goes on right until the present. The United States developed a steel industry a century ago because it radically violated the rules of the "free market," and it was able to recover its steel industry in the last decade or so by doing things like restricting imports from abroad, destroying labor unions to drive down wages, and slamming huge tariffs on foreign steel.[41] I mean, the Reaganites always talked enthusiastically about "market forces," but they refused to allow them to function—and for a very simple reason: if market forces had been allowed to function, the United States would no longer have an automobile industry, or a microchip industry, or computers, or electronics, because they would have just been wiped out by the Japanese. So therefore the Reaganites closed off American markets and poured in huge amounts of public funds. And actually, they were perfectly frank about it to the business community—though of course, not to the public. So when he was Secretary of the Treasury, James Baker proudly proclaimed to a business audience in 1987 that Ronald Reagan "has granted more import relief to U.S. industry than any of his predecessors in more than half a century"—which was far too modest, actually; Reagan probably provided more import relief to industry than all his predecessors *combined* in that period.[42]

Of course, the "free market" ideology is very *useful*—it's a weapon against the general population here, because it's an argument against social spending, and it's a weapon against poor people abroad, because we can hold it up to them and say "You guys have to follow these rules," then just go ahead and rob them. But nobody really pays any attention to this stuff when it comes to actual planning—and no one ever has.

So there was just a British study of the hundred leading transnational corporations in the "*Fortune* 500," and it found that of the hundred, every single one of them had benefited from what's called "state industrial policy"—that is, from some form of government intervention in the country in which they're based. And of the hundred, they said at least twenty had been saved from total collapse by state intervention at one point or another. For instance, the Lockheed corporation was going under in the early 1970s, and the Nixon administration just bailed them out with public funds.[43] Okay, so they're back in business. And now they *stay* in business because the public pays for C-130s [military aircraft], and upgrading F-16s, and the F-22 project, and so on—none of which has anything to do with a "free market" either.

Or take the fact that so many people live in the suburbs and everybody has to drive their own car everywhere. Was that a result of the "free market"? No, it was because the U.S. government carried out a massive social-engineering project in the 1950s to destroy the public transportation system in favor of expanding a highly inefficient system based on cars and airplanes—because that's what benefits big industry. It started with corporate conspiracies to buy up and eliminate streetcar systems, and then continued with huge public subsidies to build the highway system and encourage an extremely inefficient and environmentally destructive alternative. That's what led to the suburbanization of the country—so you get huge shopping malls in the suburbs, and devastation in the inner cities.[44]

But these policies were a result of planning—they had nothing to do with the "free market."

Actually, the most dramatic example of these "market distortions" that I can think of—which I suspect is never even taught in economics courses—concerns the reason why the United States had an industrial revolution in the first place. Remember, the industrial revolution was fueled by textiles, meaning one commodity: cotton. And cotton was cheap, that was crucially important. Well, why was cotton cheap? Was it because of market forces? No. Cotton was cheap because they exterminated the native population here and brought in slaves—that's why cotton was cheap. Genocide and slavery: try to imagine a more severe market distortion than that.

Other countries who had their own cotton resources also tried to start on industrial revolutions—but they didn't get very far, because England had more guns, and stopped them by force. Egypt, for example, had its own cotton resources, and started on an industrial revolution at about the same time as the United States did, around 1820—but the British weren't going to tolerate an economic competitor in the Eastern Mediterranean, so they just stopped it by force. Okay, no industrial revolution in Egypt.[45]

The same thing also happened in Britain's earliest "experiment" with these ideas, in what was called Bengal, in India. In fact, Bengal was one of the first places colonized in the eighteenth century, and when Robert Clive [British conqueror] first landed there, he described it as a paradise: Dacca, he said, is just like London, and they in fact referred to it as "the Manchester of India." It was rich and populous, there was high-quality cotton, agriculture, advanced industry, a lot of resources, jute, all sorts of things—it was in fact comparable to England in its manufacturing level, and really looked like it was going to take off. Well, look at it today: Dacca, "the Manchester of India," is the capital of Bangladesh—the absolute symbol of disaster.[46] And that's because the British just despoiled the country and destroyed it, by the equivalent of what we would today call "structural adjustment" [i.e. economic policies from the World Bank and International Monetary Fund which expose Third World economies to foreign penetration and control].

In fact, India generally was a real competitor with England: as late as the 1820s, the British were learning advanced techniques of steel-making there, India was building ships for the British navy at the time of the Napoleonic Wars [1803–1815], they had a developed textiles industry, they were producing more iron than all of Europe combined—so the British just proceeded to de-industrialize the country by force and turn it into an impoverished rural society.[47] Was that competition in the "free market"?

And it goes on and on: the United States annexed Texas [in 1845], and one of the main reasons for that was to ensure that the U.S. achieved a monopoly on cotton—which was the oil of the nineteenth century, it was what really fueled the industrial economies. So the American leadership figured that if they could take Texas, which was a major cotton-producing area, then they would be able to strangle England economically. See, England was the main enemy at that time, they hated England: it was much more powerful militarily than the United States, it kept us from conquering Canada and seizing Cuba the way elites here wanted to—and in fact, the only reason the American colonists had been able to defeat England in the American Revolution in the first place was that the French military had massively intervened in the colonial uprising here to help overthrow British power.[48] So England was the real enemy. And if you read the Jacksonian Democrats, Presidents Polk and Tyler and so on, they were saying: if we can get Texas, we can bring England to our feet and gain mastery of the trade of the world. In fact, the worst charges, paranoid charges, that were leveled against Saddam Hussein before the Gulf War apply precisely to the Jacksonian Democrats: they wanted to monopolize the main resource of the world so they could bring everybody else to their feet.[49]

And exactly the same lessons apply today. Today it's oil that's at the center of the industrial economies. And why is oil cheap? Well, that's what you pay your taxes for: a large part of the Pentagon system exists to make sure that oil prices stay within a certain range—not too low, because Western economies and energy corporations depend on the profits from it, but not too high, because that might interfere with what's called the "efficiency" of international trade [i.e. because transport and other costs of trade rise with the oil price]. Well, trade is only "efficient" because a lot of force and international violence keeps oil prices from going too high, so if you really wanted to measure the "efficiency of trade," you'd have to figure in all of the other costs which *make* it that way, like the costs of the Pentagon for one. And if anyone ever did that, you couldn't *possibly* say that trade is "efficient." If anybody ever bothered to calculate these things, the efficiency of trade would drop very, very low, and it would in fact prove to be extremely *inefficient*.

I mean, these market distortions are not footnotes—they are absolutely huge phenomena. Nobody ever tries to estimate them, because economics is not a serious field—but people in the business world know about them perfectly well, which is why they've always called upon a powerful state to protect them from market discipline: they don't want market discipline any more than they want democratic control, and they've always blocked it. And the same is true of just about every aspect of any developed economy there is.

## Automation

Well, let's just take one last case of this, an extremely important and revealing one: let's look at automation. I mean, it's standardly claimed these days that the reason why the population is suffering, why people have been losing jobs at a mad rate, real wages have been going down for the last twenty-five years and so on, is due to, as Ricardo said, "laws like the principle of gravitation"—inexorable market forces are making it that way, like automation, or the efficiency of international trade. That's the standard argument: these things are inevitable because the market is just imposing them on us.[50] It's all total bullshit. I mentioned one reason why the "efficiency of trade" argument is mostly a fraud, now let's look at automation.

Well, it's true that automation is "efficient"—like, by market principles, automation saves businessmen money and drives workers out of jobs. But it didn't *get* that way because of the market, not at all: it only got that way through intensive and prolonged funding and development through the state sector—that's market *distortion*. I mean, for thirty years automation was developed through the military system in the United States, and the reason why it took so long and cost so much is that automation was so *inefficient* to begin with that it couldn't possibly have survived in the market—so therefore automation was developed the same way we develop most high technology: through the public sector.

See, in the Air Force and the Navy (where most of this took place), nobody *cares* about costs—because the taxpayer's paying, so the development can be as expensive and inefficient as you like. And in that way, they were able to develop automation to the point where it could then be used to drive people out of work and make profits for corporations. For instance, take the history of automated numerical control of metal-cutting machines [i.e. translation of part specifications into mathematical information that can be fed into machines without the need for skilled machinists]. That was developed through the Air Force, it went on for decades, and finally it got efficient enough so that it could be handed over to the corporations and they could then throw out their workers. But it didn't happen through market forces, not at all—it was the result of massive state intervention.

Furthermore, if you look at the *kind* of automation that was developed, you see precisely what workers in the early labor movement were complaining about: being turned into mindless tools of production. I mean, automation could have been designed in such a way as to *use* the skills of skilled machinists and to eliminate management—there's nothing inherent in automation that says it can't be used that way. But it wasn't, believe me; it was used in exactly the opposite way. Automation was designed through the state system to demean and degrade people—to de-skill workers and increase managerial control. And again, that had nothing to do with the market, and it had nothing to do with the nature of the technology: it had to do with straight power interests. So the *kind* of automation that was developed in places like the M.I.T. Engineering Department was very carefully designed so that it would create interchangeable workers and enhance managerial control—and that was not for economic reasons.[51] I mean, study after study, including by management firms like Arthur D. Little and so on, show that managers have selected automation even when it *cuts back* on profits—just because it gives them more control over their workforce.[52]

If you're interested, there's been some very interesting work done on this; the guy who's done the best work is David Noble—for his sins he was denied tenure at M.I.T., and now he's teaching in Canada. He wrote a book called *Forces of Production*, which is a pretty specialized technical analysis mainly of the development of numerical control of machinery, but he's also got a good popular book out, called *Progress Without People: In Defense of Luddism*. Unfortunately, this is the kind of book that's published like in Katmandu or something—it's published by a very small anarchist press in Chicago. But it's very interesting, didn't make him too popular in the Faculty Club and so on.[53]

One of the things he discusses there is Luddism [a movement of English workers who wrecked industrial machines, which began in 1811]. See, the Luddites are always accused of having wanted to *destroy* machinery, but it's been known in scholarship for a long time that that's not true—what they really wanted to do was to prevent *themselves* from being de-skilled, and Noble talks about this in his book. The Luddites had nothing against machinery itself, they just didn't want it to destroy *them*, they wanted it to be developed in such a way that it would enhance their skills and their power, and not degrade and destroy them—which of course makes perfect sense. And that sentiment runs right throughout the working-class movements of the nineteenth century, actually—and you can even see it today.

Well, if economics were like a real field, these are the kinds of things they would be studying. None of it is very complicated—like, everybody knows why cotton was cheap, for instance: everybody who went to elementary school knows why cotton was cheap, and if it hadn't been for cheap cotton, there wouldn't have been an industrial revolution. It's not hard. But I'd be very surprised if anybody teaches this stuff in economics courses in the United States.

I mean, sure, there are some market forces operating—but the reality is, they're pretty much off around the edges. And when people talk about the progress of automation and free-market "trade forces" inevitably kicking all these people out of work and driving the whole world towards kind of a Third World-type polarization of wealth—I mean, that's true if you take a narrow enough perspective on it. But if you look into the factors that *made* things the way they are, it doesn't even come *close* to being true, it's not even remotely in touch with reality. But when you're studying economics in the ideological institutions, that's all just irrelevant and you're not supposed to ask questions like these: you have all the information right in front of you, but these are simply not matters that it is proper to spend time talking about.

## A Revolutionary Change in Moral Values

MAN: *Noam, given an intellectual culture like the one you've been describing—can you find any "honest" intellectuals in the U.S.?*

You can find them, but like I say, usually they're not inside the institutions—and that's for a very good reason: there is no reason why institutions of power and domination should tolerate or encourage people who try to undermine them. That would be completely dysfunctional. So typically you're going to find major efforts made to marginalize the honest and serious intellectuals, the people who are committed to what I would call Enlightenment values—values of truth, and freedom, and liberty, and justice. And those efforts will to a large extent succeed.

MAN: *Who are those people? I mean, you make the whole situation look very bleak—who would you say are the intellectuals that are going about things in the right way?*

Well, very often they're the people who have done things to make a real change in the world. Take the S.N.C.C. [Student Nonviolent Coordinating Committee] activists, for example—they were serious intellectuals, and they made a big change. Or take the people in the 1960s who did the work that's led to so many of the improvements we've seen in the country over the last twenty years—and "work" didn't just mean running around the streets waving signs, you know, it also meant thinking about things, and figuring out what the problems were, and trying to teach people about them and convince them. Despite what you always hear, that was *not* elite intellectuals: the liberal intellectual community in the United States was always *strongly* opposed to the people who protested the American aggression in Indochina on principled grounds, they were *not* the ones assisting the popular movements. Well, those people were serious intellectuals, in my view.

So you see, there is sort of an "honest" left intelligentsia, if you like—meaning intellectuals who are not serving power as either a Red Bureaucracy, or as state-capitalist commissar-equivalents. It's just that most of the time they're outside the institutions—and for almost trivial reasons: you're not going to find a militant labor activist as Chairman of the Board of General Electric, right? Yeah, how could there be? But there are people all over the place who are honest and committed, and are thinking about the world, and trying to change it—many more today than there were thirty years ago, in fact.

I mean, it's standardly claimed that there's less of a left intelligentsia around today in the United States than there was in the Fifties and Sixties—but I don't believe a word of it. I think the opposite is true, actually. Just take a look at the people who they're *calling* the big thinkers of the 1950s: who were they? They were intelligent people, like Edmund Wilson's an intelligent person—but *left intellectual*? Or Mary McCarthy: yeah, smart person, wrote some nice novels—but not a left intellectual. In fact, what you have now is much more serious activists all over the place, people who are thinking carefully about important questions, and who understand a lot.

I travel around all the time giving talks, and throughout the 1980s I was *amazed* to go to places and see it. Take the Central America solidarity movement, which was a pretty dramatic development—I don't think there's ever been anything like it in history, in fact. I'd go to a church in Kansas, or some town in Montana or Wyoming or something, Anchorage, Alaska, and find people there who know more about Latin America certainly than the C.I.A., which isn't very hard actually, but more than people in the academic departments of universities. They're people who've thought about it, and who've understood things, and brought a lot of intelligence to the issues—I can't even tell you their names, there are too many of them.

Also, I'm not even sure the word "left" is the right word for them: a lot of them were probably Christian conservatives, but they were very radical people in my view, and intellectuals who understood, and who did a lot. They created a popular movement which not only protested U.S. atrocities, but actually *engaged* themselves in the lives of the victims—they took a much more courageous stand than was ever done in the 1960s. I mean, the popular resistance that took place in the Sixties was important—but there was nobody back then who even *dreamt* of going to a Vietnamese village and living there, because maybe a white face would limit the capacity of the marauders to kill and destroy. That wasn't even an idea in your head. In fact, nobody even went to try to *report* the war from the side of the victims—that was unheard of. But in the 1980s it was common: plenty of people did it—in fact, people who were coming out of religious groups like Witness for Peace were doing that by the thousands and tens of thousands. And the people who were doing that are serious left intellectuals, in my view.[54]

Remember, what will be *labeled* "left" in the general culture and given publicity is going to be something that's ugly enough so that people can be rallied to oppose it. So books are coming out now about "left intellectuals" in France who were Stalinists—and look at the awful things they did. Okay, *that* kind of "left intelligentsia" is allowed to have publicity and prominence, in fact the elite culture will give them as much prominence as it can. Or people will say "the left" is things like the Spartacist League, or the Socialist Workers Party or something—little sectlets, the kinds of groups that anybody who's been involved in movement activities knows are the people who hang around your offices and your talks trying to see if they can disrupt things. That's not the left, that's parasites that undermine the left—but to show how lousy the left is, the elite press will say "Oh, the Spartacist League doesn't have a lot of members": yeah, big excitement.[55] On the other hand, the *real* left they don't talk about—like they don't talk about the thousands and thousands of people involved in this, that and the other cause doing serious work.

So if by "left" you mean people who are struggling for peace, and justice, and freedom, and human rights, and for social change, and elimination of authority structures, whether in personal life or in the institutions—if that's what the left is, there are more of them around than I can remember in my lifetime, at least. A lot more.

MAN: *There really has been a big change in the culture.*

Yes. If you take almost any area you can think of in life, whether it's race, or sex, or military intervention, the environment—these are all things that didn't even *exist* in the 1950s, people didn't even think they were issues, you just submitted. And people don't anymore. I mean, if I just look at pictures from the early Sixties, I can hardly believe how disciplined everything was, how deep the authority structures were—even just in personal relations, and in the way you looked and talked when you went out with your friends. Younger people may not always realize it, but life's a lot easier than it was forty years ago: there's been a big change, there are a lot of successes to point to.

Look, a lot of this stuff got started over the Vietnam War. Well, in terms of official ideology, all of us who were opposed to the war just lost, flat out: within the mainstream institutions, the only question today is, have the Vietnamese done enough to compensate us for the crimes that they committed against us? That's the only question you're allowed to discuss if you want to be a part of the educated culture in the United States. So George Bush can get up and say, "The Vietnamese should understand that we bear them no permanent grudge, we're not going to make them pay for everything they did to us; if they finally come clean, you know, devote their entire lives and every last resource they have to searching for the remains of one of those people they viciously blew out of the sky, then maybe we'll allow them entry into the civilized world"—and there won't be a single editorial writer or columnist who either falls on the floor laughing, or else says, "This guy is worse than the Nazis." Because that's the way they all are: the only issue is, will we forgive them for the crimes that they committed against us?[56] I mean, among the educated sector of the population in the U.S., there is overwhelming opposition to the war—but it's only on what are called "pragmatic" grounds: namely, we couldn't get away with it. So: "We tried, we made blundering efforts to do good, but it was a mistake." Well, at that level, we've just lost the entire discussion.

On the other hand, let's go to the general population: to this day, after twenty-five years of this endless, unremitting propaganda to which no response is ever tolerated, 66 percent of the American population still disagrees with the elite culture—that tells you there's been a victory at another level. I mean, if two-thirds of the population still says in polls, after all of this brainwashing, that the war was "fundamentally wrong and immoral," not "a mistake," well, something got through. And remember, everybody who's choosing that answer is choosing it all by themselves—because that is not what they hear in the mainstream culture, certainly not from educated people.[57]

And the thing we have to keep in mind is, the people in power know it: they might not want *us* to know it, but they know it. In fact, it's even clear from their own documents that they know it. For example, a very important early Bush administration planning document on Third World intervention was leaked to the press and published on the day of the ground attack in the Gulf War—by Maureen Dowd, incidentally, who's basically a gossip columnist for the *New York Times*. It was an inter-agency study on the general world situation, prepared by the C.I.A. and the Pentagon and others during an early stage of the Bush administration, well before the Gulf War. And it had a section on U.S. military intervention, and what they said was: in the case of confrontations with "much weaker enemies"—meaning anybody we're willing to fight—we must not only defeat them, but we must defeat them "decisively and rapidly," because anything else will "undercut political support," which is understood to be extremely thin.[58]

See, their belief is, maybe we can frighten the domestic population and get them to huddle under the flag for a couple days, but unless we get the intervention over with quickly, it's hopeless—people are going to start to rise up and pressure us to stop it. These people recognize that there can't be classical interventions anymore—you know, U.S. soldiers slogging it out in Vietnam for years and years—it has to be either clandestine warfare, as in Peru now, where not one American in ten thousand knows there are U.S. troops, or the Panama/Iraq game, with enormous propaganda about the enemy ready to destroy us, and then a quick victory without any fighting.[59]

Well, that's just a radical difference from the Kennedy period—and that difference reflects major changes in the culture. Powerful people here understand that they do not have the option of carrying out foreign interventions anymore, unless they carry out decisive, rapid victories over totally defenseless enemies, after having first gone to great lengths to demonize them. They certainly recognize that—and that's a tremendous victory for the left.

And anybody who's my age or even a little bit younger must also realize that it's a very different country today—and a much more civilized one. Just look at the issue of the rights of indigenous peoples. When I was a kid, I considered myself a radical-anarchist-this that and the other thing—but I was playing "Cowboys and Indians" with my friends: you know, shoot the Indians. That's like playing "Aryans and Jews" in Germany—you go out and try to kill the Jews. Well, that lasted for a very long time in the United States, and nobody even noticed anything curious about it.

I mean, just to tell you another story: I live in Lexington, a mainly upper-middle-class professional town near Boston, which is very liberal, everybody votes for the Democrats, they all give to the right causes, and so on. Well, in 1969—the year's interesting—one of my kids was in fourth grade, and she had a Social Studies textbook about the early history of New England, called *Exploring New England*; the book was centered on a boy named Robert, who was being shown the glories of colonial New England by some older man or something. Well, one day I decided to poke through it, because I was curious about how the authors were going to deal with the colonists' extermination of the native peoples here. So I turned to the point in the book where they got to the first really major act of genocide in New England, the Pequot Massacre of 1637—when the colonists murdered the Pequot tribe. And to my surprise, it was described quite accurately: the colonists went into the village and slaughtered all the men, women and children, burned everything down, burned out all the Pequots' crops. Then I got to the bottom line. The bottom line had this boy, Robert, who's being told all of these things, say: "I wish I were a man and had been there." In other words, it was a *positive* presentation. That was in 1969, right after the My Lai massacre was exposed.[60]

That would be *inconceivable* today—because there have been very important changes in the culture, and a real increase in civilization. And those changes are largely the result of a lot of very significant activism and organizing over the last couple decades, by people that I would refer to as "honest intellectuals."

In fact, I think all of this screaming about "Political Correctness" that we hear these days in the elite culture is basically just a tantrum over the fact that it has been impossible to crush all of the dissidence and the activism and the concern that's developed in the general population in the last thirty years. I mean, it's not that some of these "P.C." things they point out aren't true—yeah, sure, some of them are true. But the real problem is that the huge right-wing effort to retake control of the ideological system didn't work—and since their mentality is basically totalitarian, any break in their control is considered a huge tragedy: 98 percent control isn't enough, you have to have 100 percent control; these are totalitarian strains. But they couldn't get it, especially among the general population. They have not been able to beat back all of the gains of the popular movements since the 1960s, which simply led to a lot of concern about sexism, and racism, and environmental issues, respect for other cultures, and all this other bad stuff. And it's led to real hysteria among elites, so you get this whole P.C. comedy.

I mean, right now the universities are all flooded with Olin Professorships of Free Enterprise [endowed by the conservative Olin Foundation], there are glossy right-wing magazines handed out free to every student— and these are not just right-wing, but *crazy* right-wing. Meanwhile, everybody's screaming about how the left has taken over. And that's all just out of hysteria that they haven't gotten back total control—in fact, they've probably lost most of the population by now. And there's no reason to think that those changes have ended—I think there's every reason to think that they could go a lot further, and ultimately lead to changes in the institutions.

Again, people just have to remember: there is nothing in the mainstream culture that is ever going to tell you you've succeeded—they're always going to tell you you've failed. I mean, the official view of the Sixties is that it was a bunch of crazies running around burning down the universities and making noise, because they were hysterics, or because they were afraid to go to Vietnam or something—that's the official story, and that's what people always hear from the intellectual culture. They may know from their own lives and experience that that's not what really happened, but they never hear anybody saying it: that's not the message the system is always pouring into you through television, and radio, and newspapers, and books, and histories, and so on and so forth. It's beating into your head another story—that you failed, and that you *should* have failed, because you were just a bunch of crazies.

And of course, it's natural that the official culture *would* take that view: it does not want people to understand that you can make changes, that's the last thing it wants people to understand. So if there have been changes, it's because "We the elites are so great that we carried through the changes." When they bow to pressures, they're going to present that as their benevolence. Like, "We ended slavery because we were such great moral figures that we decided we didn't like slavery"—but the cause is gone, the slave revolts and the Abolitionist movement are gone.

And we've seen that on a not-so-trivial scale in the last thirty years with regard to the Sixties movements. There's been something close to a revolutionary change in moral values and cultural level in the general population, but since that change has taken place without any lasting institutional effects, the intellectual culture can just keep pounding home its moral: "You guys are worthless, you can't do anything—why don't you just shut up and go home." That's what they're always going to tell us, and we should try to remember that.

# 8

# Popular Struggle

*Based on discussions in Massachusetts, Maryland, Ontario,*
*California, and Wyoming in 1989 and between 1993 and 1996.*

### Discovering New Forms of Oppression

MAN: *Dr. Chomsky, some of your examples just reemphasize for me how power is not with popular opinion. I'm wondering, what do you think should happen if power ever gets back into popular hands?*

Well, it wouldn't be "back," because it never was there. But I think what we want to do is to extend the domains of popular power in as many areas as possible. In fact, a large part of human history is just that: a struggle to extend the domains of popular power and to break down centers of concentrated power.

Take the American Revolution, for example. There was kind of an ideological structure behind it, and that ideological structure was in part libertarian. So if you really took the rhetoric seriously—and to some extent the eighteenth-century Jeffersonians did, it wasn't nothing—what you wanted to do was to break down concentrations of power and to create a society of essentially equal participants. Now of course, their sense of "equal participants" included only a very small part of the population: white male property-owners. Today we would call that a reversion to Nazism, and rightly so. I mean, suppose some Third World country came out saying that a part of the population is only three-fifths human—that's in the U.S. Constitution, in fact.[1] That would be unacceptable.

So the American Constitution was basically for white male property-owners, because they're the only ones who are real people—but the idea was supposed to be that *they're* more or less equal, and therefore you want to break down the concentrations of power that are oppressing them. Well, in those days that meant Church power, state power, the feudal system, and so on—and what you were supposed to get was this egalitarian society for "the People," equals white male property-owners.

Well, it didn't work out that way, even for the white male property-owners, but that was the picture behind it. And to some extent it was achieved—some forms of centralized power *were* in fact dissolved. And the course of American history since then has just gone on from there. In the nineteenth century, concentrated power began to be located in corporations—that's another center of power that now has to be dissolved, and if you're an eighteenth-century-style libertarian, that's what your main critique will be of today.

But it seems to me that this is a process which goes on forever—it's not something that you ever finish with. I mean, my own suspicion is that with any victory that's won, we will then discover that there's some other form of authority and repression we didn't even notice before, and we'll try to go after that one.

And certainly there is real progress you can point to. So while from the point of view of Jeffersonian libertarians in the eighteenth century, there was no deviation from democracy and freedom if rights were limited to white male property-owners, nobody except some Neanderthal would accept that view today. Well, that's progress, that's cultural and social progress. And that progress was achieved through struggle: it didn't happen because somebody sat around and talked about it, it happened through the struggles of the Abolitionists, and the women's movement, and the labor movement, and others.

## Freedom of Speech

MAN: *But don't we need to do something to reverse the trend of revolutions falling short throughout history—don't we have to change the psychology of human beings before a really libertarian revolution would succeed?*

Well, we're not going to change people's psychology—that's a matter *for* revolution, that's not just going to happen. But I don't think the failure of revolutions reflects so much the psychology of human beings as it reflects the realities of power. Now, in general I think it's true that popular revolutions fail, and one or another elite grouping takes over afterwards. But popular revolutions also succeed—we're no longer living in the Middle Ages, after all.

Take something like freedom of speech. That's a very important right, but it has only very recently been achieved. Freedom of speech is an interesting case, actually, where popular struggles over hundreds of years have finally managed to expand a domain of freedom to the point where it's pretty good, in fact—in the United States, the best in the world. But it didn't just happen: it happened through the struggles of the labor movement, and the Civil Rights Movement, and the women's movement, and everything else. It's the popular movements which expanded the domain of freedom of speech until it began to be meaningful—if those popular movements hadn't taken place, we'd still be where we were, say, in 1920, when there wasn't even a *theoretical* right of freedom of speech. The history of this is remarkable; it's not very well known.

Take the Supreme Court: as many free speech cases came to the United States Supreme Court from 1959 to 1974 as in the entire preceding history of the Court—it was only *then* that freedom of speech was being won.[2] I mean, there had been important advances towards it through the struggles of the labor movement, which had expanded it to include the rights of picketing and labor organizing, but it wasn't until around the late 1950s that the right of freedom of speech really began to be claimed by popular movements—and because of that it found its way into the courts, and the courts began passing decisions. It wasn't until *1964* that the Supreme Court struck down the 1798 Sedition Act [which forbade spoken or written criticism of the government, Congress, or the President]—that's very recent history.

MAN: *But were there ever any prosecutions under the sedition laws?*

Oh sure, plenty of prosecutions.[3] After the First World War, for example, Eugene Debs [Socialist Party and labor leader] was put in jail for ten years for making a pacifist speech; he was prosecuted under the 1917 Espionage Act, which was another sedition law. That was a Presidential candidate— went to jail for ten years for making a speech.[4] Or take the Smith Act of 1940, for example: people went to jail under the Smith Act. That made it illegal to join a group which advocated—and didn't do anything about— changing the social order.[5] And all of these prosecutions were *upheld* by the Supreme Court, remember: they were held to be consistent with the Constitution.[6]

In fact, if you look at some of the things that are called *victories* for freedom of speech, you find that they weren't that at all. Take the famous "clear and present danger" criterion to justify repressing speech. That was from a decision by Holmes [Supreme Court Justice] in 1919, one of Holmes's first big speech decisions—it was *Schenck vs. United States*, for a long time considered one of the big victories for civil liberties. Here's the case.

Schenck was a Jewish socialist activist who put out a pamphlet in which he criticized the draft as illegal. He gave constitutional arguments, and he urged people to oppose the draft by legal means: try to oppose the draft in the courts, that's what his pamphlet said—it probably went out to twenty people or something. He was brought to court and condemned for sedition: assaulting the state with words. It went up to the Supreme Court, and this was just at the point when Holmes and Brandeis were beginning to make a crack in the authoritarian tradition. Holmes wrote the decision for a unanimous court, in which he *upheld* the conviction—that's something that people forget, he upheld Schenck's conviction—and he put forth this "clear and present danger" criterion: you can be punished if you falsely cry "Fire!" in a crowded theater. Holmes said: you can control freedom of speech when there is a clear and present danger, and when Schenck put out his document saying people should oppose the draft by legal means, that was a clear and present danger. *That's* the great victory for civil liberties.[7]

And so it goes. It wasn't until 1964 that laws punishing seditious libel were struck down. The case is interesting and instructive—it was a Civil Rights Movement case, that's what did it; it was *New York Times vs. Sullivan*. What happened was, the *New York Times* was sued by the State of Alabama for running an ad in support of Martin Luther King and the Civil Rights Movement, which accused the sheriff of Montgomery of doing a bunch of rotten things to civil rights activists.

MAN: *This is the big libel law case?*

Yes, but it was *seditious* libel—because it was criticism of a government official that was being punished. See, whether you have seditious libel is sort of at the core of whether it's a free society or not: if you're not allowed to criticize the government, if you can be punished for assaulting the government with words, even if that's in the background somewhere, the society is not really free. And *truth* is no defense to this kind of libel charge, keep in mind—in fact, traditionally truth makes the crime worse, because if what you're saying is true, then the undermining of state authority is even worse.

So this elected sheriff in Alabama sued the *New York Times* saying they had defamed him: the idea was that by publishing this ad, the *Times* had undermined his authority as an agent of the state. Well, it went up to the Supreme Court, and the Supreme Court—I think it was Brennan who wrote the opinion—for the first time said that seditious libel is unacceptable. In fact, they referred to the 1798 Sedition Act, which had never been struck down by the Court, and said this is inconsistent with the First Amendment.[8] That's the first case in which the courts struck down seditious libel.

If you want a history of this, the major Establishment legal history of freedom of speech is a book by a legal scholar named Harry Kalven, called *A Worthy Tradition*. The book's very good, except for the title—it's actually an *unworthy* tradition that he's describing. And he points out, I'm basically quoting him, that 1964 was the first time the United States met the minimal condition for a democratic society: you can't assault the state with words.[9]

It wasn't until 1969 that the Supreme Court then rejected the "clear and present danger" test—which also is awful. "Clear and present danger" shouldn't be a criterion for punishing speech. The proper criterion, if there's any, should be contribution to a crime—commission of, or maybe even incitement to, an actual criminal act. That's a plausible criterion. And the Supreme Court only reached *that* criterion in 1969 [in the case *Brandenburg vs. Ohio*].[10] So you know, freedom of speech is a very recent innovation in the United States—and the United States is unique: it doesn't exist anywhere else in the world.

For example, you might have read that in Canada they kept Salman Rushdie's book [*The Satanic Verses*] out of the country for a couple weeks while they were trying to figure out if it conflicted with a Canadian law—it's referred to as an "anti-hate" law or something. That law makes two things a crime. First, it makes it a crime to distribute "false news." That's something that goes back to 1275, I looked it up—in 1275 the first "false news" law was established in England, making it a crime to produce "false news." What that means is, the state determines what's true, and if you say anything that's not what the state says is true, that's "false news" and you go to jail. That's in Canada. The second thing the law prohibits is statements which are "harmful to the public interest." That provision was intended to stop people like Holocaust deniers, guys who say there were no gas chambers and so on, because they're harmful to the public interest—so therefore the state can repress them. And when Canadian officials stopped the Rushdie book, it was under that provision: they had to check it out to see if it was inflaming hatred of Muslims or something like that.

Well, everybody here screamed about it at the time of the Rushdie case—but nobody here raised a peep when that law was actually *applied* a few years ago to put a guy in jail for fifteen months.

MAN: *In Canada?*

In Toronto. This is in fact the guy who the law was aimed at: he's some kind of neo-Nazi who wrote a pamphlet, which he privately distributed, in which he said that there were no gas chambers, or there was no Holocaust, or one thing or another—and he was brought to court under this very same law that kept the Rushdie book out. Ernst Zundel his name is. He was convicted and sentenced by the courts to fifteen months in prison plus a three-year period in which he is not permitted to talk, publicly or privately, about anything directly or indirectly related to the Holocaust—meaning he can't talk with his friends about the Second World War. And there was a move to deport him, which the Liberal Party in Canada supported.[11]

Alright, this was reported in the American press. The *Boston Globe* had an editorial in which they praised the jury for having the courage, finally, to shut these guys up—by enforcing a law that gives the state the power to determine truth, and to punish deviation from it.[12] When the *Globe* started screaming about the Rushdie affair, I sent the editors a copy of that editorial and asked them if they would like to rethink it; well, I haven't heard anything yet. . . . And you know, you didn't have Susan Sontag [American writer] getting up in public and saying, "I am Ernst Zundel," all this kind of thing. The point is, you defend freedom of speech when it's speech you like, and when you're sure there's a half-billion Western Europeans out there between you and the Ayatollah Khomeini so you can be courageous [the Iranian leader put a $6 million price on Rushdie's head in 1989]. But when you get to a case where nobody likes what's being said, then somehow defense of freedom of speech disappears.

Well, you couldn't have a law like that in the United States anymore, but you can have it in Canada—and American intellectuals basically support it, like the liberal *Boston Globe*, the *New York Times*, the P.E.N. writers [an organization that promotes free expression for writers] who don't get excited. It's only when it's a case where we like the views being attacked that you get a big outcry about freedom of speech here.

And other countries are the same as Canada—like in England, there is no freedom of speech, by law. The police there can go into the B.B.C. [British Broadcasting Corporation] offices, as they did recently, and rifle through the files and take out anything they want, and the government can prevent people from publishing things.[13] In fact, as Alex Cockburn [British/American journalist] just noted, there's a new law in England called an "anti-terrorism" law, which makes it illegal to report statements by people the state regards as terrorists. Well, that includes Sinn Féin representatives [Northern Irish political party], people who are elected to Parliament in Britain—you're not allowed to report what they say. Cockburn pointed out that this law was recently used to block a documentary in which a couple of eighty-year-old Irish women were being interviewed about things that happened in the 1930s: the television channels were afraid to run it because of the risk of being prosecuted. So in England, you can't have a couple of Irish women talking about things that went on in the 1930s, because the state might not permit it.

In France, where there isn't even a vague tradition of freedom of speech, the government last year canceled a newspaper of Algerian dissidents in France on the sole ground that its publication was harmful to French diplomatic relations with Algeria—none of the French intellectuals even raised a peep; they were all screaming about Salman Rushdie, but not about this.[14]

In fact, the same is true wherever you go: the United States is unusual— possibly even unique in the world—in that we actually protect freedom of speech. But that was only won after long, bitter struggle—it happened because people were fighting about it for centuries. And the same is true of every other right you can think of.

## Negative and Positive Freedoms

WOMAN: *I have to say that I'm a little uncomfortable with your kind of extreme freedom of speech advocacy, though. It just seems to me that until there's a more equitable distribution of access to free speech, it's going to be used destructively more often than it's used positively. It makes me uncomfortable, so I just don't want to jump on your bandwagon.*

Well, let me see what I can say to that. Freedoms are usually distinguished between the "negative" kind and the "positive" kind. "Negative freedom" means there's no coercive force around that *prevents* you from doing something; "positive freedom" is when circumstances are such that you can actually *do it*. And those things can be quite different.

Now, freedom of speech is available today in the United States mostly as a negative freedom—meaning, nobody stops you. But it's not available as a positive freedom, because as you say, access to the channels of communication is highly skewed in our society, it's distributed roughly in accordance with power, which obviously is highly unequal. Okay, what's the way of overcoming that? One way of overcoming it—which is, say, the Catharine MacKinnon [feminist legal scholar] way—is to give the people in power even more power: give the people in power even more power, so they can use it even more inequitably. In other words, don't change the power structure, just put through some laws prohibiting speech and let the power structure enforce them. That means, give more power to the people who have power, and let them use it the way they feel like using it—that's exactly what it means. And they'll stop the speech they want to stop. Alright, that's one way. The other way is to try to change the distribution of power in the society, but not to attack the freedom of speech.

My own view is that you should save the negative freedoms, defend strongly the negative freedoms, but then try to make them positive freedoms. If the goal is to achieve positive freedom, it doesn't help to destroy negative freedom—like, giving the state the power to determine what people can say does not improve the position of people who are now powerless. And those are really the only choices you have.

I mean, to attain the negative freedom was a big achievement, I think. When the Supreme Court struck down the Sedition Act, it didn't grant anybody positive freedom, that's true. But it was a very important victory for popular movements—because that kind of law strikes right at the core of protest and dissidence. I don't think you expand those victories by assigning more power to the state authorities to control speech. And there is no other way to control it: if speech is controlled, it's controlled by police power.

WOMAN: *Acknowledging that, I still have two concerns. One is, don't we have an obligation to the victims of free speech?*

Sure . . .

WOMAN: *The second is, what about people who are saying speech that they know to be false, but are hiding behind "free speech" to promulgate their own interests?*

Well, that's what they'll say about you. Look, ultimately the question is, who gets to make that decision and enforce it? And there is only one independent structure that can do that, that's the state, that's state power, government power, the police, you know, the cops, F.B.I. *They* can make that decision, nobody else can. So the question is, do you want them to be in a position to decide what speech is acceptable? That's essentially what it comes down to. And I would say, no, we don't want them to have any right to make any decision about what anybody says. And of course, that's going to mean that a lot of people are going to say things that you think are rotten, and you're going to say things that a lot of other people think are rotten.

As to the obligation to the victims, sure—but that's a matter of building up and extending the positive freedoms. In fact, here's a case where I think the left is off on really marginal issues. Take the question of pornography: I mean, undoubtedly women suffer from pornography, but in terms of people suffering from speech in the world, that's hardly even a speck. People suffer a lot more from the teaching of free-trade economics in colleges—huge numbers of people in the Third World are dying because of the stuff that's taught in American economics departments, I'm talking about tens of millions. That's harm. Should we therefore pass a law that says that the government ought to decide what you teach in economics departments? Absolutely not, then it would just get worse. They'd force everybody to teach this stuff.

MAN: *What about things like shouting "Fire!" in a movie theater, or commanding people to assault somebody? Don't you think there should be a limit there?*

Well, the people who attack free speech rights typically say, "Look, speech is an act"—which is true, speech is an act. But therefore it ought to be treated like other acts. I mean, let's agree, speech is an act, it certainly is. But then let's treat it like any other act. For example, if you throw a bomb into a crowded theater, yeah, that's a crime, somebody ought to stop you. And if you participate in the act of somebody else throwing one, even if your participation is with words, somebody also ought to stop you. Like, if you and I go into a grocery store with the intent to rob it, and you have a gun, and I'm your boss, and I say "Fire!" and you kill the owner, that's speech. But it shouldn't be *protected* speech, in my opinion—because that statement is participation in a criminal act.

MAN: *What about things like sexual harassment?*

That's a different story. See, there *are* conflicting rights. Rights aren't an axiom system [i.e. where there are no contradictions], and if you look closely at them, they often conflict—so you just have to make judgments between them in those cases. And like freedom of speech, another right that people have is to work without getting harassed. So I think laws against sexual harassment in the workplace are perfectly reasonable, because they follow from a reasonable principle—namely, you should be able to work without harassment, period. Sexual or any other kind. On the other hand, sexual harassment in the streets is another story, and I think it has to be treated differently.

Look, in the real free speech discussions, there is nobody who's an absolutist on free speech. People may pretend to be, but they're not. Like, I've never heard of anybody who says that you have a right to come into my house and put up a Nazi poster on the wall. Well, okay, blocking you from doing that is an infringement on your freedom of speech, but it's also a protection of my right to privacy. And those rights sometimes conflict, because rights do conflict, so therefore we just have to make judgments between them—and those judgments are often not easy to make. But in general, I think we should be extremely wary about placing the power to make those determinations in the hands of authorities, who are going to respond to the distribution of power in the society as they carry them out.

MAN: *In my university, we had an architecture professor who in the course of his class was telling people that if they wanted to buy a camera they should bring a Jew with them, all sorts of racist things like that. People were wondering if they should censor him or not.*

Yeah, it's a hard question. For instance, I was an undergraduate right after the Second World War, and I happened to have a German class taught by a guy who was a flat outright Nazi—he didn't even hide it. There were a lot of war veterans around in those days, so guys were ready to kill him and stuff, because these things were very live in people's minds. But should the university have fired him? I didn't think so. I think it's dangerous to impose such constraints on what people are allowed to say. There are other ways of dealing with it.

MAN: *You might say that someone else in the classroom has a right not to hear it, though.*

Yes, but see, if a student gets up and denounces him, the student has a right to do that, and then if the student is punished you've got a straight case—because the guy in authority has no right to do anything except sit and listen. But should you stop the teacher from talking about things? I think that's tricky.

Even there, though, it's not totally straightforward. Like, there's a contractual arrangement when you go to a class: namely, you want to study chemistry or whatever it is, that's why you're there, and if the teacher starts talking about fundamentalist religion or something, you have a right to say, "He shouldn't be paid, get rid of him, because I came here to study chemistry, that was our common agreement, and he violated that agreement—so throw him out." On the other hand, if the teacher just says things you don't like, that's different.

Again, rights aren't an axiom system, so there are conflicts between them, and people just have to make their own judgments. But my own judgment, at least, tends to be that a lot of leeway ought to be allowed. Often the cases are quite hard, though—because our moral codes simply aren't clear enough to give answers in a lot of situations, and people come up with different ones.

MAN: *You think there's some ambiguity with sexual harassment, then?*

Oh yeah, a fair amount of ambiguity. For example, sexual harassment by words in the streets—like if somebody makes a nasty crack about some woman's dress or something—I don't think they should be put in jail.

WOMAN: *What about violence on television? Does that also conflict with other rights?*

Violence on television raises quite hard questions, I think. But I don't know: if you look at the literature on whether T.V. violence or pornography cause a demonstrable harm—you know, result in violence in the real world—it doesn't show anything convincing. So maybe it's too hard to study or something like that, but there are almost no probative results that I know of one way or the other: the facts just aren't there. There's *psychic* harm, that's undoubtedly true, but that you can't measure. As for the kinds of things you can measure, like increase in acts of violence—I mean, you probably get more acts of violence coming after things like sports events; not huge amounts more, but there's a notable increase in domestic violence, say, after things like the Superbowl.[15]

## Cyberspace and Activism

WOMAN: *Mr. Chomsky, on a very different note, I'd like to talk a bit about some of the recent computer technologies like the Internet, and e-mail, and the World Wide Web and so on, and how significant an impact you think they are going to have on political activism and organizing in the future. Do you see the Internet as more of a force for democracy, or a force for diverting the population from engaging themselves politically in the world?*

Well, my feeling is that the Internet is pretty much the same sort of phenomenon as radio and television were—or for that matter, as automation. Look, in most cases technology isn't predisposed to help people or harm people—there's very rarely anything inherent in it which requires that either of those things be the case, it just depends on who gets control of it.

So take radio, for example. You might ask why popular movements in the United States have to look to small community-controlled radio stations to get programming which addresses their interests and needs and goals, why doesn't any mainstream radio do that? Well, the reason is, the United States just diverged from the rest of the world on this back around the late 1920s and early Thirties, when radio was first coming into existence.

See, radio has a limited frequency band, which necessarily has to be rationed—so the question is, how is that rationing going to be done? Well, in every major country in the world—and maybe in *every* country except the United States—radio was turned into a public forum to some degree, meaning it's as democratic as the country is. Like, in Russia, it's not democratic, in Great Britain, it's as democratic as England is—but somehow it's still in the public domain. The United States went the other way: here radio was privatized, it was put into private hands—and furthermore, that was called a *victory* for democracy here.[16] So now if you want radio that's not under corporate control in the United States, you have to go to small local community radio stations—which are very important, but of course are on the margins, and have only extremely limited resources.

Or take television: when television came along in the 1940s, the same thing happened in the United States. In fact, in the case of television, there wasn't even a battle about it—it was just completely handed over to private power at once.[17]

Well, I think the Internet is going to be the same basic story: if it's put in the hands of private power, like T.V. and radio were, then we know exactly how it's going to turn out. In fact, they've been telling us about it constantly. So I remember an article in the *Wall Street Journal* about the wonders of all the new technology, and they described the great things that can be done because it's "interactive"—you know, you don't just have to be passive anymore, now you can really *do* things when you're sitting there in front of the tube. Well, they described how it would work, and they gave two examples, one for women and the other for men.

For women, it's going to be an incredible home-shopping thing: like, you're sitting there watching some model, and she shows you some ridiculous object, and you figure, "Well, I'd better have that or my kid won't grow up properly"—and now it's *interactive*, you know, so you can just push a button and they'll send it right over to your house. That's the interaction for women. For men, the example they gave was of watching the Superbowl, which every red-blooded male is supposed to do. Well, today it's passive: you just sit there and watch the gladiators fighting. But with the new technology, it's going to be *interactive*. So what they suggest is, while the team's in its huddle getting instructions from the coach about the next play, everyone in the audience—you know, the entire male population that's alive—is going to be asked to make their own decision about it: like, should it be a pass, or a run, or a kick or something. And then after the play is run (which is going on completely independently of this, of course) they'll flash on the screen what people thought the coach should have done—that's going to be the interaction for men.

And that's probably the way it's going to go in general: it'll be used as another technique for control and manipulation, and for keeping people in their roles as mindless consumers of things they don't really want. Sure—why should the people who own the society do things any differently?

But of course, none of these technologies *have* to be used like that—again, it just depends who ends up controlling them. I mean, if the general public ever ended up controlling them, they could be used quite differently. For example, these information-processing systems could be used as methods by which working people could come to control their own workplaces without the need for managers and bosses—so every person in the workplace could have all the information they need in order to make all the decisions themselves, in real time, when it counts. Well, in that kind of circumstance, the same technology would be a highly democratizing device—in fact, it would help eliminate the core of the whole system of authority and domination. But obviously it's not just going to develop like that on its own—people will have to organize and fight to make that sort of thing ever happen, in fact fight very strenuously for it.

As to the effects of all of this on activism, I think it's a complicated story. I think we can be certain that there's a lot of thinking going on about whether to even allow things like the Internet to exist—because from the point of view of power, it's just too democratic: it's very hard to control what's in it, and who can gain access to it. For example, I have a daughter living in Nicaragua, and during the U.S. contra war in the 1980s it was impossible to telephone or send letters there. The only way I could stay in contact with her was through the ARPAnet, which is basically a Pentagon computer system I was able to get access to through M.I.T.—so we were corresponding thanks to the Pentagon. Well, that's the kind of thing that happens on the Internet, and a lot of powerful people obviously don't like that aspect of it.

And they don't like the fact that you can get the text of the G.A.T.T. [General Agreement on Tariffs and Trade] treaty, and the latest news that doesn't appear in the U.S. newspapers, and so on—in fact, if you look around on the Internet, you can find virtually everything I talk about somewhere in there. And on some issues, like say, East Timor, it's also been an invaluable political organizing tool—because most of the information about what happened there was simply silenced by the U.S. press for years and years. Well, those are all bad things from the perspective of private power, and they surely would like to stop that side of it.

On the other hand, it has a number of other advantages for power. For one thing, it diverts people, it atomizes people. When you're sitting in front of your tube, you're alone. I mean, there's something about human beings that just makes face-to-face contact very different from banging around on a computer terminal and getting some noise coming back—that's very impersonal, and it breaks down human relations. Well, that's obviously a good result from the point of view of people with power—because it's extremely important to drive human sentiments out of people if you just want them to be passive and obedient and under control. So if you can eliminate things like face-to-face contact and direct interaction, and just turn people into what's caricatured as kind of an M.I.T. nerd—you know, somebody who's got antennae coming out of his head, and is wired into his computer all the time—that's a real advantage, because then you've made them more inhuman, and therefore more controllable.

Another thing I've found is that there's a kind of degraded character to e-mail messages. People are just too casual about them—they send you any half-baked idea they haven't even thought through yet, whenever the impulse hits them. And the result is, it ends up being a tremendous burden even to *read* everything that comes across, let alone to answer it—so that can easily end up being all you do with your time. And people do put *huge* numbers of hours into it. In fact, there are friends of mine whose quality of work I think is seriously declining, because of their overwhelming involvement in e-mail interactions. It's extremely seductive just to sit at the computer screen and bang at it all day.

Furthermore, I think there are still other aspects to it which are very threatening to popular movements. For instance, one thing I've noticed is that a lot of activists have been dropping subscriptions to left journals recently. Why? Because they can get them through the Internet. Now, see, if I was in the C.I.A. or something, right now I'd be saying, "Look, let's encourage this—it's true it has the negative effect of allowing people to get more information, but it also has the positive effect of destroying alternative institutions. So let's let it go on—because when all these people stop paying their subscriptions to, I don't know, *Z Magazine* or something, that is going to destroy those institutions, and that's going to separate and fragment the left even more, and maybe even destroy it."

Well, I doubt that anybody in the C.I.A. has this much brains, but if they had enough brains, I think they would just want the whole thing to go on, because it's probably going to destroy the dissident organizations—and it'll destroy them because we're so anti-social that we don't even see the *point* of supporting popular institutions. Remember, even if you're an activist on the left, what you've constantly been taught from childhood, and what you've still got ingrained in your head is: "I'm just out for myself, and therefore if I can get the information for nothing, why should I help to build an institution?" Well, that's obviously a very anti-social attitude—but you find it's very hard to break out of: we've just got it. So there are a number of aspects to these technologies that are highly dangerous, in my view—and I hope people will soon start to recognize and resist those aspects of them.

## "Free Trade" Agreements

MAN: *You mentioned that people with power probably don't like it that the G.A.T.T. treaty got onto the Internet. It just emphasized for me how these international trade agreements are being forced on us, and yet nobody even knows what they're about. I'm wondering what you think of that?*

Well, plenty of people know what they're about—there are plenty of people working for big corporations who know what the G.A.T.T. treaty is about, for example. But you're right, the general population here doesn't have the slightest idea about it—I mean, overwhelmingly the general population of the United States hasn't even *heard* of G.A.T.T., and certainly they don't know what its likely effects are going to be. [G.A.T.T. was first established in 1947, but the "Uruguay Round" of negotiations to modify it concluded in December 1993; the treaty then was signed in April 1994.]

What do I think of that? I think it's ridiculous—grotesque, in fact. Look, G.A.T.T. is something of major significance. The idea that it's going to be rammed through Congress on a fast track without public discussion just shows that anything resembling democracy in the United States has completely collapsed. So whatever one thinks about G.A.T.T., at least it should be a topic for the general public to become informed about, and to investigate, and to look at, and think about carefully. That much is easy.

If you ask what should *happen* in that public discussion—well, if that public discussion ever comes along, I'll be glad to say what I think. And what I think is in fact mixed. It's like N.A.F.T.A.: I don't know of anyone who was opposed to a North American trade agreement in principle—the question was, *what kind?*[18] So before N.A.F.T.A. got passed [in 1993], mainstream groups like the Congressional Office of Technology Assessment—can't get more centrist than that—came out with very sharp and intelligent critiques of the Executive version of N.A.F.T.A., the one that finally went through. And they pointed out that in fact N.A.F.T.A. was designed to be an *investor rights* agreement, not a "free trade" agreement—and that it was going to drive the economies of each of the three participating countries [the U.S., Canada and Mexico] down towards a kind of low-wage, low-growth equilibrium; they didn't say it of course, but it'll also be a *high-profit* equilibrium. And they suggested very constructive alternatives.[19]

Well, those sorts of constructive critiques never even entered the mainstream discussion about N.A.F.T.A. here: all you ever heard in the media was, "Crazy jingoists don't like Mexican workers."

The same was true of the American labor movement: its proposals were nothing like what was constantly being denounced in the press with virtually 100 percent uniformity.[20] The Labor Advisory Committee, for example—which by law is required to give its opinion on these things, but was illegally cut out of the discussion—came out with quite a constructive report on N.A.F.T.A.: it wasn't against *an* agreement, it was against *that* agreement. In fact, the story of the Labor Advisory Committee report tells you a lot about the way that N.A.F.T.A. was passed in the U.S., a lot about American democracy.

Twenty years ago, Congress enacted a Trade Act requiring that before any trade-related legislation or treaty is passed, there has to be consultation with a "Labor Advisory Committee" they set up which is based in the unions, such as they are. That's by law: the Labor Advisory Committee has to give an analysis and a critique of any American trade-related issue, so obviously that would include N.A.F.T.A.[21] Well, the Labor Advisory Committee was informed by the Clinton White House that their report was due on September 9th; they were not given an inkling of what was in the treaty until September *8th*—so obviously they couldn't even convene to meet. Then on top of that, they weren't even given the whole text of the treaty— it's this huge treaty, hundreds and hundreds of pages.

But somehow they did manage to write a response to it anyway, and it was a very angry response—both because of the utter contempt for democracy revealed by these maneuvers, but also because from the glimmerings of what they could get out of N.A.F.T.A. when they sort of flipped through it for a couple of hours, it was obvious that this thing was just going to have a *devastating* effect on American labor, and probably also a devastating effect on Mexican labor too, though of course it will be highly beneficial to American investors, and probably also to Mexican investors.[22] It's also certain to have a highly destructive effect on the environment—because its laws supersede federal and state legislation. So obviously there are really major issues here, crucially important issues, which in a functioning democracy would have been the subject of intensive public consideration and debate.

Actually, if you looked closely, even N.A.F.T.A.'s *advocates* conceded that it was probably going to harm the majority of the populations of the three countries. For instance, its advocates in the United States were saying, "It's really good, it'll only harm semi-skilled workers"—footnote: 70 percent of the workforce.[23] As a matter of fact, after N.A.F.T.A. was safely passed, the *New York Times* did their first analysis of its predicted effects in the New York region: it was a very upbeat article talking about how terrific it was going to be for corporate lawyers and P.R. firms and so on. And then there was a footnote there as well. It said, well, *everyone* can't gain, there'll also be some losers: "women, blacks, Hispanics, and semi-skilled labor"— in other words, most of the people of New York.[24] But you can't have everything. And those were the *advocates*.

In fact, it's kind of striking that about a day or two after N.A.F.T.A. was passed, the Senate approved the most onerous crime bill in U.S. history [the Violent Crime Control and Law Enforcement Act], which the House then made even worse. Now, I don't know if that was just a symbolic coincidence or what—but it makes sense. I mean, N.A.F.T.A. was clearly going to have the effect of reducing wages for probably three-quarters of the American population, and it's going to make a lot more of the population superfluous from the point of view of profits—so the Crime Bill just will take care of a lot of them, by throwing them in jail.

Okay, that's N.A.F.T.A.—what about G.A.T.T.? Well, in India, for example, there were hundreds of thousands of people demonstrating in the streets about some of the G.A.T.T. provisions—which *they* know about. I mean, we may be very ignorant about it in the United States, but people in the Third World know a lot about G.A.T.T.: Indian peasants understand what's being done to them, even if people here don't, which is why G.A.T.T. has to be passed virtually at gunpoint in countries like India.[25]

Well, what are those people so upset about? Here's one thing. One of the protections codified in the current G.A.T.T. agreements, as in N.A.F.T.A., is what's called "intellectual property rights" [i.e. rights to registered trademarks, patented technologies, and copyrights of valuable "information" products ranging from music to genes]. Intellectual property rights are a protectionist measure, they have nothing to do with free trade—in fact, they're the exact *opposite* of free trade. And they'll do a lot of things, but two really crucial ones.

First of all, they're going to increase the duration of patents: meaning, if Merck Pharmaceutical patents some drug, thanks to publicly-subsidized work in American universities, for example, now they can get a much longer patent for it under G.A.T.T.—much longer than any of the rich countries ever accepted during the periods when *they* were developing, incidentally. In fact, it's only in very recent years that the rich countries have even honored patent rights at all—the United States never did when it was a developing country, for instance. So, point one: patents are being much extended.

Secondly, the *nature* of patents is being shifted in character. See, up until now, patents have been what are called "process patents"—in other words, if Merck figures out a way to create a drug, the *process* of making the drug is patented, but not the drug itself. The G.A.T.T. treaty, like N.A.F.T.A., shifts that: now it's the *product* that's patented—meaning the Indian or Argentine pharmaceutical industries no longer can try to figure out a smarter way to produce the same drug at half the cost, in order to get it to their own populations more affordably. Notice that these are not only highly protectionist measures, but they're a blow *against* economic efficiency and technological progress—that just shows you how much "free trade" really is involved in all of this.

Actually, there are significant historical precedents on product patents, and I'm sure that they are perfectly well known to the G.A.T.T. designers. France, for example, once had a chemical industry, but it lost it—most of the French chemical industry moved to Switzerland, which is why Switzerland now has such a large chemical industry. The reason? France happened to have product patents, which were such a barrier to innovation and technical progress that the French chemical companies just decided to go elsewhere.[26] Well, now G.A.T.T. is trying to impose that inefficiency on the entire world. In fact, India already has been forced to accept it: a little while ago they did what's called "liberalizing" their pharmaceuticals industry, meaning they opened it up to foreign penetration. So now drug prices will shoot sky-high, more children will die, people won't be able to afford medications they need, and so on.[27]

Well, these changes in patents are just one part of G.A.T.T.: they're one piece of a whole attempt that is now being made to ensure that unaccountable transnational corporations will monopolize the technologies of the future. In my opinion, that's grotesque—I don't see any reason to push *that* through. Certainly anyone who believes in free trade would be opposed to these policies: they're a high level of protectionism, which in fact is specifically designed to be contrary to even the narrow definitions of economic efficiency they teach you in the University of Chicago Economics Department [home of well-known exponents of free-market theory]. G.A.T.T. is going to cut down on technological innovation, it's going to cut down on economic efficiency—but by some strange accident, it'll also happen to increase profits, so of course nobody will pick up on any of the contradictions.

As a matter of fact, it's not even clear that these so-called "free trade" agreements are going to increase *trade* at all, in any authentic sense. So there's a lot of talk in the papers these days about the growth of international trade, which is supposed to show everyone how wonderful the market is. But if you take a look at that international trade, you'll find that it's a very curious kind of growth: about 50 percent of U.S. trade now is *internal* to corporations, which means it's about as much "trade" as if you move something from one shelf of a grocery store to another, it just happens to cross an international border, so therefore it gets recorded as "trade." And the figures are comparable for other major countries.[28]

That means, for example, that if the Ford Motor Company sends some parts to Mexico to be assembled by super-cheap labor under essentially no environmental regulations and then they ship it back up to the United States to add more value to it, that's "trade." But that's not trade at all: those aren't exports, they didn't even enter the Mexican market—they're centrally-managed interactions by huge institutions, with a very "visible hand" pushing them around, and with all kinds of other market distortions involved that nobody here bothers to study very much but which undoubtedly are severe. And 50 percent is not a small amount—that's a lot. I mean, at the time that N.A.F.T.A. was passed, there was a lot of talk in the press about U.S. trade with Mexico soaring—but there wasn't talk about the fact that more than half of U.S. exports to Mexico were *internal* to corporations. So in fact, N.A.F.T.A. and G.A.T.T. might really end up *reducing* trade—they'll probably increase things moving across borders, but that's not the same as trade: those transfers are not market interactions.

Well, okay, these are complicated matters, and you don't just want to sloganize about them—but in my opinion, all of these international agreements are part of a general attack on democracy and free markets that we're seeing in the contemporary period, as banks, investment firms, and transnational corporations develop new methods to extend their power free from public scrutiny. And in that context, it's not very surprising that they're all being rammed through as quickly and secretly as they are. And whatever you happen to think about the specific treaties that have now been put into place, there is just no doubt that their consequences for most of the people in the world are going to be vast.

In fact, these treaties are just one more step in the process that's been accelerating in recent years of differentiating the two main class interests of the world still further—far more so than before—so that the Third World wealth-distribution model is being extended everywhere. And while the proportions of wealth in a rich country like the United States will always differ significantly from the proportions in a deeply impoverished country like Brazil, for example (deeply impoverished thanks to the fact that it's been under the Western heel for centuries), you can certainly see the effects under way in recent years. I mean, in the United States things probably aren't going to get to the point where 80 percent of the population is living like Central Africa and 10 percent is fabulously wealthy. Maybe it'll be 50 percent and 30 percent or something like that, with the rest somewhere in between—because more people are always going to be needed in the Western societies for things like scientific research and skilled labor, providing propaganda services, being managers, things like that. But the changes no doubt are happening, and they will be rapidly accelerated as these accords are implemented.

## Defense Department Funding and "Clean Money"

WOMAN: *Noam, just to go back to freedom of thought for a second—I'm curious what your feeling is about the Defense Department funding so many of our scientists today. Do you see that as a problem in terms of freedom of research and freedom of inquiry? And does it make you feel at all uncomfortable personally to be working at M.I.T.?*

To tell you the honest truth, I've always thought that's kind of a secondary issue. For instance, in the late 1960s, M.I.T. was about 80 percent funded by the Defense Department—it's less than that today, because of things like cancer research money. But what did that mean? Was M.I.T. different from, say, Harvard, which wasn't so much funded by the Defense Department? Well, about the only major differences between them were that M.I.T. was a little bit more open to radical ideas, and there was more political activism and fewer ideological controls. That's about it, as far as I could see.

Now, there was once a time when I was being funded by the Air Force myself—to do exactly the same sort of thing that I'm doing now in my scientific work. Right now I'm not, so if you asked me whether I'm funded by the Defense Department, I could in some narrow sense say no. But the fact of the matter is, I *am* funded by the Defense Department, whether I have a contract with them or not—because if the Defense Department weren't funding the Electrical Engineering Department, which M.I.T. needs, the Institute would not be able to fund my department. I mean, if you're teaching *music* at M.I.T. you're being funded by the Defense Department, because if somebody they really cared about *weren't* being funded by the Defense Department, they wouldn't have anything left to pay you to teach music. So in part the thing is kind of like a bookkeeping device.

As for its influence on what's done, that's very small: the Defense Department doesn't give a damn what you do most of the time—they just want to fund it, because they want to have a bigger bureaucracy or something like that. So there's very little reporting back by the scientists, they don't pay much attention to you, they don't care whether you did what you said you'd do or something else, and so on. In fact, back in the Sixties, there was a guy in my lab who was working on translating Humboldt [a Prussian philosopher]—he was being funded by the Office of Naval Research, they didn't care.

As far as the moral issue goes—I mean, it's not as if there's some clean money somewhere. If you're in a university, you're on dirty money—you're on money which is coming from people who are working somewhere, and whose money is being taken away, and is going to support things like universities. Now, there are a lot of ways in which that money can be taken away from those working people and get fed into the universities. One way is by diverting it through taxes and government bureaucracies. Another way is by channeling it through profits—like, some rich benefactor gives it as a gift to the university, meaning he stole it from his workers. And there are all sorts of other ways in which it happens too. But it all comes down to the same point: if you're at a university, you're there because there is a social structure which commits a certain amount of "surplus product," if you want to use a Marxist term, to funding people sitting around in universities.

Now, I don't see a whole lot of difference myself as to whether that money works its way through the Department of Defense or through some other mechanism—that's why I've never made a big fuss about this. I mean, to the extent that the Defense Department influenced what scientists *do*, it would matter. But good universities don't permit that, by and large—they don't permit it just for their own internal reasons: if you started permitting that, you'd lose the ability to *do* science altogether. Science simply can't be done under those kinds of ideological constraints.

It's sort of like what happens in cancer research: Congress is funding a lot of cellular biology because they want somebody to discover a cure for cancer by the time they get it, but what the scientists are doing is just what they know how to do—and what they know how to do has nothing to do with cancer, what they know how to do is work with big molecules. Maybe a cure for cancer will come out of it someday, but that's sort of by the side. And that's pretty much the way it goes in the sciences: you can work on what you understand, you can't work on what people tell you to solve. It's like the joke about the drunk and the streetlight: you see some drunk guy looking for something under the streetlight and you go over to him and ask, "What's the matter?" He says, "I lost my key." You say, "Where did you lose it?" He says, "On the other side of the street." You say, "So why are you looking over here?" "Well, this is where the light is." That's the way the sciences work: you look where the light is—because that's all you can do.

You understand only a certain small number of things, and you just have to work around the periphery of them. If somebody says, "I'd like to have you solve this problem out here," you say, "I'll gladly take your money"—and then you go on looking where you are. And there basically is nothing much else that can be done. If you started trying to direct the money to solving those problems, you'd just do nothing, because we don't know how to solve them. There's kind of a tacit compact between funders and recipients to overlook this . . .

## The Favored State and Enemy States

*WOMAN: Noam, people often attack you as a political commentator for focusing your criticism against the activities of the United States, and not so much against the old Soviet Union, or Vietnam, or Cuba and so on—the official enemies. I'd like to know what you think about that kind of criticism?*

Well, it's true that's one of the standard things I get—but see, if that criticism is meant honestly (and most of the time it's not), then it's really missing the crucial point, I think. See, I focus my efforts against the terror and violence of my own state for really two main reasons. First of all, in my case the actions of my state happen to make up the main component of international violence in the world. But much more importantly than that, it's because American actions are the things that I can *do* something about. So even if the United States were causing only a tiny fraction of the repression and violence in the world—which obviously is very far from the truth—that tiny fraction would still be what I'm responsible for, and what I should focus my efforts against. And that's based on a very simple ethical principle—namely, that the ethical value of one's actions depends on their anticipated consequences for human beings: I think that's kind of like a fundamental moral truism.

So for example, it was a very easy thing in the 1980s for people in the United States to denounce the atrocities of the Soviet Union in its occupation of Afghanistan—but those denunciations had no effects which could have helped people. In terms of their ethical value, they were about the same as denouncing Napoleon's atrocities, or things that happened in the Middle Ages. Useful and significant actions are ones which have consequences for human beings, and usually those will concern things that you can influence and control—which means for people in the United States, American actions primarily, not those of some other state.

Actually, the principle that I think we ought to follow is the principle we rightly expected Soviet dissidents to follow. So what principle did we expect Sakharov [a Soviet scientist punished for his criticism of the U.S.S.R.] to follow? Why did people here decide that Sakharov was a moral person? I think he was. Sakharov did not treat every atrocity as identical—he had nothing to say about American atrocities. When he was asked about them, he said, "I don't know anything about them, I don't care about them, what I talk about are Soviet atrocities." And that was right—because those were the ones that he was responsible for, and that he might have been able to influence. Again, it's a very simple ethical point: you are responsible for the predictable consequences of *your* actions, you're not responsible for the predictable consequences of somebody else's actions.

Now, we understand this perfectly well when we're talking about dissidents in the old Soviet Union or in some other enemy state, but we fail to understand it when we're talking about ourselves—for obvious reasons. I mean, commissars in the old Soviet Union didn't understand it about dissidents there either: commissars in the old Soviet Union attacked Sakharov and other Soviet dissidents because they weren't denouncing *American* crimes. In fact, an old joke fifty years ago was that if you went to a Stalinist and criticized the Soviet slave-labor camps, the Stalinist would say, "Well, what about the lynchings in the American South?" Alright, in that case the dishonesty's obvious, and we can easily understand why.

Now, just personally speaking, it turns out that I *do* spend a fair amount of effort talking about the crimes of official enemies—in fact, there are a number of people now living in the United States and Canada from the old Soviet Union and Eastern Europe who are there because of my own personal activities on their behalf. But I don't take great pride in that part of my work, particularly: I just do it because I'm interested in it. The most important thing for me, and for you, is to think about the greater consequences of your criticisms: what you can have the most effect on. And especially in a relatively open society like ours, which does allow a lot of freedom for dissent, that means American crimes primarily.

Well, that's the main point here, I think. But there's also another consideration which is important—and which simply can't be ignored, in my opinion. Honest people are just going to have to face the fact that whenever possible, people with power are going to exploit any actions which serve their violent ends. So when American dissidents criticize the atrocities of some enemy state like Cuba or Vietnam or something, it's no secret what the effects of that criticism are going to be: it's not going have any effect whatsoever on the Cuban regime, for example, but it certainly will help the torturers in Washington and Miami to keep inflicting their campaign of suffering on the Cuban population [i.e. through the U.S.-led embargo]. Well, that is something I do not think a moral person would want to contribute to.

I mean, if a Russian intellectual had started publishing articles denouncing very real atrocities committed by the Afghan resistance forces at the time of the Soviet invasion of Afghanistan, knowing that his accurate criticism would have helped enable the Kremlin to mobilize popular support for further atrocities by the Red Army, I do not think that would have been a morally responsible thing for that person to do. Of course, this often creates difficult dilemmas. But again, honest people have to recognize that they are responsible for the predictable consequences of their acts. So perfectly accurate criticism of the regime in Cuba, say, will predictably be used by ideologists and politicians in the United States to help extend our absolutely barbaric stranglehold on Cuba. Your criticism could be perfectly correct—though obviously much of what we do hear today is in fact false. But even so, an honest person will always ask, "What are the likely consequences of this going to be for other people?" And the consequences in that case at least are clear. Well, making decisions in these circumstances can often be difficult—but these are just dilemmas that human beings have to face in life, and all you can do is try to deal with them the best way you can.

## Canada's Media

WOMAN: *I'm from Canada, Professor Chomsky, and when I come to the United States and turn on the T.V., to me the propaganda all seems so blatant—I see this woman talking about guilt and abortion, there's this black woman saying, "I'm on welfare because I'm lazy," it's just one image like that after another, there's no subtlety to it whatsoever. On Canadian T.V. it's more subtle: the C.B.C. [Canadian Broadcasting Corporation] wouldn't put on the black woman saying, "I'm lazy, I'm on welfare because I'm lazy"—they'd put up a chart or something that tries to say the same thing.*

That's right.

WOMAN: *The* Globe and Mail *[self-billed "Canada's National Newspaper"] also is more subtle than the papers I see here—it's not as obvious. What I'm wondering is, how do you explain this difference in the two countries' media systems? I mean, I don't think I could apply the "Propaganda Model" you and Edward Herman laid out in* Manufacturing Consent *to the Canadian media—it really wouldn't work.*

I think you could, actually—I think you're wrong about that. Let me just give you some examples. The first part of my book *Necessary Illusions* was made up of talks on the media that I was invited to give in Canada over C.B.C. national public radio [titled "Thought Control in Democratic Societies"]. Okay, obviously that would never happen in the United States.[29] So that's a difference.

On the other hand, in preparation for those lectures I figured that it would be interesting to compare the *Globe and Mail*, Canada's main newspaper, with the *New York Times*, and maybe I'd discuss the results in my talks. So for a year I subscribed to the *Globe and Mail*—which I must say cost about $1,500 or something in the United States, and apparently all their U.S. subscribers are rich investors, because every two weeks or so you'd get a big fat glossy book about investment opportunities in Canada. But anyhow, for about a year I read the *Globe and Mail* every day and the *New York Times* every day, plus all the other junk, and at first I figured it would be an interesting comparison. Alright, it turned out that it *wasn't* an interesting comparison. Reading the *Globe and Mail* is like reading the *Boston Globe*—it's like an ordinary, quality local newspaper in the United States: small amount of international coverage, huge amount of business news, and mostly picking stories off sources in the United States.

Now, it's true that over that year I did find things in the *Globe and Mail* which did not appear in the United States, or which appeared only in really remote places. And also I have friends in the Canadian media who clip the Canadian press regularly for me, and they often find stuff there that doesn't appear anywhere in the United States. So you're right, there are some differences. But overall, reading the *Globe and Mail* for a year, I didn't get a different picture of the world than I get from reading the *Boston Globe* or the *L.A. Times* or any other quality local newspaper in the United States. The *Globe and Mail* was more local in orientation and less international than the *New York Times*, but I didn't feel that it was qualitatively different—it's mostly a business paper like all the others.

Now, when I go to Canada, I do get asked onto mainstream national radio and television a lot, as distinct from here—a lot. But see, that's because I criticize the United States, and in Canada they like it when people come up and dump on the United States—because the United States is always pushing them around all the time, so it's nice if somebody comes and says how rotten the United States is once in a while. On the other hand, I got sick of this a couple times, and I started talking about Canada—and I was off so fast you couldn't even see it. The first time I did it was on this big morning radio show they have there, with this guy whose name I can never remember . . .

MAN: *Peter Gzowski.*

Gzowski, yeah. There's this nation-wide radio talk show in Canada which everybody tunes into some time in the morning [*Morningside*, on C.B.C.], and every time I'd go to Toronto they would invite me to come on that show. So we'd have whatever it is, fifteen minutes, and this guy would ask me some leading questions, I'd tell him how rotten the United States is, big smile.

Well, one time I really got sick of this, and I started talking about Canada. He said some line about, "I hear you just flew in." I said, "Yeah, I landed at the War Criminal Airport." He said: "What do you mean?" I said, "Well, you know, the Lester B. Pearson Airport." And he says, "What do you mean, 'war criminal'?" Lester Pearson's the big hero in Canada [he was a prominent diplomat and Prime Minister from 1963 to '68]. So I started running through Pearson's involvement in criminal activity—he was a major criminal, really extreme. He didn't have the power to be like an American President, but if he'd had it, he would have been the same—he tried, you know. And I went through some of this.[30] The guy got infuriated.

Then I said something about Canada and the Vietnam War—Canada was always denouncing the United States during the Vietnam War for its criminal actions, meanwhile Canada was probably the leading military exporter in the world per capita, enriching itself on the destruction of Indochina.[31] So I mentioned some of this stuff. He went into kind of a tantrum. I actually thought it was sort of funny, but apparently his listeners didn't—when I left, after about ten minutes of listening to this harangue, the producer, sort of quivering, stopped me and said: "Oh my God, the switchboard's lighting up, we're getting thousands of phone calls from all over Canada."

And apparently the phone calls were all just about the fact that this guy Gzowski was being impolite—I don't know if people agreed with me particularly, but there were a lot of people who were very angry at the way he was going about it. Like I said, I thought it was comical, didn't bother me.

WOMAN: *I'm sorry, they got angry at* him?

*Him*, yeah—and they were pretty upset, because there were a lot of calls. Alright, so then the producer asked me "Well, look, could you go on again?" And I said, "No, I'm leaving; I'm busy while I'm here, and then I'm going home, I don't have that kind of time." So he said, "Well, can we call you in Boston to do a follow-up?"—which they never do, it's an in-studio program. So I said, "Okay, if you can arrange it, I'll do it." Anyway, they made a big effort, they called me up in Boston, and we went through another show—in which Gzowski was very contrite and quiet, just to make up to the audience. But that was the last time I ever heard from them; I've never been asked on that show with him again.

And that's happened to me elsewhere in Canada too, I should say—I mean, I've been invited to universities in Canada where they've literally refused to pay my plane fare after I gave talks in which I denounced Canada. So you know, Canada's very nice as long as you're criticizing the United States—try going after Canada and see what happens to you.

But the point is, I think the media system works the same in both countries. I don't think it works the same in *detail*—like, there's a labor movement there, and there are other factors that are different between the two countries as well which may influence the range of coverage a bit. But I doubt that the differences in the media product are very great—and if you examine the question in detail, I'm pretty sure that's what you'll find as well.

## Should Quebec Separate from Canada?

MAN: *In Canada there's been a strong movement for Quebec to separate from the English-speaking part of the country—do you think it would be in Quebec's self-interest to become independent like that? And also, do you think it would be to the advantage of American business to see that kind of instability in Canada, or is it better for powerful interests here if Canada just remains stable?*

Well, I don't know the whole situation in detail, but my guess is that it's in Quebec's self-interest to stay part of Canada—because the alternative is to become part of the United States. Quebec's not going to be able to remain independent, so it can either become part of the United States or stay part of Canada. And given that choice, I think it's better off staying part of Canada. I mean, if Quebec became independent from Canada, it wouldn't necessarily be *called* part of the United States—like it wouldn't get colored the same as the United States on the map—but it would be so integrated into the American economy that it would effectively be a colony. And I don't think that's in the interest of the people of Quebec, I think they're better off staying part of Canada.

As for American business, I suspect that powerful interests in the United States would more or less prefer things to stay the way they are—just because it's too disruptive: you don't know what all the consequences of separation would be. The way the relationship between the two countries is now, things sort of work—and after all, all of Canada is going to become a colony of the United States anyway, through things like N.A.F.T.A., so why go and pick off one piece and have all of these other disruptive effects?

Remember, people here were trying to take over Canada as early as the 1770s—it's not a new idea. And if you look back at the history of the two countries, in 1775—before the American Revolution even began—the American colonists had already invaded Canada, and had to be driven back by the British [the Continental Congress's first act before declaring independence from Britain was to send an invasion force to Canada in the unsuccessful "Quebec Campaign"]. Then through the nineteenth century, the only reason the U.S. didn't conquer Canada was that the British forces in Canada were just too strong to allow it [e.g. invading American forces were repulsed by British and Canadian soldiers several times in the War of

1812]. And ever since then, it's just been a matter of the United States integrating Canada into our economy through other means: the so-called Free Trade Agreement of 1989 gave that a big shot forward, N.A.F.T.A. is accelerating it still further, and it is very quickly taking place.

## Deciphering "China"

MAN: *Noam, China has been in the news a lot recently, especially in light of their resistance to intellectual property rights, and worldwide concern over some of their extremely destructive environmental practices and human rights abuses. What I'm wondering is, what do you think would be viable diplomatic measures now to improve U.S. relations with China?*

Well, I don't know—do we *want* to improve relations with China? China's a very brutal society, a brutal government: I don't feel any particular interest in improving relations with it.

Look, the ways in which issues are framed for us in the media and in the mainstream culture typically involve so many assumptions and presuppositions that you're kind of trapped as soon as you get into a discussion of them—you're trapped in a discussion you don't want to be in. And I think you have to start by taking apart the assumptions.

So I don't think we should be asking the question "How do we improve relations with China?"—we should be asking other questions, like "What kind of relations do we want to have with China?" And when we talk about "China," who exactly do we mean? China has a very wealthy sector now—businessmen, bureaucrats and others, the guys who make the decisions—and when the U.S. press talks about "China," that's who they mean. But there are plenty of other people in China too. So for example, you take these Southeastern sections of China which are supposed to be "economic miracles" and huge growth areas—yeah, they're economic miracles alright, but a good deal of that growth is because of foreign investment, which means absolutely horrendous working conditions. So you have women from farms who are locked into factories where they work 12 hours a day for essentially nothing, and sometimes a couple hundred of them will be burned to death because there's a factory fire and the factory doors have been locked so no one can leave, and so on and so forth.[32] Well, that's "China" too—and the same is true of any other country. So which "China" are we talking about?

In fact, in this case there's also a geographical split, there's a geographical break between Southeast China, which is a big growth area, and Central China, where most of the population still lives, and where things are maybe even going downhill in terms of development and modernization. Well, the differences between those areas are so substantial that some China specialists suspect that China may just break apart into a more coastal area that's part of the general East Asian growth area, with a lot of Japanese capital and overseas Chinese capital and foreign investment feeding into it, and then a big area with hundreds of millions of people living in it which is kind of like a declining peasant society—surely not part of the big growth rate, and maybe even declining.[33] So even within the geographical entity that's called "China," there are regions that are like completely different countries, and in some areas things could go back, as some suspect, even to the days of peasant wars and other things like that. So, again, you have to ask what exactly you mean by "China."

And in fact, if you look still more closely, the big "economic growth" areas in China *themselves* are not so simple. So it turns out that a good deal of the economic growth in those regions is coming from cooperative structures, not from foreign-based investment—I mean, nobody's really studied these cooperatives in detail, because China's such a closed society, but they're not private enterprise and they're not foreign investment, they're some other thing. But certainly they have been picking up, and they do have kind of a cooperative structure. And you don't have to go to "lefty" magazines to find this out—there are articles about it in mainstream journals like *The Economist* and the *Asian Wall Street Journal* and so on.[34] Well, those cooperatives are a big part of the growth of Southeast China, and they represent very different interests from the foreign investment-driven industrial structures, with all their horrendously exploitative conditions. So that's yet another "China."

And like I say, within all the various "Chinas" one can identify, there always are different sectors of the population with differing interests: like, for people working in the electronics factories and toy factories in Guangdong Province, life is anything but pretty, they live under absolutely horrible conditions—but there's also a managerial elite sector that is growing and getting rich at the same time. So I think the first step in figuring out what to do about policies towards something like "China" has to be to dismantle all the assumptions and presuppositions and biases behind the issues as they're being presented by the institutions. And while I don't think there are anything like simple answers, on some of these issues of conflict that you read about in the media now, I think it's a very mixed story.

Take intellectual property rights. The Chinese leadership hasn't completely accepted intellectual property rights, it hasn't completely accepted these new developments to ensure that rich and powerful corporations have a monopoly on technology and information—so now the U.S. is using various sanctions against them to try to force compliance. Well, I don't think I'm in favor of *that*. Like, I don't think I want to improve *those* relations with China, what I would like to do is to dismantle this whole crazy system.

Or look at the fact that China is one of the only countries in the world that imprisons its population at roughly the same level as the United States—the United States is way in the lead of other countries that keep statistics on imprisonment, and while we don't have precise statistics on China, from the work that's been done by criminologists who've tried to make sense of it, it looks as though they're roughly in our ballpark.[35] Well, is that a good thing—that they throw huge amounts of their population in jail like we do? I don't think it's a great thing. And it's probable that their prison system is even as brutal as ours, maybe worse. Well, the U.S. government and U.S. power systems certainly don't care about that—any more than they care about the fact that the *United States* is imprisoning its population at a rate way beyond anyone else in the world; in fact, that's going up right now. So that can't be why U.S. relations with China are bad.

There was some talk in the U.S. media a while ago about prison labor in China—but take a close look at that discussion. The only objection to prison labor in China that you heard was that the *products* of that prison labor were being exported to the United States—hence that's state industry, and the U.S. never wants state industry to compete with privately owned U.S.-based firms. But if China wanted to have prison labor and export it somewhere else, that was fine. In fact, right at the time that the U.S. government and the media were making a fuss about *Chinese* prison labor, the *United States* was exporting products of prison labor to Asia: California and Oregon were producing textiles in prisons which were being exported to Asia under the name "Prison Blues"—didn't even try to hide it. And in fact, prison production is going way up in the United States right now.[36] So there's no objection to prison labor in principle, just don't interfere with the profits of American-based corporations—that was the real meaning of that debate, when you got to the core of it.

So what you want to do on every issue, I think, is to extricate yourself from the way the discussion is being presented in the official culture, and begin to ask these kinds of questions about it. I mean, U.S. power doesn't care much if the Chinese leaders murder dissidents, what they care about is that the Chinese leaders let them make money—and I don't think that is something which ordinary people in the United States ought to buy into. I mean, China's a very complicated, big story, and I don't think there's anything like a simple answer as to what should be done in terms of U.S. relations: like anything else, you just have to look at all the various subparts. But the first step, I think, as with everything, is to reframe in your mind what's really going on, remind yourself what the real issues are, and not get trapped in discussions you don't want to be part of in the first place.

## Indonesia's Killing Fields: U.S.-Backed Genocide in East Timor

WOMAN: *Noam, a little earlier you mentioned the East Timor massacre. I'm an organizer on that issue in Canada, and it seems to me that some encouraging things have been happening in the big picture on that in the past few years, in terms of maybe pressuring Indonesia to withdraw and stop their extermination sometime in the future. Do you agree with that kind of optimistic assessment at all?*

*[Editors' Note: Indonesia finally was forced to hold a referendum in which the East Timorese voted for independence in September 1999. The following discussion of the media, the great powers, and popular activism—given before those events—provides critical background.]*

Well, it's very hard to quantify, but I think you're right. I mean, I don't know Indonesia that well myself, but people who do, like Ben Anderson [American professor], say they definitely find something positive taking place there. I hope so—but you know, it's really up to *us* what happens in East Timor: what happens there is going to depend on how much pressure and activism ordinary people in the Western societies can put together.

First of all, does everybody know the situation we're talking about? Want me to summarize it? It's an extremely revealing case, actually—if you really want to learn something about our own society and values, this is a very good place to start. It's probably the biggest slaughter relative to the population since the Holocaust, which makes it not small. And this is genocide, if you want to use the term, for which the United States continues to be directly responsible.

East Timor is a small island north of Australia. Indonesia invaded it illegally in 1975, and ever since they have just been slaughtering people. It's continuing as we speak, after more than two decades. And that massacre has been going on because the United States has actively, consistently, and crucially supported it: it's been supported by every American administration, and also by the entire Western media, which have totally silenced the story. The worst phase of the killing was in the late 1970s during the Carter administration. At that time, the casualties were about at the scale of the Pol Pot massacres in Cambodia. Relative to the population, they were much greater. But they were radically different from Pol Pot's in one critical respect: nobody had any idea about how to stop the Pol Pot slaughter, but it was trivial how to stop this one. And it's still trivial how we can stop it—we can stop supporting it.

Indonesia invaded East Timor in 1975 with the explicit authorization of Gerald Ford and Henry Kissinger [the American President and Secretary of State].[37] Kissinger then at once (secretly, though it leaked) moved to increase U.S. weapons and counterinsurgency equipment sales to Indonesia, which already was about 90 percent armed with U.S. weapons.[38] It's now known from leaked documents that the British, Australians, and Americans all were aware of the invasion plans in advance, and that they monitored its progress as it was unfolding. Of course, they only applauded.[39]

The U.S. media have real complicity in genocide in this case. Before the invasion, news coverage of East Timor had in fact been rather high in the United States, surprisingly high actually—and the reason was that East

Timor had been part of the Portuguese Empire, which was collapsing in the 1970s, and there was a lot of concern back then that the former Portuguese colonies might do what's called "moving towards Communism," meaning moving towards independence, which is not allowed. So before the invasion, there was a lot of media coverage of East Timor. After Indonesia attacked, coverage started to decline—and then it declined very sharply. By 1978, when the atrocities reached their peak, coverage reached flat zero, literally zero in the United States and Canada, which has been another big supporter of the occupation.[40]

Around that same time, the Carter administration moved to send new supplies of armaments to Indonesia, because their army was running out of weapons in the course of the slaughter. By then they'd killed maybe a hundred thousand people.[41] The press did its job by shutting up about what was really going on—when they did have coverage, it was just repetition of grotesque lies by the State Department and Indonesian generals, a complete whitewash. In fact, media coverage *to this day* has always completely wiped out the U.S. record: the strongest criticism you'll ever find is, "We didn't pay enough attention to Timor," or "The U.S. didn't try hard enough to get Indonesia to stop its atrocities" or something like that.[42] It's kind of like saying the Soviet Union didn't try hard enough to bring freedom to Eastern Europe, or they didn't pay enough attention to it—that was their problem.

And remember, the U.S. role in all of this has never been a secret—it's in fact been acknowledged very frankly. For instance, if you read the memoirs of our U.N. ambassador at the time of the invasion, Daniel Patrick Moynihan—who's greatly praised for his defense of international law, incidentally—he says: "The Department of State desired that the U.N. prove utterly ineffective in whatever measures it undertook. This task was given to me, and I carried it forward with no inconsiderable success." Okay, then he goes on to describe the effects of the invasion, which he was fully aware of: he says, in the first couple of months it seemed "some 60,000 persons had been killed . . . almost the proportion of casualties experienced by the Soviet Union during the Second World War." Alright, that's the Nazis, and that's Moynihan, the great advocate of international law.[43] And he's right, that's how it happened: the State Department wanted things to turn out as they did, and he ensured that they did. Moynihan's at least being honest, let's give him credit for it.

Another thing that's never reported, though it's completely public and was perfectly well known at the time, is that one of the main reasons why the Western powers supported the invasion was that there's a huge offshore oil field in Timor's territorial waters, and before 1975 the Australians and the Western oil companies had been trying unsuccessfully to make a deal with Portugal to exploit it. Well, they hadn't had any luck with Portugal, and they figured an independent East Timor would be even harder to deal with—but they knew that Indonesia would be easy: that's one of our boys, we've been running it ever since the huge massacre there in 1965 that the West applauded, when they wiped out the Communist Party and killed maybe 600,000 people.[44] So for instance, leaked diplomatic records in Australia show that right around the time of the invasion, top Australian officials said that they would do better with an Indonesian takeover, and that Indonesia should be supported.[45] Again, I have yet to see a word about any of this in the U.S. media.

And actually that exploitation has been proceeding rather nicely: Australia and Indonesia signed a big treaty to start extracting Timorese oil [in December 1989], and right after the Dili massacre in 1991 [in which Indonesians killed hundreds of unarmed Timorese protesters at a funeral], the big Western reaction—apart from sending additional arms to Indonesia—was that fifteen major oil companies started exploration in the Timor Sea oil fields. Happily for Chevron, there are apparently some very promising strikes.

Well, to get back to your question: even though this virtually genocidal massacre has received almost no coverage from the U.S. press, a very small number of people started working on the issue—literally it was a tiny group of activists, probably not more than a dozen.[46] And finally, after a few years, they've gotten somewhere: around the early 1980s, just through constant pressure and organizing, they managed to get the media to start reporting on Timor very occasionally. The coverage has been highly selective, and it still always excludes the crucial role that the United States has played, both in providing arms and in giving Indonesia the diplomatic support they've needed to maintain the occupation over the years—but there has been some.[47] And they've gotten some Congressmen interested, mostly conservative Congressmen, incidentally. Wider public pressure began to develop; the East Timor Action Network was started—and there has been a real change, just thanks to this small, indeed growing, number of activists.

In 1992, the pressure actually got to the point that Congress passed legislation banning U.S. military training for Indonesian officers because of their "human rights violations," which is putting it pretty mildly. That put the Clinton administration in kind of an embarrassing position, but they got out of it alright: they announced that the law didn't mean what it said, it only meant that the United States couldn't train Indonesian military officers *with money from the United States itself*, but if the Indonesians paid for the training themselves—say, with money we gave them from some other pocket—that would be fine. With rare delicacy, the State Department picked the anniversary of the invasion to announce this interpretation, and although Congress protested, it went through.[48]

Nevertheless, the legislation was a very important development, and I think it's a sign of a real change that could take place, as you suggest. I mean, with enough popular pressure, this is one of those issues that could turn around: the Indonesians could pull out, they may well be close to it.

In fact, if we're talking about activism, this is a very revealing case—

because if you can organize successfully on an issue like East Timor, you can do it on almost anything. It's a pretty hard topic to get people interested in, you'd think, yet popular pressure here has forced things to the point of at least symbolic gestures by the U.S. government—and symbolic gestures on the part of the United States are very important. Remember, everyone in the world is scared shitless of us: we're a brutal terrorist power of enormous strength, and if you get in our way, you're in trouble. Nobody steps on Uncle Sam's toes. So when the United States Congress makes a symbolic gesture like banning military-training aid or banning small-arms sales, the Indonesian generals hear it, even if they can get whatever they want from some other country, or even from Bill Clinton in the end.

## Mass Murderers at Harvard

Actually, let me give you another example of the kinds of things that have been happening on this—this one is really relevant, it shows you can really do things. In Boston recently there was a court case, in which an Indonesian general was sued by the mother of a boy who was killed in the Dili massacre in 1991. Her name is Helen Todd, which explains why the suit went through, if you can figure that part out. . . .

What happened is, in November 1991, some Indonesian troops in East Timor opened fire on a funeral march with their U.S.-supplied M-16s, and killed about 250 people. That's fairly routine there, actually, but this time the Indonesians made a mistake: a couple of Western reporters were there filming it all, and they managed to bury the videotape in an open grave and have it smuggled out of the country a couple days later. The Indonesian soldiers also nearly beat two American journalists to death, so this one became pretty difficult for the international media to ignore.[49]

Well, as Indonesia was carrying out its cover-up after this with the help of some big public relations firm they hired in the U.S. [Burson-Marsteller, Inc.], one of the things they did was to get the generals out of the way so nobody would see them, and one of them was sent off to Harvard, to study.[50] Alright, some local people in Boston found out about this, and they checked with Harvard: Harvard claimed they'd never heard of him. But he was there, he was studying at the Kennedy School of Government at Harvard—so people started to protest his presence there. The protests began to build up, there was more and more pressure, then on the first anniversary of the Dili massacre came my favorite *Boston Globe* headline in history. It said, "Indonesian General, Facing Suit, Flees Boston." And indeed, that's what happened—he fled Boston, and hasn't been seen there since.[51]

Meanwhile, the suit continued on without him. There's a law in the United States which says that you can bring civil suits for damages against torturers and murderers and human rights abusers and so on.[52] So the judge heard the testimony of Helen Todd, journalist Allan Nairn and others, and was impressed—and the General now has a $14 million fine to pay in case he ever decides to show up here again.[53]

The same thing happened the next year with one of Guatemala's leading killers, incidentally, General Gramajo—whom the U.S. State Department was grooming to become the next Guatemalan President. He was one of the big mass murderers from the early 1980s, and he was also shipped off to Harvard to refine his skills. Well, people in Boston found out about it by reading the Central American press, so they approached Harvard. Again, "Never heard of him." But he was there. Alright, then Allan Nairn, who's a very enterprising journalist, and imaginative—one of the few journalists in the country, actually—waited until the Harvard commencement ceremonies to move in. Harvard graduations are televised locally, and as the murderer General Gramajo was walking up to the platform to receive his degree, Nairn raced in front of the television cameras and served him with a subpoena. That one, he fled Boston too. The case came to court and he was fined $47 million.[54]

Well, you know, that just shows you can do things. Indonesia is getting worried about their image here, very worried. And it's starting to get to the point where they might actually allow a referendum or something on self-determination for East Timor—it's a possibility. Alatas, their Foreign Minister, in fact made a speech a little while ago in which he described East Timor as "a piece of gravel in our shoe": you know, we have to get rid of this thing.[55] But of course, it's going to take a lot more sustained pressure and activism here to ever achieve anything like that. And in fact, if it's going to be successful, that pressure will have to be international and coordinated around the world—because Britain and Australia and places like that will be perfectly happy to take up the slack and make as much money as they can selling arms to Indonesia if the United States ever were to seriously back off.[56]

## Changes in Indonesia

But there are definitely things going on in Indonesia which are quite encouraging—and which make your sense of optimism seem justified, I think. For example, did you follow the case of this Indonesian academic, Aditjondro? There's a well-known Indonesian professor who teaches at a fairly major university there, who recently went public about his opposition to the annexation of East Timor during a visit to Australia—and it turns out that for about twenty years he's been doing research on East Timor in secret, and he released a lot of extremely interesting and detailed documentation. For instance, he had the names of about 270 people killed in the Dili massacre, and they checked out; he had done studies of other atrocities, he gave very strong statements.

Well, the Australian press silenced it. Anybody from Australia here? The only place it got published was West Perch, wherever the hell that is—probably some kind of cow-town in Australia. But it did get published there, and then it kind of seeped out into the international media, pushed on by things like the Internet. And finally it got to be kind of an international affair—though of course, as usual there was never a word about it in the U.S. media.[57]

Anyway, this guy Aditjondro went back to Indonesia—and to everybody's amazement, nothing's happened to him. I was just talking to John Pilger [an Australian political activist and filmmaker] two days ago, and he'd just seen him and been in touch with him—he's still traveling around the country, and so far they've left him alone.[58] Alright, that's a sign, you know. And there are others.

In fact, I just saw one in this morning's newspaper. This week, authorities in Indonesia arrested a bunch of labor leaders, which is not good. But what *is* good is that they arrested them for a reason—namely, they had been organizing, and carrying out strikes. See, the labor movement in Indonesia is in some ferment, and as a matter of fact, the Indonesian government recently was compelled just by internal pressures to acknowledge the existence of an independent labor union in the country. Now, I don't know how far these things will go, but they're the sign of a change.[59]

Another sign is that if you talk to students from Indonesia, it's clear that they know more than they used to. It used to be like total fascism—they didn't know anything about politics or the world. But it's become much less controlled in recent years: now they've kind of heard about things, they're more aware, they're more concerned to try to change things a bit.[60] And one could go on like this—but these are all indications of internal changes in Indonesia, and they are in part a reaction to Western pressure. And Indonesia reacts very quickly to Western pressure. In fact, if there was ever any serious pressure from the West, the occupation of East Timor would be over tomorrow.

This point was just illustrated very clearly, actually. Look: the United States, Canada, England, France, Holland, Sweden, Germany, Japan, any country that can make a buck off it, are all involved in this—so it's really not a question of us laying economic sanctions on Indonesia to pressure "them," the only real question is, can *we* stop killing Timorese? However, there *was* a case recently where the major Western powers did threaten economic sanctions against Indonesia—it's not too well known, but it's extremely instructive.

In 1993, the World Health Organization voted to request that the World Court consider the legality of the use of nuclear weapons, and issue an opinion on it. Well, obviously the United States and Britain went totally berserk when they heard about this: just the fact that the World Court might *hear* a case on the legality of nuclear weapons is already a contribution to nuclear non-proliferation. And of course, we benefit from proliferation, since we're the main producer, seller, and possessor of nuclear weapons. I mean, it's not as if anybody would *listen* to the World Court if it said that the use of nuclear weapons is illegal (which means by implication that *possession* of them is illegal too)—but it would certainly be a big publicity coup for the disarmament movement if it did. So for the big nuclear powers, this was a major issue. Actually, it's of particular significance for Britain, because one of Britain's last claims to being a country, instead of like a county of the United States, is that they have nuclear weapons—so for them it's important on a symbolic level. And nuclear weapons are important to the United States because they're part of the way we intimidate everyone—we intervene around the world under what's called a "nuclear umbrella," which serves as kind of a cover to back up our conventional intervention forces.

Well, that year Indonesia was serving as the head of the Non-Aligned Movement at the U.N. [a coalition of Third World nations in the General Assembly], and the 110 countries of the Non-Aligned Movement decided to introduce a resolution endorsing this request for an opinion—that's all that was up, endorsement of a request for an opinion from the World Court. The U.S., Britain and France immediately threatened trade and aid sanctions against Indonesia if, in their role as head of the Non-Aligned Movement for that year, they submitted this resolution at the General Assembly. So Indonesia instantly withdrew it, of course—when they get orders from the boss, they stop. And they stop fast.[61]

Well, that just shows that there are some atrocities that go too far for the Western powers: genocide in East Timor we can support, but endorsement of a request for an opinion on the legality of nuclear weapons is an atrocity we simply cannot tolerate. But it also shows you what we can do to Indonesia if we feel like it.

### Nuclear Proliferation and North Korea

MAN: *Just on the subject of nuclear proliferation—what's the real problem we've had with North Korea supposedly wanting to build their own nuclear weapons? The media and the Clinton administration say they're all horrified by that prospect—is that what you really think is bothering them?*

That's very interesting in connection with this World Court story, isn't it—because part of what we claim is the problem with North Korea is that their getting nuclear weapons would threaten the Nuclear Non-Proliferation Treaty. But if we're so concerned with non-proliferation, obviously nothing would be more of a shot in the arm for it than this World Court decision we tried so desperately to block. Okay, that tells you something about our motives in all of this. But actually, I think the problem with North Korea is in fact what they're saying: the wrong guys are getting possible power, nuclear weapons.

Look, nobody in their right mind would want North Korea to have nuclear weapons. But on the other hand, there's nothing much that they would *do* with nuclear weapons if they had them, except maybe defend themselves from attack. They're certainly not going to *invade* anybody, that's not even imaginable: if they ever made a move, the country gets destroyed tomorrow. So the only role that nuclear weapons could play for them is as a deterrent to attack—and that's not totally unrealistic.

I mean, it's a pretty crazy country, and there's not very much good— there's nothing good—you can say about the government. But no matter who they were, if they were Mahatma Gandhi, they would be worried about a possible attack. I mean, the United States was threatening North Korea with nuclear weapons at least as late as the 1960s.[62] And after all, just remember what we *did* to that country—it was absolutely flattened. Here people may not be aware of what we did to them, but *they* certainly know it well enough.

Towards the end of what we call the "Korean War"—which was really just one phase in a much longer struggle [beginning when the U.S. destroyed the indigenous nationalist movement in Korea in the late 1940s]— the United States ran out of good bombing targets. We had total command of the air of course, but there was nothing good left to bomb—because everything had already been flattened. So we started going after things like dikes. Okay, that's just a major war crime.[63] In fact, if you take a look at the official U.S. Air Force history of the Korean War, it's absolutely mind-boggling, it's like something straight out of the Nazi archives. I mean, these guys don't conceal their glee at all, it's just this account of all their terrific feelings: we bombed these dikes, and a huge flow of water went through the valleys and carved out huge paths of destruction and slaughtered people! And they say, laughingly: we don't realize how important rice is for the Asians, so naturally they were screaming with rage! I really can't duplicate, you have to read it in the original.[64] And the Koreans lived on the other end of that.

Our treatment of North Korean prisoners of war also was absolutely grotesque—again, it was kind of like the Nazis. This is all documented in the West by now, and of course *they* certainly know about it.[65] So there are plenty of things for the North Koreans to remember, and plenty of things for them to be afraid of—which is not to justify their getting nuclear weapons, but it's part of the background we should keep in mind.

The other thing is, North Korea is in a desperate situation right now: they're hemmed in politically, and they're struggling very hard to break out of their total isolation—they're setting up free-trade zones, and trying to integrate themselves into the international economic system, other things like that. Well, this is apparently one of their ways of attempting to do it. It's neither intelligent nor justifiable, but that's a part of what's motivating them, and we should at least try to understand that.

As far as Western concern about nuclear weapons goes, obviously it's highly selective—like, nobody cares that the *United States* has nuclear weapons, nobody cares that Israel has nuclear weapons, they just don't want them in the hands of people we don't control, like North Korea. And I think that's really the main issue behind the controversy these days.

WOMAN: *Could you say a few words more about the origins of the Korean War? I take it you don't accept the standard picture that it began when the U.S. moved to block a Communist expansionist invasion.*

Well, the fact of the matter is that the Korean War is much more complex than the way it's presented in mainstream circles. In this case, incidentally, the scholarship is considerably better than is usual, and if you look at the serious monograph literature on the Korean War, you'll see that a different position is presented than the one we always hear.[66]

The 1950 North Korean attack on the southern part of the country was really the tail end of a long war. In fact, before North Korea attacked the South in 1950, already about 100,000 Koreans had been killed—that's something we forget. What happened in Korea is essentially this. When the American forces landed in 1945 at the end of World War II, they found that an already functioning local government had been set up. There had been an anti-Japanese resistance, and it had established local administrations and Peoples' Committees and so on, all over North and South Korea. Well, when the United States moved into the South, we dismantled all of that, destroyed it by force—we used the Koreans who had collaborated with the Japanese, and in fact even reinstituted the Japanese police to destroy it all [Japan had occupied Korea for 35 years until its defeat in the Second World War]. And that led to serious conflict in the South, a rather bitter conflict which went on for four or five years with a lot of people killed, and also there was a lot of cross-border fighting at the time (going both ways, incidentally). Then there was sort of a lull, and *then* came the North Korean attack going south. So there was definitely a North Korean attack, but it was an intervention by the North into the South after the United States had suppressed the anti-Japanese resistance movement in a civil war.[67]

Now, that puts a slightly different color on it than the standard line we hear. For example, if some country were—let's say—to conquer the western part of the United States, and there was resistance against that conquest, and then the resistance was suppressed with say a hundred thousand people killed, and then the Eastern part of the United States "invaded" the Western part, that wouldn't be just an invasion: that would be a little too simple. And something like that happened in Korea.

## The Samson Option

WOMAN: *You mentioned Israel having nuclear weapons—would you expand on the significance of that? I remember you used the title "The Road to Armageddon" for the last chapter of your book on the Middle East,* The Fateful Triangle.

Yeah, that's something I think is quite important, actually. I mean, that book was written back in 1982, and what I was discussing at the end of it is what in Israel for the last forty years or so has been called the "Samson Complex"; later Sy Hersh wrote a book about it called *The Samson Option*, but it's an old story that goes back to the 1950s.[68]

You know the story of Samson in the Bible? At the end, Samson gets captured by the Philistines, he's blinded, he's standing in the temple between two pillars, and he pulls down the temple walls and crushes all the people inside: the Bible says, "He killed more Philistines as he died than in all of his life."[69] Well, that's the Samson Complex. What it means, translated into straight politics—and they're pretty straight about it—is: if anybody pushes us too far, we'll bring down the universe.

Now, in order to do that, Israel needed nuclear weapons—and they got them, with our help.[70] In the 1950s, when all of this stuff started, the threats were kind of empty—they couldn't bring down the temple walls. But since the early 1960s, it's been imaginable, and it's in fact something that's discussed quite openly in Israel: the idea is, push us too hard and we'll do something wild, we'll go crazy—and you'll all suffer.[71]

So for example, according to the Israeli Labor Party press, when the Arab League proposed a Saudi Arabian-initiated peace plan for the region in August 1981, Israel sent U.S.-supplied F-14 fighters over the Saudi Arabian oil fields as a warning to Western intelligence agencies—meaning, if you take this peace plan seriously, you're all going to be in trouble, we'll destroy those oil fields.[72] Also back in the early 1980s, Israeli strategic analysts were publicly saying—even in English, so everybody would hear it—that Israel was developing nuclear-tipped missiles that could reach the Soviet Union. It may have been false, but that's at least what they were saying.[73] Well, why would they need nuclear-tipped missiles that could reach the Soviet Union? They're not going to attack Russia; they're not going to deter a Russian attack—that's outlandish. But the idea was, and everybody understood it at the time, that if U.S. policy ever changes course and we decide to stop supporting Israel, they'll attack Russia and draw Russia into the Middle East—which would then probably destroy the world in a nuclear war.

Well, now it seems Russia's out of the game—maybe only temporarily, I might say. But none of the underlying considerations have changed, and there are obviously a lot of other similar scenarios like that around. So the fact of the matter is, this is just going to remain an extremely dangerous area.

Incidentally, one of the nice things about the end of the Cold War and the collapse of the Soviet Union is that top-level American planners are finally becoming a bit more honest about some things. So for example, every year the White House puts out a big glossy document explaining to Congress why we need a huge military establishment—and for a long time it was always the same story: the Russians are coming, this-that-and-the-other-thing. Well, after the fall of the Berlin Wall, they had to change the computer disk for the first time. The bottom line had to remain the same: we need a big military, a big so-called "defense" infrastructure (read: support for electronics)—but now the justification had to change. So in 1990, the reason they gave was no longer "the Russians are coming," it was what they called "the technological sophistication of Third World powers"—especially ones in the Middle East, where they said, our problems "could not be laid at the Kremlin's door."

Okay, first true statement: for the preceding fifty years, our problems always had been "laid at the Kremlin's door," but now that the Kremlin's gone, we'd might as well tell the truth about it—because we still need the same policies.[74] And in fact, just to make sure that there always *is* a real danger, we also have to *sell* all these Third World powers high-tech weaponry—the U.S. in fact very quickly became the biggest arms dealer to the Third World after the Cold War ended.[75] And the arms contractors of course *know* it: like, if you read Lockheed-Martin corporate propaganda, they say, look, we've got to build the F-22 because we're selling advanced upgraded F-16s to these Third World regimes, and we're selling them all kinds of complicated air defense systems, and who knows, they're just a bunch of dictators, maybe they'll turn against us—so we've got to build the F-22 to defend ourselves from all the high-tech weapons we're selling them.[76] And of course, that's all at the cost of the U.S. taxpayer, as usual.

## The Lot of the Palestinians

MAN: *Noam, how do you interpret the 1996 elections in Israel [in which the more right-wing Likud Party, led by Benjamin Netanyahu, defeated the Labor Party, which had negotiated the Oslo Accords in 1994]? And what do you think the effect is going to be on the peace process that the Labor Party was instituting with the Palestinians?*

I think it's going to have almost no effect on that. "Peace process" is a very funny word for what's happened, actually—it's a "peace process" in the same sense that it was a "peace process" in South Africa when they instituted apartheid [the system of official white supremacy]. So when South Africa instituted its apartheid system in the 1950s and set up the Bantustans [partially self-governing black territories], that was also a "peace process"—it stabilized the country, there was peace for a while, and so on. Well, in many ways that's similar to what's called "the peace process" in the Middle East right now, although if you look closely, that comparison is not quite fair. It's unfair to South Africa.

See, the Bantustans that South Africa set up in the 1950s were much more viable economically than any scattered fragment that may someday be allowed for a Palestinian state under the Oslo Agreements. And further-more, South Africa subsidized its Bantustans: so if you go back to, say, Transkei [Bantustan under apartheid until 1991], South Africa gave it plenty of subsidies—in fact, a large part of the South African budget went to subsidizing the Bantustans, which were relatively viable areas economi-cally. Well, Israel has never permitted any development whatsoever in the Occupied Territories—in fact, there was actually a military ordinance that no development would be allowed there if it would be competitive with Is-raeli business. They've wanted the Territories to be a captive market, and therefore there's been no development at all.[77]

Israeli reporters have covered this very well, actually. When they went to Jordan after the peace treaty with Jordan [finalized in October 1994], even they were shocked by the difference between it and the Occupied Territo-ries—and they wrote very interesting articles about it.[78] Remember, Jordan is a poor Third World country: it hasn't had any of the advantages that Israel has had in being the chief American client-state, and before the 1967 war, the West Bank was somewhat more developed than Jordan. Well, today the disparity is extraordinary in the opposite direction. So in Jordan, there's rich agriculture, and highways, and factories, and other things like that—but right across the border, the West Bank is a total disaster: Israel hasn't al-lowed a cent to go into it; in fact, they've taken a lot of money *out* of it.

For instance, the poor workers in the Israeli labor force over the years have mostly been Palestinians from the West Bank and Gaza Strip—they did the dirty work in Israel's economy. And theoretically they were paid, but mostly theoretically—because from their pay, the Israeli government deducted what is deducted from the pay of Jewish workers, like deductions for pensions and health care and so on. Except the Palestinian workers never got any of the benefits: the money for their benefits just went right to the Israeli treasury. Well, that amount is estimated to be about a billion dol-lars or so. In fact, not long ago an Israeli civil rights group, partly made up of law professors at the Hebrew University and partly just a workers' rights group [Kav La'Oved], brought a lawsuit in the Israeli courts to try to re-cover for these workers the roughly billion dollars it's estimated has been stolen from them. Well, the court recently decided the case—and it decided that the claims were null and void because of the Oslo Agreements, which it said have retroactively eliminated the basis for the suit by legalizing Israel's confiscation of the funds. And furthermore, the decision said that the pur-pose for making those deductions had never been to ensure equal rights for the Palestinian workers in the first place, it was just to ensure that their ac-tual wages would be lower than those of Jewish workers and to protect Is-raeli workers from unfair competition by cheaper Palestinian labor. Okay? That was the real purpose of taking the money from them. And then the court said that this was a worthy and legitimate action, just like introducing tariffs to protect domestic production is a legitimate action: so therefore the robbery is retroactively justified.[79]

Well, that's just one of the many ways in which Israel has taken plenty of wealth from the Territories, including its water.[80] And all of that is going to continue after the Oslo Agreements and the recent election. So if you look at the peace treaty, everything just keeps going to Israel—and that's not going to change.

Furthermore, Israel is not taking any responsibility for what it's done to the Territories during the occupation [which began in 1967]: the peace treaty in fact says explicitly that Israel has no liability for anything that was done in that time, that's all the sole responsibility of the Palestinian Authority. In fact, it's the only thing that the Palestinian Authority *does* get full responsibility for—everything else they don't get, but they do get full responsibility for paying all the costs of the occupation. And the treaty explicitly says that if there is any *future* claim against Israel for something that happened during the occupation, the Palestinian Authority also is responsible for paying that claim and for reimbursing Israel if there are any charges against Israel. So here as well, what's happened in the "peace process" is not quite like South Africa: the South African Bantustans were far more forthcoming.

Well, all of this is just going to continue after the elections—I mean, the Likud Party would be out of their minds if they didn't persist in all this; the Oslo Agreements are such an overwhelming victory for Israel that they'd be insane if they didn't maintain them. So I would not expect any of that to change.

Now, that's not the standard story about the elections in the United States, of course. For example, the *New York Times*'s lead story in their "Week in Review" section after the elections said, flat out: the peace process is dead—everything the U.S. did is finished, it's dead, it's over.[81] But I don't think that's true at all—I think that's based on a serious misunderstanding of what the "peace process" was really about. Likud would be crazy not to persist with the relations that have been established with the P.L.O. under the Oslo Agreements—just as the white South African elites would have been crazy not to continue pushing through the Bantustan process if they could have gotten away with it. In fact, the main difference between the two cases is that in the case of the Bantustans, nobody in the international community recognized the arrangement as legitimate—but in the case of the Israeli policy towards the Occupied Territories now, everybody in the world at this point basically supports it, thanks to U.S. power. In fact, the current U.S. government, the Clinton administration, has gone way beyond any of its predecessors in support for the most extremist Israeli policies. The Israeli press is constantly astonished by it. For instance, there was a big headline in a recent article in Israel, which read, "Clinton: The Last Zionist"—you know, the only one left who really believes all the bullshit.[82]

So you know, the most important part of the "peace agreement" is its complete termination of any possibility of self-determination for the Palestinians: they're finished as far as this goes, they get nothing. As far as the Palestinian refugees are concerned, it's finished. I mean, for years the United States went along with rhetorical commitments about a "just settlement" of the refugee problem; now it doesn't even do that anymore. On the issue of control of Jerusalem, while the United States used to rhetorically oppose the Israeli annexation and takeover, along with the rest of the world, now that's over—the Clinton administration doesn't even oppose it rhetorically anymore.[83]

The terms of the treaty are pretty amazing, they're really worth looking at: they were pushed by the United States in such a way that the chance of anything at all for the Palestinians is *very* minimal. So people living in the Territories used to have two options: one was to go somewhere else (which Israel hoped would happen, and did happen to a considerable extent), and the other was to commute to Israel and be kind of what in Europe are called "guest workers," what are called here "illegal migrant labor"—so they would do the dirty work in Israel that nobody wanted, for a pittance, essentially nothing. But now even that is being cut out—they're not being allowed back into Israel.[84] And Israel is now turning to another source: they have by now about 200,000 immigrants (it's maybe about 5 percent of the population) from all over the world, from Ghana, Ecuador, lots of them from Thailand, Romania, China, the Philippines. And these are people essentially brought over for this purpose—who just live under the most miserable conditions.

The ones they sort of like best are the Chinese, because they have a deal with the Chinese government that if these people get out of hand—like if they demand that they be paid their wages (which they're usually not paid), or you know, they want to stop being beaten while they're on the job or something—Israel can just call in the Chinese authorities who will, as they put it, "deal with them." China's a rough, tough government, you know, so they'll make sure that no one makes any fuss—and if they *do* make a fuss, Israel will just send them home where they'll be even worse off. So the Chinese workers are easier to discipline, because of the cooperation of the Chinese authorities, and that's something they like very much in Israel.[85]

Well, that's a very brutal system, and it ends up displacing the Palestinians—so that means one of the options for survival for the Palestinians now is gone. The other option, leaving, of course is sort of open—if they can figure out some place to go. But with immigration restrictions being what they are all over the world, that's getting harder and harder.

Basically there's nothing much left at all for the Palestinians. I mean, if Israel's smart, what they'll do is transfer some production across the border into the Territories, like the United States does with Mexico—that would be smart from the Israeli industrialists' point of view. So instead of having to hire Jewish workers and giving them wages and benefits and so on, they could just move a couple miles across the border and get what the U.S. gets in Mexico or what Germany gets in Bulgaria and so on: super-cheap labor with no real standards for working conditions, and basically no environmental regulations. But there's so much racism in Israel that they're not even considering what would at least be rational from an economic point of view.

So for the moment, things are pretty much finished in the Territories—I mean, you can't predict the future, but the point of the "peace process" was to destroy the Palestinians, crush them, demoralize them, eliminate them, ensure that the U.S. and Israel take over everything. That's why it's all so admired here. And none of this is likely to be affected by the elections—I mean, why would it be? There may be some mild differences now with regard to Israel's relationship with Syria, but that's about all as far as I can see.

See, the Labor Party was looking for some sort of arrangement with Syria by which they could maintain the Golan Heights—which remember is Syrian territory that Israel conquered after the cease-fire in the Six Day War in 1967, then drove out most of the population and took it over and settled it. And it's a very important area, partly because it has some agricultural wealth, but mainly because the Golan Heights has a big influence on controlling the headwaters of the Jordan River and other water sources, which are extremely important to Israel. So Israel doesn't want to give up the Golan Heights, but Syria won't make peace unless it formally regains control over them—and it was likely that the Labor Party was going to try to figure out some way of finessing an arrangement so that Syria could have *legal* control of them, but Israel will retain *actual* control, like maybe some 99-year lease or some deal like that that the lawyers can figure out. The Labor Party was at least likely to toy with arrangements like that, and maybe even begin to move towards them; whether Syria would have accepted or not is an open question. But now it's likely that Likud *won't* do that. Apart from that, though, I don't really see much likelihood of a difference in the international arrangements in the region as a result of the recent election.

What I *do* suspect will change are things internal to Israel—it's only there that there's likely to be an effect. And that's actually where the issues of the election were. In fact, if you look at them for a minute, there's a real irony to these elections.

Netanyahu won a big victory: the popular vote was split almost 50/50, but if you look at the *Jewish* vote (which is the only part that counts as far as policy-making goes in Israel), it was a far higher proportion, it was over 55 percent—which is a landslide victory, you know.[86] And that could have a major effect. See, the support for the Likud Party was from several sources. They got close to 100 percent of the religious vote—because there's a very big fundamentalist religious community in Israel, and since it's a very totalitarian community, they just do what the rabbis say, and the rabbis said "Vote for Likud." Then they also got a lot of the sort of chauvinist nationalist Jewish vote. And actually they got the vote of most of the working class and the poor as well—because the Labor Party in Israel, despite its name, is the party of the rich elites and professionals and the Europeanized segments of the population, and big business really likes it: I mean, they don't mind Likud, but they really like Labor. In case you were confused about this, the fact that the United States has supported the Labor Party ought to be a giveaway about its real interests: the United States does not support parties of working people and the poor.

But the point is, most of these voting blocks that joined to put Netanyahu in power have a kind of religious chauvinist element to them—you know, they want to restore and establish Jewish identity, their emphasis is on what are called in the United States "the cultural issues," that's what Likud won on. And often that does have sort of a populist appeal: so Likud got the support of poor and working people, and they got it in the same kind of way as Pat Buchanan gets their support here—and with about as much authenticity in terms of concern for their interests. And part of the irony of the elections is that the people these nationalist constituencies elected are almost pure Americans and secular—I mean, Netanyahu could run for office in the United States and nobody would notice it, he's essentially an American, just listen to him on television. Or take his leading foreign policy advisor, Dore Gold: he grew up in the United States, has an American accent, he's completely Americanized and secular—and he's the chief policy advisor. So what in fact happened is that the most Americanized element that has ever existed in Israeli politics won the election on a nationalist/religious program. And since you've got to give some crumbs to your constituency, the question now is, how are they going to do it? Well, *that's* the issue after the Israeli elections.

And right now the more secular European-types in the Israeli population are extremely worried about it—and they're extremely worried about it for the exact same reason we would be extremely worried about it if the Christian Right turned out to be the major constituency of the guy who wins the Presidential election in the United States. So suppose Bob Dole had won the Presidency here in 1996 with the overwhelming support of the Christian Right, and chauvinist fanatics, and the "militias," and so on and so forth. I mean, basic policies wouldn't change much as a result, but something would have to be done—there would have to be some kind of palliative offer to the constituency that voted him in. And that can mean things, it can have serious effects. So those are the sorts of changes I think one can expect to see in Israel, and it's not very clear how these internal factors will play out.

## P.L.O. Ambitions

MAN: *Can you add a word about the Palestinian leadership's response to the whole "peace process"? You generally characterize the P.L.O. as a bunch of conservative mayor-types—has that analysis changed at all?*

Well, you know, I've always thought that the P.L.O. is the most corrupt and incompetent Third World movement I've ever seen.[87] I mean, they've *presented* themselves all these years as, you know, revolutionaries waving around guns, Marx, etc.—but they're basically conservative nationalists, and they always *were* conservative nationalists: the rest was all pretense.

In fact, part of the reason for the failure of the whole Palestinian cause is that the P.L.O. is the only Third World leadership I've ever seen that didn't try to stimulate or support—or even help—any kind of international solidarity group. Even the North Koreans, crazy as they are, have made efforts to try to get popular support in the United States. But the Palestinian leadership never did. And it's not because they weren't *told* that it would be a good idea—I mean, there were people like, say, Ed Said [Palestinian-American professor], who were trying to get them to do that for years, and I was even involved in it myself. But they just couldn't hear it. Their conception of the way politics works is that it's arranged by rich guys sitting in back rooms who work out deals together, and the population's irrelevant. They haven't the slightest conception of the way a democratic system functions. So while it's true we don't have like a stellar democracy in the United States, what the population thinks and does makes a difference here—a big difference—and there are mechanisms to influence things. But the P.L.O. leadership has just never understood that.

The extent of this is really astonishing, actually. Just to give you one example of it, back in the early 1980s, when South End Press [a radical American publishing collective] was first coming along, it was publishing some books which could have been very useful for Palestinians. So one of the books it published was a very good war diary about the 1982 Lebanon war, written by a well-known Israeli military officer who was one of the founders of the Israeli army actually, a guy named Dov Yermiya, who's a very respected guy and a decent human being—and he was absolutely horrified by what was going on during Israel's attack on Lebanon. So he wrote a war diary which was published in Hebrew and was very different from anything you ever heard here in the mainstream, giving an accurate picture of what was going on, which was massive atrocities.[88] Well, obviously no publisher in the United States was going to touch it, but South End did publish it in English translation—and of course, it never got reviewed, no library would pick it up, nobody knows it exists, and so on; I had a book on the Middle East which was the same story, and there were a couple others like that.

Well, there was an approach to the P.L.O. about all of this—and incidentally, the P.L.O. had tons of money. I mean, part of their problem was that they were way too rich for their own good: they had a ton of money because the rich Arab states were trying to buy them off so they wouldn't cause them any trouble. So you know, Arafat was able to broker billion-dollar loans to Hungary, and all this kind of crazy business. But anyway, the P.L.O. had tons of money, and there was a proposal to try to get them just to purchase books—like, say, Yermiya's book—and send them to libraries so the book would be in American public libraries: it was nothing more than that.

Okay, it got up to the P.L.O. leadership, and they refused. Or rather, they would agree to do it only if the book was published with a P.L.O. imprint on it, saying, you know, "Published with the support of the P.L.O." Well, you can guess what it would mean if you published a book in the United States with that imprint on it—so that was the end of that idea. But just to do something like buying books which never would be reviewed and putting them in libraries which aren't going to buy them on their own, as a way to maybe help Palestinians in refugee camps who are being smashed to pieces in Beirut [the Lebanese city that was the focus of Israel's attack]—that they wouldn't do. And in fact, that's just symbolic: they would do *nothing* that would help to build up support for the really suffering people who they were supposed to represent—just because they were playing a different game. Their game was, "We're going to make a deal with Kissinger or Nixon, or some rich guy in a back room, and then our problems will be over." Well, of course that will never work.

Actually, the corruption of the P.L.O. has just infuriated Palestinians in the Territories, I should say. I was in the Territories back in 1988 or so, and when you went into, say, the old city of Nablus, or villages, and talked to organizers or activists, their hatred and contempt of the P.L.O. was just extraordinary. They were very bitter about it—about the robbery and the corruption and everything else—but they just said: look, it's the best we've got, that's our international image, you want to talk diplomacy you've got to talk to them.

However, by about 1992 or '93 even that kind of grudging acceptance had begun to collapse. There was a lot of opposition to the Arafat leadership in the Territories—and in the refugee camps in Lebanon, there were open calls for his resignation, calls for democratizing the P.L.O., and so on. The Israeli press knew all about it—they cover the Territories pretty well—and certainly Israeli intelligence knew about it, because they've got the place honeycombed. So there were articles by doves in the Israeli press around the summer of 1993 or so, saying: now's a good time to deal with the P.L.O., because they're going to give away everything—since their support is so weak inside the Occupied Territories, the last chance the P.L.O. leadership has to hang on to power is to be our agents, Israeli agents. Israeli *doves* wrote articles about that, and of course the Israeli government knew it.[89]

Well, okay, that whole phenomenon led to the Oslo Agreements—and now where the P.L.O. leadership fits in is just as part of the standard Third World model: they are the ruling Third World elite. So take a classic case, look at the history of India for a couple hundred years under the British Empire: the country was run by *Indians*, not by British—the bureaucrats who actually ran things were Indians, the soldiers who beat people up and smashed their heads were Indians. There was an Indian leadership which became very rich and privileged by being the agents of the British imperial system—and it's the same thing everywhere else. So for example, if you look at Southern Africa in the more recent period, the most brutal atrocities were carried out by black soldiers, who were basically mercenaries for the white racist South African regime. And every Third World country is like that. Whatever you want to call it, the whole American sort of "neocolonial system"—El Salvador, Brazil, the Philippines, and so on—is not run by *Americans*. The U.S. may be in the background, and when things get out of hand you may send in the American army or something—but basically it's all being run by local agents of the imperial power, whose internal power depends on their support from the outside, but who very much enrich themselves by their client ruler status. Alright, that's the standard colonial relationship, and the P.L.O. is intending to play that role.

So they have a huge security force—nobody really knows how big it is, because it's secret, but they may have thirty or forty thousand men enlisted. They surely have one of the highest densities of police per capita in the world, if not the highest. They work very closely with the Israeli secret services and the Israeli army. They're very brutal.[90] And they're making a ton of money. So you go to places like Gaza which are just collapsing, there are people starving in the streets—and there's also a ton of construction, new fancy restaurants, hotels, a lot of Palestinian investors going in and making plenty of money: it's the standard Third World pattern, that's the way the whole Third World is organized. And you see it everywhere these days—Eastern Europe is becoming that way too right now. I mean, about a year ago the per capita purchasing rate of Mercedes-Benzes in Moscow was higher than it was in New York, because there is tremendous wealth. Meanwhile, half a million more people are dying every year in Russia than in the 1980s; mortality for men has gone down seven or eight years on average in the last few years; and on and on.[91]

Okay, that's the Third World. And that's the way the P.L.O. leadership sees its future—and with some justice too, you know, because otherwise they probably would have been kicked out. So now that's their role, to oversee all of this, and they'll put up with any humiliation, it doesn't matter what. I mean, you look at the terms of the peace treaty, it was just gratuitous humiliation. But the P.L.O. is perfectly happy to take it. And they'll get rich, they'll have the guns, and they'll be the equivalent of the elite in India, or Mexico, Thailand, Indonesia, or any other place that you see in the Third World.

## The Nation-State System

WOMAN: *Noam, the problems you describe in the world sound almost chronic to me—systematic underdevelopment and exploitation in the Third World, proliferation of nuclear weapons, the growing environmental crisis. What means of social organization do you think would be necessary for us to overcome these things?*

Well, in my view what would ultimately be necessary would be a breakdown of the nation-state system—because I think that's not a viable system. It's not necessarily the natural form of human organization; in fact, it's a European invention pretty much. The modern nation-state system basically developed in Europe since the medieval period, and it was extremely difficult for it to develop: Europe has a very bloody history, an extremely savage and bloody history, with constant massive wars and so on, and that was all part of an effort to establish the nation-state system. It has virtually no relation to the way people live, or to their associations, or anything else particularly, so it had to be established by force. And it was established by centuries of bloody warfare. That warfare ended in 1945—and the only reason it ended is because the next war was going to destroy *everything*. So it ended in 1945—we hope; if it didn't, it *will* destroy everything.

The nation-state system was exported to the rest of the world through European colonization. Europeans were barbarians basically, savages: very advanced technologically, and advanced in methods of warfare, but not culturally or anything else particularly. And when they spread over the rest of the world, it was like a plague—they just destroyed everything in front of them, it was kind of like Genghis Khan or something. They fought differently, they fought much more brutally, they had better technology—and they essentially wiped everything else out.[92]

The American continent's a good example. How come everybody around here has a white face, and not a red face? Well, it's because the people with the white faces were savages, and they killed the people with red faces. When the British and other colonists came to this continent, they simply destroyed everything—and pretty much the same thing happened everywhere else in the world. You go back to about the sixteenth century and the populations of Africa and Europe were approximately comparable; a couple centuries later, the population of Europe was far higher, maybe four times as high. Why did that change? Well, you know, those were the effects of European colonization.[93]

So the process of colonization was extraordinarily destructive, and it in turn imposed the European nation-state system on the world, kind of a reflection of internal European society, which of course was always extremely hierarchical and unequal and brutal. And if that system continues, I suppose it will continue to be hierarchical and unequal and brutal.

So I think *other* forms of social organization have to be developed—and those forms are not too difficult to imagine. I mean, the United Nations was an attempt to do something about it, but it didn't work, because the superpowers won't let it work. International law is the same story. International law is a method by which you might regulate the aggressive and destructive tendencies of the nation-state—the trouble is, international law doesn't have a police force: there are no Martians around to enforce it. So international law will only work if the powers subjected to it are willing to accept it, and the United States is not willing to accept it. If the World Court condemns us, we simply disregard it, it's not our problem—we're above the law, we're a lawless state.[94] And as long as the major powers in the world are lawless and violent, and are unwilling to enter into international arrangements or other kinds of mechanisms which would constrain force and violence, there's very little hope for human survival, I would think.

Now, my own feeling—I mean, big story—is that the reasons for all of this have to do with the way that power is concentrated *inside* the particular societies; that's the source of this extreme violence in the world. Remember that every existing social system has a vast disparity of power internally. Take the United States: the United States was not founded on the principle that "the people" ought to rule—that's freshman Civics, it's not what happened in history. If you look back at the actual record, you'll find that the principles of the American Founding Fathers were quite different.

Keep in mind, all of the Founding Fathers hated democracy—Thomas Jefferson was a partial exception, but only partial. For the most part, they hated democracy. The principles of the Founding Fathers were rather nicely expressed by John Jay, the head of the Constitutional Convention and the first Chief Justice of the Supreme Court. His favorite maxim was, "The people who own the country ought to govern it"—that's the principle on which the United States was founded.[95] The major framer of the Constitution, James Madison, emphasized very clearly in the debates at the Constitutional Convention in 1787 that the whole system must be designed, as he put it, "to protect the minority of the opulent from the majority"—that's the primary purpose of the government, he said.[96]

Now, Madison had kind of a theory behind that, which was that the "minority of the opulent" would be elevated Enlightenment gentlemen, who would act like some kind of ancient Roman republicans of his imagination—benevolent philosophers who would use their opulence to benefit everybody in the country. But he himself quickly recognized that that was a serious delusion, and within about ten years he was bitterly denouncing what he called the "daring depravity of the times" as "the minority of the opulent" were using their power to smash everyone else in the face.

In fact, still in the eighteenth century, Madison made some insightful comments about the interactions between state power and private power. He said, we've designed a system in which the "stock-jobbers" (what we would today call investors) are simply using state power for their own ends—we thought we were going to create a system which would put enlightened gentlemen in control so that they would protect everyone from the tyranny of the majority, but instead what we've got is gangsters in control using state power for their own benefit.[97]

Well, that's the way the system was originally designed in the United States—and over the next two centuries, that basic design hasn't changed a lot. The "minority of the opulent," who share a very definite class interest, still have control of the government institutions, both the parliament and the Executive, while the general population remains highly dispersed, separated, and as Madison also recommended, fragmented so that people will not be able to unite together to identify and press their interests.[98] And the principle that "The people who own the country ought to govern it" continues to be the dominant feature of American politics.

Alright, it's not a very big secret who owns the country: you look at the "*Fortune* 500" every year and you figure out pretty well who owns the country. The country is basically owned by a network of conglomerates that control production and investment and banking and so on, and are tightly inter-linked and very highly concentrated—*they* own the country. And the principle of American democracy is that they also ought to govern it. And to a very large extent, they do. Now, whenever you have a concentration of power like that, you can be certain that the people who *have* the power are going to try to maximize it—and they're going to maximize it at the expense of others, both in their own country and abroad. And that's just an unviable system, I think.

Let's put international violence aside for a minute and take environmental issues, which people are finally beginning to look at. Well, it's been obvious for centuries that capitalism is going to self-destruct: that's just inherent in the logic of system—because to the extent that a system is capitalist, that means maximizing short-term profit and not being concerned with long-term effects. In fact, the motto of capitalism was, "private vices, public benefits"—somehow it's gonna work out. Well, it *doesn't* work out, and it's *never* going to work out: if you're maximizing short-term profits without concern for the long-term effects, you are going to destroy the environment, for one thing. I mean, you can pretend up to a certain point that the world has infinite resources and that it's an infinite wastebasket—but at some point you're going to run into the reality, which is that that isn't true.

Well, we're running into that reality now—and it's very profound. Take something like combustion: anything you burn, no matter what it is, is increasing the greenhouse effect—and this was known to scientists decades ago, they knew exactly what was happening.[99] But in a capitalist system, you don't care about long-term effects like that, what you have to care about is tomorrow's profits. So the greenhouse effect has been building for years, and there's no known technological fix on the horizon—there may not be any answer to this, it could be so serious that there's no remedy. That's possible, and then human beings will turn out to have been a lethal mutation, which maybe destroys a lot of life with us. Or it could be that there's some way of fixing it, or some ameliorating way—nobody knows.

But just keep in mind what we're dealing with: the predictable effect of an increase in the world's temperature through the greenhouse effect will be to raise the sea level, and if the sea level begins to rise a few feet, it's not clear that human civilization can continue. A lot of the agricultural lands, for example, are alluvial—they're near the seas. Industrial centers, like New York City, could be inundated. The climate is going to change, so the agricultural-producing areas of the United States could become dust-bowls.

And when these changes start to be recognized, they're going to set into motion social conflict of a sort that we can't even imagine—I mean, if it turns out that agricultural areas in the United States are becoming unviable and that Siberia is becoming the next great agricultural producer, do you think that American planners are going to allow the Russians to use it? We'll conquer it, even if we have to destroy the world in a nuclear war to do it. That's the way they think, and have always thought. And those conflicts are going to be growing up all over the world—you can't even predict what they'll be like.

Alright, right now we do not have the forms of internal democracy or international organization which will allow us even to begin to cope with these sorts of problems. The very concept of social planning, of rational planning for human concerns—that's regarded as virtually subversive. And that's the only thing that could possibly save people: rational social planning, carried out by accountable people representing the whole population rather than business elites. Democracy, in other words—that's a concept we don't have.

# 9

# Movement Organizing

*Based primarily on discussions at Woods Hole, Massachusetts, between 1993 and 1996.*

### The Movie <u>Manufacturing Consent</u>

*Editors' Note: The 1992 movie* Manufacturing Consent: Noam Chomsky and the Media *was the most successful Canadian feature documentary ever made and played in more than 32 countries. Although Chomsky cooperated with the directors and liked them very much, he has not seen the film and does not intend to, for reasons that follow.[1]*

MAN: *Noam, watching your reactions to the documentary they made about your critique of the media, you've shown a lot of discomfort . . .*

You should see the letters I write him [indicating Mark Achbar, one of the directors].

MARK ACHBAR: *He's a good letter-writer.*

MAN: *Again earlier today you said something critical about it. I'm sure you realize the politically potent effect that the film is having.*

Oh yes.

MAN: *And I was just wondering, if this were a film about Bertrand Russell [British philosopher and socialist] and his powerful ideas, and how he helped to change society with his ideas, would you be as critical of it, or would you see it as a powerful political organizing tool?[2]*

Both, both.

MAN: *Then I guess I'd love to hear you say something positive about the film.*

Well, what I would say is exactly what you said—I mean, the positive impact of it has been astonishing to me. Mark can give you the details, but outside of the United States, the film is shown all over the place, and even inside the United States it was shown to some extent.

MAN: *It was in a lot of cities.*

Yeah, but in every other country it's been on national television.

MAN: *It came to Seattle four times and sold out every screening.*

Okay, but everywhere else it was on national television. I didn't realize this myself until I was traveling around Europe giving talks last year, and I'd be in Finland and "Oh yeah, we all saw it on television"—it was that sort of thing all over the place. As a matter of fact, it's gotten to the point where I'm invited to film festivals all over the world—literally.

Well, one result of that is there's been a ton of reviewing, and the reviewing is extremely interesting. The reviews are often written just by guys who write T.V. criticism for the newspapers, you know, completely apolitical people. And their reaction is extremely positive, I'd say about 98 percent of the time it's *very* positive. In fact, about the only thing that got a lot of people pissed off, including Phil Donahue, was some remarks I made about sports: people got kind of angry about that.[3] But most of the time the reaction is very positive; they say, "Yeah, really interesting."

In fact, I get a ton of letters about it—like I get a letter from some steelworker in Canada saying, "I took my friends three times, we all saw it and it's great," and so on and so forth. Well, that's all fine. But the standard letter, the *standard* letter, is something like this: it says, "I'm really glad they made this film; I thought I was the only person in the world who had these thoughts, I'm delighted to know that somebody else actually has them and is saying them." Then comes the punch-line: "How can I join your movement?" That's why I'm ambivalent.

Now, I don't think it's anything Mark and Peter [the directors] did wrong; I mean, I haven't seen the movie, but I know that they were very well aware of this problem, and tried very hard to overcome it. But somehow it's just inherent in the medium, I don't think the medium allows an escape from this—or if it does, I don't think that anybody's yet found it. I mean, I don't think the medium can make people understand that if they film me giving a talk somewhere, that's because somebody else *organized* the talk, and the real work is being done by the people who organized the talk, and then followed it up and are out there working in their communities. If they can bring in some speaker to help get people together, terrific, but that person is in no sense "the leader." That somehow doesn't get across in a movie—what gets across is, "How can I join your movement?" And then I've got to write a letter which is a big speech about this. So I am ambivalent about it.

Incidentally, one more comment about the reviews: the reviews in the United States were intriguingly different. First of all, there weren't many, because it wasn't shown a lot here. But they were very interesting. Do you remember the *New York Times* review? That was really fascinating, that was the most intriguing one.

MARK ACHBAR: *They left your name out of the title of the film.*

Well, yeah, right. But actually, the *New York Times* to my surprise wrote a very favorable review, or what I'm sure they took to be a favorable review. They assigned it to Vincent Canby, who's kind of an old-time New Dealer, he was the big cultural critic at the *Times* forever, and he wrote a review which I'm sure everybody at the *Times* took to be very favorable. It said something like, oh yeah, really interesting guy, wonderful film, so on and so forth. Then it said, obviously there's nothing to what he's saying, of course it's all nonsense—but it was very sympathetic.

Then it got really interesting. It said, though what he's saying is all non-sense, nevertheless the leading idea is worth taking seriously, even though it sounds crazy. And the leading idea, Canby said, is that the government is only responsive to the fifty percent of the population who vote, not to the fifty percent who don't vote, so therefore we ought to try to register more people. He said, yeah, this sounds pretty far out in left field, but neverthe-less we shouldn't discount it totally, something like that.[4] It just flew by him completely—he didn't see what the film was about. I mean, the most illiter-ate T.V. reviewer in Tasmania didn't miss the point like that, it's only in the *United States* that it has to be completely missed. And that's what it means to "think properly."

But I do think the film is double-edged. It's certainly energized a lot of ac-tivism. I think it did a tremendous amount of good just for East Timor alone [the film includes extensive coverage of the unreported East Timor genocide as a case study of Edward Herman's and Chomsky's "Propaganda Model"[5]]. And it's had a good impact in other respects. But it also has this negative aspect, which seems to me almost unavoidable. But you wanted to say something more . . .

MARK ACHBAR: *I'm sure you're aware that we have you saying in the film, almost verbatim, what you just said: that the reason you can give talks all over the place is because people are organizing.*

Yeah, I know—but it just doesn't get across. There's something about the medium which prevents it from getting across. I mean, I know that it was tried, I know that that was the idea, but . . .

MARK ACHBAR: *Was it really the majority of letters that said, "I want to join your movement"?*

Well, they say something like that: the general picture is that it's about *me*—and it isn't. The whole point is, it's not. And I don't know how you get that across to people in a film.

MAN: *But it is about you, just the ideas aren't about you.*

Nooo!

MAN: *The ideas are for the world to think about.*

But see, it really *isn't*—because if I'm somewhere giving a talk, it's precisely because somebody organized a meeting. Like, I'm here, but I didn't do anything—Mike and Lydia [Albert and Sargent, co-editors of *Z Magazine*] did something. I didn't do anything. And that's the way it is everywhere else too.

MAN: *But you're also here because of the way you grew up, and that school that you went to.*

But the same is true of everybody else who's here too. Yeah, sure. Everybody's got their own story.

WOMAN: *But the critique of the media in the film is taken from speeches that* you *gave.*

Yeah, but that's because other people are doing important things and I'm not doing important things—that's what it literally comes down to. I mean, years ago I used to be involved in organizing too—I'd go to meetings, get involved in resistance, go to jail, all of that stuff—and I was just no good at it at all; some of these people here can tell you. So sort of a division of labor developed: I decided to do what I'm doing now, and other people kept doing the other things. Friends of mine who were basically the same as me—went to the same colleges and graduate schools, won the same prizes, teach at M.I.T. and so on—just went a different way. They spend their time organizing, which is much more important work—so they're not in a film. That's what the difference is. I mean, I do something basically less important—it *is*, in fact. It's adding something, and I can do it, so I do it—I don't have any false modesty about it. And it's helpful. But it's helpful to people who are doing the real work. And every popular movement I know of in history has been like that.

In fact, it's extremely important for people with power not to let anybody understand this, to make them think there are big leaders around who somehow get things going, and then what everybody else has to do is follow them. That's one of the ways of demeaning people, and degrading them, and making them passive. I don't know how to overcome this exactly, but it's really something people ought to work on.

WOMAN: *As an activist for East Timor, though, I have to say that the film put our work on a completely different level. Even if you have some trouble with it personally, it has gotten people doing a lot of real work out there.*

I think that's true; I know that's true.

ANOTHER WOMAN: *Now I've got to admit it—I felt odd having you sign a book for my friend earlier today.*

Yeah, it's crazy—it's just completely wrong. In a place like San Francisco, it gets embarrassing: I can't walk across the Berkeley campus—literally—without twenty people coming up and asking me to sign something. That doesn't make any sense.

WOMAN: *It does feel unnatural.*

It is, it's completely missing the point. It's simply not factually accurate, for one thing—because like I say, the real work is being done by people who are not known, that's always been true in every popular movement in history. The people who are known are riding the crest of some wave. Now, you can ride the crest of the wave and try to use it to get power, which is the standard thing, or you can ride the crest of the wave because you're helping people that way, which is another thing. But the point is, it's the wave that matters—and that's what people ought to understand. I don't know how you get that across in a film.

Actually, come to think of it, there are some films that have done it. I mean, I don't see a lot of visual stuff, so I'm not the best commentator, but I thought *Salt of the Earth* really did it. It was a long time ago, but at the time I thought that it was one of the really great movies—and of course it was killed, I think it was almost never shown.

WOMAN: *Which one was that?*

*Salt of the Earth.* It came out at the same time as *On the Waterfront*, which is a rotten movie. And *On the Waterfront* became a huge hit—because it was anti-union. See, *On the Waterfront* was part of a big campaign to destroy unions while pretending to be for, you know, Joe Sixpack. So *On the Waterfront* is about this Marlon Brando or somebody who stands up for the poor working man against the corrupt union boss. Okay, things like that exist, but that's not unions—I mean, sure, there are plenty of union bosses who are crooked, but nowhere near as many as C.E.O.s who are crooked, or what have you. But since *On the Waterfront* combined that anti-union message with "standing up for the poor working man," it became a huge hit. On the other hand, *Salt of the Earth*, which was an authentic and I thought very well-done story about a strike and the people involved in it, that was just flat killed, I don't even think it was shown anywhere. I mean, you could see it at an art theater, I guess, but that was about it. I don't know what those of you who know something about film would think of it, but I thought it was a really outstanding film.

## Media Activism

WOMAN: *Noam, I agree with you that alternative media activists have to be very careful not to re-create authoritarian structures like the ones that exist now—like, not have a "Z Channel" [i.e. after Z Magazine] that goes about things in the same way as A.B.C. and C.B.S. But I'm not quite sure how we can disseminate information effectively and still be egalitarian as we do it: it seems to me there is this tendency to try to speak from a position of authority, and we really have to fight against that.*

I think that's exactly right—that's a crucial point. I don't completely know what the answer is to that, actually—I'd be interested in what some of you have to say about it.

MAN: *Well, let's just take you personally for a second. When people ask you where to turn for more truth and for accuracy of information, what do you tell them?*

What I usually say is that they're not phrasing the question the right way. I mean, people should not be asking me or anyone else where to turn for an accurate picture of things: they should be asking *themselves* that. So someone can ask me what reflects my interpretation of the way things are, and I can tell them where they can get material that looks at the world the way I think it ought to be looked at—but then *they* have to decide whether or not that's accurate. Ultimately it's your own mind that has to be the arbiter: you've got to rely on your own common sense and intelligence, you can't rely on anyone else for the truth.

So the answer I give is, I think the smartest thing to do is to read everything you read—and that includes what I write, I would always tell people this—skeptically. And in fact, an honest writer will try to make it clear what his or her biases are and where the work is starting from, so that then readers can compensate—they can say, "This person's coming from over here, and that's the way she's looking at the world, now I can correct for what may well be her bias; I can decide for myself whether what she's telling me is accurate, because at least she's making her premises clear." And people *should* do that. You should start by being very skeptical about anything that comes to you from any sort of power system—and about everything else too. You should be skeptical about what I tell you—why should you believe a word of it? I got my own ax to grind. So figure it out for yourself. There really is no other answer.

And in fact, if you're an organizer who's serious about it, what you're going to try to do is help people *themselves* find their own answers. And then if you can be a resource, or point them in some direction that might be useful, or help put them in touch with somebody, or take care of their kids while they're out looking for a job or something—okay, that's organizing.

MARK ACHBAR: *Noam, one of the best things you said that didn't end up in the film was, "It's not so much a matter of what you read, it's a matter of how you read." When people ask me about sources for information, I recommend the* New York Times *as quickly as I recommend* Z Magazine.

Yeah, I do too—I absolutely agree with that. Take, say, *Business Week*: it's useful to read it, it's useful to read what the ruling class tells its people. You can learn an awful lot from the *Wall Street Journal* and the *New York Times* and so on.

In fact, I think in general that people tend not to read the business press as much as they should. Most of it is very boring, but there are things in there that you do not find elsewhere—they tend to be more honest, because they're talking to people they don't have to be worried about, and to people who need to know the truth so that they can go out and make decisions about their money. I mean, you can lie as much as you want in the *Boston Globe* or something, but the people who read the *Wall Street Journal* have to have a tolerable sense of reality when they go out to make money. So in journals like *Business Week* and *Fortune*, you'll typically find an awful lot of very useful information. These are journals that you shouldn't *buy*, incidentally, they're too expensive; but you should steal them if you can. They're also in the library.[6]

As a more general matter, though, if you really want to educate yourself politically, what you have to do is become part of a group—because unless you're a real fanatic about it, you're just not going to be able to do it all by yourself. I mean, *I* do it, but I know I've got a screw loose, and I don't expect anybody else to be that crazy. On the other hand, a group working together can do it very well. Take a look at the Central America solidarity movements in the 1980s, for example—they were usually church-based groups around the country, and they just kept working at it together. They had people going down there, they had their own literature, they circulated information around, and the result was, there were people I met in those groups who knew more about Central America than I do—and I work on it hard. They certainly knew more about it than the C.I.A., which is no big thing actually, or than people in a lot of the academic departments. But that's what can happen when you start working together—and I think that's just got to be the answer, except for a few crazed individuals here and there.

And in fact, what I just said about my own work isn't really accurate—because I certainly don't find all the information I use on my own. The fact is, there are a lot of people around the world who are in a similar position, and we share information together. A good deal of my time is actually spent just clipping newspapers and periodicals and professional journals, and photocopying them to send to people—and they do the same for me. And the result is, I can easily get to know more than people in the C.I.A., or in any academic research center—mainly because I have smart agents, not dumb agents, and they know what's important and can dig things out. I mean, mainstream scholars and national intelligence agencies don't have very smart and perceptive people scanning the journals and the press in other countries and around the United States, and finding what's important, doing an analysis of it and sending it to them. The countries I'm especially interested in, like say Israel, I could never cover the press well enough by myself, it's just too much of a job. But if I have friends there clipping it and sending me articles, and picking out what's important, we can share understanding. And it's the same with other places—for instance, a lot of the work I've done on Southeast Asia and East Timor has used mostly material from the Australian press: I just get tons of stuff from there.

And again, it's reciprocal: you do this for a number of people, they do it for you, and the end result is, informal networks of cooperation develop through which people can pool their efforts and compensate for a lack of resources. That's exactly what organization is all *about*, in fact.

WOMAN: *Noam, I remember in the movie you criticized the U.S. media for insisting on "concision"—restricting news analysis to concise sound-bites, so only conventional wisdom can be presented coherently. But in the organizing I've done, I've found that it's important to use both "concision" and a more in-depth type of analysis, to use the two in combination. I'm thinking specifically of trying to get people's attention through fact-sheets and quick blurbs of information that you can digest easily, and then go on to find out more. I'm wondering what you think about that kind of combined use?*

Sure, oh yeah—it's very useful to do it that way. Actually, I should say that this term "concision" is kind of like a joke—it's a word I learned from the media P.R. guys when I heard one of them use it, I forget who . . .

MARK ACHBAR: *Jeff Greenfield.*

Yeah, what is he, manager of *Newsweek*?

MARK ACHBAR: *Producer at* Nightline.

Producer at *Nightline* or something. He used the word "concision" to describe what they do—you know, find people who can make their points in 600 words, or between two commercials.[7] It was the first time I'd ever heard the term. But yeah, it's around, and it's a technique of thought control. But you can use it quite constructively too.

For example, during the Gulf War, *Z Magazine* ran a couple pages of just short factual statements of what the basic story was—I think every good organizing group does things like that. I mean, people need to have information in the front of their minds, so that they know what the general structure is—it's just that then you should fill in the depth. So I think you should use the techniques in combination: there's nothing wrong with slogans if they lead you to something. But of course, we should also be making people aware that *any* presentation of facts is a selection and an interpretation—I mean, we're picking the facts that *we* think are important, maybe they'll think something else is important.

WOMAN: *A common response when you give people a fact-sheet is, "Why should we trust you? Where did you get this information?" Not enough people ask those questions, actually.*

They should, yeah. But that distrust still is something that's very hard to overcome as an organizer. I don't know how many of you have been following the Z online Bulletin Board lately [a computer network discussion forum], but there's been an ongoing conversation there in which people have pointed out—and they're right, I don't know any answer to it—that they'll come to people with, not necessarily just fact-sheets, but even detailed, elaborate arguments with a lot of evidence and data, but it's different from what everyone has always heard, and the standard response is, "Well, why should I believe you?"

And that's not an unreasonable response. I mean, if somebody came to you with a three-volume work with a lot of footnotes and statistics and mathematical calculations which proved that the world is flat, you'd be very wise to be cautious, no matter how impressive it looked. And that's the way we're coming to people most of the time—we're telling them that the world is flat, and they're not going to believe all your evidence. They *should*, in fact, ask questions like that. And that's just a hard situation for organizers to overcome: you only really overcome that by winning confidence, and helping people gain a broader understanding for themselves, bit by bit.

## Self-Destruction of the U.S. Left

MAN: *You travel around the country doing a lot of speaking engagements, Noam. I'm wondering, just from going to all these different communities,*

*what do you think things look like in general as far as the movement goes,
as far as politics go—what's your assessment?*

Well, over the years I think there's sort of like a tendency you can see—a
tendency towards, on the one hand, much larger groups of people getting
engaged in political activism in some fashion, or at least *wanting* to become
involved in some sort of progressive activity, roughly speaking. On the
other hand, the opportunities for it are declining at the same time—and
people are becoming extremely isolated. I just got a sense of it yesterday af-
ternoon. I was getting ready to go off for a couple of weeks, so I did my
monthly making out of checks to all the, you know, worthwhile organizations around the world. And it's amazing when you see it. You take any
topic you like, no matter how narrow it is—I mean, health rights in the
southern part of Guatemala, let's say—and there are fifteen separate organizations working on it, maybe right next door to one another, so you have
to make out fifteen checks.

Well, that's what I happened to notice yesterday, but it's characteristic of
what's happening: everybody's got their own little operation, everything is
extremely narrowly focused and very small, and often the groups don't
even know about each other's existence. And partly that's the result of, and
partly it contributes to, a sense of real isolation, and also a kind of hopelessness—a sense that nothing's going on, because after all it's just me and
my three friends. And it's true, it's you and your three friends, except down
the block there's somebody else and their three friends. The success in at-
omizing the population has been extraordinary; I think that's in fact the
major propaganda achievement of recent years—just to isolate people in a
most astonishing fashion. And the left has done a lot to help that along, in
my opinion.

So what you find all around the country is huge mobs of people showing
up at talks and wanting to get involved, but nobody around with anything
for them to do, or any sense that there could be any follow-up. I mean, the
standard question after a talk where thousands of people have shown up is,
"What can I do?" That's a terrible condemnation of the left, that people
have to ask that question. There ought to be fifty booths outside with people saying, "Look, join up, here's what you can do." And there aren't—or if
there are, the groups are so narrow that people just have a feeling, "Look, I
don't want to do anything this narrow; I mean, I'm all in favor of gay and
lesbian rights in Western Massachusetts, say, but I don't want to devote my
whole life to that."

WOMAN: *What exactly has the left done that you think is so self-destructive?*

In part the problem is just divisiveness—it's passionate commitment to a
very narrow position, and extreme intolerance of anyone who doesn't see it

exactly the way you do. So if you have a slightly different view from the person next door on, say, abortion rights, it's a war—you can't even talk to each other, it's not an issue that you can even discuss. There's a lot of that on the left, and it's been very self-destructive. It's made the progressive movements, the sort of "left" movements, kind of unwelcome—because people don't like it; they see it, and they don't like it.

Also, there's just a huge amount of frittering away of energy on real absurdities. There are parts of the country, like California, where *incredible* amounts of energy go into things like trying to figure out exactly which Mafia figure might have been involved in killing John F. Kennedy or something—as if anybody should care. The energy and the passion that goes into things like that is really extraordinary, and it's very self-destructive.

Or take a look at the intellectual left, the people who ought to be involved in the kinds of things we're doing here. If you look at the academic left, say, it's mired in intricate, unintelligible discourse of some crazed postmodernist variety, which nobody can understand, including the people who are involved in it—but it's really good for careers and that sort of thing. That again pulls a ton of energy into activities which have the great value that they are guaranteed not to affect anything in the world, so therefore they're very useful for the institutions to support and to tolerate and to encourage people to get involved with.

Another thing is, there are just extreme illusions about what's going on in the world—and that's the fault of all of us, in fact: we just can't seem to get over them. Take the so-called "Gulf War"—it wasn't really a war, it was a slaughter, but take the Gulf Slaughter. It led to tremendous depression on the left, because people felt like they weren't able to do anything about it. Well, if you just think about it for a minute, you realize that it was exactly the opposite: it was probably the greatest victory the peace movement has ever had. The Gulf War was the first time in history that there were huge demonstrations and protests *before* a war started—that's never happened before. In the case of the Vietnam War, it was five years before anybody got out in the streets; this time, there were massive demonstrations with hundreds of thousands of people involved *before* the bombing even started. And if you just look at the attitudes of the general population, up until the day the bombing started it was about two to one in favor of a negotiated settlement involving Iraqi withdrawal from Kuwait in the context of an international conference on regional issues, Israel-Palestine issues and so on.[8]

Well, at the time, the left couldn't do anything about it. First of all, it didn't know it, and didn't know that there were alternatives—like it didn't know that a week earlier high U.S. officials had rejected an Iraqi offer to withdraw from Kuwait on exactly those terms.[9] But nevertheless, there is a huge reservoir of support in the general population—it's just the left isn't dealing with it.

In fact, the attitudes of the general population are absolutely astonishing. For example, 83 percent of the American population thinks that the economic system is inherently unfair, "the rich get richer and the poor get poorer"—meaning things should just be radically changed.[10] Well, what is the left doing about that mere 83 percent of the population that thinks everything has to be radically changed? What we're doing is alienating them, or making them feel that we have nothing to say to them, or something like that.

Or I remember in 1987, when there was a big hoopla about the bicentennial of the Constitution, the *Boston Globe* published one of my favorite polls, in which they gave people little slogans and said, "Guess which ones are in the Constitution." Of course, nobody knows what's in the Constitution, because everybody forgot what they learned in third grade, and probably they didn't pay any attention to it then anyway—so what the question really was asking is, "What is such an obvious truism that it must be in the Constitution?" Well, one of the suggestions was, "What about 'From each according to his ability, to each according to his needs'?" [a slogan from Karl Marx]. Half the American population thinks that's in the Constitution, because it's such an obvious truth—it's so obviously true that it must be in the Constitution, where else could it come from?[11] If you think about what this means and what we're doing about it, it's mind-boggling, the chasm.

Or take the whole Ross Perot phenomenon during the 1992 election [Perot is an American billionaire who ran for President on an independent ticket]. Ross Perot appeared on the political scene and had no program, nobody knew what he stood for, he could have come from Mars for all anybody knew, and within a couple days he was running even with the two major candidates. I mean, if a puppet was running it probably would have come out even.

Or do you remember the whole business with Dan Quayle and Murphy Brown? That was taken very seriously in the United States, it was treated as if these were two real people—a debate between the Vice President and a television actress; actually, not an actress, a character on a television show, who then responded through the show [Quayle had criticized the character for deciding to have a child out of wedlock]. Well, there was a poll done at that time in which people were asked who they would prefer as President, Dan Quayle or Murphy Brown—and you can guess who won.[12] There wasn't a poll done as to who they thought was real; I'm not sure what the result of that one would have been.

But what these things demonstrate is something that is shown over and over again in careful public opinion studies: the population is what's called "alienated." People think that none of the institutions work for them, everything's a scam, a crooked operation; they feel they have no way of influencing anything, the political system doesn't work, the economic system doesn't work, everything is being done somewhere else and it's all out of their control. And this feeling goes up across the board pretty regularly.[13] I mean, they're not aware how much it's true—like, they're not aware that in the current G.A.T.T. [General Agreement on Tariffs and Trade] negotiations, major decisions are being made that will have a tremendous impact on the world and on their lives, and neither they, nor the unions, nor Congress knows anything about them. But they get a sense of it, they sort of have a feel for it.

And the point is, the left is doing virtually nothing to try to take advantage of this situation and turn the tremendous discontentedness in some kind of constructive direction. What I see on the left at least is pretty much the same story everywhere: tremendous divisiveness, narrowness of focus, intolerance, unwillingness to meet people on their own terms, plus inertia, and just madness of various kinds.

And the reason for a lot of that is—well, I think you could sort of see some of the reasons. If you just take the Civil Rights Movement and look at its course, I think you get a pretty good idea of some of the reasons. In the early part of the Civil Rights Movement, in the late 1950s and early Sixties, there was tremendous courage and dedication, and huge numbers of people finally got involved, including all the way up to middle-class America. And it was successful: there were big victories in the South. And then somehow it stopped. Well, what happened? What happened was, you got restaurants integrated, and you got things like the Voting Rights Act of 1965—it was a little bit like what's going on in South Africa now, although there it's much more dramatic. And you were able to establish the forms that in general are accepted by the mainstream Establishment culture, and even by the business community—like, General Motors doesn't have any stake in having restaurants segregated, in fact they'd rather have them not segregated, it's more efficient. So all of that stuff worked, at least to a certain extent. It wasn't easy—a lot of people got killed, it was very brutal and so on. But it worked. And then it stopped, and it frittered away, and in fact probably it's regressed since then. And the reason is, it ran into class issues—and they're hard. They require institutional change. There the Board of Directors of General Motors is *not* going to be happy, when you start dealing with class issues in the industrial centers.

So at that point it stopped, and it frittered away, and also it went off into pretty self-destructive things—revolutionary slogans, carrying guns around, smashing windows, this and that—just because it ran into harder issues. And when you run into harder issues, it's easy to look for an escape. And there are a lot of different escapes. You can escape by writing meaningless articles on some unintelligible version of academic radical feminism, or by becoming a conspiracy buff, or by working on some very narrowly focused issue, which may be important, but is so narrow that it's never going to get anywhere or have any outreach. There are a lot of these temptations. And as the number of people becoming interested and involved has increased, since the issues are indeed hard, they're not easy, there's been a kind of chasm developing between the potentialities and the actual achievements.

WOMAN: *You don't think the left is dealing with class issues?*

Not much. I mean, it's not that nobody is. And they're not the only issues that have to be dealt with, it's just that they're the most important ones—because they're right at the core of the whole system of oppression. And also, they're the hardest ones, because there you're dealing with solid institutional structures where the core of private power is involved. I mean, other issues are hard too—like issues of patriarchy are hard. But they're modifiable without changing the whole system of power. Class issues aren't.

MAN: *Do you have any strategies for the left to be able to get more on common ground with the working class?*

Well, first of all, "working class" is pretty broad. I mean, anybody who gets a paycheck is in some sense "working class," so there's a sense in which a lot of managers are working class too—and in fact, they have pretty much the same interests these days: they're getting canned as fast as everybody else is, and they're worried about it. See, in the United States the word "class" is used in an unusual way: it's supposed to have something to do with wealth. But in its traditional usage, and the way the word is used everywhere else, what it has to do with is your place in the whole system of decision-making and authority—so if you take orders, you're "working class," even if you're wealthy.

And how should the left be dealing with class issues? Well, we have to take that 83 percent of the population that thinks that the system is inherently unfair, and increase it to a larger percentage, then we simply help people get organized to change it. There are no special tactics for that, it's just the usual education and organizing. Okay, so you get started doing it.

## Popular Education

WOMAN: *One thing that I've noticed in reading a number of your books, and a number of books by people like Holly Sklar and Michael Albert, is that it's a standard practice on the left in trying to help educate people—because we are in the minority position—to document everything very thoroughly, to lay out very precise scholarly arguments, to marshal a lot of evidence and have a ton of citations. But the thing that bothers me about that is there are a lot of people who are shut out of that world.*

That's right.

WOMAN: *They're not academics, they haven't been trained in this way of making arguments. I really wish that there was something out there in the middle ground that would not just try to persuade, but would also teach about argumentation. Somebody told me they used to do things like that in the 1930s, with popular education.*

Absolutely—in fact, that was one of the big things in the 1930s for left intellectuals to be involved in. I mean, good scientists, well-known, important scientists like Bernal [British physicist] and others just felt that it was a part of their obligation to the human species to do popular science. So you had very good popular books being written about physics, and about mathematics and so on—for instance, there's a book called *Mathematics for the Million* which is an example of it.[14]

WOMAN: *Yeah, I've heard of that.*

Well, that guy came out of the left. And the point is, those people just felt that this kind of knowledge should be shared by everyone. In fact, one of the things I find most astonishing about the current left-intellectual scene is that what the counterparts of these people today are telling the general public is, "You don't have to know about this stuff, it's all just some white male power-play—and besides, astrology's the same as physics: it's all just a discourse, and a text, and this that and the other thing, so forget about it, do what comes natural; if you like astrology, it's astrology." I mean, this is so different in character from what was just assumed automatically in the days when there were live popular movements, it's amazing.

If you're privileged enough to, say, know mathematics, and you think you're a part of the general world, obviously you should try to help other people understand it. And the way you do it, for example, is by writing books like *Mathematics for the Million*, or by giving talks in elementary schools and things like that. In fact, involvement in popular education goes well beyond writing books: it means having groups, giving talks, workers' education, all sorts of stuff. And the fact that people on the left *aren't* doing those things today I think is a real tragedy—and also part of the really self-destructive aspect of a lot of what's been happening, in my opinion. These are things that have always been a part of live political movements.

In fact, workers' education used to be a huge thing in the United States. For example, A. J. Muste [American pacifist and activist] worked in workers' education for a long time, and the working-class schools he helped set up were significant and big—people who hadn't gone through elementary school came to them, and really learned a lot. Incidentally, Muste was one of the most important people of this century in the United States—of course, nobody knows about him, because he did the wrong things, but he was really a leading figure in the sort of left-libertarian movement.[15]

John Dewey [American philosopher and educator] was also very much involved in popular education, and part of it was an attempt to do just this kind of thing. So Dewey worked with Jane Addams [American social worker and suffragist] and others in Chicago during the Progressive Period on community development programs and so on—in fact, the whole progressive school movement came out of that, and it very much had this kind of democratizing commitment and a commitment to industrial democracy, which was considered a central part of it all.[16]

In fact, there were schools like this set up all over the place—for example, in England several of the colleges in the big universities, including Oxford, are working-class colleges: they came out of the labor movement, and are directed to educating working people. And even right around here there's Cape Cod Community College, which like a lot of community colleges has people teaching in it whose interests really are this. Community colleges and urban colleges in general have mostly working-class students, and they can be a very good way to reach people. A lot of activists have in fact chosen to do that—there are people teaching in community colleges all over the place for precisely these reasons.

So you're right: there really ought to be more efforts put into things like these—they would be a very important step towards reconstituting the kinds of popular movements we need.

## Third-Party Politics

WOMAN: *What do you think about working through the electoral process as a strategy for activists to pursue at this point? Is that a viable way to spend one's energy, if ultimately what we're trying to change is the basic structure of the economy?*

Well, I think it's possible to work through the electoral process. But the point we have to remember is, things will happen through the electoral process only if there are popular forces in motion in the society which are active enough to be threatening to power.

So for example, take the Wagner Act of 1935 [i.e. the National Labor Relations Act], which gave American labor the right to organize for the first time.[17] It was a long time coming—most of Europe had the same rights about fifty years earlier—and it was voted through by Congress. But it wasn't voted through by Congress because Franklin Roosevelt liked it, or because he was a liberal or anything like that—in fact, Roosevelt was a conservative, he had no particular interest in labor.[18] The Wagner Act was voted through by Congress because the people who do have power in the society recognized that they'd better give workers something, or else there was going to be real trouble. So therefore it was voted through, and workers got the right to organize—and they kept that right as long as they were willing to struggle for it, then they basically lost it, it doesn't get enforced much anymore.

So you can get things through the electoral process, but the electoral process is really only a surface phenomenon: a lot of other things have to be happening in the society for it to be very meaningful.

MAN: *What about trying to get proportional representation in the United States as a way of maybe developing a viable labor party, which could help articulate more popular interests and broaden the range of political debate generally? [Proportional representation refers to an electoral system by which legislative seats are assigned according to the proportion of votes that each party receives rather than by majority vote in each district, which encourages the proliferation of parties and gives minority voters better representation.[19]] It seems to me that in Canada, the fact that they have a labor party makes people somewhat more attuned to issues that Americans largely miss, like workers' issues for example.*

That's right—Canada's an interesting case: it's a pretty similar society to us, except different somehow. It's much more humane. It has the same corporate rule, the same capitalist institutions, all of that's the same—but it's just a much more humane place. They have a kind of social contract that we don't have, like they have this national health-care system which makes us look bad because it's so efficient. And that *is* related to their having a labor-based party, I think—the New Democratic Party in Canada [N.D.P.] isn't really a *labor* party, but it's kind of labor-based. However, that party's ability to enter the political system in Canada wasn't a result of having proportional representation, it was due to the same thing that would be necessary to *get* any kind of change like proportional representation in the first place: a lot of serious popular organizing.

Look, if you have a political movement that's strong enough that the power structure has to accommodate it, it'll get accommodated in some fashion—as in the case of union organizing rights here, the Wagner Act. But when that movement stops being active and challenging, those rights just aren't going to matter very much anymore. So I think that pushing for something like proportional representation could be worth doing if it's part of a wider organizing campaign. But if it's just an effort to try to put some people into Congress and that's it, then it's pretty much a waste of your time. I mean, there is never any point in getting some person into office unless you can continue forcing them to be *your* representative, and they will only continue to be *your* representative as long as you are active and threatening enough to make them do what you want, otherwise they're going to stop being your representative.

This point has been understood forever, actually. So if you go back to James Madison, who framed a lot of the Constitution and the Bill of Rights and so on, he pointed out that, as he put it, a "parchment barrier" will never stand in the way of oppression—meaning, writing something down on paper is totally worthless by itself: if you fight for it, you can make it real, otherwise you'll just have really nice things on paper.[20] I mean, Stalin's constitution was just about the nicest constitution around—but it was a parchment barrier. And the same is true of every other part of politics too, including having your representative in Congress.

So you can vote for Gerry Studds [liberal Massachusetts Congressman] if you're from around here, and he'll do some nice things—but he also voted for N.A.F.T.A. [the North American Free Trade Agreement]. And that was against the will of a lot of his constituents—just because those constituents weren't making it clear enough to their representative what he had to do. I mean, the anti-N.A.F.T.A. activity that went on in the country was important, and it went way beyond anything I ever thought it would, but it still wasn't enough to get people like Gerry Studds to come along when it was needed—and he's a good guy, like I gave money to the Studds campaign. It's just that when you weighed all of the pressures, there wasn't enough of a popular movement to get them to come through when it mattered.

This was also part of the problem with the Rainbow Coalition, in my opinion [progressive political organization led by Jesse Jackson]. I mean, Jesse Jackson was in a very strong position a couple years ago with the Rainbow Coalition, and he had a choice. His choice was, "Am I going to use this opportunity to help create a continuing grassroots organization which will keep on working after the election, or am I going to use it as my own personal vehicle of political promotion?" And he more or less chose the latter—so it died. Therefore it was a complete waste of time: anybody who spent time working on that campaign was wasting their time, because it was used as an electoral platform, and that never makes sense. I mean, whenever somebody says "I want to become President," you can forget it— as President, they won't be any different from George Bush.

So as far as I can see, getting proportional representation in the United States today would have basically no effect, the effect would be essentially zilch—just because there's nothing around to take advantage of it. On the other hand, if it was passed at a time when you had popular grassroots organizations of the kind that developed, say, in Haiti in the late 1980s, sure, then it could make a difference. But of course, it's only under those circumstances that you would ever *get* proportional representation in the first place.

So in my view, any of these things could be fine if they're being used as organizing tools to try to get things going: they're a waste of time if you actually take them seriously in themselves, but if they're understood simply as a part of larger popular struggles—so this is what you're focusing on right now, but the purpose isn't to get some words written down somewhere or some person into office, but rather it's to get people to understand the *importance* of the words and the need to keep fighting for them—yeah, then it can mean something.

WOMAN: *So you think that trying to develop a third party here might be worth doing?*

Sure, absolutely—I think that could be a very important step. Take Canada again: why does Canada have the health-care program it does? Up until the mid-1960s, Canada and the United States had the same capitalist health service: extremely inefficient, tons of bureaucracy, huge administrative costs, millions of people with no insurance coverage—exactly what would be amplified in the United States by Clinton's proposals for "managed competition" [put forward in 1993].[21] But in 1962 in Saskatchewan, where the N.D.P. is pretty strong and the unions are pretty strong, they managed to put through a kind of rational health-care program of the sort that every industrialized country in the world has by now, except the United States and South Africa. Well, when Saskatchewan first put through that program, the doctors and the insurance companies and the business community were all screaming—but it worked so well that pretty soon all the other Provinces wanted the same thing too, and within a couple years guaranteed health care had spread over the entire country. And that happened largely because of the New Democratic Party in Canada, which does provide a kind of cover and a framework within which popular organizations like unions, and then later things like the feminist movement, have been able to get together and do things.

Now, in the United States there are also a lot of popular organizations, but they're all separate, there's no framework to start bringing them together. So developing a popularly-based third party here could be a very important step towards that, and I think it should be pursued.

In fact, there have even been some encouraging developments in recent years in getting something like that off the ground—I'm thinking of the emergence of the New Party, specifically, which is sort of trying to follow the Canadian model. So again, I don't think that we should have any illusions about working through the political system, and I'm not much of a fan of political parties—but the New Party is really the first serious third-party alternative that I've seen in the United States: seriously thought-out, trying to create grassroots structures, using politics the way it ought to be used, as an organizing and pressuring technique, and hoping ultimately to get to the point where it could have real influence. Now, they're not going to make structural reforms—that requires much bigger changes, changes in the institutions. I mean, when the N.D.P. got into power in Ontario in 1990, they couldn't really do anything, they just carried out the normal right-wing policies, and in the next national election [in 1993] they got like two votes, nobody wanted to bother with them anymore. But even given those limitations, I still think it's important for a country to have something like that—there's a lot of potential to help make people's lives better, and it certainly could be a basis for moving further and pressing for larger changes.

In fact, that same kind of thinking extends to electoral politics in general, in my view. I mean, right now voting decisions in the United States are pretty subtle tactical matters, in which the policy differences between the two major parties are not great. But just because I say they're "tactical," I don't mean to demean it: the decisions that have serious human consequences and matter for people are *mostly* tactical judgments, after all. Like, we can have big discussions about what society ought to look like in the future, which is fine, but that doesn't affect what happens to people in their lives right now, except extremely indirectly. What happens to people in their daily lives usually depends on small, difficult, tactical assessments about where to put your time and energy—and one of those decisions is whether you should vote, and if so, who should you vote for. And that can be an extremely important decision, with significant implications.

So for example, we have a national election coming up in the United States soon [in 1996], and I don't really know of any very strong arguments one way or another about who to vote for—but that's not to say that that judgment is an unimportant one: I think it's very important. I mean, I'll vote for Clinton, holding my nose—but the reason has nothing at all to do with big policy issues; there I can't really see too much difference. What it has to do with are things like who's going to get appointed to the judiciary: there are some differences between the Republicans and Democrats on questions like that, and who's appointed to the judiciary happens to have a big effect on people's lives. They may be small policy differences when you look at the big picture—but remember, there's a huge amount of power out there, and small policy differences implementing a huge amount of power can make big differences to people. Or there might be a slight difference in things like the earned income tax credit [a tax refund program for poor working individuals and families]. Okay, that makes a lot of difference for people whose kids are hungry in downtown Boston, say. So that'll be my decision in this election—again, holding my nose. And that's the way it is at the upper levels of our political system generally, I think.

Actually, one way for third parties to address this situation is to run "fusion" candidates—meaning, you have your own third-party ballot-line which stands for whatever you stand for, say for social-democratic-type programs, but then you have that ballot-line vote go to one of the main-party candidates in the election, based on these sort of tactical decisions. That's possible in some jurisdictions. And it's a compromise way for a third party to preserve a genuine policy identity and commitment, while nevertheless letting people make the small tactical voting choices that can make a real difference to people—and I think it's a very plausible compromise.

## Boycotts

MAN: *Do you think it would help to undermine corporate power if people were to begin making consumer choices that directly affect companies like United Fruit [renamed Chiquita], which are the most actively involved in exploiting Third World countries—like, stop buying their bananas, say, stop buying their coffee?*

Again, if only a few people do it, it isn't going to have any effect—it just means that some guy picking bananas in East Costa Rica isn't going to have enough money to feed his children tomorrow. But if it's done on a large enough scale that it can have an impact on the corporate structure, sure, then it could mean something.

I mean, suppose you stopped consuming altogether—you can live on subsistence farming in the United States in a lot of places, so suppose you did that. The effect on the general society would be exactly as if you decided to commit suicide: it would simply go on as before, but without you. Bear in mind that a lot of these things about "let's really make a change by withdrawing from the world and living a decent life" have precisely the social effect of suicide—well, that's a little too extreme, because people might notice and become interested and involved, so maybe it's a little bit more than suicide. But not a lot. And in fact, the only thing that does differentiate it from suicide is when you use it as an organizing tool.[22] Otherwise not, otherwise in fact it is just like suicide.

WOMAN: *Would you ever advocate a boycott as a tactic, though, assuming that it was coordinated and on a large enough scale?*

Well, tactics depend on the specific situations you're faced with—I don't think you can say very much worthwhile about them in the abstract. So there might be a particular moment when a boycott of something would be helpful. But as a general matter, I don't think they really make a lot of sense, frankly.

I mean, suppose we got millions of people to stop buying: what would happen? The economic system barely functions as it is—I mean, the contemporary economic system is a complete catastrophe, an absolutely catastrophic failure. For instance, the International Labor Organization recently gave its latest estimate of unemployment worldwide—"unemployment" they define as meaning not having enough work to meet a subsistence level, so maybe you can sell some handkerchiefs at a street corner or something, but you don't have enough work to survive on your own. They estimate that at about 30 percent of the world's population—which makes it a lot worse than the Great Depression.[23] Alright? Now, there's a ton of work to be done in the world—everywhere you look there's work that ought to be done. And the people who don't have work would be delighted to do it. So what you've got is a huge number of idle hands, a vast amount of work that ought to be done, and an economic system that is incapable of putting those two things together. Okay, absolutely catastrophic failure. Boycotts aren't going to overcome that failure, they're just going to make it worse.

So you know, they may be worthwhile as a tactic at some point, but what's really required is just a complete rethinking of the entire nature of economic interactions and structures—there really is no other way to overcome this whole massive failure of the economy.

## "A Praxis"

MAN: *Dr. Chomsky, as I listen to you talk and give your marvelous analysis of the destructions of capitalism and American foreign policy, and even as I hear you today give us some of your perspectives on more practical issues of activism, I'm often struck by what I hear to be an underlying generality to your advice: it seems there's almost the absence of a concrete program. Don't you think that it would be helpful to give people a little bit more guidance about what to do specifically, especially since people are so directionless these days?*

*What I'm saying is, I don't see a revolutionary "praxis" in your politics—and I'm wondering why that is.*

Well, when you say there's no "praxis," I don't exactly know what that means. There are plenty of things that can be done; I don't think they have to be described with fancy terms. And we just do the things that can be done, the kinds of things that are the next stage. There aren't any general formulas about that—you just ask where you are, what are the problems that exist, where are people ready to move? And then you try to do something with them. There's a whole spectrum of actions you can take, and there's no simple answer as to which ones should have the priority—people judge differently.

But I'd be very skeptical if somebody comes along with a "praxis"—you know, some formula saying, "Here's the way we're supposed to do it." I'd be *really* skeptical about that, if I were you.

## The War on Unions

WOMAN: *Noam, I know a lot of people fighting for Workmen's Compensation [i.e. for on-the-job injuries] and things like that, and sometimes they've said to me, "If I try to get together with other workers to press for changes, I'm going to get in trouble, I'll lose my job—what the hell can I do except look out for Number One?" They're not happy about that option, nobody's happy about saying, "All I can do is duck and cover and look out for myself, never be loyal to anybody else or support other workers"—it's just that there are these consequences that they can't deal with. I don't have an answer for them, I really don't know what to say to that.*

Yeah, there really *is* no answer, unless there are organizations—in this case, unions—that are strong enough to fight for them. I mean, if you don't have solidarity and organization and you're just out there alone fighting a big system of power, there's not very much that you can do. It's like if you're walking down the streets of Haiti [under the military junta] and somebody comes up to you and says, "What should I do?"—the answer "Go attack the police station" is not very helpful.

The only thing that these people looking for workmen's comp can do is be involved in strong enough organizations, and in this case that means unions—or maybe they can get somebody from the National Lawyers Guild [progressive law organization] or something to help them work through the legal structures. Short of having an organization that you can be part of that will defend you, though, there's really not much you can do—and that's precisely why there's been such a passionate effort by the business world and the government to try to destroy unions. I mean, ever since the Wagner Act first got passed in 1935, there has been a sustained campaign in the United States to destroy the labor movement and to overcome this tragedy. And there's a very good reason for that: if people are all alone, they really are defenseless, they just assume "I can only look out for myself," and then that builds up a real privatization of interests, which in turn contributes to their oppression. But of course, the dynamic also goes the other way too—when you organize with other people, you develop your sense of solidarity and sympathy, and that helps break down the oppression.

In fact, this all goes back to James Madison's point again: there are "parchment barriers" which say that you *can't* fire workers for trying to organize, there are federal laws that make that completely illegal. But because for whatever reason people have not been able to fight to maintain those laws, the government just doesn't enforce them anymore. I mean, the reason the people you're talking about *can* be fired is that the government is a criminal operation: it doesn't enforce the laws. Therefore employers have this real weapon over people's heads, which is a very powerful one, as you say.

Actually, there was an interesting article about this in *Business Week* a little while ago. It was about the destruction of unions in the United States, and what they pointed out—kind of casually, not making a big point of it— is that part of the way that unions have been destroyed here is just by a huge increase in illegal firings, particularly during the 1980s. The Wagner Act makes that flatly illegal, but since the federal government is a criminal operation and doesn't enforce the laws, employers just do whatever they feel like. The same thing was true with industrial accidents: they shot way up in the 1980s, because the Reagan administration just refused to enforce the laws regulating workplace safety. And this is all right out in the open— like, *Business Week* says it straight out: "illegal firings," nobody's trying to cover it up.[24]

WOMAN: *Can't employers fire employees "at will" in the U.S., though?*

No—if employees are trying to organize and they get fired, that's against the law, it's flatly illegal.[25]

WOMAN: *It's tough to prove, though.*

It's tough to prove if the government won't prosecute, or if the courts won't hear it, or if the National Labor Relations Board is set up in such a way that you've got to work for five years before your case ever gets heard—by which time everybody's either gone away or dropped dead or something. I mean, these are all just various techniques of state criminality to evade very clear legislation. In fact, the United States has been censured by the International Labor Organization for violating international labor standards—it's probably the only industrial society the I.L.O. has ever censured, because this is a U.N. agency, so it's largely paid for by the U.S., and they never say anything bad about the people who pay their wages. But the I.L.O. in 1991 censured the United States for violating international labor standards at the time of the Caterpillar strike, when the government permitted the corporation to bring in scabs [workers who cross the picket-line] to break the strike.[26]

And the same sorts of things are happening under Bill Clinton too. So one of the campaign issues that got Clinton a lot of labor support in 1992 was that he promised to put some teeth in the law that makes it illegal for employers to hire scabs—which basically destroys any strike. I mean, when you've got a huge unemployed labor force, and you don't have a sense of working-class solidarity in the population, and a ton of people are desperate, if you go on strike and get replaced by scabs, okay, that's the end of the strike—so that kills strikes. Now, this is unheard of: no modern country permits this. In fact, at the time that the I.L.O. censured the U.S., only the U.S. and South Africa allowed it, though by now I think it's spreading for all kinds of reasons, especially in England. But one of Clinton's big campaign promises in '92 was that he was going to put a stop to this practice—and just now he's sort of backed off from that, under the threat of a filibuster [the practice of blocking legislation in Congress by indefinitely prolonging debate]. The people in Congress who were pushing it said, rightly or wrongly, that they couldn't overcome a filibuster—and so he stopped.[27]

Well, that's again the same interaction: there are already laws on the books that make hiring scabs illegal, but laws only get enforced if people are willing to fight for them, otherwise they don't get enforced. I mean, it's nice to have the laws, but it's nice partly because it makes it easier to struggle for your rights—it's not that the laws *give* you the rights. Laws can be on the books and mean absolutely nothing, as in this case.

There are also a number of other tricks which are being used all around the world to destroy unions. So for example, in England under Margaret Thatcher [Prime Minister from 1979 to '90], which was very similar to Reaganite America in many ways, there was also a major effort to try to destroy the labor movement—and by now it's pretty much gone there too. It's not quite as bad as the United States yet, but it's going that way. And remember, the labor movement used to be very strong in England, just like in Canada. In fact, the British labor movement led the way in a lot of respects in pushing through the wave of modern social reform after the Second World War. But now employers in England are allowed to pay differential wages to workers depending on whether or not they unionize—in other words they can say, "If you refuse to join the union I'll increase your wages; if you join the union I'll lower your wages." Well, that's devastating for unions.

Or take another trick they just instituted there, which is absolutely lethal for organizing. Union dues have traditionally been paid by a check-off: you agree that some part of your salary is going to be deducted for union dues, just like some part of it gets deducted for Social Security. Well, the Conservative John Major government in England just passed an administrative regulation or something that requires all union members to regularly renew their authorization for this check-off—meaning the British labor movement now has to reach six million people somewhere and periodically get them to sign a statement saying, "I agree to continue doing this." Alright, that is just an *incredible* burden. Even the mainstream British press pointed out that if you tried to do that to banks, like make banks regularly get written agreements from everybody they've ever lent money to or something that they're still going to pay it back, the financial system would probably collapse.[28] And the labor movement mostly runs by unpaid volunteers— they don't have the money to pay people, so it's usually volunteers who keep the unions going. So now those volunteers have to take time off from their other activities to try to round up six million people from all around the country, who've moved since you last heard of them and this and that, just to get them to sign some statement they've already signed before allowing the unions to make this check-off of dues.

Well, that's the kind of thing that's been happening all over the place in recent years—and it's all going to keep on going. I mean, there are all kinds of ways in which power can try to destroy popular organizations: it doesn't have to be death squads like it is in the Third World. And unless there is enough popular pressure and organizing to overcome it—and in fact, *progress*—they'll win. So I don't know how many of you have tried to organize these days, but it's extremely hard—partly just because there are a lot of barriers that have been set up to make it very difficult to do, many of them instituted in the 1980s. But they're obstacles we're just going to have to overcome.

## Inner-City Schools

WOMAN: *Noam, a number of activists I know are on welfare, and their children are going to public schools that increasingly are resembling prisons: there are armed guards in the halls, there's a high level of violence. And I know some of these kids, they're really brutalized—if they're not chroni-*

*cally depressed, then they're violent: violent in language, violent in fact. One of the mothers recently told me—and she's a pretty radical person— that the conservative "School Choice Movement" [whereby the state would subsidize tuition at private institutions instead of administering public schools] really is appealing to her. It surprised me, but she said, "The left isn't addressing the problem of the schools, the left is sentimental about public education." I'm wondering what you think about that?*

I think there's a lot of truth to it. I mean, it's the same with crime—people are really scared, especially people in poor neighborhoods. It's not so bad where I live, in the fancy suburbs, but if you live in a poor neighborhood, it's frightening—unpleasant things can happen to you and your children. And when it's frightening, people want something to protect themselves—and if protecting yourself means having armed guards all around, or calling for more use of the death penalty or something, well, then you'll go for that. If the choices are narrowed to your child being attacked in the halls and getting a rotten education, or having "private choices"—sure, people will pick the "private choices." But the task of the left is to *extend* those options, to let people know that there is another option, the option of a decent life: which is neither schools as prisons, nor pull yourself out and let everybody else stay in the prison—which is what the whole "privatization of education" story is really about.

But sure: if people can't see any other alternatives, they'll say "I'll pull myself out." In fact, I did the same thing. Why do I live in the suburbs? Because my wife and I wanted our kids to go to a good school, first person to tell you. Of course I did that, and people who have that option will do it— but the idea is to set up a system in which people don't ever have to face that narrow set of alternatives, all of them awful.

I do think it's true, though, that at this point the left is basically offering nothing in the way of alternatives. What it *ought* to be getting across is the message, "Look, this is *not* the full range of alternatives, there are others"—and then it should present the others. And the others are not utopian. I mean, just look at the history of inner-city schools in the United States: there was a period, not so far back, when many of the inner-city schools here were extremely good—in fact, some of the black inner-city schools in Washington had among the highest college-acceptance rates in the country.[29] Or take my own family, for example: they were immigrants from Eastern Europe—not peasants, but from a very poor Eastern European background—and they went through ordinary city schools in New York, some of them went to the City College, and they got very good educations. In fact, the City College of New York used to be one of the best schools in the country: public city school, no reason why it shouldn't be.

So good public education can certainly be achieved—but of course, like everything else, it's going to depend on the general social and economic structure in which it operates. I mean, it's true that things like violence and rotten schools are destroying the cities—but they're destroying them because of a social structure that we've just got to change, from the bottom up. And yes, until people can see some hope of changing it, they're going to pick from within the rotten set of options that are being presented to them.

## Defending the Welfare State

WOMAN: *Noam, since you're an anarchist and often say that you oppose the existence of the nation-state itself and think it's incompatible with true socialism, does that make you at all reluctant to defend welfare programs and other social services which are now under attack from the right wing, and which the right wing wants to dismantle?*

Well, it's true that the anarchist vision in just about all its varieties has looked forward to dismantling state power—and personally I share that vision. But right now it runs directly counter to my goals: my immediate goals have been, and now very much are, to defend and even strengthen certain elements of state authority that are now under severe attack. And I don't think there's any contradiction there—none at all, really.

For example, take the so-called "welfare state." What's called the "welfare state" is essentially a recognition that every child has a right to have food, and to have health care and so on—and as I've been saying, those programs were set up in the nation-state system after a century of very hard struggle, by the labor movement, and the socialist movement, and so on. Well, according to the new spirit of the age, in the case of a fourteen-year-old girl who got raped and has a child, her child has to learn "personal responsibility" by not accepting state welfare handouts, meaning, by not having enough to eat. Alright, I don't agree with that at any level. In fact, I think it's grotesque at any level. I think those children should be saved. And in today's world, that's going to have to involve working through the state system; it's not the only case.

So despite the anarchist "vision," I think aspects of the state system, like the one that makes sure children eat, have to be defended—in fact, defended very vigorously. And given the accelerating effort that's being made these days to roll back the victories for justice and human rights which have been won through long and often extremely bitter struggles in the West, in my opinion the immediate goal of even committed anarchists should be to defend some state institutions, while helping to pry them open to more meaningful public participation, and ultimately to dismantle them in a much more free society.

There are practical problems of tomorrow on which people's lives very much depend, and while defending these kinds of programs is by no means the ultimate end we should be pursuing, in my view we still have to face the problems that are right on the horizon, and which seriously affect human lives. I don't think those things can simply be forgotten because they might not fit within some radical slogan that reflects a deeper vision of a future society. The deeper visions should be maintained, they're important—but dismantling the state system is a goal that's a lot farther away, and you want to deal first with what's at hand and nearby, I think. And in any realistic perspective, the political system, with all its flaws, does have opportunities for participation by the general population which other existing institutions, such as corporations, don't have. In fact, that's exactly why the far right wants to *weaken* governmental structures—because if you can make sure that all the key decisions are in the hands of Microsoft and General Electric and Raytheon, then you don't have to worry anymore about the threat of popular involvement in policy-making.

So take something that's been happening in recent years: devolution— that is, removing authority from the federal government down to the state governments. Well, in some circumstances, that would be a democratizing move which I would be in favor of—it would be a move away from central authority down to local authority. But that's in abstract circumstances that don't exist. Right now it'll happen because moving decision-making power down to the state level in fact means handing it over to private power. See, huge corporations can influence and dominate the federal government, but even middle-sized corporations can influence state governments and play one state's workforce off against another's by threatening to move production elsewhere unless they get better tax breaks and so on. So under the conditions of existing systems of power, devolution is very anti-democratic; under other systems of much greater equality, devolution could be highly democratic—but these are questions which really can't be discussed in isolation from the society as it actually exists.

So I think that it's completely realistic and rational to work within structures to which you are opposed, because by doing so you can help to move to a situation where then you can challenge those structures.

Let me just give you an analogy. I don't like to have armed police everywhere, I think it's a bad idea. On the other hand, a number of years ago when I had little kids, there was a rabid raccoon running around our neighborhood biting children. Well, we tried various ways of getting rid of it— you know, "Have-A-Heart" animal traps, all this kind of stuff—but nothing worked. So finally we just called the police and had them do it: it was better than having the kids bitten by a rabid raccoon, right? Is there a contradiction there? No: in particular circumstances, you sometimes have to accept and use illegitimate structures.

Well, we happen to have a huge rabid raccoon running around—it's called corporations. And there is nothing in the society right now that can protect people from that tyranny, except the federal government. Now, it doesn't protect them very *well*, because mostly it's run by the corporations, but still it does have some limited effect—it can enforce regulatory measures under public pressure, let's say, it can reduce dangerous toxic waste disposal, it can set minimal standards on health care, and so on. In fact, it has various things that it can do to improve the situation when there's this huge rabid raccoon dominating the place. So, fine, I think we ought to get it to do the things it can do—if you can get rid of the *raccoon*, great, then let's dismantle the federal government. But to say, "Okay, let's just get rid of the federal government as soon as we possibly can," and then let the private tyrannies take over *everything*—I mean, for an anarchist to advocate that is just outlandish, in my opinion. So I really don't see any contradiction at all here.

Supporting these aspects of the governmental structures just seems to me to be part of a willingness to face some of the complexities of life for what they are—and the complexities of life include the fact that there are a lot of ugly things out there, and if you care about the fact that some kid in downtown Boston is starving, or that some poor person can't get adequate medical care, or that somebody's going to pour toxic waste in your backyard, or anything at all like that, well, then you try to stop it. And there's only one institution around right now that can stop it. If you just want to be pure and say, "I'm against power, period," well, okay, say, "I'm against the federal government." But that's just to divorce yourself from any human concerns, in my view. And I don't think that's a reasonable stance for anarchists or anyone else to take.

## Pension Funds and the Law

MAN: *Mr. Chomsky, if what I've been told is correct, almost half of publicly-owned stock in the United States is in privately-held pension trusts, such as union trust funds. I'm wondering, if restrictions like those under E.R.I.S.A. [the Employee Retirement Income Security Act] can be modified so that workers could control their own funds, do you think that it would be possible to support a collaborative or union-based or popularly-based effort to direct that money towards socially responsible investment—like away from companies that are breaking unions and so on?*

Well, notice that whatever the numbers are, it's huge—but that money is *not* in the hands of labor unions, it's in the hands of Goldman Sachs [investment firm]. And in fact, if the government enforced the laws, the trustees of those pension funds would be in serious trouble right now—because they have violated their legal responsibility to invest those funds in safe investments. For instance, they are investing your pensions in things like junk bonds in Mexico—and the people making those investment decisions would be legally liable for that, if we applied our laws, because they have a trust to invest those funds in secure investments, and they don't do it. They just do whatever they want with them. Now, they're *not* going to be in trouble, because we don't have a real justice system—we only go after poor people. But they should be, and in fact, I think the labor movement ought to ask for that now: like, Rubin, the guy who's Secretary of the Treasury, he should probably be in jail just because of the Mexican economic collapse alone [in December 1994], which he allowed to happen.[30]

But the point is, you could democratize the unions enough so that they could actually take *control* of their own resources. And that would be a very important step. I mean, there's a lot of potential for activism and popular-based efforts there, you're right. And it doesn't have to stop at their own pensions, you know: what about the factories in which they work? Why should they be in the hands of private investors? That's not a law of nature. Why should a corporation have the rights of an individual?[31] A corporation is a public trust: you go back just a century, and governments were taking away corporate charters because corporations weren't living up to the "public interest." [32] It's a very recent idea that these totalitarian institutions should be totally unaccountable.

So, yes, workers ought to have control of their pension funds—but also everything else too: that is, the society ought to be democratized. And this is not a particularly radical idea, actually: you go back to the guys who founded the American Federation of Labor a century ago—the A.F.L. is not a flaming radical organization—they said, look, working people ought to control the places where they work, there's no reason why they should be controlled by some rich guy out there who put some money into it and has nothing to do with it.[33] That's true too, just like it's true of pension funds—and that would be a move towards a democratic society, as was always understood in fact, until the independent working-class culture was eliminated in the United States. So pension funds are only a part of it: a big part, but only part.

MAN: *What do you think the role of law is generally in the whole scheme of control?*

Well, law is a bit like a printing press—it's kind of neutral, you can make it do anything. I mean, what lawyers are taught in law school is chicanery: how to convert words on paper into instruments of power. And depending where the power is, the law will mean different things.

MAN: *So you don't think there's any legal basis for the hegemony of American corporations, especially in the way that the Fourteenth Amendment was interpreted to consider them individuals, with individual rights?*

Well, you know, "legal basis" is a funny notion: what has a legal basis is a matter of power, not law—like, the Fourteenth Amendment doesn't say anything about corporations. During the nineteenth century, there was just a change in the legal status of corporations—a change which would have absolutely appalled Adam Smith, or Thomas Jefferson, or any other Enlightenment thinker. In fact, Smith warned against it, and Jefferson lived long enough to see the beginnings of it—and what he said is, if what he called the "banks and moneyed incorporations" got the rights that they in fact ended up receiving, we would have a form of absolutism worse than the one we thought we were fighting against in the American Revolution.[34] And those rights simply were granted—they weren't granted by Congress, and in other countries they weren't granted by Parliaments; they were granted by judges, lawyers, corporate representatives, and others, completely outside the democratic system. And they simply created another world—they created a world of absolutist power which was very new.[35]

There's a lot of good work on this by what are called Critical Legal historians, Morton Horwitz at Harvard and others. Also, Oxford University Press has a book by a historian at the University of California named Charles Sellers, who discusses some of this: it's called *The Market Revolution*.[36] That's the basic story, though: these laws were made by a big power-play, completely outside of popular control. Okay, as usual, the guys with the guns are the ones that decide what the law is.

## Conspiracy Theories

MAN: *Noam, you mentioned earlier how "conspiracy theories" take up a lot of energy in the left movements these days, particularly on the West Coast and with respect to the Kennedy assassination—and you said that in your view, it's a totally wasted effort. Do you really feel there's nothing at all worthwhile in that kind of inquiry?*

Well, let me put it this way. Every example we find of planning decisions in the society is a case where some people got together and tried to use whatever power they could draw upon to achieve a result—if you like, those are "conspiracies." That means that almost everything that happens in the world is a "conspiracy." If the Board of Directors of General Motors gets together and decides what kind of car to produce next year, that's a conspiracy. Every business decision, every editorial decision is a conspiracy. If the Linguistics Department I work in decides who to appoint next year, that's a conspiracy.

Okay, obviously that's not interesting: all decisions involve people. So the real question is, are there groupings well outside the structures of the major institutions of the society which go around them, hijack them, undermine them, pursue other courses without an institutional base, and so on and so forth? And that's a question of fact: do significant things happen because groups or subgroups are acting in secret outside the main structures of institutional power?

Well, as I look over history, I don't find much of that. I mean, there are *some* cases—for instance, at one point a group of Nazi generals thought of assassinating Hitler. Okay, that's a conspiracy. But things like that are real blips on the screen, as far as I can see. Now, if people want to spend time studying the group of Nazi generals who decided it was time to get rid of Hitler, that's a fine topic for a monograph—maybe somebody will write a thesis about it. But we're not going to learn anything about the world from it, at least nothing that generalizes to the next case—it's all going to be historically contingent and specific; it'll show you how one particular group of people acted under particular circumstances. Fine.

And if you look at the place where investigation of "conspiracies" has absolutely flourished, modern American history, I think what's notable is the *absence* of such cases—at least as I read the record, they almost never happen. I mean, occasionally you'll find something like the Reaganites, with their off-the-shelf subversive and terrorist activities, but that was sort of a fringe operation—and in fact, part of the reason why a lot of it got exposed so quickly is because the institutions are simply too powerful to tolerate very much of that stuff. As far as the Pentagon goes, sure, the Services will push their own interests—but typically they do it in pretty transparent ways.

Or take the C.I.A., which is considered the source of a lot of these conspiracies: we have a ton of information about it, and as I read the information, the C.I.A. is basically just an obedient branch of the White House. I mean, sure, the C.I.A. has done things around the world—but as far as we know, it hasn't done anything on its own. There's very little evidence—in fact, I don't know of any—that the C.I.A. is some kind of rogue elephant, you know, off on its own doing things. What the record shows is that the C.I.A. is just an agency of the White House, which sometimes carries out operations for which the Executive branch wants what's called "plausible deniability": in other words, if something goes wrong, we don't want it to look like we did it, those guys in the C.I.A. did it, and we can throw some of them to the wolves if we need to.[37] That's basically the role of the C.I.A., along with mostly just collection of information.

It's the same with the Trilateral Commission, the Council on Foreign Relations, all these other things that people are racing around searching for conspiracy theories about—they're "nothing" organizations. Of course they're *there*, obviously rich people get together and talk to each other, and play golf with one another, and plan together—that's not a big surprise. But these conspiracy theories people are putting their energies into have virtually nothing to do with the way the institutions actually *function*.

The Kennedy-assassination cult is probably the most striking case. I mean, you have all these people doing super-scholarly intensive research, and trying to find out just who talked to whom, and what the exact contours were of this supposed high-level conspiracy—it's all complete nonsense. As soon as you look into the various theories, they always collapse, there's just nothing there.[38] But in many places, the left has just fallen apart on the basis of these sheer cults.

MAN: *There's perhaps one exception, though—what about Martin Luther King's assassination?*

That's interesting—see, that's the one case where you can imagine pretty plausible reasons why people would have wanted to kill him, and I would not be in the least surprised if there in fact *was* a real conspiracy behind that one, probably a high-level conspiracy. I mean, the mechanisms were there, maybe they would have hired somebody from the Mafia or something to do it—but that conspiracy theory is perfectly plausible, I think. And interestingly, I'm not aware that there's been very much inquiry into it—or if there has been, I haven't heard about it.[39] But in the case of the one that everybody's excited about—Kennedy—I mean, nobody's even come up with a plausible *reason*.

In fact, that's a pretty dramatic contrast, isn't it: the case of the King assassination is on its face very plausible, and the case of the Kennedy assassination is on its face extremely implausible—yet look at the difference in treatment.

WOMAN: *Do you have any ideas why that might be?*

Well, there are a lot of things in a way "conspiring" to make the Kennedy assassination an attractive topic these days. I mean, the Kennedy administration was in many ways very similar to the Reagan administration—in policy and programs—but they did do one smart thing that was different: they sort of buttered up the intellectual class, as compared with the Reaganites, who just treated them with contempt. So they gave sort of an *appearance* of sharing power (it was never real) to the kinds of people who write books and articles, and make movies, and all of those things—and the result is, Camelot has always had a very beautiful image. And somehow it's all succeeded in getting most of the population to believe the lies about Kennedy. I mean, even today you can go down to poor rural black areas in the South and find pictures of him on the walls. Kennedy's role in the Civil Rights Movement was not pretty. But somehow the imagery has succeeded, even if the reality was never there.[40]

And certainly a lot of things have gone wrong in the last thirty years, for all sorts of independent reasons. I mean, the Civil Rights Movement made great achievements, but it never lived up to the hopes that many people invested in it. The anti-war movement made achievements, but it didn't end war. Real wages have been declining for twenty years.[41] People are working harder, they have to work longer hours, they have less security—things are just looking bad for a lot of people, especially young people. I mean, very few people expect the future for their children to be anything like what they had, and entry-level wages in the United States have just declined radically in the last fifteen years—for instance, wages you get for your first job after high school are now down 30 percent for males and 18 percent for females over 1980, and that just kind of changes your picture of life.[42] And one could easily go on. But the fact is, a lot of things have happened that aren't very pretty. And in this kind of situation, it's very easy to fall into the belief that we had a hero, and we had a wonderful country, and we had this guy who was going to lead us, we had the messiah—then they shot him down and ever since then everything's been illegitimate. So really there have to be serious efforts to get past this, I think.

## The Decision to Get Involved

MAN: *Noam, we've been discussing a number of activist strategies and problems—I'd like to talk for a moment about some of the reasons why people* don't *get involved in activism. Suppose somebody convinced you, at the level of your belief in most things, that it was impossible to change the country, that the basic institutional structures we have now are going to remain in place for the next 200 years—you know, more or less adapted, but the same basic structures. I'm wondering, would you behave any differently?*

Zero.

MAN: *You would behave exactly the same way?*

Same way. In fact, you don't even have to make it hypothetical—when I first got seriously involved in anti-Vietnam War activity, I was a hundred percent convinced that absolutely nothing could be done. I mean, into 1965 and '66, if we wanted to have an anti-war meeting in Boston, we'd have to find six topics—you know, "Let's talk about Venezuela, Iran, Vietnam, and the price of bread, and maybe we can get an audience that'll outnumber the organizers." And that went on for a long time. It looked impossible.

MAN: *So if you thought that the current situation was going to continue, just persist forever, you would still do it?*

Yes.

MAN: *Why, exactly?*

Well, for a number of quite simple reasons. For one thing, if somebody convinced me of that, it would be because I'm totally irrational—there's no *way* to convince anybody of such things rationally. Look, we cannot predict the weather two weeks ahead, and that's something relatively simple, it's not like human society.

MAN: *It's a hypothetical question, it gets to motivations—I'm sure none of us believe it, none of us believe you could prove it . . .*

Not only could you not prove it, you couldn't even say anything convincing about it.

MAN: *But, nevertheless, because in fact a great many people not understanding that point do feel this way, or tend to feel this way sometimes, and get depressed at those moments—what I'm wondering is, anyway, in any event, what gets you up each morning to do the things you do? Is it that you think in terms of winning a little way down the road, or is it something else?*

Well, it's hard to introspect, but to the extent that I introspect about it, it's because you basically have two choices. One choice is to assume the worst, and then you can be guaranteed that it'll happen. The other is to assume that there's some hope for change, in which case it's possible that you can help to effect change. So you've got two choices, one guarantees the worst will happen, the other leaves open the possibility that things might get better. Given those choices, a decent person doesn't hesitate.

MAN: *But is it really true that a decent person will only go that one way? I'm remembering a friend of mine who was an activist in the Sixties and intended to move into a working-class neighborhood to do organizing, and finally he decided not to. Somewhat later he went back to graduate school and became a psychiatrist, and now I'm sure he has progressive values, but he's certainly not involved in any significant way in political activity. But the choice he made back then was a very conscious one: he looked around and said, "The impact that I personally am going to have is so small, because I'm not So-and-so and So-and-so, that I feel it's just not worth giving up what I think I'll be giving up."*

I know plenty of people like that too. But see, that person now, let's say he's a rich psychiatrist somewhere—okay, he's got a lot of options, he's simply deciding at some point not to face them. They're always there. For example, he's got money: if he doesn't want to do things himself, he can give money to people who do. In fact, movement groups have existed because people who were doing other things were willing to fund them—something as trivial as that. And you can go way beyond that, of course, and still live your elegant lifestyle and do the work you want to do. I know plenty of people who have in fact divided their lives that way.

Now, of course, it's extremely easy to say, "The heck with it—I'm just going to adapt myself to the structures of power and authority, and do the best I can within them." Sure, you can do that. But that's not acting like a decent person. Look, if you're walking down the street and you see a kid eating an ice-cream cone, and you notice there's no cop around and you're hungry, you can take the ice-cream cone because you're bigger and just walk away. You can do that—probably there are people who do. But we call them pathological. On the other hand, if they do it within existing so-cial structures, we call them normal—but it's just as pathological, it's just the pathology of the general society.

Again, people always have choices, so you can decide to accept the pathology—but then do it honestly at least. If you have that grain of hon-esty in you, say: "Okay, I'm going to honestly be pathological." Or else just try to break out of it somehow.

*MAN: For a lot of people, though, it appears that there's an all-or-nothing choice—it appears that there's the choice between being "normal," patho-logical as you describe, but a normal member of society with its normal benefits and costs, having a reasonably average or perhaps elite existence, one that's accepted. And then there seems to be the "all" choice. I think the reason why it's so hard for people even just to take a leaflet, or to give a do-nation at a relatively low level which means nothing to them financially—which is less money than they're going to spend on dinner Friday night when they go out—seems to me to be because there is this psychologically very powerful effect. At some level people know that it's right, but they also know that to do it somewhat leads to doing it more—so they just close the door right at the very beginning. I'm not sure how as organizers we can manage to overcome that situation.*

I think you're right that just giving your contribution of a hundred dol-lars to the Central America Support Center or whatever is a statement that you know that that's the right thing to do—and then once you've stated that it's the right thing to do, the question arises, "How come I'm only doing this when I could be doing a million times more?" And it's very easy just to say, "Look, I'm not going to face that problem, I'm just going to for-get it all." But that's like stealing the ice-cream cone from the kid.

The reality is that there's a whole range of choices in the middle, and all of us have made them—none of us are saints, at least I'm not. I haven't given up my house, I haven't given up my car, I don't live in a hovel, I don't spend 24 hours a day working for the benefit of the human race, or any-thing like that. In fact, I don't even come close: I spend an awful lot of my time and energy just doing scientific work.

*MAN: And you don't feel guilty about that.*

Well, that's not so clear. But I certainly do devote an awful lot of my en-ergy and activity to things that I just enjoy, like scientific work. I just like it, I do it out of pleasure. And everybody else I know does the same thing.

*MAN: Do you fool yourself into believing that it increases your effective-ness as a political person somehow?*

No, that's ridiculous—it has no effect on that. And I certainly don't do it for that reason. I do it because I like it, and I think it's getting somewhere.

Look, you're not going to be effective as a political activist unless you have a satisfying life. I mean, there *may* be people who are really saints, but I've never heard of one. Like, it may be that the political activities themselves are so gratifying that they're all you want to do, and you just throw yourself into them. Okay, that's a perfectly fine thing to be—it's just that most people have other interests: they want to listen to music, they want to take a walk by the ocean, they want to watch the sunset. Any human being is too rich and complex just to be satisfied with these things, so you have to hit some kind of a balance.

Well, the choices are all there, but I think you've identified precisely why it's psychologically difficult for people to recognize that—because once you've recognized that the choices are there, you're always going to be faced with the question, why am I not doing more? But that's just the reality of life: if you're honest, you're always going to be faced with that question. And there are plenty of things to do, and also plenty of successes to point to. In fact, it's *amazing* how many successes there have been, if you really think about it.

For example, take the issue of East Timor, a big massacre. At the time that I got involved in that over a decade ago, nobody even wanted to hear about it—but after years of organizing by some pretty tireless activists, things finally got to the point where the U.S. Congress barred military aid to Indonesia. That's a tremendous change—you could save hundreds of thousands of lives that way. How many people can look back and say, "Look, I helped to save hundreds of thousands of lives"? And that's one tiny issue. So all of it was going on in secret, nobody was interested, everybody in power wanted to let it go on—but half a dozen or so people finally managed to break through.

MAN: *I'm inclined to think that most of the people who are involved in that effort, instead of feeling elated, or at least feeling a degree of satisfaction over the accomplishment, rather view it as a horrendously long campaign with very little achieved over the years.*

Suppose you're on your deathbed: how many people can look back and say, "I've contributed to helping *one* person not get killed"?

MAN: *I'm not disagreeing with you—but there's just something about our culture that causes people on the left not to see the successes.*

See, I'm not so convinced of this. If you go back to the 1960s movements, when a lot of the current ferment started, the people involved overwhelmingly were young people—and young people have a notoriously short perspective. That's part of being twenty years old: you're thinking about what's going to happen tomorrow, not what life is going to be like twenty years from now.

So look at something like the Columbia strike, which was the big thing in 1968 [hundreds of students took over Columbia University buildings for eight days to protest war-related research and the school's relations with the surrounding community]. If you remember what it was like back then, you'll recall that the sense on the Columbia campus—quite literally, I'm not exaggerating—was: "If we close down Columbia and have fun smoking pot for three weeks, the revolution will be here, and then it'll all be over and everybody will be happy and equal and free, and we can go back to our ordinary concerns." Well, you waited three weeks, the cops came in and smashed you up, and nothing changed. And there were a lot of results from that. One result was just that a lot of people gave up, said, "Well, we couldn't do it." In fact, it's rather striking that '68 around the world is considered a crucially important date—but it was really the end.

So the fact that it was dominantly a youth movement in the Sixties had good and bad aspects, and one bad aspect was this sense that if you don't achieve quickly, you'd might as well quit. But of course, that's not the way changes come. The struggle against slavery went on forever, the struggle for women's rights has been going on for centuries, the effort to overcome "wage slavery"—that's been going on since the beginnings of the industrial revolution, we haven't advanced an inch. In fact, we're worse off than we were a hundred years ago in terms of understanding the issues. Well, okay, you just keep struggling.

## "Human Nature Is Corrupt"

*MAN: Noam, another view I frequently encounter lying behind people's reticence to become involved in political activity stems from the idea that human nature is corrupt: egotistical, self-centered, anti-social, and so on— and that as a result, society will always have oppressors and oppressed, be hierarchical, exploit people, be driven by individual self-interest, etc. I often find that you can get agreement on the inhumanity of the system, or on the injustice of a war, or on some specific set of policies, but that people will refrain from becoming active about it because of a sense of hopelessness having to do with this view of human nature. Again, it may just be an excuse, a last line of defense against getting involved—but in order to deal with it as an organizer, you still have to address the claim. I'm curious what you would say to someone like that.*

Well, there's a sense in which the claim is certainly true. First of all, human nature is something we don't know much about: doubtless there is a rich and complex human nature, and doubtless it's largely genetically determined, like everything else—but we don't know what it is. However, there is enough evidence from history and experience to demonstrate that human nature is entirely consistent with everything you mentioned—in fact, by definition it has to be. So we know that human nature, and that includes our nature, yours and mine, can very easily turn people into quite efficient torturers and mass-murderers and slave-drivers. We know that—you don't have to look very far for evidence. But what does that mean? Should people therefore not try to stop torture? If you see somebody beating a child to death, should you say, "Well, you know, that's human nature"—which it is in fact: there certainly are conditions under which people will act like that.

To the extent that the statement is true, and there is such an extent, it's just not relevant: human nature also has the capacity to lead to selflessness, and cooperation, and sacrifice, and support, and solidarity, and tremendous courage, and lots of other things too.

I mean, my general feeling is that over time, there's measurable progress—it's not huge, but it's significant. And sometimes it's been pretty dramatic. Over history, there's been a real widening of the moral realm, I think—a recognition of broader and broader domains of individuals who are regarded as moral agents, meaning having rights. Look, we are self-conscious beings, we're not rocks, and we can come to get a better understanding of our own nature, it can become more and more realized over time—not because you read a book about it, the book doesn't have anything to tell you, because nobody really knows anything about this topic. But just through experience—including historical experience, which is part of our personal experience because it's embedded in the culture we enter into—we can gain greater understanding of our nature and values.

## Discovering Morality

Take the treatment of children, for example. In the medieval period, it was considered quite legitimate to either kill them, or throw them out, or treat them brutally, all sorts of things. It still happens of course, but now it's regarded as pathological, not proper. Well, it's not that we have a different moral *capacity* than people did in the Middle Ages, it's just that the situation's changed: there are opportunities to think about things that weren't available in a society that had a lower material production level and so on. So we've just learned more about our own moral sense in that area.

I think it's part of moral progress to be able to face things that once looked as if they weren't problems. I have that kind of feeling about our relation to animals, for example—I think the questions there are hard, in fact. A lot of these things are matters of trying to explore your own moral intuitions, and if you've never explored them, you don't know what they are. Abortion's a similar case—there are complicated moral issues. Feminist issues were a similar case. Slavery was a similar case. I mean, some of these things seem easy now, because we've solved them and there's a kind of shared consensus—but I think it's a very good thing that people are asking questions these days about, say, animal rights. I think there are serious questions there. Like, to what extent do we have a right to experiment on and torture animals? I mean, yes, you want to do animal experimentation for the prevention of diseases. But what's the balance, where's the trade-off? There's obviously got to be some. Like, we'd all agree that too much torture of animals for treating a disease would not be permissible. But what are the principles on which we draw such conclusions? That's not a trivial question.

MAN: *What about eating?*

Same question.

MAN: *Are you a vegetarian?*

I'm not, but I think it's a serious question. If you want my guess, my guess is that if society continues to develop without catastrophe on something like the course you can see over time, I wouldn't in the least be surprised if it moves in the direction of vegetarianism and the protection of animal rights.

Look, doubtless there's plenty of hypocrisy and confusion and everything else about the question right now, but that doesn't mean that the issue isn't valid. And I think one can see the moral force to it—definitely one should keep an open mind on it, it's certainly a perfectly intelligible idea to us.

I mean, you don't have to go back very far in history to find *gratuitous* torture of animals. So in Cartesian philosophy, they thought they'd proven that humans had minds and everything else in the world was a machine— so there's no difference between a cat and a watch, let's say, just the cat's a little more complicated. And if you look back at the French Court in the seventeenth century, courtiers—you know, big smart guys who'd studied all this stuff and thought they understood it—would as a sport take Lady So-And-So's favorite dog and kick it and beat it to death, and laugh, saying, "Ha, ha, look, this silly lady doesn't understand the latest philosophy, which shows that it's just like dropping a rock on the floor." That was *gratuitous* torture of animals, and it was regarded as if it were the torturing of a rock: you can't do it, there's no way to torture a rock. Well, the moral sphere has certainly changed in that respect—gratuitous torture of animals is no longer considered quite legitimate.

MAN: *But in that case it could be that what's changed is our understanding of what an animal is, not the understanding of our underlying values.*

In that case it probably was—because in fact the Cartesian view was a departure from the traditional view, in which you didn't torture animals gratuitously. On the other hand, there are cultures, like say, aristocratic cultures, that have fox-hunting as a sport, or bear-baiting, or other things like that, in which gratuitous torture of animals has been seen as perfectly legitimate.

In fact, it's kind of intriguing to see how we regard this. Take cock-fighting, for example, in which cocks are trained to tear each other to shreds. Our culture happens to regard that as barbaric; on the other hand, we train humans to tear each other to shreds—they're called boxing matches—and that's *not* regarded as barbaric. So there are things that we don't permit of cocks that we permit of poor people. Well, you know, there are some funny values at work there.

## Abortion

MAN: *You mentioned abortion—what's your view about that whole debate?*

I think it's a hard one, I don't think the answers are simple—it's a case where there really are conflicting values. See, it's very rare in most human situations that there's a clear and simple answer about what's right, and sometimes the answers are very murky, because there are different values, and values do conflict. I mean, our understanding of our own moral value system is that it's not like an axiom system, where there's always one answer and not some other answer. Rather we have what appear to be conflicting values, which often lead us to different answers—maybe because we don't understand all the values well enough yet, or maybe because they really are in conflict. Well, in the case of abortion, there are just straight conflicts. From one point of view, a child up to a certain point is an organ of the mother's body, and the mother ought to have a decision what to do—and that's true. From another point of view, the organism is a potential human being, and it has rights. And those two values are simply in conflict.

On the other hand, a biologist I know once suggested that we may one day be able to see the same conflict when a woman washes her hands. I mean, when a woman washes her hands, a lot of cells flake off—and in principle, each of those cells has the genetic instructions for a human being. Well, you could imagine a future technology which would take one of those cells and create a human being from it. Now, obviously he was making the argument as a reductio ad absurdum argument, but there's an element of truth to it—not that much yet, but it's not like saying something about astrology. What he's saying is true.

If you want to know my own personal judgment, I would say a reasonable proposal at this point is that the fetus changes from an organ to a person when it becomes viable—but certainly that's arguable. And besides, as this biologist was pointing out, it's not very clear when that is—depending on the state of technology, it could be when the woman's washing her hands. That's life, though: in life you're faced with hard decisions, conflicting values.

## Moral Values

MAN: *Where do you think "values" come from in the first place?*

That's an interesting question. Any answer we give is based on extremely little understanding, so nothing one says is very serious. But just from the conditions of moral judgment, I don't see how it can fail to be true that moral values are basically rooted in our nature—I think that must be true. And the reason why I say that is pretty elementary.

I mean, undoubtedly the way in which we look at things and make judgments about them and assess them has a significant and notable cultural factor. But that aside, we certainly are capable, and everybody does it, of making moral judgments and evaluations in entirely *new* situations—we do that all the time; we may not be *consciously* evaluating all the new circumstances we're faced with, but we're certainly at least tacitly doing it, and the results of those evaluations are the basis for our choices of action, our doing one thing and not another. So we're constantly making all kinds of judgments, including moral judgments, aesthetic judgments, and all sorts of others, about new things and new situations. Well, either it's being done just randomly, sort of like pulling something out of a hat—which certainly doesn't seem to be true, either introspectively or by observation—or else we're doing it on the basis of some moral system that we have built into our minds somehow, which gives answers, or at least partial answers, to a whole range of new situations.

Well, nobody knows what that system actually *is* of course—we don't understand it at all—but it does seem to be rich and complex enough so that it can apply to indefinitely many new situations.

MAN: *Obviously one couldn't map it out in detail, but how do you think such a system might be set up?*

Well, again, we really don't know at all. But a serious proposal for such a system, I think, would be that it might be something like what we know about language—and a lot is known. For example, there is a framework of basic, fundamental principles of language that are invariant in the species, they're just fixed in our biological nature somehow—they hold for all languages, and they allow for only a very limited degree of modification, which comes from early experience. Then as soon as those wired-in options for variation are fixed, children have a whole linguistic system which allows them to say new things, and to understand new things, and to interpret new expressions that nobody's ever heard before—all kinds of things like that.

Well, qualitatively speaking, that's what our system of moral judgment looks like, so it's conceivable that it has a similar kind of basis—but again, you have to find the answer, you can't just guess.

MAN: *Obviously the underlying principles can't be simple—they can't just be something like, "Thou shalt not kill."*

No—because we decide much more complex things than that. I mean, we really don't know what the fundamental principles of moral judgment actually *are*, but we have very good reason to believe that they're *there*. And that's simply because we can, in fact, make relatively consistent moral judgments, judgments which are understood by other people, and appreciated by them (sometimes with disagreement, in which case we can have moral discourse), and we can do all of that under new conditions that we've never seen before, and facing new problems and so on. Okay, unless we're angels, the structures that perform those functions got into the organism the same way other complex things did—namely, they're largely part of a genetically-determined framework, which gets marginally modified through the course probably of early experience.

Well, that's what our moral system might look like. How much variation can there be in such moral systems? Well, without understanding, we don't know. How much variation can there be in languages? Without understanding, we don't know. I mean, in the case of languages, we know that it's not much variation, and in the case of moral values I think we can make a fair guess that it also can't be much variation—and the reason is quite elementary. Our moral system appears to be complex and determinate, and there are only two factors that can enter into determining it: one is our fixed biological nature, and the other is individual experience. Well, we know that experience is extremely impoverished, it doesn't give a lot of direction—the logic being pretty much the same as when someone asks, "Why do children undergo puberty at a certain age?" Actually, nobody knows the answer to that: it's a topic that's unknown. But there are only two possible factors that can enter into it. One is something in children's pre-puberty experience which sort of sets them off undergoing puberty—say, some effect of the environment such as peer pressure, or somebody told you it would be a good idea or something. And the other is that we're just genetically designed so that under certain conditions and at a certain level of maturation, hormones take over, and at that point we undergo puberty: it's wired in.

Well, without knowing anything, everyone just assumes the second possibility. Like, if somebody came along and said they think it's peer pressure that causes puberty—it's because you see other people doing it, and you want to be like them—without knowing anything, you'd just laugh. And the reason you'd laugh is very simple: the environment is not specific enough or rich enough to determine these highly specific changes that take place. And that logic also holds for just about everything else in growth and development too—that's why people assume, without knowledge, that an embryo will become a chicken rather than a human being depending on its biological nature, not depending on the nutrition that's fed in: because the nutrition doesn't have enough information to cause those highly specific changes. Well, it looks as if moral values and our moral judgment system are of that character too.

Actually, contributing to this conclusion is just the fact that we can *have* moral discourse to begin with. So take an issue on which people were really split, take slavery. It wasn't just an intellectual debate, obviously—there was a huge amount of struggle involved—but insofar as there *was* an intellectual debate, it had a certain shared moral ground to it. In fact, the slave owners' arguments are not so simple to answer—some of them are valid, and have a lot of implications. They were taken very seriously by American workers in the late nineteenth century, for example.

For instance, the slave owners argued, "You take better care of a slave if you own it than if you rent it." Like, you take better care of your car if you own it than if you rent it, so you take better care of your worker if you own it than if you rent it—so slavery's benevolent and "free market" is morally atrocious. And the slave owners in fact said, "Look, we're a lot more benevolent than you guys with your capitalist wage-slave system." And if you look back at the literature by workers who organized into, say, the Knights of Labor and other working-class organizations of the late nineteenth century, you'll also see a strain running through their position which said: "We fought to *end* slavery, not to impose it" [i.e. the industrial wage-labor system became dominant after the Civil War].[43] So the point is, on all sides of debates like these, people understand that they have to appeal to the same basic moral principles, even if what they're doing is totally venal.

I mean, it's extremely rare even for an S.S. guard or a torturer to say, "I'm doing this because I like to be a son of a bitch." We all do bad things in our lives, and if you think back, it's very rare that you've said, "I'm doing this just because I feel like it"—people reinterpret things in order to fit them into a basic framework of moral values, which in fact we all share.

Now, I don't want to suggest that moral values are *uniform*—if you look across cultures, you do find some differences. But when you look at different languages, you also appear to find radical differences. You know they can't be there—because if the differences *really* were great, it would be impossible to acquire any of the languages. So therefore the differences have to be superficial, and the scientific question is to prove what must be true by the basic logic of the situation. Well, I think the same must be true in the case of moral judgment as well. So to go back to the original question, I don't think we can reasonably doubt that moral values are indeed rooted in our nature.

MAN: *Then if people do have this shared set of moral values, you still have to explain why everything is as corrupt and hierarchical and war-laden as it is.*

But why not ask another question? Why not ask how come there's so much sympathy, and care, and love, and solidarity? I mean, that's also true.

MAN: *That's the way I always answer the objection—there should be none of those things, because the institutions don't breed them.*

Well, there's no such thing as, "why is there so much of this and so much of that?"—there is what there is. But what there is doubtless is conditioned by the opportunities and choices that are imposed and available to people under particular social, cultural, economic, and even physical settings. So the point is to try to get to a situation where the society and all its institutions and arrangements are set up so as to maximize the options for people to pursue the healthier alternatives. And I really don't think there's been a better period in modern history for organizing towards that than there is right now, actually.

I mean, there's tremendous disillusionment all across the country—and it's world-wide incidentally: there have been cross-national studies of this, and the level of pessimism across the entire industrial world is just extraordinary. In the United States, for example, about three-quarters of the population thinks that the future is going to be "objectively worse" than the past—in other words, that their children won't live like they do.[44] About half the American population thinks that both political parties just ought to be disbanded, they're useless.[45] The disaffection from institutions is always high, and it's been going up very consistently in past years.[46] These are conditions under which organizing for social change ought to be very much possible—if we're not doing it, it's our own fault: these factors have not been true in the past.

But at the same time, it's also true that people feel hopeless. I mean, part of the disillusionment is that they just don't see anything else—they don't see a solution, or any alternatives. Even at the depths of the 1930s Depression, which was objectively much worse than today, people were never hopeless the way they are today. Most people felt it's going to get better, we can do something about it, we can organize, we can work. I mean, they had illusions too, like there were a lot of illusions about Roosevelt, for example—but the illusions were combined with something real going on. Today what people mainly feel is, it's going to get worse, and there's nothing we can do about it.

So what we're faced with is a combination of a very high degree of disillusionment, and a very low degree of hope and perception of alternatives. And that's exactly where serious organizers ought to be able to step in.

# *10*

## Turning Point

*Based on discussions in Illinois, New Jersey, Massachusetts,
New York, and Maryland in 1994 to 1996 and 1999.*

### Bringing the Third World Home

WOMAN: *What would have to happen for people to be able to do more of
the real work of society—like supporting each other and educating children—instead of just spending our whole lives working at lame jobs for
corporations?*

Actually, a lot of countries tend to emphasize those things, even today—
we don't have to look very far for models. For example, take Western Europe: those are societies not very different from ours, they have the same
corporate-run economy, the same sort of limited political system, but they
just happen to pursue somewhat different social policies, for various historical reasons. So Germany has a kind of social contract we don't have—one of
the biggest unions there just won a 35-hour work-week, for example.[1] In the
Netherlands, poverty among the elderly has gone down to flat zero, and
among children it's 4 percent, almost nothing.[2] In Sweden, mothers and fathers both get substantial parental leave to take care of their children, like a
year or something—because taking care of children is considered something
that has value in that society, unlike in the United States, where the leadership elements *hate* families.[3] I mean, Newt Gingrich and the rest of these
people may *talk* about supporting "family values," but they actually want
families destroyed—because families are not rational from the point of view
of profit-making.

So even within the range of existing societies set up almost exactly like
ours, there are plenty of other social policies you could have—and I think
our system could tolerate those things too, it really just depends if there's
enough pressure to achieve them.

Actually, you might want to take a look at an interesting volume published recently by U.N.I.C.E.F. [the United Nations Children's Fund], about treatment of children in the rich countries—it's yet to be reviewed in the *New York Times*, or anywhere else in the United States, but it's really quite revealing. It was written by a very good American economist named Sylvia Ann Hewlett, and she identifies two basic patterns of treatment, a "Continental-European/Japanese" model and an "Anglo-American" model—which just are radically different. Her conclusion is, the Continental-European/Japanese pattern has improved the status of children and families; the Anglo-American pattern has been what she calls "a war" against children and families. And that's particularly been true in the last twenty years, because the so-called "conservatives" who took over in the 1980s, aside from their love of torture and misery abroad, also happen to be passionately opposed to family values and the rights of children, and have carried out social policies which have destroyed them.[4]

Well, that's just the wrong story for the *New York Times*—so that study never gets reviewed. Instead what the *Times* editors devote the cover-story of their *Book Review* to is another extremely deep problem the United States is facing—in case you aren't aware of it, you'd really better read this. We're facing the problem that "bad genes" are taking over the United States—and part of the proof of that is that scores on S.A.T.s and I.Q. tests have been steadily declining in recent years, children just aren't doing as well as they used to.

Well, somebody who's really unsophisticated might think that the problem could have something to do with social policies that have driven 40 percent of the children in New York City below the poverty line, for example—but that issue never arises for the *New York Times*.[5] Instead the problem is bad genes. The problem is that blacks, who evolved in Africa, evolved in kind of a hostile climate, so therefore they evolved in such a way that black mothers don't nurture their children—and also they breed a lot, they all breed like rabbits. And the effect is, the gene pool in the United States is being contaminated, and now it's starting to show up in standardized test scores.[6]

This is real hard science.

The *Times*'s review starts off by saying, well, maybe the facts in these books aren't quite right, but nonetheless, one thing is clear: these are serious issues, and any democratic society which ignores them does so "at its peril."[7] On the other hand, a society doesn't ignore "at its peril" social policies that are depriving 40 percent of the children in New York City of the minimal material conditions which would offer them any hope of ever escaping the misery, destitution and violence that surround them, and which have driven them down to levels of malnutrition, disease and suffering where you can predict perfectly well what their scores are going to be on the "I.Q." tests you give them—none of that you even mention.

In fact, according to the last statistics I saw about this, 30 million people in the United States are suffering hunger. 30 million is a lot of people, you know, and that means plenty of children.[8] In the 1980s, hunger declined in general throughout the entire world, with two exceptions: sub-Saharan Africa and the United States—the poorest part of the world and the richest part of the world, *there* hunger increased. And as a matter of fact, between 1985 and 1990, hunger in the United States increased by *50 percent*—it took a couple years for the Reagan "reforms" to start taking hold, but by 1985 they were beginning to have their effects.[9] And there is just overwhelming evidence, in case it's not obvious from common sense, what the effects of this kind of deprivation are on children—physically, emotionally, and mentally. For one thing, it's well known that neural development simply is reduced by low levels of nutrition, and lack of nurturance in general. So when kids suffer malnutrition, it has permanent effects on them, it has a permanent effect on their health and lives and minds—they never get over it.[10]

And the growing hunger here isn't just among children—it's also been increasing among the elderly, to name one group. So as the *Wall Street Journal* recently pointed out in a front-page story, hunger is "surging" among the elderly: about five million older Americans, about 16 percent of the population over 60, are going hungry, they're malnourished, many of them are literally starving to death.[11] Now, in the United States we don't have starvation the way they do in Haiti or Nicaragua or something—but the deprivation is still very real. In many places it's probably worse than it is in Cuba, say, under the embargo.

So just take Boston, for example, where I live—which is a very rich city, and also maybe the world's leading medical center. There are some very fancy hospitals there, but there's also a City Hospital, which serves the rest of the population. Well, that hospital, which is not a bad hospital I should say, established a malnutrition clinic a few years ago—because after the impact of the Reaganite economic policies began to be felt, they were starting to find Third World levels of malnutrition in Boston. And it gets worse over the winter, because then families have to make the choice: do you let your kids starve, or do you let them die of the cold? Okay? That's in one of the richest cities in the world, a major medical center. That's just criminal in a country as rich as this—or anywhere, for that matter.[12]

And it's not just hunger: it turns out that contact time between parents and children has declined by about 40 percent in the United States since the 1960s—that means that on average, parents and children have to spend about 10 or 12 hours less time together a week.[13] Alright, the effects of that also are obvious: it means television as supervision, latch-key kids, more violence by children and against children, drug abuse—it's all perfectly predictable. And this is mostly the result of the fact that today, *both* parents in a family have to put in 50- or 60-hour work-weeks, with no child-support system around to help them (unlike in other countries), just to make ends meet.[14] And remember, this is in the 1990s, a period when, as *Fortune* magazine just pointed out, corporate profits are at a record high, and the percentage of corporate income going into payrolls is near a record low—that's the context in which all of this has been happening.[15]

Well, none of these things are discussed in the *New York Times Book Review* article either. They *are* discussed in the U.N.I.C.E.F. book I mentioned, but the *Times* chose not to review that one.

So to return to your question, you ask: what would have to happen for us to get social policies different from all of these? I don't think there's any reason why the "Anglo-American model" Hewlett identifies has to continue—and be extended by things like the Contract With America [a Republican Congressional policy platform launched in 1994] and the Welfare Reform Act [the "Federal Personal Responsibility and Work Opportunity Reconciliation Act," which President Clinton signed in August 1996]. These aren't laws of nature, after all; they're social-policy decisions—they can be made differently. There's a lot of space for changing these things, even in a society with the same corporate control as ours.

But why not ask another question. Why not ask why absolutist organizations have any right to exist in the first place? I mean, why should a corporation—technically a fascist organization of enormous power—have any right to tell you what kind of work you're going to do? Why is that any better than having a king tell you what kind of work you're going to do? People fought against that and overthrew it, and we can fight against it again and overthrow it.

There's plenty of challenging, gratifying, interesting, productive work around for people to do, and there are plenty of people who want to do it—they simply aren't being allowed that opportunity under the current economic system. Of course, there's also plenty of junky work that has to get done too—but in a reasonable society, that work would just be distributed equally among everybody capable of doing it. If you can't get robots to do it, fine, then you just distribute it equally.[16]

Okay, I think that's the kind of model we have to try to work towards now—and frankly, I don't see any reason why that's an impossible goal.

WOMAN: *Mr. Chomsky, I just wanted to say that I saw the* New York Times *review you were discussing, and I was absolutely appalled by it. If I was a black man in this country, I wouldn't know what to do with myself—it would just be a burning fire inside, I would feel such rage.*

How about if you were a black woman? That article took seriously the idea that black women don't nurture their children—because they evolved in Africa, where the environment was such-and-such. It was pure racism, something straight out of the Nazis.

But look: it's really not even worth talking about it. The right way to respond is just to ask, what are they doing it for? And they're doing it for a very simple reason. 30 million people in the country go hungry. 40 percent of the children in New York City, most of them black and Hispanic, live below the poverty line—which means they're destroyed, okay? And that is the result of very definite social policies that these people are supporting. Well, you want to keep making all your money, but you don't want to face any of the rest of it, so you need some kind of a cover. And what's the cover? "Bad genes." Okay, once you understand what's really motivating all of this, then at least you're in a position to deal with it.

The point is, just as it was proper at some point for the Nazis to say, "Jews are a virus that's destroying our society," it is now proper for the *New York Times* to run articles taking seriously the idea that black mothers don't nurture their children, and for the mainstream intellectual culture to pretend that these farcical books on I.Q. have any kind of scientific legitimacy.[17]

But these are such transparent ideological weapons we shouldn't even waste our time arguing about them. We should just understand them transparently for what they are: the product of a real commissar culture that is dedicated to obscuring the most elementary truths about the world, and rich, powerful people trying to justify the fact that they are pursuing social policies which are forcing children to die. It's understandable why nobody would want to face that—but it's also clear how we can change it.

### Welfare: the Pea and the Mountain

WOMAN: *You mentioned the "Contract With America" and the "Welfare Reform Act" [which replaced the Aid for Families With Dependent Children program, ending receipt of public assistance benefits by families that include an adult who has received welfare for five years, and requiring all "able-bodied" adult recipients to secure a job within two years]. I'm wondering, how do you explain the surge to the right in Washington over the past several years, beginning with the Republicans' big Congressional triumph in 1994? And what do you think is the real point of these new programs?*

Well, let me just begin with the 1994 elections, and the so-called "Contract With America." You're right that in the media that whole election was called a "landslide for conservatism" and a "political earthquake" and so on—but you really have to look at that kind of rhetoric a lot more carefully. There was an interesting fact about the Republicans' agenda, the so-called "Contract With America"—that is, only a very small number of voters even knew what it was, and when people were asked about most of its specific provisions, big majorities opposed it. So there was never really a vote on it, nobody knew what it was. And even after months of intensive and unremitting propaganda about it, less than half of the U.S. population said they had even *heard* of the Contract With America.[18] And it wasn't hidden, it was in the headlines every day. *That's* the "landslide for conservatism." And that's just a way of saying that democracy has collapsed.

As far as what it's been about, that couldn't be more obvious: it's standard free-market doctrine—huge state-subsidies for the rich, cut out everything for the poor. Very brazen. So just take a look at some of the specific provisions. For example, they had one section in the "Contract" called the "Job Creation and Wage Enhancement Act"—the things under it were, subsidies to business, tax cuts to business, and then there was one little line at the bottom which said that the "program to increase wages and create jobs" will be to eliminate "unfunded mandates," which are one of the main mechanisms to ensure that States do things like provide social programs, set regulatory standards, and so on [i.e. the "mandates" are imposed on state and local governments by Congress].[19] Okay, that's the program to "raise wages and create jobs"—and that's kind of like a symbol for the whole thing.

The main target that they've gone after, both Clinton and Congress, is what's called "welfare"—meaning that tiny component of welfare that goes to poorer people, which is approximately the size of a pea on a mountain. Meanwhile, they continue to enhance the *real* welfare—that is, the mountain of welfare that goes to richer people. And they're continuing to enhance it in the traditional two ways: first, by straight handouts to business; and second, through regressive fiscal measures [i.e. ones having a greater adverse impact on those with less money].

So first take the straight handouts part, which is the bulk of welfare. The straight handouts part is things like military spending, for example. Now, the United States isn't *defending* itself from anybody—that's not even a joke. We have almost half the military spending in the world, and who's attacking us?[20] The United States hasn't been attacked since the War of 1812—there is no country in the world that has as limited security threats as we do.[21] But we *are* defending rich people, that's true—the rich are defending themselves against the poor and the poor are paying for it, so for that, it's true, you have to keep increasing military spending. In fact, that's the main reason we have the Pentagon system in the first place: it's a vehicle to channel hundreds of billions of taxpayer dollars to the wealthy, through military contracts and technology research and so on.

Look, the Pentagon's never really been about defense: the Pentagon is about the fact that rich people can have their own computers, after decades of development paid for by the public through the state-sector—and it's about the fact that I.B.M. and other private corporations and investors are making huge profits off them. Or it's about the fact that the biggest civilian exporter in the country is the Boeing corporation, and the biggest single industry in the world, tourism, is founded largely on technology that was developed through the American military system—namely, airplanes—and that it's been pouring huge sums of money into sectors of the American economy for decades.[22] Well, the Clinton administration and Congress have increased all of those subsidies—in fact, Clinton's military budget is well above the Cold War average—and the Contract With America programs include plenty of other forms of direct handouts and subsidies to the wealthy as well.[23]

The second kind of welfare payment that's being extended is regressive fiscal measures—which are just another way of disguising welfare to the rich. So for example, if you increase tax deductions for business expenses, let's say, that is the exact financial equivalent of giving out a welfare check. I mean, suppose there's a mother with six kids and no job, and she gets a hundred-dollar check—okay, that's welfare. Now suppose it's me, somebody who's rich, and I get a hundred dollars of tax relief because I have a home mortgage: it's the same government payment. I mean, one of them is a direct sum of money and the other is hidden in regressive fiscal measures, but from an economic standpoint, they're exactly the same thing—like, it would come out exactly the same if they gave me the hundred dollars and took a hundred dollars off her taxes.

Well, if you take a look at all of the welfare that goes to the rich through regressive fiscal measures like these, it is absolutely huge. Take tax write-offs for charitable contributions: almost all of that goes to the rich, it's a way for them to cut down on their taxes—which means it's a subsidy, exactly the equivalent of a welfare check. Or take tax deductions for home mortgages: about 80 percent of that welfare goes to people with incomes of over $50,000 a year, and the deductions get disproportionately greater the higher your income—like, if you have a million-dollar home, you get a much bigger write-off than if you have a two hundred thousand-dollar home or something.[24] Or just look at income-tax deductions for business expenses: that is a massive welfare program, and it all goes to the rich. So there's a book by a Canadian writer, Linda McQuaig, which estimates that the tax loss in Canada for what are called "business entertainment deductions"—like taking your friends out to hundred-dollar seats at the baseball game, and to fancy dinners and all that kind of stuff—is not far below what would be needed to give daycare to 750,000 Canadian kids who now can't get it.[25] And remember, Canada's a far smaller country than the United States is, far smaller. Well, those are all welfare handouts too—and what's happening is they're being increased, while at the same time anything that might help poor people is being cut back.

It's striking to see the way they're doing it, actually. For instance, they decided not to go after Medicare for now—they probably will sooner or later, but for now they're not. And the reason is, rich people get Medicare. But they *are* going after Medicaid right away, because that only goes to poor people [Medicare is a federal health insurance program for the elderly and disabled, and Medicaid is a federally-funded health care program for those with low incomes]. In fact, there were three big programs that they intended to go after right from the time of the '94 election: one was Medicaid, one was Aid for Families with Dependent Children, and the third was Food Stamps. Well, Food Stamps quickly got kicked off the list. You know why? Because there's a big agri-business lobby behind it. See, Food Stamps does happen to feed poor people, but it's also a major handout to high-tech commercial agriculture and big commerce, so those interests immediately started to lobby for it—because they want it. So that was taken off the list.[26]

What about Aid for Families with Dependent Children? Well, for one thing, it's dropped very sharply since 1970, even without "Welfare Reform." I mean, compared to 1970, maximum A.F.D.C. benefits for an average family had fallen by about 40 percent in real terms by 1995.[27] In fact, we always hear in the media and from politicians how there's so much welfare for the poor in the United States, but the reality is that the United States is completely off the international spectrum in this respect—we give *far* less than any other industrialized country.[28]

Well, A.F.D.C. still has around nine million young children on it; these guys want to take five million of them off. Alright, those are *children*—average age: seven.[29] And if you just look at the families who are receiving welfare under the program, what you find is that a substantial number of the mothers are young women who've been raped, or abused, or never had any educational opportunities, and so on. Well, under the current dogmas, their children, seven-year-old children, *they* have to be taught "fiscal responsibility"—but not Newt Gingrich's constituents. They have to keep being funded by the public.[30]

So Bill Clinton and all these others are talking about "welfare reform" these days—but no one's suggesting that we put *executives* to work: they're going to keep getting welfare, it's only poor mothers who are supposed to be forced into "work obligations" [i.e. parents must obtain jobs or lose benefits after receiving welfare for a specified period]. It's these seven-year-old kids who now have to be forced to internalize our values: that there are no human rights, they don't exist, the only human rights people have are what they can gain for themselves on the labor market. And the way they're going to be forced to learn those lessons is by driving their mothers to work—instead of all this non-work like raising children. I mean, it's astonishing the sexism that has been so institutionalized in the culture that people just accept the idea that raising children isn't "work"—"work" is things like speculating in financial markets. Child-care's just taken for granted, it's supposed to come free because you don't get a paycheck for it.

## Crime Control and "Superfluous" People

The other thing the Clinton "New" Democrats and Gingrich Republicans both want is to build up crime control—and there's a very simple reason for that: you've got a big superfluous population you aren't letting survive in your system, what are you going to do with them? Answer: you lock them up. So in Reagan America, the jail population in the U.S. more than tripled—*tripled*—and it's been going up very fast ever since.[31] In the mid-1980s, the United States passed its main competitors in per capita prison population: South Africa and Russia (though now that Russia's learned our values, they've caught up with us again). So by this point, well over a million and a half people are in prison in the United States—it's by far the highest per capita prison population of the Western countries—and it's going to go way up now, because the 1994 Crime Bill was extremely harsh.[32] Furthermore, the prisons in the United States are so *inhuman* by this point that they are being condemned by international human rights organizations as literally imposing torture.[33] And these people all want to increase that—they're statist reactionaries, remember: what they really want is a very powerful and violent state, contrary to what they might say.

Also, if you just look at the *composition* of the prison population, you'll find that the crime-control policy that's been developed is very finely honed to target select populations. So for example, what's called the "War on Drugs," which has very little to do with stopping the flow of drugs, has a lot to do with controlling the inner-city populations, and poor people in general. In fact, by now over half the prisoners in federal prisons are there on drug charges—and it's largely for possession offenses, meaning victimless crimes, about a third just for marijuana.[34] Moreover, the "Drug War" specifically has been targeted on the black and Hispanic populations—that's one of its most striking features. So for instance, the drug of choice in the ghetto happens to be crack cocaine, and you get huge mandatory sentences for it; the drug of choice in the white suburbs, like where I live, happens to be powder cocaine, and you don't get anywhere near the same penalties for it. In fact, the sentence ratio for those drugs in the federal courts is 100 to 1.[35] Okay?

And really there's nothing particularly new about this kind of technique of population control. So if you look at the history of marijuana prohibitions in the United States, you'll find that they began with legislation in the southwestern states which was aimed at Mexican immigrants who were coming in, who happened to use marijuana. Now, nobody had any reason to believe that marijuana was dangerous or anything like that—and obviously it doesn't even come *close* to alcohol, let alone tobacco, in its negative consequences. But these laws were set up to try to control a population they were worried about.[36] In fact, if you look closely, even Prohibition had an element of this—it was part of an effort to control groups like Irish immigrants and so on. I mean, the Prohibition laws [which were part of the U.S. Constitution from 1919 to 1933] were intended to close down the saloons in New York City, not to stop the drinking in upper New York State. In Westchester County and places like that, everybody just continued on drinking exactly as before—but you didn't want these immigrants to have saloons where they could get together and become dangerous in the urban centers, and so on.[37]

Well, what's been going on with drugs in recent years is kind of an analog of that, but in the United States today it also happens to be race-related, for a number of reasons, so therefore it's in large part aimed against black and Latino males. I mean, this is mainly a war against the superfluous population, which is the poor working class—but the race/class correlation is close enough in the inner cities that when you go after the poor working class, you're mostly going after blacks. So you get these astonishing racial disparities in crime statistics, all across the board.[38] And the point is, the urban poor are kind of a useless population from the perspective of power, they don't really contribute to profit-making, so as a result you want to get rid of them—and the criminal justice system is one of the best ways of doing it.

So take a significant question you never hear asked despite this supposed "Drug War" which has been going on for years and years: how many bankers and chemical corporation executives are in prison in the United States for drug-related offenses? Well, there was recently an O.E.C.D. [Organization for Economic Cooperation and Development] study of the international drug racket, and they estimated that about a half-trillion dollars of drug money gets laundered internationally every year—more than half of it through American banks. I mean, everybody talks about Colombia as the center of drug-money laundering, but they're a small player: they have about $10 billion going through, U.S. banks have about $260 billion.[39] Okay, that's serious crime—it's not like robbing a grocery store. So American bankers are laundering huge amounts of drug money, everybody knows it: how many bankers are in jail? None. But if a black kid gets caught with a joint, he goes to jail.

And actually, it would be pretty easy to trace drug-money laundering if you were serious about it—because the Federal Reserve requires that banks give notification of all cash deposits made of over $10,000, which means that if enough effort were put into monitoring them, you could see where all the money's flowing. Well, the Republicans deregulated in the 1980s—so now they don't check. In fact, when George Bush was running the "Drug War" under Reagan, he actually canceled the one federal program for this which did exist, a project called "Operation Greenback." It was a pretty tiny thing anyway, and the whole Reagan/Bush program was basically designed to let this go on—but as Reagan's "Drug Czar," Bush nevertheless canceled it.[40]

Or why not ask another question—how many U.S. chemical corporation executives are in jail? Well, in the 1980s, the C.I.A. was asked to do a study on chemical exports to Latin America, and what they estimated was that more than 90 percent of them are not being used for industrial production at all—and if you look at the kinds of chemicals they are, it's obvious that what they're really being used for is drug production.[41] Okay, how many chemical corporation executives are in jail in the United States? Again, none—because social policy is not directed against the rich, it's directed against the poor.

Actually, recently there've been some very interesting studies of urban police behavior done at George Washington University, by a rather well-known criminologist named William Chambliss. For the last couple years he's been running projects in cooperation with the Washington D.C. police, in which he has law students and sociology students ride with the police in their patrol cars to take transcripts of what happens. I mean, you've got to read this stuff: it is all targeted against the black and Hispanic populations, almost entirely. And they are not treated like a *criminal* population, because criminals have Constitutional rights—they're treated like a population under military occupation. So the *effective* laws are, the police go to somebody's house, they smash in the door, they beat the people up, they grab some kid they want, and they throw him in jail. And the police aren't doing it because they're all bad people, you know—that's what they're being told to do.[42]

Well, part of the Contract With America was to increase all of this. They weren't satisfied with the 1994 Crime Bill—and the reason is, the original 1994 Crime Bill still allowed for things like Pell Grants for people in prison [i.e. college subsidies available to capable, low-income students], which are a very small expense. See, most of the people who are in jail have never completed high school, and Pell Grants help give them some degree of education. Alright, there are many studies of this, and it's turned out that the effect of Pell Grants is to cut back on recidivism, to cut back violence. But for people like the Gingrich Republicans, that doesn't make any sense—they *want* people in jail, and they want violence, so they're going to cut out small expenses like that so that we can have even more people thrown into jail.[43]

Also, all of this "crime control" spending is another huge taxpayer stimulus to the economy—mainly to parts of the construction industry, and to lawyers, and other professionals. Well, that's another very useful way to force the public to keep paying off the rich—and by now "crime control" spending is approaching the Pentagon budget in scale; it's still not quite as favored as the Pentagon, because the spending's not as sharply skewed towards the wealthy, but nevertheless it's useful.[44] And as the society keeps taking on more and more Third World-type characteristics, we should certainly expect that the repression will continue—and that it will continue to be funded and extended, through the Contract With America or whatever other technique they can come up with.

## Violence and Repression

MAN: *Dr. Chomsky, around where I work out in Fresno, California, the local government has instituted a policy where they have three S.W.A.T. teams roving the streets with rifles, to reduce the level of violence. My question for you is, as an organizer, how can one deal with the fact that this is what the people really want?*

What is what the people really want? They want S.W.A.T. teams?

MAN: *Yeah.*

Who wants them—the people in the slums?

MAN: *Well, the mayor ran his election campaign on this; it's a pilot project in California.*[45]

And who voted for him—the people in the slums?

MAN: *I don't really know . . .*

Well, there are a couple of points to be made. First of all, I don't know Fresno specifically, but the way it usually works is, voting in the United States is a very skewed affair: the wealthy have a huge amount of clout, largely because of business propaganda, but also through a whole range of other methods, including things like gerrymandering. So that's one point.

But another thing is, this whole bit about "combating violence" is something you've really got to look at more closely. So I don't know the particular area you're talking about very well, but the fact is, a large portion of the country's population is being dismissed as superfluous because they do not play a role in profit-making—and those people are increasingly being cooped up in concentration camps, which we happen to call "slums." Now, it's true that internal to those concentration camps there's a lot of violence—but that's kind of like violence internal to a family or something: wealthier sectors are pretty well insulated from it.[46]

So take me: I live in a mostly lily-white, very liberal professional suburb just outside Boston, called Lexington. And we have our own police force, which is mostly for finding stray cats and things like that. Except for one thing: it's also a Border Patrol. I mean, nobody there will tell you this, but if you want to find it out, just get some black friend of yours to drive a broken-down car into Lexington and watch how many seconds it takes before he's out.

Well, that's how the panic about combating violence tends to play out. But if you actually look at the *facts* about the general level of violence in the U.S., there's really no evidence that it's increased over the past twenty years—in fact, the statistics say it's actually decreased.[47] Furthermore, contrary to what a lot of people believe, crime rates in the United States are not all that high relative to other countries—if you look at other developed countries, like Australia and France and so on, U.S. crime rates are sort of at the high end, but not off the spectrum. In fact, about the only category in which U.S. crime rates are way off the map is homicides with guns—but that's because of crazy gun-control laws here, it doesn't particularly have to do with "crime."[48]

Now, the popular *perception* certainly is that violence is greater today— but that's mostly propaganda: that's just a part of the whole effort to make people frightened, so that they'll abandon their rights. And of course, it all has a real racist undertone to it, there are little code words that are used, "Willie Horton" kinds of things, to try to get everyone to think there's some black man out there trying to rape their daughter. [Horton was a black prisoner who raped a white woman while on furlough from prison; his image was used by the Republicans in T.V. ads to portray the Democrats as "soft on crime."] Yeah, that's the kind of image you want to convey if your goal is to keep people divided and calling for more repression in the society. And the success of it all in the last few years has been very dramatic.

In fact, the perception of more violence is rather like what's happened in the case of welfare: people's *image* is that welfare has gone way up, but the reality is, it's gone way, way down.[49] So I don't know if you've looked at the polls on this, but people's attitudes are really quite striking. For example, when you ask them, "Do you think we're spending too much on welfare or too little?," 44 percent say we're spending too much, and 23 percent say we're spending too little. But if you take exactly the same question and you just replace the word "welfare" with "assistance to the poor"—so now you're saying, "Are we giving too much or too little assistance to the poor?"—the numbers change radically: 13 percent say it's too much, and 64 percent say it's too little.[50] Alright, that's kind of funny: what's welfare? It's assistance to the poor. So how come you get this strange result? Because people have bought the racist line. The image they have of "welfare" is black mothers driving Cadillacs past some poor white guy who's working: Reaganite propaganda. And I think it's pretty much the same kind of story with the perception of more violence.

Look: the public relations industry doesn't spend billions of dollars just for the fun of it.[51] They do it for reasons, and those reasons are to instill certain imagery, and to impose certain means of social control. And one of the best means of controlling people has always been induced fear: for Hitler it was Jews and homosexuals and Gypsies; here it's blacks.

So yes, there *is* violence—but it's mostly the kind of violence that results from being cooped up in concentration camps. I mean, if you look at Hitler's concentration camps during World War II, there was also internal violence. That happens: if people are sufficiently deprived, they'll turn on one another. But when you say that people in California want S.W.A.T. teams, I doubt that the people in the concentration camps do—because those S.W.A.T. teams are at war with them. It's just that those people typically are not a part of the "public" that actually decides on things in the United States; more powerful elements do. And they decide the way they do for the same reason the liberals out in Lexington want a Border Patrol, although they won't say so of course: because you want to confine the violence somewhere else, so your own family won't be affected.

Like, take Cobb County, Georgia, the rich suburb outside Atlanta that's Newt Gingrich's district—which gets more federal subsidies than any suburban county in the United States, incidentally, despite its leader's calls to "get government off our backs" (only Arlington, Virginia, the home of the

Pentagon, and Brevard County, Florida, where the Kennedy Space Center is, get more). Well, in Cobb County, I'm sure they're also very afraid of violence and want S.W.A.T. teams to insulate them from any urban infection that might make its way out from downtown Atlanta.[52] Sure, and it's the same thing all over the place. So I suspect that's probably what you're seeing in Fresno as well.

Now, if you *really* want to talk about violence, there's plenty of it—but not the kind you're talking about. For example, take the biggest killer of them all: tobacco. Compared with tobacco, hard drugs don't even *exist*. Deaths from tobacco *far* outweigh deaths from all hard drugs combined, probably by a factor of more than a hundred.[53] Do you see Jesse Helms in jail? I mean, there used to be a House Committee that regulated among other things the tobacco industry—it's gone now, because it was flat taken over by a tobacco company—but in its last meeting, its members released a study that made it to the back pages of the newspapers, and was very interesting. It turned out that the data that everybody had been using for the last couple years on the effects of passive smoking [i.e. breathing of smoke from other people's cigarettes] were coming from tobacco-industry studies—and they were faked. People re-did the studies and found that they were a total fraud, they made the problem look far less significant.[54] Alright, that means these tobacco-industry executives and their U.S. government puppets have been killing thousands and thousands of people—they're killing young children, say, whose mothers are smoking. Are they in jail? Why isn't that violence?

In fact, right now U.S. state power is being used to force Asian countries to open their markets to advertising for American tobacco. For instance, we're telling China, "You don't allow us to advertise tobacco to the emerging markets of women and youth, and we'll close off your exports"— so then they just have to do it. Alright, recently there was a study done at Oxford University which estimated that of the kids under 20 alive today in China, about fifty million of them are going to die from tobacco-related diseases.[56] Killing fifty million people is fairly impressive, even by twentieth-century standards—why isn't that "violence"? That's the violence of the American state working for the interests of American tobacco manufacturers. You wouldn't need S.W.A.T. teams to go after that kind of violence, you'd just need to apply laws. The trouble is, it's the rich and the powerful who enforce the laws, and they don't want to apply them to themselves.

WOMAN: *Noam, you just mentioned that Gingrich's county in Georgia is one of the leading recipients of federal government subsidies—I was wondering, why didn't the Democrats make that an issue during the 1994 elections? I've never heard it before, but you'd have thought that would be a very strong tactic for them to use at the time, given the Gingrich group's campaign strategy?*

That's an interesting side-light to the '94 election story, isn't it—the absolute silence of the Democrats about that? I mean, during the whole campaign, Newt Gingrich was just slaughtering them with the line that they're always pushing the "welfare state" and the "nanny state" and all this government spending all the time—but no one in the press or in the political system ever once made the obvious rejoinder that would have wiped him out in three minutes: that *Newt Gingrich* is the leading advocate of the welfare state in the entire country. I mean, that would have been the end of the entire discussion—but the Democrats never even raised a peep. Like, nobody raised the fact that the largest employer in Cobb County is the Lockheed corporation [an armaments contractor], a publicly-subsidized/private-profit corporation that wouldn't *exist* except for taxpayer subsidies. Or nobody pointed out that 72 percent of the jobs in Cobb County are white-collar jobs in industries like electronics and computers—which are all very carefully tended by the "nanny state," and in fact wouldn't be around in the first place if it hadn't been for massive public subsidies through the military system for decades.[56]

And I think the reason for that lack of comment is pretty obvious, actually. I think the reason is that class interests overpower narrow political interests, and there's a real and very important class interest, shared right across the board in the United States, that the rich always must be protected from market discipline by a very powerful welfare state—that simply can't be called into question at all. I mean, the *poor* can be subjected to the market—that's perfectly fine. But not the rich: they need constant subsidies and protection, like they get in Cobb County.

Well, you can't say any of that *publicly*, of course, because then people might start to get the idea—and that would be very dangerous. So therefore, even if they get smashed in the elections, the Democrats still won't tell you the truth: that Newt Gingrich is the leading advocate of the "nanny state," and that what he wants is a big, powerful, interventionist government that will keep providing the rich with constant economic subsidy and protection. The 1994 elections were a perfect illustration of the point—and again, it's another sign of the kind of democracy we really have in the United States that nobody even mentioned it.

## International Capital: the New Imperial Age

MAN: *In the past twenty-five years, there has been such a massive expansion of multinational finance capital being used for speculation in international stock markets, rather than for investment and trade, that it seems by now the United States is just a colony at the mercy of the movements of international capital—it doesn't much matter who's in office, they're not the ones really setting the agenda anymore. What's the significance of that phenomenon on the international scene right now?*

Well, first of all, we really ought to be a bit more cautious with our language—including myself, because I talk this way all the time. We shouldn't talk about things like "the United States"—because there is no such entity, just like there's no such entity as "England" or "Japan" or anything like that. The *population* of the United States may be "colonized," but the *corporate interests* that are based in the United States aren't "colonized" at all. So you sometimes hear about "America in decline"—and if you look at the share of the world's manufacturing production that happens to *take place* in the United States, it's true, that is in decline. But if you look at the share of the world's manufacturing production that's done by *U.S.-based corporations*, that's not in decline at all: in fact, it's doing extremely nicely. It's just that that production is now taking place mostly in the Third World.[57] So you know, one can talk about the geographical entity "the United States"—but that is not what functions in world affairs. To be brief about it, unless you begin with an elementary class analysis, you aren't even in the real world: things like "the United States" aren't entities.

But you're right, most of the *population* of the United States is being driven towards kind of a Third World "colonized" status—it's just that we should remember, there's another sector in the world, which includes rich corporate executives and investors, plus their people in the Third World, like some Mafia thug in Russia who's running their local thing for them or some rich guy in São Paulo, and they're a much different grouping. Those people have never been doing better.

Now, about speculative capital—that's an extremely important part of this. You're absolutely correct that it's having a huge impact on national governments. This is really a major phenomenon. Just the numbers themselves are dramatic.

Back around 1970, about 90 percent of the capital involved in international economic transactions was being used for more or less productive commercial purposes, like production and trade, and about 10 percent was being used for speculation. Today those figures are reversed: by 1990, about 90 percent was being used for speculation, and by 1994 it was up to 95 percent. Furthermore, the absolute *amount* of speculative capital has just exploded: the last estimate I saw from the World Bank was that there is now about $14 trillion involved—which means there's now $14 trillion free to transfer from one national economy to another, an amount which just overwhelms any national government's resources, and leaves governments with only an extremely narrow range of choices when it comes to setting policies.[58]

Well, why has this huge growth of speculative capital happened? There have been two key reasons. The first had to do with the breakdown of the post-war world economic system, which occurred in the early 1970s. See, during the Second World War, the United States basically reorganized the world economic system and made itself into sort of the "global banker" [at the Bretton Woods United Nations Monetary and Financial Conference of

1944]—so, the U.S. dollar became the global reserve currency, it was fixed to gold, and other countries' currencies were fixed relative to the dollar. And that system was pretty much what lay behind the very substantial economic growth rate that followed in the 1950s and Sixties. But by the 1970s, the "Bretton Woods" system had become unsustainable: the U.S. no longer was strong enough economically to remain the world's banker, primarily because of the huge costs of financing the Vietnam War. So Richard Nixon at that point made a decision to just dismantle the whole arrangement: in the early 1970s he took the United States off the gold standard, he raised import duties, he just destroyed the whole system totally. Well, after this international regulatory apparatus had been destroyed, we started to get speculation against currencies on an unprecedented scale, and fluctuating financial exchanges, all these other things that have kept growing ever since.

The second main factor behind this explosion of speculative capital has been the technological revolution in telecommunications—which took place in the same period, and which suddenly made it very easy to transfer currencies from one country to another. So for example, today virtually the whole of the New York Stock Exchange moves overnight to Tokyo: the money is in New York in the daytime, then they just wire it over to Japan every night, and since Japan is 14 hours ahead of us, the same money is used in both places. And by now, about a trillion dollars a day moves around in international speculative markets like that—and that has just a huge effect on national governments.[59] In fact, by this point, what it means is that the international investing community has virtual veto-power over what any national government can do.

We're seeing it in the United States right now, actually. The United States has had a very sluggish recovery from the last recession—it may be the slowest recovery ever; certainly it's the slowest one since the end of the Second World War. But it's been sluggish in only one respect: there's been very low economic growth, very little job creation (in fact, for many years wages were actually going *down* in this "recovery"), but profits have been absolutely zooming.[60] So every year *Fortune* magazine has an issue devoted to the well-being of the important people of the world, the "*Fortune* 500," and what it's reported during this period is that profits went through the sky: in 1993 they were very happy, in 1994 they were euphoric, and 1995 just broke all records. Meanwhile real wages were going down, growth was very low, production was low—and even the slow growth that's been taking place has been halted at times because the bond market, as they put it, "signaled" that it didn't like the growth.

See, financial speculators don't want growth: what they want is stable currencies, meaning *no* growth. In fact, the business press talks very openly now about "the threat of too much growth," "the threat of too much employment": they're perfectly open about all of this, to one another.[61] And the reason for it is, people who speculate against currencies are afraid of inflation—because it decreases the value of their money, so therefore it's a big threat to them. And any kind of growth, any kind of stimulation of the economy, any decline of unemployment all threaten to increase inflation. Well, currency speculators don't like that, so if they see signs of stimulative economic policies or anything that may bring economic growth, they'll just take their capital out of that country's economy—and even a slight withdrawal of that sort can easily trigger a recession in those countries.

So what's happened as a result of all of this is a big drift internationally towards low-growth, low-wage, high-profit economies—because national governments trying to make economic and social policy decisions just have very little leeway to do so by now, or else their economies will be wrecked by capital flight. I mean, Third World governments have no chance at all of doing so at this point—they don't even have any possibility of carrying out a national economic policy. But by now, it's even a question whether big countries can—including the United States. I mean, I don't think that any administration we've had in the United States has *wanted* to do things much differently here—but if they *had* wanted to, I think it would have been extremely hard, if not impossible.

Just to give you an indication, right after the 1992 election, the *Wall Street Journal* ran a front-page article just informing its readers that there was no reason to fear that any of the alleged "lefties" around Clinton would do things differently when they got into office. Of course, the business community already knew that perfectly well, as you can see by taking a look at the stock markets towards the end of the election campaign. But in any event, the *Wall Street Journal* explained why, if by some accident Clinton or any other candidate *did* try to initiate a program of social reform in the United States, it would immediately be cut off. They simply stated what's obvious, and they gave the numbers.

The United States is deeply in debt—that was part of the whole Reagan/Bush program, in fact: to put the country so deeply in debt that there would be virtually no way for the government to pursue programs of social spending anymore. And what "being in debt" really means is that the Treasury Department has sold a ton of securities—bonds and notes and so on—to investors, who then trade them back and forth on the bond market. Well, according to the *Wall Street Journal*, by now about $150 billion a day worth of U.S. Treasury securities alone is traded this way. The article then explained what this means: it means that if the investing community which holds those securities doesn't like any U.S. government policies, it can very quickly sell off just a tiny signal amount of Treasury bonds, and that will have the automatic effect of raising the interest rate, which then will have the further automatic effect of increasing the deficit. Okay, this article calculated that if such a "signal" sufficed to raise the interest rate by 1 percent, it would add $20 billion to the deficit overnight—meaning if Clinton (say in someone's dream) proposed a $20 billion social spending program, the international investing community could effectively turn it into a *$40* billion program instantly, just by a signal, and any further moves in that direction would be totally cut off.[62]

Similarly, there was a great article in the London *Economist*—you know, the big free-trade pop-ideology journal—about the fact that Eastern European countries have been voting Socialists and Communists back into power. But the basic line of the article was, don't worry about it, because as they said, "policy is insulated from politics"—meaning, no matter what games these guys play in the political arena, policy's going to go on exactly the way it is, because we've got them by the balls: we control the international currencies, we're the only ones who can give them loans, we can destroy their economies if we want to, there's nothing they can do. I mean, they can play all of the political games they want to, they can pretend they have a democracy if they like—anything they please—so long as "policy remains insulated from politics." [63]

What's been happening in the contemporary period is really something quite new in history, actually. I mean, in recent years a completely new form of government is being pioneered, one designed to serve the developing needs of this new international corporate ruling class—it's what has sometimes been called an emerging "de facto world government." That's what all of the new international trade agreements are about, N.A.F.T.A., G.A.T.T., and so on; it's what the E.E.C. [European Economic Community] is about; it's increasingly taking shape in international financial organizations like the International Monetary Fund, the World Bank, the Inter-American Development Bank, the World Trade Organization, the G-7 planning meetings of the rich industrial countries, and so on and so forth. These are all efforts to try to centralize power in a world economic system geared towards ensuring that "policy is insulated from politics"—in other words, towards ensuring that the general populations of the world have no role in decision-making, and that the level of policy planning is raised to be so remote from people's knowledge and understanding and input that they have absolutely no idea about the various decisions that are being made that will affect their lives, and certainly couldn't influence them if they did.

The World Bank has its own term for the phenomenon: they call it "technocratic insulation." So if you read World Bank studies, they talk about the importance of having "technocratic insulation"—meaning a bunch of technocrats, who are essentially employees of the big transnational corporations, have to be working somewhere in "insulation" from the public to design all the policies, because if the public ever gets involved in the process they may have bad ideas, like wanting the kind of economic growth that does things for people instead of profits, all sorts of stupid stuff like that. So therefore what you want to have is insulated technocrats—and once they're insulated enough, then you can have all the "democracy" you like, since it's not going to make any difference. In the international business press, this has all been described pretty frankly as "The New Imperial Age." And that's quite accurate: it's certainly the direction things are going in.[64]

## The Fairy Tale Economy

MAN: *A few moments ago, you described the 1990s economy as "sluggish," with low growth and low wages. Usually we hear that this is a "fairy tale" economy and everything's wonderful. Can you say something more about that?*

Well, there's a very important book that comes out every two years, called *The State of Working America*. It's kind of the main, standard database for what's going on for working people—meaning most everybody in the economy. The latest data goes up through 1997. And it tells you just what the "fairy tale" economy is. It's nothing that everybody doesn't know, they just give all the data.

Since the mid-Seventies, the economy has slowed down: there's been a period of much lower growth than the post-war period. Virtually all the wealth that's been created has gone to the very top part of the income distribution. The typical family is now working about fifteen weeks a year more than they did twenty years ago, at stagnating or declining real incomes. The United States now has the heaviest workload in the industrial world. It's also the only country in the industrial world that doesn't have legally mandated vacations. And with that, incomes are at best stagnating for the majority of the population.[65]

Now, it *is* a "fairy tale" economy—and the reason it's a "fairy tale" economy is because for the top few percent of the population, incomes have gone through the roof. The book points out that essentially the only gains in the past twenty years have been to C.E.O.s, and through asset inflation in the stock market. Well, you take a look at assets on the stock market, they also give figures for that: it turns out that roughly half are owned by the top one percent of the population—and of that, most is owned by the top one-half percent. So one percent owns roughly half the stock; the top ten percent own most of the rest. About 85 percent of the total increase in stock values in this great stock-boom have gone to the top ten percent of the population, mostly to the top one-half percent.[66] In fact, the second decile—you know, the 90th to 80th percentiles in income levels—have actually lost net worth during the Clinton recovery (net worth meaning assets minus debt). Below that, it's mostly worse.[67] The ones who have been hit hardest are the youngest. So entry-level wages are about 20 to 30 percent lower than they were twenty years ago, which tells you what's going to happen up the road. It's now even true for white-collar workers, even scientists and engineers. Unless they're in a very high bracket, their wages and incomes are declining.[68] So that's the "fairy tale" economy.

This Clinton recovery—which one kind of wonders about—is the first one certainly in post-war history, maybe in American history, in which most of the population has been left out. I mean, it wasn't until the end of 1997 that median real income reached the level of 1989, which was the peak of the last business cycle.[69] That's unheard of: in every other recovery, median income has been way higher this many years after the peak of the last business cycle.

But for some sectors, it's fantastic. And part of the reason is just intimidating working people with job insecurity.

So this is a very good book—it's put out by the Economic Policy Institute. It's out in paperback, and it's not that expensive. I think the data won't surprise you, because I think you sort of know it from your lives and your neighborhoods and so on.[70] But it's not what you're reading in the *New York Times* and the *Wall Street Journal*. Actually, in the *Wall Street Journal* you *do* read it sometimes—but not in the popular press.

## Building International Unions

WOMAN: *Noam, facing an international power structure like the one you describe, which seems to be showing no signs of letting up as it extends its grip, clearly the response has to be organized and coordinated on a mass scale internationally. But given the size of the problems and just the scale of the task we're faced with, it seems nearly impossible to me, frankly. Even just building the kinds of unions we need to develop in the United States seems like a daunting prospect. Do you think it's really possible in today's world?*

Reconstructing a democratic trade-union movement in the United States? Sure, I don't see why that's an impossible task, it's certainly something that's been done before. But you're right that it's not going to be so simple.

For one thing, in the contemporary period something that's surely going to be required, which does make it a lot harder than before, is that a real labor movement simply *has* to be international today. I mean, in the old days, labor activists used to talk about "Internationals," but that was mostly a joke. Now the labor movement just *has* to be international— because there has to be something to prevent Daimler-Benz, for example, from destroying German work standards by shifting production over to Alabama, where wages are much lower, and the labor's not unionized, and legislative protections for workers are much weaker. Or take the original Free Trade Agreement with Canada [implemented in 1989]: in the first few years of that, Canada lost a couple hundred thousand manufacturing jobs to the Southeastern United States for the same reasons.[71]

In fact, it's gotten to the point where some major corporations don't even worry about strikes anymore, they see them as an opportunity to destroy unions. For instance, the Caterpillar corporation recently broke an eighteen-month strike in Decatur, Illinois [from June 1994 to December 1995], and part of the way they did it was by developing excess production capacity in foreign countries. See, major corporations have a ton of capital now, and one of the things they've been able to do with it is to build up extra overseas production capacity. So Caterpillar has been building plants in Brazil—where they get far cheaper labor than in the United States—and then they can use that production capability to fill their international orders in the event of a strike in the U.S. So they didn't really mind the strike in Decatur, because it gave them an opportunity to finally break the union through this international strategy.[72] That's something that's relatively new, and given this increasing centralization of power in the international economy, and the ability of big transnational corporations to play one national workforce against another to drive down work standards everywhere, there just has to be international solidarity today if there's going to be any hope—and that means *real* international solidarity.

Another thing that has to happen for an international trade union movement to really be successful, in my opinion, is that it is simply going to have to be started from the ground up and be run by its participants. And that kind of serious organizing is something that is very difficult to do. It's going to be particularly tricky in the United States—because the labor leadership here has traditionally been almost completely divorced from the workforce. So take a look at the world-wide destruction of unions after the Second World War: that's had a really major impact on working conditions throughout the world, and some of the people who were doing it were in fact the American labor leadership at the time—they were a big part of the whole effort to break up the Italian unions, and the Japanese unions, and the French unions, and so on.[73]

If you look back to the history of the reconstruction of post-World War II Europe, American planners were very intent on preventing the rise of popular-democratic movements there which would have been based in the former anti-fascist resistance, which had a lot of prestige right then. And the reason was, the world in general was very social-democratic after the war, especially as a result of the anti-fascist struggles that had taken place. And with the traditional order discredited and a whole lot of radical-democratic ideas around, powerful interests in the United States were extremely concerned that a unified labor movement could develop in a place like Germany or Japan.

Actually, the same kind of problem also existed at home right then as well: the U.S. population was very social-democratic after the war—it was extremely pro-union, it wanted more government involvement in regulating industry, probably a majority thought there should even be *public* industry—and business was terrified by it, they were very scared. They in fact said in their publications things like, "We have about five or six years to save the private enterprise system."[74] Well, one thing they did was to launch a huge propaganda program in the United States, aimed at reversing these attitudes.[75] It was actually called at the time part of "the everlasting battle for the minds of men," who have to be "indoctrinated in the capitalist story";

that's a standard straight quote from the P.R. literature.[76] So in the early 1950s, the Advertising Council [an organization begun during World War II and funded by the business community to assist the government with propaganda services at home] was spending huge amounts of money to propagandize for what they called "the American way."[77] The public relations budget for the National Association of Manufacturers I think went up by about a factor of twenty.[78] About a third of the textbooks in schools were simply provided by business.[79] They had 20 million people a week watching propaganda films about worker-management unity, after the Taft-Hartley Act of 1947 allowed propaganda to be shown to basically captive audiences in companies.[80] They continued on with the "scientific methods of strike-breaking" that had been developed in the late 1930s: devoting huge resources into propaganda instead of goon-squads and breaking knees.[81] And it was all tied up with the "anti-Communist" crusade at the time—that's the true meaning of what's referred to as "McCarthyism," which started well before Joseph McCarthy got involved and was really launched by business and liberal members of the Democratic Party and so on.[82] It was a way of using fear and jingoism to try to undermine labor rights and functioning democracy.

And the point is, the leadership of the U.S. labor movement was right in the center of the whole post-war destruction of unions, internationally. In fact, if you look back at their records, which are very fascinating, one of the things that they were most afraid of when they helped to smash the Italian unions, for example, was that they were just too democratic—they wanted them to be more like American unions, and they said so. "American unions" means the A.F.L. leadership sits in a room somewhere and none of the workforce knows what's going on, the leaders make the decisions, then they go out and have lunch with some guy in the government or a corporation—that's the way a union's supposed to work here. The trouble is, the Italian unions weren't like that. I might be exaggerating it a little—but if you look back at these guys' records, they say it in roughly those words, actually.[83]

Well, when you have a history of labor leadership like that, it's another reason why reconstituting a union movement here is simply going to have to start from the bottom up—and I don't think that's an impossible job. It's certainly been done under much harsher conditions than we face. I mean, if it's possible in El Salvador to organize a union when you've got death squads running after you and murdering you, and then we ask, "Is this too hard for us?"—it's kind of like a joke. If it's not happening, it's because people aren't doing it: it's not because it's too hard, it's because people aren't doing it.

So take Haiti, the most impoverished country in the Hemisphere. I don't know if any of you have ever traveled to Haiti, but if you go there, you can barely believe it—I've gone to a lot of parts of the Third World, and Haiti is just something else. But in Haiti in the late 1980s, under extremely repressive and impoverished conditions, Haitian peasants and slum-dwellers were able to create an organized civil society: they succeeded in creating unions, and grassroots organizations, and a whole network of popular groupings which achieved such strength that, with no resources at all, they were able to take over the government. Now, it turns out they immediately got smashed by a military coup which we were assisting—but that shows you what people can do in the world.[84] If you read the American press when the coup collapsed [in 1994], they were all saying, "Now we have to go down and teach lessons in democracy to the Haitians"—but anybody except a complete commissar ought to have burst out in ridicule at that. We have to *learn* about democracy from the Haitians, Haitian peasants have a lot to teach *us* about democracy, they show how it really works.

But the point is, if you can do it in Haiti, and if you can do it in El Salvador, you can certainly do it right now in the United States—we are much better off than those people.

So you're right, it's certainly not going to be a walk-over—but I don't really see any reason why these things are beyond our reach. And I should say that if they *are* beyond our reach, we're all in trouble—*bad* trouble. Because if it turns out that building genuine mass popular movements on an international scale can't be done, it's not so obvious that there will continue to be human civilization for very long—because part of the whole capitalist ethic is that the only thing that matters is how much money you make tomorrow: that's the crucial value of the system, profit for tomorrow. Not just profit, but the bottom line has to look good *tomorrow.* And the result is that planning for the future, and any kind of regulatory apparatus that would sustain the environment for the long-term, become impossible—and that means the planet is going to go down the tubes very fast.

In fact, this was just demonstrated kind of dramatically in the United States a little while ago. Right as the "Gingrich army" was coming into office in 1994 and describing how they're going to destroy the country's environmental regulatory system, right at that very same time a number of scientific reports of considerable significance were released.[85] One had to do with New England—or really, the world: it had to do with the Georges Bank fishing ground, an offshore shelf off the coast of New England. Georges Bank has always been the richest fishing area in the world, and it remained so through the 1970s. But in the 1980s, the Reaganites deregulated the fishing industry and at the same time subsidized it—because that's how the "free market" works: you deregulate so the industries can do anything they want, and then the public pays them off to make sure they stay in business. Well, when you deregulate and you subsidize the fishing industry, it doesn't take a great genius to figure out what's going to happen—what happened is, they wiped out the ground-fish.

Well, now New England is importing cod from Norway. Anybody from New England knows what that means—it's unimaginable. And the reason we're importing cod from Norway is that in Norway, they continued to regulate their fishing grounds; here we deregulated them, so of course they were destroyed. So now a large part of Georges Bank is closed off to fishing, and nobody knows if it can recover.[86] Well, if they eliminate the rest of the country's regulatory apparatus, it's going to be the same kind of thing all over the place. So if this task of organizing a democratic society *does* prove to be impossible, we're all going to be in very serious trouble: very serious.

## Initial Moves and the Coming Crisis

MAN: *Do you see any steps being taken right now towards building these kinds of international movements?*

Well, I think one can see some things happening—and you can imagine them extending to a much larger scale. Most of the things you see today are so small that they're not really making an impact, but they're real, and they could potentially become the start of bigger things.

For example, the first shreds of any positive move in the union movement that I'm aware of occurred right after N.A.F.T.A. was passed [in 1993]. Immediately after the N.A.F.T.A. vote, like within weeks, General Electric and Honeywell both fired workers for trying to organize unions in their plants in Northern Mexico. Okay, normally when that happens, that's the end of it. This time, for the first time ever I think, two American unions, United Electrical Workers and the Teamsters, intervened to defend the organizers and protested to the Clinton administration. And they have some clout: they're not like corporations, but they've got a lot more power than Mexican unions. I mean, there really *are no* Mexican unions, because Mexico's like a fascist state—there's just a government union (kind of like in the old Soviet Union) and then essentially one other one, which of course opposed N.A.F.T.A. but is under such terrific controls that it couldn't do anything. But the big American unions still can't be completely ignored, and in this case they were able to get the U.S. Labor Department to investigate these firings in Mexico.[87]

Well, the thing went to a U.S. Labor Department panel, which was supposed to determine whether there had in fact been an infringement of labor rights—and of course Robert Reich's department discovered that there had been no violations. What they said is, the fired workers had Mexican law behind them, they still had legal recourse under Mexican law, so therefore there was no issue for the U.S. Labor Department. I mean, you have to *read* this thing—I don't know if any of you are familiar with Mexican labor law, but this doesn't even rise to the level of hilarity. But that was the decision, so the firings went through. The fired workers are allowed to apply for severance pay, very happy; I'm sure G.E. is mourning.[88] But at least in this case American unions got to the point of defending the rights of Mexican workers for the first time—at this point out of their own interests, because they recognize they're really getting crushed. But that's the kind of thing that has to start taking place on a massive scale, if there are going to be significant moves against these problems.

Beyond that, serious changes in the economy will simply require dismantling private power altogether—there just is no way around that in the end. And you can even see some rudimentary steps towards it here and there, I think. Weirton Steel was one recent effort [workers own a portion of the company through an Employee Stock Ownership Plan]; and there are others which could be turned into something meaningful. Even things like the negotiations at United Airlines could be meaningful initial steps, though ultimately it depends on whether the settlements are just in terms of stock ownership by workers or actual employee management, which would be something very different [United's employees traded steep pay cuts for 55 percent ownership of the company's stock and 3 of its 12 board seats in 1994].

So the *methods* for starting to move towards real change are quite clear, it's just a question of whether enough people are willing to start pursuing them. There are all sorts of options for how to begin building popular movements, and they could be developed on a very substantial scale. Then if they're coordinated, with genuine community efforts to take control over whatever resources and industries are within them, and they begin to link up internationally, anything at all is possible, I think. I mean, sure, the scale is enormous—but with any major social change the scale has been enormous. You could raise the same doubts about the women's movement, or getting rid of slavery in Haiti in 1790—it must have looked impossible. There's nothing new about that feeling.

MAN: *I just get the sense that we're waiting for some ecological disaster before people really start to get active in these movements on a massive scale.*

Well, if we wait for an ecological disaster, it'll be too late—in fact, we might not even have such a long wait.

Look, it's certainly true that as the threats mount, it may energize people—but you don't *wait* for that to happen: first you have to prepare the ground. For example, suppose it was discovered tomorrow that the greenhouse effect has been way underestimated, and that the catastrophic effects are actually going to set in 10 years from now, and not 100 years from now or something. Well, given the state of the popular movements we have today, we'd probably have a fascist takeover—with everybody agreeing to it, because that would be the only method for survival that anyone could think of. I'd even agree to it, because there just are no other alternatives around right now.

So you don't *wait* for the disasters to happen, first you have to create the groundwork. You need to plant the seeds of something right now, so that whatever opportunities happen to arise—whether it's workers being fired in Mexico, or an ecological catastrophe, or anything else—people are in a position that they can do something constructive about it.

MAN: *Dr. Chomsky, I'm actually wondering whether the corporate elites can't turn the environmental crisis to their benefit—use it as a new technique of taxpayer subsidy, another form of welfare like the others you were describing? So now the public will pay them to salvage the environment they've been primarily responsible for destroying?*

Yeah, sure, you don't even have to predict it—it's already been happening. Take DuPont: they weren't all that upset about the fact that they can no longer sell fluorocarbons [which destroy the ozone layer and have been closely regulated since the late 1980s], because now they can just get big public subsidies to produce other things that will replace them.[89] I mean, at least in this respect these people are rational, so they are going to try to take advantage of whatever techniques happen to be around to ensure that the public is forced to keep subsidizing their profits. And if the environmental crisis reaches the point where some changes have to be introduced—as it already *has*, in fact—they'll be sure to profit off them.

Actually, people are really worried about the destruction of the ozone layer—even the *Wall Street Journal* editors, who are usually out in space on these issues, have started getting worried about it. I mean, it wasn't so bad when it was just killing people in Chile and Argentina who are near the South Pole [i.e. where the first hole in the ozone layer was discovered], but when they detected another hole over the Arctic in the north—meaning white people are going to suffer someday—then even those guys finally noticed it.[90] And when the ocean starts rising to the level of whatever building they're in and whatever floor they're on as they write their editorials, yeah, then they'll agree that there's a greenhouse effect and we'd better do something about it. Sure, no matter how lunatic people are, at some point or other they're going to realize that these problems exist, and they are approaching fast. It's just that the next thing they'll ask is, "So how can we make some money off it?" In fact, anybody in business who *didn't* ask that question would find themselves out of business—just because that's the way that capitalist institutions work. I mean, if some executive came along and said, "I'm *not* going to look at it that way, I'm going to do things differently," well, they'd get replaced by someone who *would* try to make more money off it—because these are simply institutional facts, these are facts about the structure of the institutions. And if you don't like them, and I don't, then you're going to have to change the institutions. There really is no other way.

So yes, within the framework of the institutions that currently exist, the environmental crisis will be yet another technique of public subsidy to ensure continued private profits, and they'll keep capitalizing on it exactly as you describe.

## Elite Planning—Slipping Out of Hand

MAN: *How much of this do you attribute to a conspiracy theory, and how much would you say is just a by-product of capital near-sightedness and a shared interest in holding on to power?*

Well, this term "conspiracy theory" is kind of an interesting one. For example, if I was talking about Soviet planning and I said, "Look, here's what the Politburo decided, and then the Kremlin did this," nobody would call that a "conspiracy theory"—everyone would just assume that I was talking about planning. But as soon as you start talking about anything that's done by power in the *West*, then everybody calls it a "conspiracy theory." You're not allowed to talk about planning in the West, it's not allowed to exist. So if you're a political scientist, one of the things you learn—you don't even make it into graduate school unless you've already internalized it—is that nobody here ever plans anything: we just act out of a kind of general benevolence, stumbling from here to here, sometimes making mistakes and so on. The guys in power aren't idiots, after all. They do planning. In fact, they do very careful and sophisticated planning. But anybody who talks about it, and uses government records or anything else to back it up, is into "conspiracy theory."

It's the same with business: business is again just operating out of a generalized benevolence, trying to help everybody get the cheapest goods with the best quality, all this kind of stuff. If you say: "Look, Chrysler is trying to maximize profits and market share," that's "conspiracy theory." In other words, as soon as you describe elementary reality and attribute minimal rationality to people with power—well, that's fine as long as it's an enemy, but if it's a part of domestic power, it's a "conspiracy theory" and you're not supposed to talk about it.

So, the first thing I would suggest is, drop the term. There are really only two questions. One is, how much of this is *conscious* planning—as happens everywhere else. And the other is, how much is *bad* planning?

Well, it's all conscious planning: there is just no doubt that a lot of very conscious planning goes on among intelligent people who are trying to maximize their power. They'd be insane if they didn't do that. I mean, I'm not telling you anything new when I tell you that top editors, top government officials, and major businessmen have meetings together—of course. And not only do they have meetings, they belong to the same golf clubs, they go to the same parties, they went to the same schools, they flow up and back from one position to another in the government and private sector, and so on and so forth. In other words, they represent the same social class: they'd be crazy if they didn't communicate and plan with each other.

So *of course* the Board of Directors of General Motors plans, the same way the National Security Council plans, and the National Association of Manufacturers' P.R. agencies plan. I mean, this was a truism to Adam

Smith: if you read Adam Smith [classical economist], he says that every time two businessmen get together in a room, you can be sure there's some plan being cooked up which is going to harm the public. Yeah, how could it be otherwise? And there's nothing particularly new about this—as Smith pointed out over two hundred years ago, the "masters of mankind," as he called them, will do what they have to in order to follow "the vile maxim": "all for ourselves and nothing for anyone else."[91] Yeah, and when they're in the National Security Council, or the Business Roundtable [a national organization composed of the C.E.O.s of 200 major corporations], or the rest of these elite planning forums, they have extreme power behind them. And yes, they're planning—planning very carefully.

Now, the only significant question to ask is, is it *intelligent* planning? Okay, that depends on what the goals are. If the goals are to maximize corporate profits for tomorrow, then it's very intelligent planning. If the goals are to have a world where your children can survive, then it's completely idiotic. But that second thing really isn't a part of the game. In fact, it's institutionalized: it's not that these people are stupid, it's that to the extent that you have a competitive system based on private control over resources, you are forced to maximize short-term gain. That's just an institutional necessity.

I mean, suppose there were three car companies: Chrysler, General Motors, and Ford. And suppose that one of them decided to put its resources into producing fuel-efficient, user-friendly cars which could be available ten years from now, and which would have a much less destructive impact on the environment—suppose Ford decided to put a proportion of its resources into that. Well, Chrysler *wouldn't* be putting its resources into that, which means that they would undersell Ford today, and Ford wouldn't be in the game ten years from now. Well, that's just the nature of a competitive system—and that's exactly why if you're a manager you've got to try to make sure that in the next financial quarter your bottom line shows something good, whatever effects it may have a year from now: that's just part of the institutional irrationality of the system.

In fact, here I must say I would like to complain about a recent cover of *Z Magazine*. I had an article in there, and on the cover there was the title: "Corporate Greed." But that's just an absurd phrase.[92] I mean, to talk about "corporate greed" is like talking about "military weapons" or something like that—there just is no other possibility. A corporation is something that is trying to maximize power and profit: that's what it *is*. There is no "phenomenon" of corporate greed, and we shouldn't mislead people into thinking there is. It's like talking about "robber's greed" or something like that—it's not a meaningful thing, it's misleading. A corporation's purpose is to maximize profit and market share and return to investors, and all that kind of stuff, and if its officers *don't* pursue that goal, for one thing they are legally liable for not pursuing it. There I agree with Milton Friedman [right-wing economist] and those guys: if you're a C.E.O., you must do that—otherwise you're in dereliction of duty, in fact dereliction of official legal duty.[93] And besides that, if you don't do it, you'll get kicked out by the shareholders or the Board of Directors, and you won't be there very long anyway.

So in a sense the planning is "bad," if you like—like it's stupid to destroy Georges Bank if you're thinking about five years from now. But it's *not* stupid if you're thinking of tomorrow's profits. And I think the question we need to ask is, which of those things are we concerned about?

In fact, it's interesting to look at the history of the government regulatory system in the United States in this context—things like the I.C.C. [Interstate Commerce Commission] and so on. Keep in mind that these governmental regulatory agencies were mostly instituted by business itself, particularly capital-intensive, internationally-oriented big business—because they recognized that the predatory nature of capitalism was just going to destroy everything if they didn't bring it under control somehow. So they *wanted* regulation to keep things kind of organized—just like they wanted labor unions, and they wanted the New Deal programs. In fact, if you look at many of the things that have really improved the country, like the New Deal programs in the 1930s, for example (which at least partially brought the United States into the main framework of industrial societies with respect to social programs), a lot of the drive behind them was coming from big business, as opposed to small business.

See, big corporations like General Electric and so on—which are capital-intensive, and have relatively small labor forces and an international orientation—they supported the New Deal measures. It was more mainstream businesses who opposed the New Deal, like medium-level industry, members of the National Association of Manufacturers and so on—because they weren't capital-intensive, and they had large labor forces, and didn't sell to international markets, therefore they didn't benefit particularly from New Deal programs. But for a big corporation like G.E., it was better to have an organized workforce that wouldn't carry out wildcat strikes, and that you could be sure was going to work pretty regularly even if you had to pay them a little bit more, and so on and so forth.[94] That's also why big business has tended to support the existence of unions—American-style unions—to a certain extent: because they know the system's going to self-destruct if there aren't devices around to bring things under control.

As a matter of fact, one aspect of the recent shift we've seen in American politics is that big business is *not* in such good shape in this respect. The guys who took over Congress in 1994 are *not* pro-big business in this way—they are not the sort of people who want an organized, planned society. See, big business is kind of Communist: they want a powerful state organizing things in their long-term interests. And the guys who came into power with Newt Gingrich in 1994 are a somewhat different breed. They're more like the old National Association of Manufacturers-types who opposed the New Deal, and there's also this freakish fundamentalist element among them, which is extremely powerful in the United States. I mean, this is not so much true of Gingrich himself—Gingrich is sort of more reasonable, he's just a flak for big business. But the people he organized are fanatics, especially what they call the "Christian Right"—they're people who want money tomorrow, they don't care what happens to the world two inches down the road, they don't care what happens to anybody else, they're deeply irrational. And they're totalitarian: despite what they say, they in fact want a very powerful state, but only to order people around and tell them how to live, and to throw them in jail if they step the wrong way, and so on, a National Security State basically. Well, that's a real basis for fascism—and big business and a lot of other powerful people are very worried about it.

In fact, if you looked at the funding for the whole Gingrich movement, it was quite interesting. The *Wall Street Journal* had an article on it after the Congressional elections in 1994, and it turned out that the main people who were funding them were at the fringes of the economy: I think the biggest funder was Amway [a direct-sales company somewhat like a pyramid scheme], which is basically a scam operation, and the other big ones were things like "hedge funds"—not the real brokerage houses, but the ones around the fringe of Wall Street who lend you huge amounts of money for very risky loans. And then there was lots of money coming from gun interests, and alcohol interests, and gambling interests, and so on. I mean, these are sectors of business where there's a ton of money, but they are not really a part of the mainstream economy. The Gingrich group wasn't getting its funding from General Electric, let's say. In fact, the only big corporation that was funding them was Philip Morris [a cigarette manufacturer], and the guys at Philip Morris are mass murderers, so they need government protection and yeah, they'll fund Newt Gingriches.[95] But if you look at who was really backing them, it's mostly what are called "small businessmen"— they're people in the top two percent of income levels, let's say, instead of the top one-half percent; they're what's referred to as "Main Street," like their businesses have about fifty employees or something like that. Well, those people really *do* want the government out of their hair, they don't want a lot of regulations holding them back from making as much money as they can.

Just to give you an example, there's a contractor painting my house right now, and I've been talking to him—*he's* the kind of guy they represent. He hates the government, because the government doesn't let him use lead in the paint, and it makes him pay workers' compensation to his workers when they get hurt, things like that. He just wants to get all this stuff out of his hair so he can go out there and make money, do whatever he feels like. You tell him, "Well, kids will die of lead poisoning if you use leaded paint." He says, "Ahh, a lot of government bureaucrats made that up, what do they know? I've been breathing lead all my life and look at me, I'm healthy as a horse." That's the sort of attitude that's been supporting this movement—and I think big business is very worried about it.

If you want to get a sense of what it's like, *Fortune* magazine in its February '95 issue had a cover-story on the attitudes of C.E.O.s towards what's been going on in Washington. These guys are worried—and the reason why they're worried is quite simple: these C.E.O.s are what's called "liberal." I mean, they love the fact that wages are going down, and that profits are shooting through the roof, and that environmental laws are being loosened, and that welfare is being cut—all that stuff is just great to them. But if you look at some of their personal attitudes, they're about as far away from the Christian Right as the Harvard faculty is.[96] They are militantly pro-abortion on demand. They believe in women's rights—like, they want their daughters to have career opportunities. They don't want their kids to have to study Lucifer and Beast 666 in school. They don't want maniacs running around with assault rifles because the black helicopters are bringing aliens in, or whatever the latest frenzy is. But the troops that they've mobilized are in that domain. The so-called Christian Right, for one, just have a different agenda. And I think big business is worried about them: the C.E.O.s don't want *that* kind of fascism. And that's why by now, if you take a look, you'll see that big corporations have tended to line up with the Clinton administration.

Take something like science policy. These "Gingrich army"-types don't see any point in science—it's just a bunch of pointy-headed intellectuals, who needs that? On the other hand, big corporations understand that if they want to keep making profits five years from now, there'd better be some science being funded today—and of course, they don't want to pay for it themselves, they want the public to pay for it, through university science departments and so on. They want the government to keep funding science, so when some discovery comes along they can then rip it off and make the money off it. Well, just a little while ago, a bunch of the big corporate heads wrote a joint letter to the House science committee asking them to continue high levels of funding for university-based science and research programs—just the thing the Republican Congress wants to cut—because their job *isn't* just to pour lead paint on somebody's house: these guys know that they are not going to be in the game a couple years from now unless U.S. science continues to produce things for them to exploit. So by this point, they are getting very worried that these Newt Gingrich-types might go too far and start cutting down the parts of the state system that are welfare for *them*—which of course is unacceptable.

What's happened is actually pretty intriguing, if you think about it. I mean, for the past fifty years American business has been organizing a major class war, and they needed troops—there *are* votes after all, and you can't just come before the electorate and say, "Vote for me, I'm trying to screw you." So what they've had to do is appeal to the population on some other grounds. Well, there aren't a lot of other grounds, and everybody always picks the same ones, whether his name is Hitler or anything else—jingoism, racism, fear, religious fundamentalism: these are the ways of appealing to people if you're trying to organize a mass base of support for policies that are really intended to crush them. And they've done it, business had to do it—and now after fifty years they've got a tiger by the tail.

Actually, the German businessmen who supported Hitler were probably thinking about the same thing in 1937 and '38. They'd been perfectly happy to pay off the Nazis to organize the population on the basis of fear, hatred, racism, and jingoism, in order to beat down the German labor movement and kill off the Communists there—but of course, once the Nazis got into power, they had their own agenda. The big industrialists in Germany did *not* want a war with the West—but by then it was too late.

Now, I don't want to say that this is Nazi Germany, but there is a similarity—just as there's a similarity to post-Khomeini Iran. I mean, Iranian business strongly opposed the Shah [the Iranian monarch who ruled the country until 1979], because they didn't like the fact that he controlled the state monopolies, especially the National Iranian Oil Company—and as a result they wanted to see him overthrown, and they needed somebody to do it. Well, the only forces they could appeal to were the movements in the streets, and those guys were being organized by fundamentalist clerics. So as a result they overthrew the Shah alright, but they also got Khomeini and all these fundamentalist maniacs running around, which they didn't like.

Well, something similar has been happening in the United States and people are worried about it. Incidentally, I think this is also why we're now starting to get editorials in the *New York Times* defending the counterculture.[97] And just to tell you a personal thing, recently there was a favorable review of a book of mine in the *Boston Globe*. That is unbelievable.[98] I mean, it couldn't *possibly* have happened a couple years ago. There have even been some discussions in the press of "class war"—that's a concept that is usually unmentionable in the U.S.[99] And I think it's because a lot of elites are really running scared these days. They think: "Look, we've unleashed the demon—now it's going to go after the interests of really rich people." The only way they've been able to keep their power is by waging a huge propaganda war, and that has now brought up guys who are like suicide bombers, and who think that women ought to be driven back to the home and shut up, and who want to have twelve assault rifles in their closets, and so on. Well, they don't like that, and now they're starting to get scared.

### Disturbed Populations Stirring

WOMAN: *How do you think it's all going to play out, then—do you see the American political system heading for a civil war?*

Well, in general I don't think you can make predictions like that—when we talk about predictions, we're just talking about intuitions, and mine are no better than anybody else's. But I do feel this period is kind of a turning point. I mean, you can see very clearly where policy is driving people, and you know exactly what its goals are. The only question you can't answer is how the population is going to react as they get slammed in the face—and they *are* getting slammed in the face. One way it could go would be like the building of the C.I.O. [an integrated mass union formed in 1935], or the Civil Rights and feminist movements, or the Freedom Rides [whites and blacks rode buses together into the American South in 1961 to challenge segregation laws]. Other ways it could go would be Nazism, Khomeini's Iran, Islamic fundamentalism in Algeria—those are all ways people could go too.

But the country is very disturbed. You can see it in polls, and you can certainly see it traveling around—and I travel around a lot. There's complete disaffection about everything. People don't trust anyone, they think everyone's lying to them, everyone's working for somebody else. The whole civil society has completely broken down. And when you talk about the mood of people—well, whether it's on right-wing talk radio, or among students, or just among the general population, you get a very good reception these days for the kinds of things I talk about. But it's scary—because if you came and told people, "Clinton's organizing a U.N. army with aliens to come and carry out genocide, you'd better go to the hills," you'd get the same favorable response. That's the problem—you'd get the same favorable response. I mean, you can go to the most reactionary parts of the country, or anywhere else, and a thousand people will show up to listen, and they'll be really excited about what you're saying—no matter what it is. That's the trouble: it's *no matter what it is.* Because people are so disillusioned by this point that they will believe almost anything.

Take these guys in what are called the "militias"—I mean, obviously they're not militias in the Second Amendment sense: "militias" are things raised by states, these are just paramilitary organizations.[100] But if you look at who's involved in them, they are people from a sector of the population that has really gotten it in the neck in the last twenty years: they're high school graduates, mostly white males, a segment of the society that has really taken a beating. I mean, median real wages in the United States have dropped about 20 percent since 1973—that's a substantial cut.[101] Their wives now have to go to work just to put food on the table. Often their families have broken up. Their kids are running wild, but there's no social support system anywhere to help them deal with that. They don't read the "*Fortune* 500" and put together an analysis of what's really going on in the world, all they've had rammed into their heads is, "The federal government's your enemy." If you come to them with a political framework that could lead to some kind of productive change, it's all just another power-play as far as they're concerned—and with some justice: everything else they've been told is a crock, so why should they believe you? You tell them to read declassified National Security Council documents, or to look at things in the business press that would really mean something to them—I mean, a lot of people don't even read. We should bear in mind how illiterate the society's become. It's tough.

So these groups certainly represent something: they're a response to sharply worsening conditions. I mean, they're called "right-wing," but in my view they're sort of independent of politics—there could be people on the left in there too. All of this is not so different from people believing conspiracy theories about Kennedy's assassination, or about the Trilateral Commission [an elite think-tank], or the C.I.A. and all the rest of that stuff—the things that are just tearing the left to shreds.

Or take this guy called the "Unabomber" [a serial mail-bomb killer who espoused an anti-industrial worldview]. When I read his manifesto, I thought, if I don't know him, I know his friends—they're the kind of people I run into on the left all the time. They're demoralized, they're fed up, they're desperate, but they don't have a constructive response to all the problems we've got to face. Then again, the L.A. riots [in 1992] also weren't a constructive response. In fact, all these reactions, from the "militias," to conspiracy theories, to the Unabomber, to the L.A. riots, they're all the result of a kind of collapse of civil society in the United States. The vestiges of an integrated, socially cohesive, functioning society, with some kind of solidarity and continuity to it, have just been destroyed here. It's hard to imagine a better way to demoralize people than to have them watch T.V. for seven hours a day—but that's pretty much what people have been reduced to by now.

In fact, all of these things really illustrate the difference between completely demoralized societies like ours and societies that are still kind of hanging together, like in a lot of the Third World. I mean, in absolute terms the Mayan Indians in Chiapas, Mexico [who organized the Zapatista rebellion in 1994], are much poorer than the people in South Central Los Angeles, or in Michigan or Montana—much poorer. But they have a civil society that hasn't been totally eliminated the way the working-class culture we used to have in the United States was. Chiapas is one of the most impoverished areas of the Hemisphere, but because there's still a lively, vibrant society there, with a cultural tradition of freedom and social organization, the Mayan Indian peasants were able to respond in a highly constructive way—they organized the Chiapas rebellion, they have programs and positions, they have public support, it's been going somewhere. South Central Los Angeles, on the other hand, was just a riot: it was the reaction of a completely demoralized, devastated, poor working-class population, with nothing at all to bring it together. All the people could do there was mindless lashing out, just go steal from the stores. The only effect of that is, we'll build more jails.

So to answer your question, I think it's very much up in the air what's going to happen in the United States. See, there's an experiment going on. The experiment is: can you marginalize a large part of the population, regard them as superfluous because they're not helping you make those dazzling profits—and can you set up a world in which production is carried out by the most oppressed people, with the fewest rights, in the most flexible labor markets, for the happiness of the rich people of the world? Can you do that? Can you get women in China to work locked into factories where they're burned to death in fires, producing toys that are sold in stores in New York and Boston so that rich people can buy them for their children at Christmas?[102] Can you have an economy where everything works like that—production by the most impoverished and exploited, for the richest and most privileged, internationally? And with large parts of the general population just marginalized because they don't contribute to the system—in Colombia, murdered, in New York, locked up in prison. Can you do that? Well, nobody knows the answer to that question. You ask, could it lead to a civil war? It definitely could, it could lead to uprisings, revolts.

## The Verge of Fascism

And there are other things to worry about too, like the fact that the United States is such an extremely fundamentalist country—and also such an unusually frightened one. I mean, we became kind of a laughingstock to the rest of the world during the 1980s: every time Reagan would announce some Libyan terrorist action or something, the entire tourism industry in Europe would collapse, because everybody in the United States was afraid to go to Europe—where they're about a hundred times as safe as in any American city—for fear there might be some Arab lurking around the corners there trying to kill them. That's literally the case, it became a real joke around the world—and it's just another sign of how much extreme irrationality and fear there is in the U.S. population.

And that's a very dangerous phenomenon—because that kind of deep irrationality can readily be whipped up by demagogues, you know, Newt Gingriches. These guys can whip up fear, hatred, they can appeal to fundamentalist urges—and that's been scaring most of the world for a while, I should say. For example, if you recall the Republican National Convention in 1992, it opened with a "God and Country" rally, which was televised and seen around the world. In Europe particularly it really sent chills up people's spines—because they remember Hitler's Nuremberg rallies, at least older people do, and it had something of that tone. Well, the Republicans were able to insulate the Convention from it that time around and keep most of that stuff confined to the first night, but in the future they might not be able to do that—in the future those people might take the Convention over, in which case we'd be very close to some American version of fascism; it may not be Hitler Germany, but it'll be bad enough.

It's in fact a very similar situation: Germany in the 1930s was maybe the most civilized and advanced country in the world, though with plenty of problems, and it was quite possible there to whip up hatred and fear, to mobilize people, and in fact to carry out what from their point of view was social development—with consequences that you're familiar with. Yeah, why are we different? We've got the same genes, and the conditions in the culture which might be a part of the background for it certainly already exist.

Actually, I think that the United States has been in kind of a pre-fascist mood for years—and we've been very lucky that every leader who's come along has been a crook. See, people should always be very much in favor of corruption—I'm not kidding about that. Corruption's a very good thing, because it undermines power. I mean, if we get some Jim Bakker coming along—you know, this preacher who was caught sleeping with everybody and defrauding his followers—those guys are fine: all they want is money and sex and ripping people off, so they're never going to cause much trouble. Or take Nixon, say: an obvious crook, he's ultimately not going to cause that much of a problem. But if somebody shows up who's kind of a Hitler-type—just wants power, no corruption, straight, makes it all sound appealing, and says, "We want power"—well, then we'll all be in very bad trouble. Now, we haven't had the right person yet in the United States, but sooner or later somebody's going to fill that position—and if so, it will be highly dangerous.

On the other hand, though, I think you can also imagine things going quite differently. The situation just is very pliable at this point in the United States. I mean, these same guys who are blowing up Oklahoma City government buildings [in 1995] could be doing what they would have been doing sixty years ago, which is organizing the C.I.O.—the same guys. It really just depends on whether people start doing something about it. And there are also other things here that are very healthy as well, and can be built on. For instance, there's a streak of independence and opposition to authority in the United States which probably is unique in the world. Obviously it can show up in anti-social ways, like running around with assault rifles and so on. But it can show up in very healthy ways too, and the trick is to make it show up in the healthy ways, like opposition to illegitimate authority.

So you know, it's complicated. Could there be a civil war? It could be very unpleasant. A lot of very ugly things could happen, they're not inconceivable. But they're also not inevitable.

*WOMAN: I've often heard you end talks by saying basically, "We can't give up hope." But do you really see any hope—for the future of democracy, or for the United States, or for the people in the Third World?*

Well, I'll quote my friend Mike Albert [co-editor of *Z Magazine*], who was listening to one of my gloomy disquisitions and said: "You know, what you're describing is an organizer's dream." And I think that's true. The country is in a state where people are disillusioned, frightened, skeptical, angry, don't trust anything, want something better, know that everything's rotten. That's a perfect place for organizers to come and say, "Okay, let's do something about it. If they could do something about it in the hills of El Salvador, we can certainly do something about it here." And I think he's right: it just depends whether you decide it's time to start doing something about it.

## The Future of History

WOMAN: *But what do you think personally, Noam—will the general population of the United States remain marginalized for the rest of history, or do you actually feel that there's going to be a movement to prevent that?*

Look, I really don't know, but I think we can predict one thing with fair certainty: if the U.S. public remains marginalized, there isn't going to be much history left to worry about. We're not living in the eighteenth century anymore. The problems may be sort of similar, but they're quite different in scale, and the problems now have to do with human survival. So if the general population in the most powerful country in the world remains marginalized, we aren't going to have to worry very much about history, because there isn't going to be any. And that's not very far away at this point.

Take Central America, which is the region where we have the most control—we've been controlling things there for a hundred years, so it really tells us what we are. It's quite possible that much of Central America will become uninhabitable in another couple decades. For instance, Nicaragua's losing its water supply. Why? The reason is, in the aftermath of the American attacks of the 1980s, people are starving, and they're doing the only thing they can do—they go up into the hills to cut wood and try to find some land to work, they do whatever they can do to survive. Well, that eliminates the forest cover, streams start drying up, the land can't absorb water, lakes are drying up, and on top of it all, there happens to have been a drought. So Nicaragua's water supply may disappear—and as the pressures continue, it may become a desert. The same could be true of Haiti.[103]

Haiti, in fact, is a parable of Western savagery. That was one of the first places Columbus landed, and he thought it was a paradise—it was the richest place in the world, and also probably the most densely populated place in the world. And in fact, it remained that way: France is a rich country in large measure because it stole Haiti's resources, and even early in the twentieth century, before Woodrow Wilson sent the U.S. Marines to invade and wreck the country in 1915, American scholarship and government studies on Haiti were still describing it as a major resource center—it just happened to be an extremely rich place.[104] Well, take a look if you fly into Haiti today. The island consists of Haiti and the Dominican Republic—the Dominican Republic we've also brutalized, but Haiti much more so—and you can just see it if you look down from the plane: on one side it's brown, on the other side it's sort of semi-green. The brown side is Haiti, the richest place in the world. It may not last another couple decades—literally it may become un-inhabitable.

Well, that's extending elsewhere now, and it involves us too. The rich and the powerful are going to survive longer, but the effects are very real—and they're getting worse very quickly as more and more people get mar-ginalized because they play no role in profit-making, which is considered the only human value. Well, the environmental problems are simply much more significant in scale than anything else in the past. And there's a fair possibility—certainly a possibility high enough so that no rational person would exclude it—that within a couple hundred years the world's water-level will have risen to the point that most of human life will have been de-stroyed. Alright, if we don't start to do something about that now, it's not impossible that that'll happen. In fact, it's even likely.

So whatever *I* happen to think, that's irrelevant. The answer to your question is: if you remain marginalized, there's not going to be much his-tory to worry about. Whether people will react or not, who knows? You know? Everyone's got to decide.

# Index

Note that additional material on these topics can be found in the online footnotes at **www.understandingpower.com**.